Advanced FileMaker® Pro 5.5 Techniques for Developers

Chris Moyer
and Bob Bowers

Wordware Publishing, Inc.

Library of Congress Cataloging-in-Publication Data

Moyer, Chris.
Advanced FileMaker pro 5.5 techniques for developers / by Chris Moyer and Bob Bowers.
p. cm.
ISBN 1-55622-859-7
1. FileMaker pro. 2. Database management. I. Bowers, Bob. II. Title.

QA76.9.D3 M688 2002
005.75'65--dc21 2002002983
CIP

2320 Los Rios Boulevard
Plano, Texas 75074

Printed in the United States of America

ISBN 1-55622-859-7
10 9 8 7 6 5 4 3 2
0204

All inquiries for volume purchases of this book should be addressed to Wordware Publishing, Inc., at the above address. Telephone inquiries may be made by calling:

(972) 423-0090

Dedication

For Rebecca

Bob Bowers

For my wife, Laura, and my son, Devlin, and for any future kids who would be really ticked that their big brother got mentioned in this book and they didn't.

Chris Moyer

Contents

Foreword

We almost never read forewords or introductions, so we'll try to be as brief as possible. There were several reasons for writing this book. As time has gone by and FileMaker has evolved into a more sophisticated development tool, the need for more advanced FileMaker reference materials has grown as well. We felt that while advanced FileMaker users could find some things in existing materials, there weren't any books available that were dedicated to this area.

Also, FileMaker has a base of more than 7 million users. Much of the FileMaker development community is home grown and/or self taught. This is a great testament to the utility of FileMaker the product, but it has meant that large numbers of developers are going about their work without a good grasp of relational design principles.

This book is the first in what will be a series of FileMaker books. It covers areas of knowledge required for building more complex FileMaker systems; topics such as relational theory, data modeling, security implementations, audit trails, recursive relationships, advanced portal tricks, and advanced scripting control techniques are discussed in depth.

The second book in the series, *Advanced FileMaker Pro Web Development* (1-55622-860-0), will cover all aspects of web publishing with FileMaker Pro, including sections on FDML, Lasso development, PHP, implementing a RAIC, JavaScript, XML, and conducting secure web transactions with SSL. The third book, *Advanced FileMaker Pro Integrated Applications* (1-55622-861-9) will cover a variety of methods for integrating FileMaker with other technologies, including ODBC, ActiveX, Visual Basic, AppleScript, Microsoft Terminal Server, and Adobe Acrobat.

Acknowledgments

We'd like first to thank all of the people who helped make this book possible and lent their support and assistance during its creation. In particular, we'd like to thank Andy LeCates, who actually worked on some of the early drafts of the book many moons ago. The security section is more thorough because of his efforts. Our editors at Wordware Publishing, Jim Hill, Wes Beckwith, and Beth Kohler, deserve a parade in their honor for being so patient and understanding when we missed a few deadlines and had all sorts of last-minute changes. Thanks to Molly Thorsen for being our technical editor and friend. And thanks to Andrew Nash, who created some of the illustrations, and the rest of the crew at Chris Moyer Consulting who put up with us (and covered for us) while we were working on this project. Many of them read and commented on chapters, and we're grateful to Debbie Asquith, Josie Graham, Aaron Holdsworth, Steve Lane, Greg Lane, Jesse LaVere, Scott Love, David Outten, Rick Sabatino, Bruce Schmoetzer, Jamie Thomas, Steve Thoms, and Adrienne Vasquez for keeping things running smoothly. Last, but by no means least, thanks to all of the clients we've had the privilege of working with over the years. Virtually every example in this book was inspired by one project or another.

I would like to thank first and foremost my wife, Rebecca Moore. I couldn't have finished this project without her love and support. Thanks also to Jasper, Sandy, and Helix, for presenting me with so many opportunities for procrastination and walking all over my keyboard. Thanks to John Overton for his moral support, and to Steve Lane for always being willing to lend a hand. And finally, thanks to my father, who sparked my interest in databases at quite an early age, though I didn't know it at the time. I wish he could have seen where that interest has led.

Bob Bowers

Acknowledgments

I want to give a huge thanks to Bob Bowers, who dragged me and this book kicking and screaming over the finish line. I still remember when we sketched out the original outline on a restaurant table in Island Falls, Maine, in the winter of 1997. I want to thank my wife, Laura LeDuc, who also has been good at keeping my nose to the grindstone. I'd also like to single out Jay Welshofer for being a major dude and an all-around asset to the FileMaker community. He's always pushing important directions and generally guarding the flank. I'd especially like to salute the spirit of the FileMaker community. Countless people dedicate a lot of time and energy to helping others along. You all know who you are.

Chris Moyer

Chapter 1

The Relational Model

When we first started working with FileMaker, we just thought it was cool that we could get the program to do what we wanted (more or less). We didn't really think about the fact that we were, like it or not, database designers. From time to time, though, we'd run into problems that seemed to take more work than they should have. We'd have to create a whole bunch of fields, such as Month1, Month2, etc., and it just seemed like there was probably a better way to do some things. Our early problem-solving techniques relied on instinct more than anything else, and we, like many other developers we've talked to, often look back on some of our early work and cringe.

As we started dealing with more complex data problems, we began to read up on relational design techniques and theory, and a whole series of "Aha!" moments happened. ("So that's why that was such a pain in the backside… ") Even though problems often seemed unique to us, they were often classic database problems. What's more, the techniques and solutions used to address these problems had been kicking around for quite a while, and we were just wasting time by not taking some time to educate ourselves on the information that was out there. For those of you who haven't started this process, you should take a look at some of our recommended readings in Appendix A. A little study goes a long way when you do database work.

There was one area, however, that seemed pretty dry and uninviting, and that was the relational model itself. Most books that deal with this topic read like textbooks. Not surprisingly, that's because they are textbooks. We craved a plain English explanation of the relational model, and we haven't found one. Being FileMaker developers (Don't have a kitchen timer for the turkey? I'll just whip one up in FileMaker…), the obvious answer was to write our own. You now have it in your hands, and you can judge for yourself if we succeeded in making it clear and understandable.

Some other points: FileMaker's ODBC capability allows it to venture into the world of client/server technology. This world has pretty good conformance to the relational model, and it therefore uses the terminology of the relational model. If you're going to be working with client/server people, they'll probably give you blank looks when you start talking about FileMaker's match fields. Learning their terminology will make your job much easier.

This chapter is divided into three sections:

- A discussion of the purpose of database systems and why problems in meaningfully representing data can best be achieved by implementation of the relational model
- A quick survey of the concepts that constitute the roots of the relational model
- The relational model itself

Databases as Vessels of Meaning

In a nutshell, the relational model is all about ensuring the integrity of a database system's meaning. If you stop and think about it, the databases that you create are really tools for sharing meaningful information within an organization, or sometimes across multiple organizations. "Meaningful" is the important word to emphasize because if your data doesn't convey its intended meaning, the database system has failed. Below are some examples to prove this point.

Imagine a database with the following values:

Field 1	Field 2
2	4
1	1
3	1
2	3

What do these numbers mean? Hard to say, isn't it? Whoever created this information didn't think through the idea that it might someday be shared with someone who wouldn't know what the author was thinking when he created the data. This is a fundamental point of database design: Data is shared among multiple users, and there must be consensus on what the data means. Another idea to keep in mind is that data structures themselves are often shared with other database developers who may come into a project after the original designer has left. The meaning should be clear and even obvious.

Let's say we told you that these numbers came from a table called Baseball and that Field 1 was our score and Field 2 was the other team's score. That gives you some context for the data, some meaning. Things aren't crystal clear, though. One user may think that each record represents the score of a baseball game, and another user may think that each record represents the score of an inning of a baseball game. We offer this example to show that the naming of tables contributes to perceived meaning and should not be taken too lightly.

Let's make the following changes:

- Change the name of the table to "Baseball Game."
- Change the name of Field 1 to "Our Score."
- Change the name of Field 2 to "Opponent Score."

With these changes, a casual observer could wander up and figure out what the data means. He could figure out that the above records mean that the home team won one game, lost two games, and tied one game. By investing the data with some basic meaning, logical conclusions can follow. It's a basic concept, and it points out how important it is to get your names right.

Let's consider a different example of meaning. We have a customer table with one record in it:

Name	Address	City	State	Zip
CMC	833 West Chicago	Chicago	IL	60622

A user enters another record as follows:

Name	Address	City	State	Zip
30305	CMC	GA	Atlanta	123 Main Street

Intuitively, you know this is wrong. But your average FileMaker database (and lots of other database products) will accept this as a valid entry. Why shouldn't it? Let's say that all of these fields are text fields. All of those entry items are text, so everything is fine as far as the database is concerned. You, however, know that the company name doesn't belong in the Address field. You know that the zip code doesn't belong in the Name field. Meaning has been lost because the structural rules of this record have been violated.

Just what are those rules, though? A rudimentary rule might be that certain types of data should go into certain fields. This is where things get interesting because the kind of developer who learned how to create databases by fumbling around in FileMaker probably isn't equipped to come up with a rule system that can address this problem. Happily, the relational model addresses this issue through the idea of domains. We'll get to that in due course, however. Let's look at another kind of problem:

Invoice ID	**Invoice Date**	**Customer**
3	12/21/93	Gary DeSorbo
3	1/3/97	Steve Whitlow
4	2/28/98	Boo Boo the Cat

In this case, we have two invoices with the same invoice ID. If Steve Whitlow called with his invoice number and wanted to discuss invoice 3, your search in FileMaker would result in a found set that contained two invoices. Since Gary's invoice was created first, that would be the one you saw first. Once again, meaning has been compromised. Invoice ID 3 refers to both Steve Whitlow's invoice on 1/3/97 and Gary's invoice on 12/21/93.

Let's instead suppose that you didn't know it was Steve who had called. All you know is that someone left a garbled message about a problem with invoice 3. You'd have a problem determining which invoice the caller was talking about.

You'd also have a problem trying to summarize payments against these invoices because a payment against either invoice would apply to both of them. If that happened and they were both paid in full, it would look like you had an overpayment on both of them and that you should write checks for the amount that was overpaid. At that point, the database can cause the company to lose money, and that's generally considered to be a bad thing. The root cause of this bad thing is that you can't uniquely identify a record in your invoice database. Lots of people aren't too concerned about being able to uniquely identify a record until you tell them that it can make them lose money.

Here's another example. We have two database files:

An Invoice database:

Invoice ID	Invoice Date	Customer	Address
11	9/29/98	CMC	833 West Chicago
12	8/14/98	Tex's Dog Wash	1 Hound Dog Way
13	10/2/98	CMC	833 West Fullerton

...and a Line Item database:

Invoice ID	Product ID	Description	Quantity
11	31	Cabbage Brush	10
12	33	Granola Dispenser	2
13	35	Dandelion Juice	8

We could create a relationship between Invoice ID in the Invoice database, and Quantity in the Line Item database. The relationship would be valid as far as FileMaker was concerned, but it would be, you guessed it, meaningless. Line items that belonged with the invoice would not be grouped with the invoice unless by some fluke the quantity was the same as the Invoice ID. It would also be likely that the wrong items would be grouped with an invoice. At this point, we hope you're getting the drift that loss of meaning = bad.

Note also that the two CMC invoices have slightly different addresses. Is one right and one wrong? Do they represent two different company locations? This is a problem that arises when you have redundancy, or multiple copies of the same piece of information. Eliminating redundancy eliminates yet another problem with accurately communicating meaning.

If you're an experienced database designer and you've run into problems like these before, you can anticipate them and avoid them in future designs. In this case, you'd be relying on experience to keep you out of trouble, but until you've experienced every possible problem, you won't be experienced enough to anticipate everything. It's better if you can follow a process that will guarantee a proper outcome.

While you intuitively understand the problems with all of the above examples, you would probably be hard pressed to come up with some kind of comprehensive logic to define their "wrongness." The relational model provides a conceptual framework that will enable you to say exactly why each of the above examples is wrong. Also note that these are examples of obvious errors; a lot of errors aren't so obvious. Familiarity with the relational model will enable you to detect more subtle errors.

Until now, you may have been relying on your experience and talent to create databases. Database development is an art rather than a science for most FileMaker programmers. Interestingly enough, this was the state of all database programming back in the 1960s. Since programming was an art, there was no real technique for evaluating the superiority of one approach over another.

This situation eventually led to an effort to give database development a more theoretical footing, and it culminated in the publication of "A Relational Model of Data for Large Shared Data Banks" by Dr. E.F. Codd in 1970. This paper introduced the relational model. The principles of the model grew out of two branches of mathematics: set theory and first order predicate logic. This grounding in existing mathematical theory made it possible to apply scientific rigor to the art of database development. The relational model has been refined over the years, but even when it was first proposed, it made it possible to create rules based on mathematics rather than intuition. That in turn made it possible to say why one design approach was superior to another. By conforming to the relational model, you can guarantee the accurate representation of meaning.

Having said that, we now say that there is no relational database product on the market that completely conforms to the relational model. It's a theoretical ideal, and the closer you are, the better you are at representing meaning. Unfortunately, experience shows that the closer you get, the more likely it is that your database will have lousy performance. You need to strike a balance between the ideal structure and practical performance. We'll return to this issue later in the book.

Anyway, certain parts of the relational model are difficult to implement without severely limiting the performance of a database system, and for that reason, no relational database product (including FileMaker) on the market today fully conforms to the relational model. Don't freak out and think that FileMaker is deficient just because it doesn't meet all the criteria. No other system does either.

Roots of the Relational Model

Let's touch briefly on the branches of mathematics that are the basis of the relational model. They have their own vocabulary of terms that have come to be applied to relational databases. We thought it would be helpful to see where these terms came from. Even if you fear advanced mathematics, press on; we'll keep this section as simple as we can. These concepts will help your understanding of the relational model later on.

Set Theory

The primary object of the relational model is the *relation*, which is roughly equivalent to a table. A relation is a special type of *set*, and for that reason, it's helpful for your understanding of relations if you understand some basic set theory. Ready? Time to dust off those old memories of math class. A set is a collection of objects. You can describe a set with an equation like this:

Bones = {femur, tibia, patella}

You can also represent them with a diagram as shown in Figure 1.1.

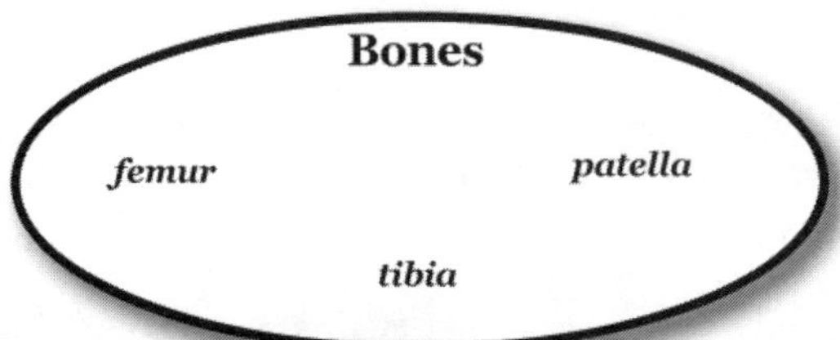

Figure 1.1 A set is an unordered collection of objects.

An important thing to note is that sets have no definite order, so that even though these bones were listed in a certain order, any order constitutes an equivalent set:

Bones = {femur, tibia, patella} = {tibia, patella, femur} = {patella, femur, tibia}

Members of a set are, by definition, distinct, so that even if we have duplicate values in the list, the set itself only recognizes one:

Bones = {femur, tibia, patella} = {femur, femur, tibia, tibia, patella}

Note that this is the same way that FileMaker stores values in its index: each record's field value is only stored in the index once. An index is a set. The above set was described by using a list, but large or infinite sets can also be described by a membership criteria:

States = {x| x is a state in the United States}

The "|" character is read "such that." This entire expression would be read as "States equals the set of all x such that x is a state in the United States." When you have a criteria like this, you need to evaluate whether or not some value of x meets the criteria, and if it does (as x = Georgia would), this would be expressed as x ∈ States. The "∈" symbol can be read as "is a member of," and thus this expression would read "x is a member of States." If x is not a member of the set, we would use the "∉" symbol, which means "is not a member of." In the case of x = turnip, we would express membership as x ∉ States, and we would read this as "x is not a member of States."

An empty set (a set with no objects) is also called a null or void set, and is represented by the ∅ symbol. When a field in a database is empty, it is said to contain a null or a null value. Believe it or not, the concept of nulls is quite complex. Rather than get into all that here, we'll come back to the topic later in the chapter and show you why.

Given these three sets:

States = {x| x is a state in the United States}
Midwestern States = {Illinois, Michigan, Ohio, Indiana, Wisconsin}
∅ = { }

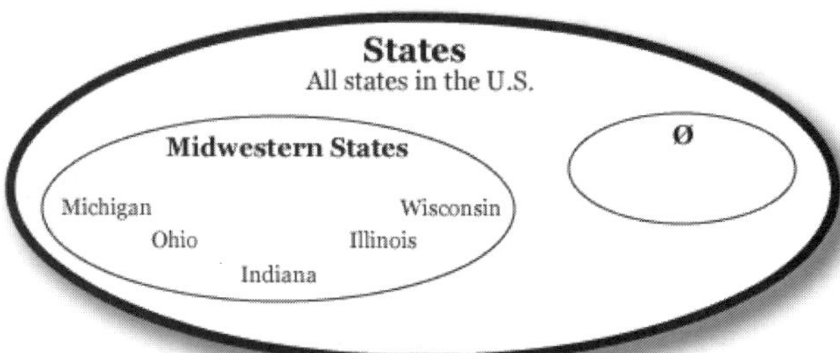

Figure 1.2 Both Midwestern States and the empty set are subsets of States.

You can say that the set Midwestern States is a subset of States since every value in Midwestern States is also contained in States. Conversely, States is a superset of Midwestern States. This is expressed as States ⊇ Midwestern States. By the way, the empty set is a subset of every set, so we could also say that States ⊇ ∅. Remember this, because it will have some significant implications when we start talking about empty field values.

Now we need to get into set operators. Set operators are used to add, subtract, divide, etc. When we first showed this chapter to proofreaders, they started getting agitated right about here. For those of you who are getting agitated, we have this to say: Don't freak out about the funny symbols. It's important for you to understand set operations because they are the foundation for relational operators and thus relational algebra. You'll have a better understanding of relationships in FileMaker Pro if you have a grasp of relational algebra. If you're math challenged and all of this makes you approach hysteria, relax. It's not that bad. If you keep on reading and decide that yes, it is that bad, I guess you should flip to another chapter. There's plenty of straight FileMaker stuff in the rest of this book. However, if you want to become a good relational database developer and not just a good FileMaker developer, you really need to have a handle on the fundamental concepts. Be brave and read on.

If you add the elements of two sets together, this is called a union. Union is represented by the "∪" symbol. For example:

O States = {Ohio, Oklahoma, Oregon}
V States = {Vermont, Virginia}
O States ∪ V States = {Oklahoma, Oregon, Ohio, Vermont, Virginia}

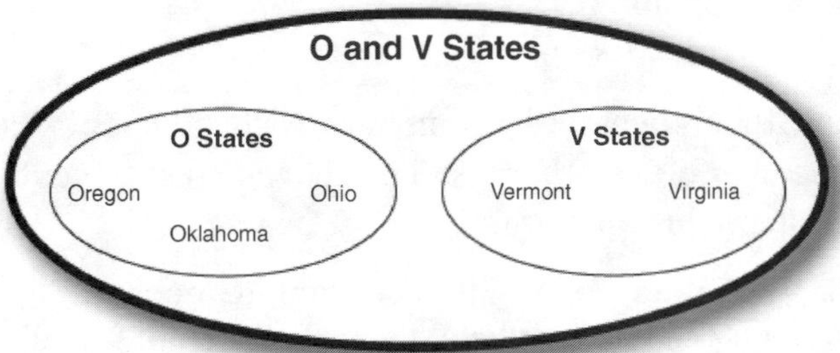

Figure 1.3 The union of O States and V States yields a larger set containing both O States and V States as subsets.

If you create a set by using only the members that two or more sets have in common, you have an intersection. Intersection is represented by the "∩" symbol, as shown below:

O States ∩ Midwestern States = {Ohio}

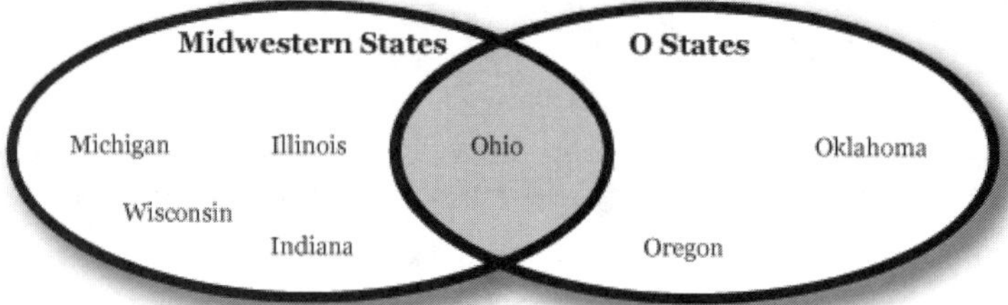

Figure 1.4 The intersection of O States and Midwestern States is a set containing one item: Ohio.

NOTE This chart shows the set operators.

Set Operator	Meaning
∈	is a member of
∉	is not a member of
⊇	superset
∪	union
∩	intersection

If you multiply two or more sets together, the result is called the Cartesian product of these sets. The notion of multiplying collections of things together is a little funky, but it works like this. Given these sets:

Shirts = {Green, Red, Blue}
Shorts = {Yellow, Tan, Black}

we can multiply them together by combining each member of each set with every other member of the other set. The above two sets would yield the following Cartesian product of outfits:

Shirts X Shorts = {(Green, Yellow), (Green, Tan), (Green, Black), (Red, Yellow), (Red, Tan), (Red, Black), (Blue, Yellow), (Blue, Tan), (Blue, Black)}

If we multiplied three or four sets together, we'd have three or four items in each piece of the result. An important thing to note about all of these set operators is that when we use them, we start with sets, and we wind up with sets. Sets in, sets out. This is known as the *closure property*. Remember this term because you'll see it again later.

From this concept of a set, we're going to jump to the concept of a relation. A relation is just a set of ordered pairs. Given the following people from our baseball team:

Player Name	**Position**
Chris	Catcher
Bob	First Base
Andy	Pitcher

there is a relationship between the value in the first column and the value in the second column. This relationship has to be expressed in an ordered pair. We would mathematically define the relation Team as follows:

relation Team = {(Chris, Catcher), (Bob, First Base), (Andy, Pitcher)}

Each argument in each pair is said to be *related* to the other argument, thus Chris is related to Catcher, and so on.

This set of ordered pairs represents the relationship between two distinct sets of values, a set of players and a set of positions. The team roster is basically a set of variables that we can plug in to the relation, and when we do, the result is the position. I can ask you what position Bob plays, and you can look at the relation and answer that he plays first base. The set of variables (the team roster) has a special name: the domain. The *domain* is a set of all possible variable values. The set of results also has a special name: the range. The domain of Team is {Chris, Bob, Andy}, and the range of Team is {Catcher, First Base, Pitcher}. If we had a slightly different version of this relation showing how each player batted:

relation Team = {(Chris, Right), (Bob, Right), (Andy, Left)}

the domain of Team would still be {Chris, Bob, Andy}, but the range of Team would be {Right, Left}.

The relational model has an extended version of this concept of a relation. We'll get into that shortly, but first, let's take a look at the other main root of the relational model.

First Order Predicate Logic

You don't need to have any understanding of predicate logic in order to understand the relational model, although you probably already have an intuitive understanding of the basic ideas. What an understanding of predicate logic will give you is a conceptual framework from which you can evaluate the "rightness" or "wrongness" of database entries. Ensuring that only acceptable data gets entered into your database means that you can ensure that your database maintains fidelity to its intended meaning. This is obviously important, and therefore this topic is worth knowing something about.

Before we go wading in here only to get bushwhacked by incomprehensible math jargon and expressions, let's figure out what we're talking about. Logic is the study of deductive argument. It's that fun branch of mathematics that doesn't even care what you're being logical about; it only cares about whether or not your sentence structure is right. This can be confusing sometimes. Take this example:

If 1 > 4 and 6 = 4, then 1 > 6

The trick to logic is to ignore the truthfulness of the premise involved. Just see if the conclusion is a logical consequence of the premise. It doesn't matter if a premise is "true" or not. This makes a great framework for declaring the meaning of something. The above logical expression declares that 1 is greater than 4. This is inconsistent with our normal understanding of number values, so we're actually declaring a new meaning for these values. We start with a clean slate. We're in a new universe where their traditional meanings are not yet understood, so we need to declare them. A seemingly paradoxical expression like the one above is a good example to drive that point home.

Think about this idea of being in a new universe. This is somewhat analogous to a person working with a database for the first time. They have no idea what's going on or what all this stuff in the database means. We need to declare meaning so that the user will understand the rules of the database system. Hold this thought. We're going to pick it up again later in the chapter.

A *predicate* is, in a nutshell, an expression that uses one or more singular arguments to form a true or false sentence. "Jake dislikes math" is a sentence containing a *two place* predicate: x dislikes y. We can substitute other arguments in for the dislikes predicate, such as "Cat dislikes dog." You describe a predicate by the number of places it has for terms. We can turn this into a *three place* predicate by saying something like this: "Giraffe dislikes pudding more than turnips." Okay. That part's not too tough. Let's carry this a bit farther.

Suppose you have a population of people {Fred, Sue, Anne} and the one place predicate "is weird." If we evaluate all of these propositions one at a time, we can find out whether they are true or false.

For the sake of this example, we will define the following:

Fred is weird is true
Sue is weird is true
Anne is weird is false

Since our end result is just a set of true or false results, we don't really need to see all of the gory details of how we got them. This being the case, you can save yourself a lot of time and effort by simplifying the above set of propositions to a single predicate that allows you to test a set of values instead of testing them one at a time. Let's express the predicate as Weird(x), and then we substitute our set of people for x to get our set of true/false results.

Again, the set of all possible values (the variables) of x is called the *domain* of Weird. Since the domain is a set, we can specify it either by listing each member of the set separately, or by describing the characteristics of the entire set. While we specified the exact values of x, we could also have said that the domain of Weird consists of every person in my neighborhood who's wearing purple socks. In other words, we can define the domain by rules rather than by specifically listing its members.

Sometimes you just need to know one thing about the entire result set. Maybe you need to know if any value of x evaluates to true, or if all values of x evaluate to true. To address these issues, we have *quantifiers*. The existential quantifier "E" indicates that for all possible values of x, at least one evaluates to true. For example:

```
(Ex) Weird(x)
```

is true if any of the people in my neighborhood who are wearing purple socks are weird. To be more formal about it, this expression is true if there exists any value of x such that Weird(x) is true.

Another quantifier is the universal quantifier "A." This one indicates that for all values of x, all of them evaluate to true:

(Ax) Weird(x) is true if Weird(x) is true for all possible values of x.

Let's map this concept into the world of relational databases. Just as the predicate Weird is a one place predicate, the customer relation (database) mentioned at the beginning of the chapter has five fields and is therefore a five place predicate: Customer (a,b,c,d,e). If a database conforms to the relational model, the field structure of the database is actually a predicate, with each field having its own underlying domain. The zip code field, for example, has a domain of all possible zip codes. They may not all be in the database yet, but only values coming from that list are allowed. When values from that list are entered, they evaluate to true. When values not in that list are entered, they evaluate to false. To enforce the accuracy of the database's meaning, every variable value (a,b,c,d,e) in a given record needs to evaluate to true before it can be deemed acceptable. In other words, for the relation Customer to be true (to accurately represent meaning), all values of (a,b,c,d,e) need to be true in the predicate. If any item in the set of (a,b,c,d,e) is false, it should be rejected by the database. In other words, if a user tries to enter this:

Name	**Address**	**City**	**State**	**Zip**
30305	CMC	GA	Atlanta	123 Main Street

which might be mathematically represented as this:

Customer (30305, CMC, GA, Atlanta, 123 Main Street)

the database system should evaluate it as false and not accept it, thereby preserving the true meaning of the database.

This seems nice and tidy, but you're probably wondering how a database might determine that the above attempted entry is false. That's an excellent question, and we're going to answer it in the next section.

Overview of the Relational Model

Okay, now that we've been through the roots, we think you'll find that the ideas in the relational model naturally follow. There are three sections of the relational model: objects, operators, and integrity.

Objects

The list of objects in the relational model is as follows:

- Relation
- Tuple
- Attribute
- Key — candidate key, primary key, foreign key
- Domain

The main object is the relation, and before we go on, we need to distinguish between relation variables and relation values. Just as you can refer to some value x (a variable) in algebra, you can also say that x (a variable) = 6 (a value). The same goes for relations. You can speak abstractly of some relation R, and in doing so you refer to a relation variable. It can change over time and be redefined. That's what variables do. When we define the relation Customer as having certain attributes (also known as fields), we're then talking about a relation value. It now has been declared as having a certain structure. For the rest of this book, when we refer to a relation, we'll actually be referring to a relation value. While knowledge of this detail will probably have no place in your database discussions, isn't it nice to be armed in case you run into a real math wonk?

NOTE Just to make sure that everyone's clear on this concept, we want everyone to know that a relation in the relational model (or in set theory) has nothing to do with a relation(ship) in FileMaker Pro. A relation in this chapter is an abstract mathematical concept, while a FileMaker relationship is a link from one FileMaker database file to another.

The next item of business is that a relation in the relational model is a bit different from a relation in standard set theory. If you'll recall, a regular relation is a set of ordered pairs, something like this:

Team = {(Chris, Catcher), (Bob, First Base), (Andy, Pitcher)}

In the relational model, such a set is actually a *tuple* (rhymes with couple), and a relation is a set of tuples:

Team = {{(Name : Chris), (Position : Catcher)}, {(Name : Bob), (Position : First Base), {(Name : Andy), (Position : Pitcher)}}

These two structures are significantly different. A *set theory* is a set of ordered pairs while a *relational model relation* is a set of sets of ordered pairs. For the rest of this chapter, when we refer to a relation, we'll be referring to a relation as described in the relational model. As you can see, it's not a very big jump from this type of relation to a database table. A relation is a more formal mathematical expression of a table, and a table roughly corresponds to a file in FileMaker Pro. We say roughly because FileMaker's file structure has some quirks that make a file more than just a table. Layouts, for example, don't belong in a table. We'll get into more on this topic in Chapter 3.

Name	Position
Chris	Catcher
Bob	First Base
Andy	Pitcher

Figure 1.5 It's easier to view the contents of a relation in spreadsheet form.

Figure 1.5 shows a different representation of our Team relation. A relation consists of a heading and a body. The heading is comprised of the set of attributes, while the body consists of a set of tuples. A tuple is a row of a relation, or a record of a database. The number of attributes is the *degree* of the relation. If you have a database with three fields, you could say that it represented a relation of degree 3. The number of tuples is the *cardinality* of the relation.

Now let's talk about domains again. Domains are probably the most important conceptual part of a relation. Recall that a domain is a set of every possible value that a given attribute can have. For example, if a domain is defined to be whole numbers between 1 and 5, then only those values can be entered in a row for that attribute. We're talking about predicate logic again. Membership in the underlying domain of an attribute makes a value acceptable or unacceptable, because it makes that instance of the attribute true or false. For example, given an attribute City that is defined on the domain of U.S. cities, the value 781 would make that instance of the attribute City false, while Atlanta would make it true. Every attribute in a relation has to be defined on a domain, and it is this fact which makes a relation of degree 5 (such as the Customer relation mentioned earlier) into a five place predicate. For every tuple of the relation, it must be true that the value in every attribute be a member of the underlying domain.

This is an extremely powerful concept. It provides a mathematical basis for determining whether a piece of data is an acceptable entry or whether a record is a valid record. If any attribute of a row has an invalid entry (an entry that is not found in the underlying domain of that attribute), then the record is invalid as well.

It might help to think of a domain as a sophisticated data type. In FileMaker, you have data types such as text, number, date, time, etc. Using the domain concept, think of having city, state, color, or atomic weight as additional data types. Let's think back to one of the examples at the beginning of this chapter. We talked about creating a relationship between Invoice ID in the Invoice database and Quantity in the Line Item database. This relationship would be meaningless because the two fields are defined on different domains, and they therefore have different data types. A relationship between Invoice ID in the Invoice database and Invoice ID in the Line Item database "makes sense" because both fields are defined on the domain Invoice ID. By the way, it's customary to name the attribute and the domain that it's defined on with the same name.

There's something else you need to know about domains, and that is that all values in a domain need to be atomic. (What a great term, huh? Captain Attribute and the Atomic Domains — now available from Predicate Records...) A value that is said to be atomic has no internal structure. Actually, it would be better to say that it has no meaningful internal structure. Let's look at an example. If you have a field called Location that contained the value "Chicago, Illinois," that value would not be atomic, since it can be broken down into two meaningful values: "Chicago" and "Illinois." Putting those two values in separate fields would still give you the same meaning. Of course, we can break "Chicago" down into its constituent letters, but when we go that far, we lose meaning. So, when we say that an atomic value has no internal structure, we really mean that we can't break the structure down any more without sacrificing meaning. You might say that domains contain the smallest possible units of meaning within a relation.

Having said that, we now have to say that the complexity or simplicity of an atomic value is arbitrary. You could decide that atomic values for a particular domain consist of phone books. Each phone book may have hundreds of thousands of individual phone numbers in it, but since you've decided that that's the smallest unit that you care about, then for the purposes of that domain, the phone book's internal structure is irrelevant. You get to decide what an atomic value is. It may be a map or a short story or anything you want. In the example above, you could decide that since different states can have cities of the same name, and since you never need to deal with city and state information independently of each (in a report, for example), then it's perfectly valid to designate a city-state pair as an atomic value. It's your party. Set it up however you like, but always think of the possible consequences of updating information, reporting information, and so on. The bottom line is that once you decide on the complexity of an atomic value, you can properly determine the membership in a domain.

Domains are therefore a way — actually the way — of embedding and enforcing meaning within a relation. If a user can only enter "proper" values for a field, they can't help but preserve the intended meaning and usage of that field. Practically speaking, you can also impart meaning via labels and instructions, but in terms of an abstract relation, the domain embodies the meaning of an attribute.

This is all fabulous, of course, but unfortunately, most relational database products out there don't support domains well, if at all, and FileMaker is no exception. Think of the technical difficulties in allowing database designers to specify data types of such a huge variety. It boggles the mind. If you can't define the domain mathematically (U.S. Cities, for example), you need to have separate tables to hold the values for each domain. A large system would require a staggering number of domain tables.

The only answer is to do the best you can. You have what you might consider crude support for domains in FileMaker Pro in the form of the existing data types. You can also use calculated validation to enforce those domains that can be defined mathematically. If your domain will fit into a reasonably sized database, you could validate that a field value is a member of a value list. That value list would draw its values from the domain database. We'll discuss all of these approaches in detail in Chapter 2.

The strategies mentioned above are workable solutions, but just because you can rig something up to support the notion of domains doesn't mean that FileMaker supports domains. You have to build that support into your database designs. Most other systems have the same problem, so FileMaker is not uniquely deficient in this regard.

We're going to hold off on the discussion of keys for now. We'll pick up that topic later in the chapter when we discuss integrity.

Now that we have our relation anatomy specified, let's discuss the four properties of a relation as specified in the relational model.

No duplicate tuples. Remember that a relation is really just a special kind of set, and sets do not recognize duplicate values. Still, rules are meant to be broken, right? If you want a few duplicates, why should anyone care? Here's why: In a single-user database system, you know the meaning of your database system. As soon as that becomes a shared database system, though, the meaning of that database system needs to be correctly interpreted by multiple people. The obstacles to getting everyone to agree on the correct meaning of duplicate rows are so high that it would be virtually impossible for you to guarantee the correct interpretation. You seem skeptical. Then answer this: How can you guarantee that every user will interpret a duplicated row in the same way? How would a user distinguish between an accidentally duplicated row versus one that was intentionally created? If the rule is that there will never be duplicate tuples, a duplicate row should be rejected by the system. Even if you couldn't enforce such a rule, the very existence of that (alas, breakable) rule would help users understand that duplicate rows are invalid. The intended meaning would be clear, and there would never be any such confusion.

Tuples have no order. Again, because a relation is a set, and because sets are defined by their unordered contents (allowing set A = {x,y,z} to equal {z,y,x}), relations also have no internal order. Information within a relation is accessed via the use of logical predicates (i.e., Invoice ID = 36), not by some record number. This property is a good example of why tables and relations aren't quite the same thing. A FileMaker table stores records in the order in which they were created. Since a relation is an abstract concept that has no dependence on the system required to "operate" the relation, a relation can't have any such storage order.

Note that a relation might possess an attribute that describes creation order. Make sure that you don't misinterpret such an attribute to mean that the relation has an order. FileMaker may need to assign its own internal creation order data to records, but this is a practical consequence of trying to make the software function and has no relevance to the properties of relations.

Attributes have no order. For the same reason that tuples have no order, attributes have no order. Both are just examples of sets. The relation Customer still has the same meaning whether you have {Customer Name, City, State} or {City, State, Customer Name}. We can express meaning mathematically by saying:

Customer = {(Customer ID : 1), (Name : Fred)} = {(Name : Fred), (Customer ID : 1)}

If you think about this in FileMaker terms, it really makes no difference how you arrange fields on a layout. You're still looking at the same database file (relation).

Attribute values are atomic. This follows naturally from the fact that domains can only contain atomic values and that attributes must be defined on a domain. You can also refer to atomic values as scalars. You'll find both of these terms if you decide to look into the relational literature. When a relation contains only scalar (atomic) values, it is normalized, or in first normal form. There are more normal forms, but we'll get into those in Chapter 3.

Operators

Operators allow you to manipulate relations. A key thing to remember is that in the same manner that set operators take sets as arguments and yield sets as results, relational operators take relations as arguments and yield relations as results. This is known as the relational closure property. Another important point about relational operators is that the results must have consistent headers all the way through. For example, it would be meaningless to import a product database into a contact database. The two relations have different types of tuples. Results of relational operations must have consistent tuples throughout; otherwise, the results will be sets but not relations, and this would violate the relational closure property.

Dr. Codd's original presentation of the relational model contained eight relational operators. Four were based on the standard set operators: union, intersection, subtraction, and product. The other four were join, project, restrict, and divide. Together, these comprise the relational algebra. There's also a relational calculus, but it's really an equivalent of the algebra, just in a sentence, or descriptive, format. We'll stick with describing the algebra. If you'd like to read up on relational calculus, see Appendix A. Following is a description of each operator.

Union

The union of two relations will yield a new relation that consists of all tuples from both relations by vertically stacking them. Tuples common to both source relations will only appear once in the new result relation since all tuples in a relation must be unique. This would be analogous to importing all records from one file into another file, then purging duplicates.

Figure 1.6 Union combines all tuples from two or more relations.

Intersection

The intersection of two relations will yield a new relation that contains only those tuples that appeared in both relations. Again, even though the tuples are being drawn from two relations, each common tuple will only appear once in the resulting relation to preserve tuple uniqueness.

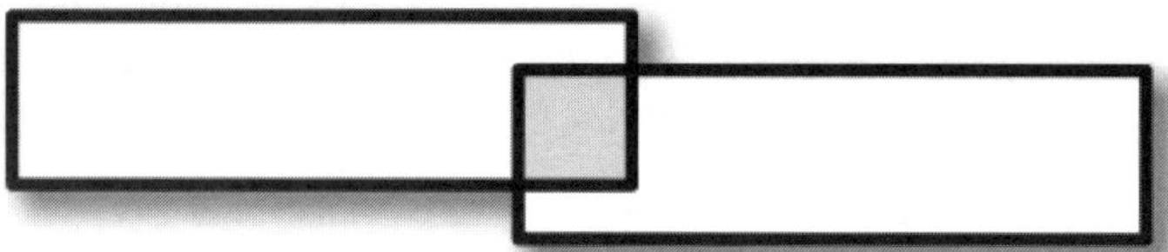

Figure 1.7 Intersection results in only those tuples that two or more relations have in common.

Subtraction

Subtracting one relation from another yields a relation that contains all of the tuples from the first relation that were not found in the second relation. Just like in regular math, order matters. Subtracting relation B from relation A is different from subtracting relation A from relation B, just like 6 – 3 is different from 3 – 6. The first argument is the one that has tuples subtracted from it.

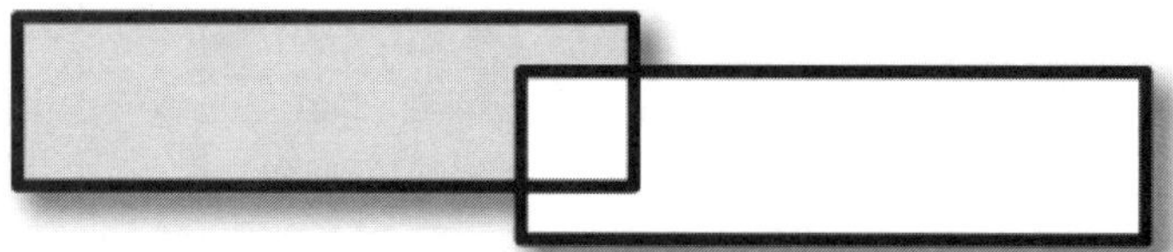

Figure 1.8 Subtraction removes the intersection of the two (or more) relations from the first relation.

Product

This is similar to the Cartesian product in set theory. The product of two relations yields a new relation that has all possible combinations of tuples from the first two relations.

Invoice ID	Invoice Date	Customer ID
2002	3/21/2002	33
2003	4/12/2002	36
2004	4/24/2002	51

Product ID	Product Name	Price
1	Rosetta Stone	$33.00
2	Tarot Cards	$12.95
3	Amethyst Geode	$22.00

Figure 1.9 These are the Invoice and Product relations.

Given two relations, you take each tuple from the first relation and combine it with every tuple from the second relation, yielding the result in Figure 1.10.

Invoice ID	Invoice Date	Customer ID	Product ID	Product Name	Price
2002	3/21/2002	33	1	Rosetta Stone	33.00
2002	3/21/2002	33	2	Tarot Cards	12.95
2002	3/21/2002	33	3	Amethyst Geode	22.00
2003	4/12/2002	36	1	Rosetta Stone	33.00
2003	4/12/2002	36	2	Tarot Cards	12.95
2003	4/12/2002	36	3	Amethyst Geode	22.00
2004	4/24/2002	51	1	Rosetta Stone	33.00
2004	4/24/2002	51	2	Tarot Cards	12.95
2004	4/24/2002	51	3	Amethyst Geode	22.00

Figure 1.10 The Cartesian product combines all attributes from both relations. The degree of the resulting relation is the degree of the two arguments added together, while the cardinality is the cardinality of the two arguments multiplied together.

Again, it's important to note that every tuple in the resulting relation has the same structure. Does this table look kind of familiar? It's pretty similar to the kind of line items file that you would have between an invoice database and a product database. Hmm. Could our old familiar Line Item file actually be some kind of Cartesian product relation? We'll revisit this question in the next chapter.

Join

A join actually yields a result that's similar to the result produced by the product operator. In both the product and join operations, you combine the attributes of two relations to come up with a whole new (larger) structure in the result relation. This is analogous to creating a relationship in FileMaker Pro. When two relations are joined, they yield a new relation that has combined tuples from each relation where the two corresponding tuples met some criteria for one or more attributes.

Invoice ID	Product ID
2002	1
2003	3
2004	2
2004	3

Product ID	Product Name	Price
1	Rosetta Stone	$33.00
2	Tarot Cards	$12.95
3	Amethyst Geode	$22.00

Invoice ID	Product ID	::Product Name	::Price
2002	1	Rosetta Stone	$33.00
2003	3	Amethyst Geode	$22.00
2004	2	Tarot Cards	$12.95
2004	3	Amethyst Geode	$22.00

Figure 1.11 These Line Item and Product relations can be joined on their one common attribute: Product ID.

This particular type of join is based on both attributes being equal, and it's called an equijoin. An equijoin is a type of Θ-join (theta join). Θ is just a stand-in for some type of operator. You might create the join based on A being equal to B, greater than B, less than B, etc., where Θ is =, >, or <, respectively. We'll cover these other types of joins in the next chapter.

Even though two columns of Product ID (one from each table) went into the operation, only one came out. Note that in this case the two relations used as arguments were joined on a single attribute. Relations can also be joined on multiple attributes.

Project

The project operator takes only a subset of attributes from a relation. This result would be analogous to having a FileMaker database that contained six fields, but only four were showing on a layout. While the viewable result is the same, remember that in the relational model, the project operation will yield a completely new relation that has fewer attributes than the original argument relation.

Restrict

Sometimes referred to as the SELECT operator, a restrict is analogous to performing a find in FileMaker. The operation returns a relation containing a subset of rows from a source relation based upon selection criteria in one or more attributes. The selection criteria will generally be an expression that contains a comparison operation (equality, greater than, or less than) and a value (literal, range of values, or another expression).

Divide

This one is a little tricky to understand, and even harder to describe. You start with two relations, one of which is a superset of the other. The larger relation is the dividend, and the smaller relation is the divisor. They both must have an attribute in common. The division operation results in a relation that contains only the non-common attributes from the dividend. Furthermore, it only contains tuples from the dividend where the attributes matched with all values in the other relation. We know that's tough to follow. You'll have a much easier time of it if you just take a look at the example in Figure 1.12.

Invoice ID	Product ID	::Product Name	::Price
2002	1	Rosetta Stone	$33.00
2003	3	Amethyst Geode	$22.00
2004	2	Tarot Cards	$12.95
2004	3	Amethyst Geode	$22.00

Divided by

Product ID	Product Name	Price
2	Tarot Cards	$12.95
3	Amethyst Geode	$22.00

Yields

Invoice ID
2004

Invoice ID	Product ID	::Product Name	::Price
2002	1	Rosetta Stone	$33.00
2003	3	Amethyst Geode	$22.00
2004	2	Tarot Cards	$12.95
2004	3	Amethyst Geode	$22.00

Divided by

Product ID	Product Name	Price
1	Rosetta Stone	$33.00

Yields

Invoice ID
2002

Figure 1.12 The division operator is useful if you want to find all of one thing that contained another. These two examples show all invoices that contained Products 2 and 3 and all invoices that contained Product 1.

Integrity

Integrity rules are designed to force users to enter only meaningful data into a database system. We hesitate to equate meaning with an actual representation of reality. For example, if a large software manufacturer created a database system that tracked software sales through every possible sales outlet — computer superstores, tiny shops that buy through distribution, and everything in between — it would be almost impossible for the manufacturer to fill the database with complete information. There would be gaps in the data, and those gaps would only allow the system to imperfectly represent reality.

The main integrity rules are those enforced by the domain of an attribute. The rule might be that values in the State attribute must come from the pool of U.S. states, or that Cities must come from the pool of valid U.S. cities. Again, enforcing domains is something that FileMaker doesn't do naturally, so we'll defer further discussion of this topic until Chapter 2.

The other integrity rules are based on the concept of keys, but before we get into that topic, we need to address an issue that straddles both the concepts of domains and keys.

Null Values

One aspect of domains that we haven't touched on is whether or not they can be defined to contain blank or null values. Conceptually, these are not the same thing. Let's consider two scenarios. In a contact database, it's common to have an Address 1 and an Address 2 field. This setup comes in handy when someone has a two-part address such as 123 Main Street, Suite 33 (or Accounting Department). One piece of the street address would go in Address 1, the other in Address 2. If there's only one part to the address, Address 2 will be left blank. Then again, if you have problems with data entry, maybe Address 1 will be left blank. It happens. For the sake of this example, let's say Address 2 is left blank, and in this case it is intentionally left blank. The meaning of this blank is that there is no Address 2.

In the second scenario, you receive a letter from someone, and you enter the address from the letter into your contact management database. Unfortunately, the writer did not include a phone number, so you need to leave the Phone Number field blank because it is unknown at this time. This is a very different meaning than the one conveyed by the blank Address 2 field in the first scenario.

Again, the agreement by all users of the database on what things mean is at the heart of this issue. It's common practice to have the implicit understanding that if an "important" field like Phone Number is empty, it's unknown, while if Address 2 is missing, it probably doesn't exist. Strictly speaking, this is unacceptable enforcement of meaning. Practically speaking, it probably works well enough. This chapter is about a theoretical construct, though, not the practical demands of daily living, so for the moment we have to frown on such practices.

Since the whole point of the relational model is to codify and enforce meaning, null values are a big hairy deal. There is disagreement among relational model theorists on how nulls fit into the relational model. At one end of the spectrum you have Codd, the inventor of the relational model, who says that nulls are an integral part of the model. At the other end, you have C.J. Date, another giant in the field, who says that nulls are not completely understood and that they have no place in the relational model. Given this lack of consensus, it may seem like the slipshod approach alluded to earlier is as good as any, but that doesn't address the fundamental goal, which is the preservation of meaning.

If you take Date's approach and disallow nulls, a record would not be acceptable by the database system until all values were present. Date's way of getting around this is a default value scheme. In other words, a user designates some default value to indicate what the null means right in the field. For example, if a phone number exists but is unknown, you could use the default value "Unknown" instead. For this to be valid, the value "Unknown" would also have to be added to the domain. This would be awkward since it would lead to a mixed data type within the domain, which would be a combination of valid phone numbers and a non-phone number that indicates that the real one is out there somewhere but is missing in action. Practically speaking, if you do something like a mail merged letter with the phone number included, you need to create "special case" logic to omit the "Unknown" value when it's encountered. There are other problems with putting the responsibility for meaning into the hands of the users, but let's not go there. Suffice it to say that it gets messy in a hurry.

Codd's approach accepts nulls as a fact of life. He advocates a kind of purgatory for incomplete tuples. If a tuple is missing critical information (such as part of its primary key — covered later in this chapter), it is not subject to the integrity mechanisms until the complete information is entered. Unfortunately, there are no relational database products that have this kind of two-step entry process capability. In other words, a tuple is supposed to be "true," according to the predicate of domain membership, in order to be added to the relation. While nulls are technically a member of every set, and therefore a member of every domain, a tuple that contains only null values might be technically valid, but its meaning is ambiguous. Also, allowing null values in every attribute makes it impossible to uniquely identify a record. This approach seems to have as many practical problems as the first one.

Candidate Keys

We mentioned earlier that relations are unordered. We can't refer to a specific row number to reference a specific tuple in the relation, so we need to have some other way of referencing a specific tuple. If we can't do this, we can't perform an operation on a specific tuple. If that's the case, any operations we need to perform on only a specific tuple may affect innocent bystander tuples, thus compromising their integrity (destroying their meaning). For that reason, it is essential that we are able to construct some kind of predicate that can reference a specific tuple. For example, in an Invoice relation we might want to see a row where:

Invoice ID = 37

This predicate will either be true or false for every tuple in the relation. We need to look at the tuple where this predicate is true. We don't need to worry about the criteria too much if we don't care what we get back, but if we want to find a single tuple, we need to be able to uniquely identify a tuple. That is, find a predicate that is true for a single row.

We know that since every tuple has to be unique, all of the attributes in a given relation will form a unique combination in every tuple. Given this Invoice relation:

Invoice
Invoice ID   Invoice Date   Customer

We can construct a predicate where:

Invoice ID = 37 AND Invoice Date = 9/29/98 AND Customer = CMC

Obviously, the more complex your relation, the more unwieldly this method becomes. In some cases, using all attributes will be the only way to uniquely identify a tuple, but in others, there will be some subset of all of a relation's attributes that will also uniquely identify a tuple. When you get to the point where such a subset can't be reduced any further while still uniquely identifying a tuple, you've found a candidate key.

A *candidate key* consists of a group of one or more attributes in a relation that is unique for every possible tuple of the relation. Furthermore, no subset of this group of attributes can also be unique for every possible tuple of the relation. This last part is worth an example.

Given an invoice system (shown here with some friends):

Invoice

Invoice ID	Invoice Date	Customer

Line Item

Invoice ID	Product ID	Quantity	Price

Product

Product ID	Product Name

Let's say that the Invoice ID in the Invoice table and the Product ID in the Product table are both serial numbers, and are therefore unique in each record of their respective relations. Since the Invoice ID has the uniqueness property all by itself in the Invoice table, the Invoice Date and Customer are unnecessary for identifying uniqueness with the Invoice ID. Therefore, the Invoice ID comprises an entire candidate key by itself.

In the Line Item table, we have a similar situation, except that the subset of Invoice ID and Product ID have the uniqueness property. Since any given invoice might have multiple line items, the Invoice ID attribute by itself won't have the uniqueness property, and since a given product can appear on many invoices, the Product ID won't have the uniqueness property either. A key containing multiple attributes like this one is called a compound key, while a single attribute key is called a simple key. For the set of attributes {Invoice ID, Product ID}, no subset of this set can be unique for every possible tuple of the relation; therefore, it's a candidate key.

Every relation will always have at least one candidate key, again because every tuple has to be unique. It's possible for a relation to have more than one candidate key as well. Suppose that the Line Item table also contained a serial number Line Item ID. Assuming that you couldn't enter the same Product ID on an invoice more than once, the Line Item table would then have two candidate keys: {Line Item ID} and {Invoice ID, Product ID}.

Since candidate keys have to have the uniqueness property, permitting a null in the candidate key causes big problems. Let's look at the Invoice table described above. If we have two or more tuples where the Invoice ID is null, then we can't uniquely identify those rows. Permitting the null value destroys the candidate key. In fact, permitting a null in all attributes makes it possible for two tuples with all null values to exist. Since the definition of a relation mandates unique tuples, permitting nulls in all attributes destroys the relation.

Referring back to the end of the last section, Codd gets around this problem by positing a kind of non-member status to any tuple in the relation that has incomplete (containing nulls in any attribute) data. Again, this is nice in theory, but there are no relational database products that can recognize certain tuples as "not being in the club yet." If a tuple exists, it's in the relation. For practical purposes and given the functionality of current relational database products, the rule is that candidate keys cannot contain nulls. By the way, we refer to all relational database products and not just FileMaker Pro because FileMaker's ODBC capability means that it can exchange data with other relational systems. Since FileMaker is no longer an island, issues that affect all relational database systems also need to be taken into consideration by FileMaker developers.

Primary Keys

The relational model requires that one candidate key be designated as the *primary key*. Since there is usually only one candidate key, this is usually an easy call. In the cases where you have multiple candidate keys, the relational model doesn't specify any rules or guidelines for picking the "best" one. A good rule of thumb is to pick the one with the fewest attributes. If you have a tie, pick the one with the simplest attributes. Any candidate key that is not chosen as the primary key is called the alternate key.

NOTE There is some disagreement in the relational database literature about whether it's actually necessary to mandate that one of the candidate keys be designated as the primary key. There is also disagreement about whether a foreign key should only reference a related primary key, or if any of the candidate keys will do just as well. Since most database systems that you're likely to come into contact with reflect the "primary key school of thought," this chapter will follow the more conventional thinking.

Foreign Keys

Let's take another look at the invoice system discussed earlier:

Invoice

Invoice ID	Invoice Date	Customer

Line Item

Invoice ID	Product ID	Quantity	Price

Product

Product ID	Product Name

If you were to build this in FileMaker Pro, you'd have a portal in the Invoice database that created records in the Line Item database. The relationship that linked the two files would be built on Invoice ID in the Invoice database and Invoice ID in the Line Item database. In this case, the Invoice ID field in Line Item is what's known as a foreign key.

A *foreign key* references the primary key in another database or, in terms of the relational model, in another relation. The foreign key must always reference a primary key that actually exists in the other relation. This is known as *referential integrity*. As you might guess, a foreign key that references a nonexistent primary key in another relation is meaningless. Therefore, enforcing referential integrity is tantamount to protecting meaning. Preserving referential integrity has implications when we consider updating and deleting records.

Imagine what happens if you try to update a primary key that is referenced by an existing foreign key in another table. Let's revisit our trusty Invoice example and ponder this. If we had an invoice in FileMaker that had related line items in a portal, those line items would vanish if we changed the Invoice ID. We would have destroyed the referential integrity of the foreign key Invoice ID in the Line Item file. We have two options for maintaining that foreign key's referential integrity: We can either disallow changes to a primary key when it's referenced by some foreign key, or we can alter the foreign key so that it once again matches the primary key value. These two options are known as restricted update and cascading update, respectively. It's beyond the scope of this chapter to describe how to implement these features in FileMaker Pro, but the next chapter will cover the techniques for implementing these features in full detail.

NOTE Updating even part of a compound primary key is equivalent to updating the entire key. Because a primary key consists of a set (possibly a set containing only one attribute, but more than one attribute if we're talking about a compound primary key), changing the value of any member of the set changes the value of the set itself.

If we delete a tuple that contains a primary key that is referenced by an existing foreign key in another table, we'll again destroy the referential integrity of the foreign key. We again have two options for maintaining that foreign key's referential integrity: We can either disallow the deletion of a tuple when its primary key is referenced by some foreign key, or we can delete both the tuple in question as well as any tuples in another file that have foreign keys referencing that primary key. These two options are known as restricted delete and cascading delete, respectively. Again, the next chapter will cover the techniques for implementing these features in full detail.

Summary

This chapter took you through a discussion of why the relational model came into being and how it's the best tool you have to preserve the intended meaning of your database system. By "meaning" we mean that the database faithfully indicates what it's supposed to indicate. If your system tracks payments against invoices, it should never misrepresent someone's past due status according to the data in the system.

Prior to delving into the relational model itself, we reviewed some concepts from the two parent branches of mathematics that gave rise to the relational model: set theory and first order predicate logic. (Doesn't that sound impressive? Aren't you impressed with yourself that you know what that means now?) A relation in set theory is a special kind of set, a set of ordered pairs. First order predicate logic gives us a conceptual true/false framework for evaluating whether or not the data in a new record is acceptable.

The relational model consists of three parts: objects, operators, and integrity. Objects are things like relations, attributes (fields), tuples (records), domains, and keys. Operators allow you to manipulate relations, and they include some standard set operators like union, intersection, difference, and Cartesian product, as well as some different operators like restrict, project, join, and divide. Integrity rules are designed to force users to enter only meaningful data into a database system. Implementation of these rules relies on being able to uniquely identify records by the use of candidate/primary keys, and being able to uniquely identify related records by the use of foreign keys.

Chapter 2

The Relational Model and FileMaker Pro

In the first chapter, we went over the relational model in some detail — why it's important, how it came into being, and what its features are. At this point, we need to discuss the relational model as it's been implemented in FileMaker Pro. We'll also get into the details of how you can implement the features (or a close approximation thereof) of the relational model in your FileMaker Pro database systems. The first part of this chapter will deal with issues at the table level, and the second half will deal with issues at the field level. Specific topics include:

- Relational operators
- Domains
- Scalar values
- Primary keys
- Referential integrity

Building Relational Systems with FileMaker Pro

Before we get started, we need to make a transition. Chapter 1 was all about the relational model — all theory. We need to move from the concept of a model to a living, breathing system — a relational system. A *relational system* is a system built on the principles of the relational model. It's worth your while to try to develop FileMaker systems that are as close as is practical to being relational systems.

The best way to convince you that this is the case is to consider some examples.

Imagine the following two tables:

Invoice

Invoice Number	**Invoice Date**
1	8/3/2001
3	9/29/2001

Invoice Item

Invoice Number	**Product Number**
1	47
1	54
1	19
2	76
2	23
3	18

The problem here is that the Invoice Item file contains two records that refer to invoice 2, an invoice that no longer exists. Most people recognize that this isn't right. Most database designers know that this is bad. The question is, Do you know how to build a system where this can't ever happen? If you build a FileMaker system that's also a relational system, this won't be possible.

One more example just for fun:

Customer

Customer Number	**Customer Name**	**City**	**State**
1	Tom	Mentor	Ohio
2	Dick	Columbus	Ohio
3	Harry	Jasper	Saturn

Saturn isn't a state (in the United States anyway), but in most FileMaker systems that we've seen, there wouldn't be anything stopping a user from entering Saturn in the State field.

By constructing your FileMaker system as a relational system, you ensure that your FileMaker system won't even accept data that doesn't accurately represent reality (as defined by your design). If any of your past database implementations allow a user to have a customer ID that references a nonexistent customer, or a product ID that references multiple products, or a repeating field that is almost useless for reporting, then you have a problem that can be solved by redesigning the system as a relational system.

Let's start with the basics. In a relational system, the user "perceives" the data to be organized into tables called *base tables*. We emphasize the word "perceives" because it doesn't matter how the data is really stored. Several tables' worth of data could be lumped into a word processing document for all the user knows. The important thing to note is that the system hides physical organization issues from the user. The user doesn't need to know how the inner mechanisms work. This seems obvious to FileMaker developers because such an organizational scheme (i.e., data organized into files/tables) and ease of use are hallmarks of FileMaker. In the old days, though, programmers who actually used a programming language to work with their databases needed to have an intimate knowledge of its inner workings.

The concept of a relational system posits a higher level of abstraction. Messy technical stuff may still be going on behind the scenes, but the user experience is one of dealing with tables. Tables constitute the organizing structure of a database, and not some variable array or physical location on a hard drive.

Base tables roughly correspond to database files in FileMaker Pro. We say "roughly" because there are some other non-table items in FileMaker files that come along for the ride. To better explain this statement, it would be instructive to get a broader perspective and look at how things work in other relational database systems. Let's make a brief digression.

In larger database management systems such as those made by Oracle or IBM, the only thing in the actual database tables is raw data (well, almost). No field can be dependent on another field for its field value, so there are no such things as calculation fields that have an underlying mathematical definition. Typical field types in these systems are:

- Char (fixed-length text field)
- Date
- Decimal
- Float (floating-point decimal number)
- Integer

- Long (takes long character data, 2 GB long in the case of Oracle)
- VarChar (variable-length character string)

There are many other field types, but this should give you a feel for the situation. FileMaker's text field type would correlate to a VarChar field type, but while that's the extent of FileMaker's text field types, there are several more (such as the Char type) in the larger environments. You can be very surgical in your data typing methodology in these larger systems.

In a typical client/server environment, a user never interacts with the main system directly. The interaction is always by means of some "front-end" application — the client in a client/server paradigm. These days that front-end application is often a web browser, which in turn communicates with an intermediate application that converses with the database system. Fields that users see in these applications may or may not really exist in the underlying database tables. Since calculation fields can't exist in the base tables, they need to be derived on the fly by the client application (or by the intermediate application logic in the case of web browsers).

This construct is very different from the way that FileMaker files are structured. Leaving FileMaker's web publishing capabilities aside for the moment, the client application roughly corresponds to the collection of FileMaker layouts, buttons, and scripts, as well as calculation, summary, and global fields that are found in most FileMaker systems. For the purposes of this chapter, we'll refer to these field types as view fields. In the typical client/server environment, these view fields usually have a very short life span. They get calculated within the client application and then are presented to the user in the form of a table (even a single record is a single-row table). Since this table contains data that is not found in an underlying base table, it is said to be a *derived table*. To frame this in terms of FileMaker concepts, a derived table is any table that includes calculation or summary field values. A subsummary report would be a good example. In our client/server scenario, once the client application quits or drops the derived temporary table, the table and the values in it are destroyed. In similar fashion, FileMaker's summary field values change depending on the sort order or found set. They're very transient.

Data in a derived table is said to be *materialized*. If the base table stores 1 or 0 and the user sees Yes or No, this direct reinterpretation of a single field is called *direct materialization*. When a field in a derived table uses several records or fields to derive a value, as in an invoice subtotal, this lack of a direct correlation between a single field value in the base table and the field value that the user sees is called *indirect materialization*. This is also an example of a *virtual field* since it doesn't even exist in the base table. These virtual fields correspond to FileMaker's calculation and summary fields, which also use multiple field values to derive a single value.

Let's ponder this for a moment. We can roughly match up FileMaker's components to those found in larger relational systems, but only a small part of a FileMaker table would actually be considered a table in the other systems. Layouts would be considered views in a client application (and not part of the table), while calculation fields, summary fields, and global fields would only be found in the client application as virtual fields. Only text, number, date, time, and container fields could be found in the base tables of these other systems. Things such as scripts or layouts have nothing to do with table data in the relational model. For our purposes, let's consider a FileMaker file to be more than a table, which it is. It includes one table and a potentially large number of views with their materialized fields.

One thing we haven't addressed yet is the notion of scripts. FileMaker scripts actually have their parallels in larger database systems; in some systems, scripts even live in tables as they do in FileMaker. Again, this cohabitation has nothing to do with table data in the relational model, but it's a practical reality of relational database systems. The types of scripts that live with the tables are called triggers or stored procedures, and they usually fulfill some sort of validation function analogous to what we can do with FileMaker's calculated validation. Other sorts of scripts exist in client applications, so that's why we say that FileMaker scripts don't neatly map to the larger relational database systems. Suffice it to say that they have their counterparts in both server tables and client applications.

Relational Closure Property

Remember the relational closure property from Chapter 1? It says that operations on relations need to have other relations as outputs. A relation is a more strictly defined version of a table, and the whole point here is that when you perform an operation on a table (restrict, for example, which amounts to a find in FileMaker), you get another table as the result of that operation.

We know that base tables are the actual building blocks of a relational system, and we know that derived tables are literally new tables (usually temporary) that are derived from the base tables. We mentioned one way that the tables are derived, but the derivation may not be strictly about reinterpreting stored data.

For example, in FileMaker you might have a database with 60 records in it. If you want to see a subset of all the rows in the table that meet some criteria, you would perform a find and get a found set. The found set is really a new table as perceived by you, the user. It is a row subset of the underlying table, and for viewing and printing purposes, it's a table in its own right. In a similar fashion, layouts are used to restrict the number of columns in this virtual table, so they can be considered a column subsetting tool. The user's various views (layouts) of the table are representations of temporary new tables that are distinct from the base table that actually contains the found set or layout that is being employed. Yes, we know that layouts are persistent and don't go away when you stop looking at them. We say "temporary" because you temporarily "delete" that particular view of the data (at least your ability to view or print it) when you change layouts. It's a nuance, we know, but play along with us for a bit.

This is an important concept, and it's probably more difficult for FileMaker users to grasp because of the way that layouts exist in the same file as the data. If you're having trouble with it, humor us on this point: Whenever you perform a find in FileMaker, you're creating a new derived table. When you discard that found set, you're discarding that derived table, but your actions have no effect on the data in the base table.

Similarly, when you create a new layout or switch to an existing layout in a FileMaker database, you're invoking a view by which you can see a derived table even though it may or may not contain the same number of fields as the underlying base table. When you exit the layout, you destroy that derived table. These are novel ways of thinking about working with FileMaker, but they really make sense in terms of the relational model and thus a relational system.

The bottom line is that even though the base tables and derived tables reside within the same physical file in FileMaker, FileMaker supports the relational closure property. No matter how you operate on a FileMaker table, you can't help but get a table as a result. This leads us directly to the means of manipulating table data: relational operators.

Relational Operators

Relational operators are the means by which you create a derived table from one or more base tables. As we mentioned in the last chapter, just as you have +, –, /, and * as operators in algebra, you have the Cartesian product (multiplication), difference (subtraction), division, intersection, join, project, restrict, and union as the original operators in the relational model. There are other relational operators, but we'll limit our discussion to the original operators just mentioned.

As we stated before, you use relational operators to manipulate relations in mathematical expressions. Some of these operators are easy to do in FileMaker, while others are pretty difficult. Let's start with the easy ones.

Project

The project operator is used to display only specific columns (as opposed to displaying all columns in a table). A FileMaker Pro user can perform a project operation by dragging fields onto a layout. They would be "drawing" the project operation graphically, instead of specifying it mathematically. FileMaker's specific support of column subsetting in its layout capabilities qualifies as a project operator. While this isn't technically an operator, in practice it is a project operation. It's kind of like sculpting data. Think of it: FileMaker layout development as data sculpture.

Restrict

The restrict operator is used to get a subset of all of the rows in a table. In FileMaker Pro, the restrict operation is performed by means of a find or its equivalent — the Go to Related Records script step, for example. Using the Omit Menu command is also tantamount to restricting rows. The restrict operator is implemented in SQL as the SELECT command, so think of restrict and SELECT as the same thing. Selecting rows (a found set) is the same thing as restricting your view of the entire set of rows. Finding all records can also be considered a restrict operation since the set of all records is technically a subset of itself. In general, any FileMaker operation that manipulates the found set of records can be considered to be a restrict operation. This means that we don't have a single formal operator; we have several ways to perform the operation. FileMaker is very accommodating in this regard. At any rate, the Find command is closest to the real meaning of the restrict operator.

Before we go on, we want to emphasize that these operators can be used in tandem to produce complex results. You can simultaneously perform restrict and project operations to look at a subset of columns for a subset of records. The operators are intended to give you great flexibility in manipulating your data.

Joins

The join operator is roughly equivalent to creating a relationship in FileMaker Pro. A Θ-join (theta join) is one in which you use an operator such as <, >, =, and ≠. A Θ-join in which you use the = symbol is called an equijoin, and it's really the only type of join that FileMaker supports. This is a weakness in the program, so if any of you are the gadfly type, agitate FileMaker, Inc. for support of more join operators. You'll have a lot more enthusiasm for the task after you see what you have to do to mechanically produce the results of other types of joins.

Let's review each of the join types and explore how they can be produced in FileMaker.

Natural Join (aka Inner Join)

A natural join is an equijoin between a foreign key in a child table and the parent key in the corresponding parent table. For example, if you had an Invoice table that was related to a Customer table (its parent), the join between Invoice and Customer (as shown in Figure 2.1) would be a natural join.

If you had any invoices that didn't have a customer number assigned or that had a customer number that didn't appear in the Customer table, they would not be included in the join result. Since the view that displays the resulting join "lives" with the Invoice table (and you thought this was a family program ...) due to FileMaker Pro's file format, you'll need to omit any records with an empty or non-matching Customer ID.

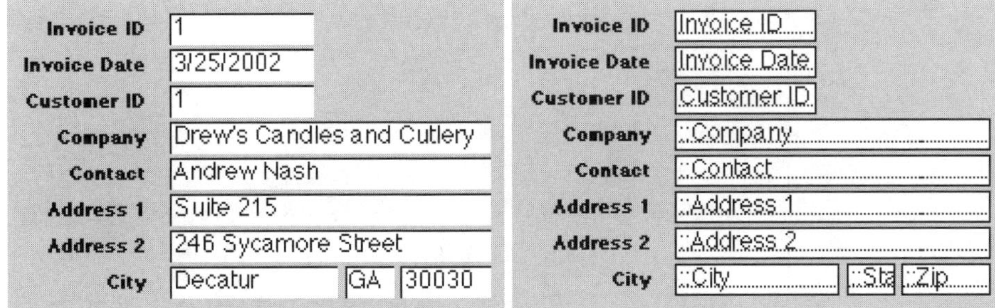

Figure 2.1 Result of a join: The invoice information on this layout comes from the Invoice table, while the customer information is from the Customer table.

It's easy enough to omit records with an empty Customer ID. Just enter Find mode, put an = sign in the Customer ID field, check the Omit box, and find. To also omit records that don't have a valid Customer ID, you need to do one of two things:

- Add the related Customer ID field (from the Customer file) to the layout that you'll be using for the find. Assuming that all Customer IDs are 1 or greater, you can then search for values >0 in the related field. By searching on just this one field, you'll only find records with a valid Customer ID, thereby omitting records without a Customer ID by default. If your Customer ID were a text field (instead of a number field as in this case), you could search using the * (wildcard) character, but you don't have to. In text fields, FileMaker treats letters as having a greater value than numbers. If you have any fields that contain only punctuation, those values can only be found using a literal text search (e.g., ";").

- Create a new calculation field in the Invoice table called Valid:

  Valid [number] = IsValid (Customer by Customer ID::Customer ID)

  Add the Valid field to the layout that you'll be using for the find. The IsValid function returns a Boolean result (1 or 0), so searching for 1 will again turn up only those records with a valid Customer ID.

Outer Join

An outer join combines two tables like the inner join, but where a tuple in one table is missing its counterpart in the other table, that information will be filled in with nulls and the resulting hybrid tuple will appear in the result. This join can be broken down into three subtypes, discussed next.

Left Outer Join

Given tables A and B, the join result will contain all rows from A joined with any matching rows from B. Where there are no corresponding rows in B, the values will be filled in with nulls. For example, consider again Invoice and Customer, where Invoice is A and Customer is B. If we have any invoices with an invalid Customer ID value, the customer information will be presented with blanks, as shown in Figure 2.2.

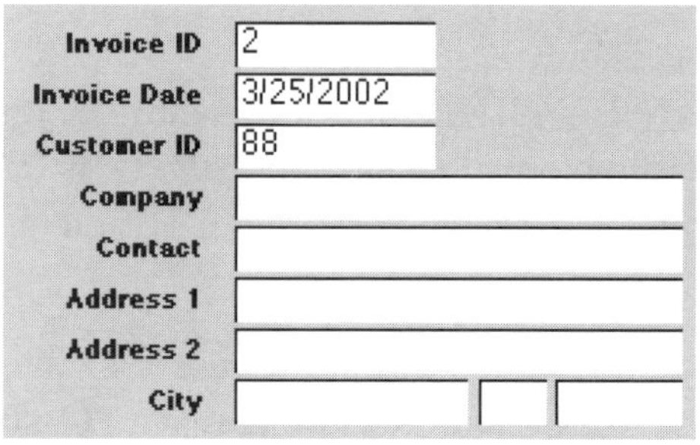

Invoice ID 2
Invoice Date 3/25/2002
Customer ID 88
Company
Contact
Address 1
Address 2
City

Figure 2.2

Right Outer Join

Given tables A and B, the join result will contain all rows from B joined with any matching rows from A. Where there are no corresponding rows in A, the values will be filled in with nulls.

Right and left outer joins can be created in FileMaker simply by creating the layout that will display the join results in the A or B table. For a left outer join, create the layout in table A, and include related fields from table B. You'll be able to show all rows in A, and you have blanks in the related fields where you don't have matching data in table B. Create the layout in table B for a right outer join.

Full Outer Join

Given tables A and B, the join result will contain all rows from A and B joined with their matching rows from the other table. Where there are no corresponding rows in the other table, the values will be filled in with nulls.

This one is trickier to do in FileMaker. It can be done two different ways, neither of which is particularly elegant. First, the bad way: Given tables A and B, start in A, then go to related records in B (showing only related records). Find the omitted records in B, then import only the foreign key values into A. A will now contain records for all rows in A and B, and will represent a full outer join of the original A and B. The problem with this method is that it compromises the integrity of A. The base table has been altered. Table A has been changed.

A better method is to have a third "utility" file that imports all records from A, then imports only the non-matching rows from B (using the same method that was described in the previous paragraph). This truly represents a derived table, but it's not as easy to get rid of a table in FileMaker as it is in other systems. To destroy this table, a user needs to physically delete it from the hard drive. In other systems, a DROP TABLE command would suffice.

Union Join

The opposite of an inner join, a union join results in only those rows where no match was found between the two tables. Since it's still a join yielding fields from both tables, nulls are used to fill in the nonexistent values from the missing table.

You can create a union join in FileMaker by using a layout that displays related fields. Perform a find that yields all records where there is no related information. You can do this by searching in all related fields for values (>0 works well) and checking the Omit box. You'll need to do the same in the related table.

The next step is to export the found records and all related fields to a new table. Open that new table and import the found set from the other table; the combination of the two sets of unmatched records will constitute a union join.

Cross Join

This join type is actually a Cartesian product, so we'll cover that next.

Cartesian Product (Multiplication, or Product)

The Cartesian product, or product, is derived by taking all possible combinations of the rows of those tables. For instance, if table X contained {A,B,C} and table Y contained {1, 2, 3}, the Cartesian product would be {(A,1), (A,2), (A,3), (B,1), (B,2), (B,3), (C,1), (C,2), (C,3)}. If you have tried to create filtered portals, you've likely run into this. Suppose you have a portal that displays real estate listings. Suppose also that you want to allow a user to select the number of bedrooms, the number of bathrooms, and the city in global fields so that the portal will only display those listings that meet that criteria. If a user isn't interested in a particular criteria, they can just use the value All.

If you concatenate those global values together, you'll get a field (a compound key) that you'll need to match to a single field in the listing table. You can't just combine the Bedroom, Bathroom, and City fields, though. If the user selects All for any of the values, the match will break. What you need to do is generate a Cartesian product for three tables:

Table 1	Table 2	Table 3
All	All	All
Bedroom	Bathroom	City

The result will be a match field that might look like this:

Bedroom-Bathroom-City
All-Bathroom-City
Bedroom-All-City
All-All-City
Bedroom-Bathroom-All
All-Bathroom-All
Bedroom-All-All
All-All-All

which is the Cartesian product of Tables 1, 2, and 3. (Chapter 8 contains a complete example of implementing filtered portals.)

Let's look at a different example. Suppose you were running a conference and you had a day allocated so that attendees could play golf at one of two courses. Before people can sign up for tee times, you need to create a table that lists all possible tee times at each course. This table will be the Cartesian product of the Course table and the TeeTime table.

One method of actually creating this in FileMaker involves an interesting use of value lists as arrays. You would begin by creating a new table called TimeSlot with the following fields:

CourseID	Number
TeeTime	Time
UserID	Number
gCourseIDList	Global, text
gCourseID	Global, number

The CourseID field should be formatted to auto-enter the value of gCourseID. You will need to import records from TeeTime once so that you can align the TeeTime fields and check the import option to perform auto-enter options while importing.

Next, create a value list called Courses in TimeSlot that uses the CourseID values from Course. You could then use the following script (which will work with any number of courses) to populate the table:

```
Show All Records
Delete All Records [No dialog]
Set Field ["gCourseIDList", "ValueListItems(Status(CurrentFileName),
        "Courses") & "¶""]
If ["not isEmpty (gCourseIDList)"]
     Loop
          Set Field ["gCourseID", "Left(gCourseIDList,
                    Position(gCourseIDList, "¶", 1, 1) - 1)"]
          Import Records [Restore, No dialog, "TeeTime.FP5"]
          Set Field ["gCourseIDList", "Right(gCourseIDList,
                    Length(gCourseIDList) - Position(gCourseIDList, "¶",
                    1, 1))"]
          Exit Loop If ["IsEmpty (gCourseIDList)"]
     End Loop
     Show All Records
Else
     Show Message ["There are no records in the Course database, so no slots
               can be created."]
End If
```

This script has a very basic error check in it that makes sure course records exist before it does anything. It would be appropriate to add an error check to make sure that some TeeTime records existed as well, and that the found set in TeeTime consisted of all records (since an import acts on the found set).

Difference

The difference operator is for subtracting one relation from another. Imagine that you had two tables full of customers (and we're not talking about a party of six in a restaurant…) — Table A and Table B. These two tables started out as identical files, but Table B was put on a laptop and was taken out into the great big world. Records were added, and when the laptop came back, you needed to import only the new records into Table A. What you really wanted was the difference between Table B and Table A. You literally needed to subtract Table A from Table B so that only the new records would be left.

There's an interesting way of getting this result in FileMaker. It completely violates the "one fact per field" rule, but since the field in question isn't a base table field (it's a global), and since it works like a dream, it's really hard to find fault with it. Let's flesh out a little bit more of these tables before we get into the process.

Table A
Customer ID
Customer Name

Table B
Customer ID
Customer Name

Here's the process:

1. Add a global text field to Table A called **gID List**.
2. Create a relationship in Table A called **Table B by gID List** that matches from gID List to Customer ID in Table B.
3. Create a script in Table B called **Sub:Show Omitted**. The script itself needs to have only one step: Show Omitted.
4. Create the following script in Table A:

```
Find All
Set Field ["gID List", """"]
Go to Record/Request/Page [First]
Loop
     Set Field ["gID List", "gID List & Customer ID & "¶""]
     Go to Record/Request/Page [Exit after last, Next]
End Loop
Go to Related Record [Show, "Table B by gID List"]
Perform Script [Sub-scripts, External: "Table B"]
```

The Perform Script step on the last line calls Sub:Show Omitted in Table B as an external script. How this works is that the script in Table A loops through every record and adds the Customer ID to the gID List field. Each ID is separated by a carriage return, so that when you jump to the related records, you get a found set that includes every record in the list. (This is buggy in FileMaker Pro 4.0, but it works fine in 3.0, 5.0, and 5.5. The 4.0 fix is to perform the Go to Related Record step twice, and then it works. Weird, huh?) When you find omitted records, you wind up with the difference.

Would we say that you have a difference operator in FileMaker Pro? Nope. However, you can certainly build one in the form of the above script. The script itself constitutes a difference operator. This is another example of where FileMaker falls short of the relational model. It's also a nice example of how the sheer flexibility of FileMaker allows you to overcome this problem.

Division

Imagine you have an invoicing system. It's easy enough to find every invoice that contains granola bars, but it's a bit trickier to find every invoice that contains granola bars and tofu jerky and seaweed snacks all on the same invoice.

This sort of situation, one in which you want to find all distinct values of an attribute (in this case, all invoice IDs) that correspond to a set of attributes (granola bars, tofu jerky, seaweed snacks), is tailor made for the divide operator, because that's exactly what it does. We could represent it graphically as follows:

```
1 A
1 C
1 D
2 B
2 C
3 A
3 D
```

Divided By

```
A
D
```

Equals

```
1
3
```

Only 1 and 3 correspond to both A and D. Keeping in mind the relational closure property, wherein every operation on a relation or relations yields a relation as a result, we need to end up with a table containing our values. Going back to the example we started with, there are a few different options for getting that result table. If we're literally trying to find all the invoices that meet our criteria, the most useful place for us to end up is in the Invoice table with a found set of the appropriate invoices.

There are other possibilities though. If we're trying to integrate the result into a report, we may want to end up in the Line Item table. In that case we would have to subsummarize by Invoice ID to get the distinct Invoice ID values. Technically, we have more records in the result set, but the representation to the user (and in a summarized export, if necessary) is that of a table containing only single instances of the correct values.

Given these different possible goals for the use of the result, we're going to show you two very different techniques for performing a divide operation in FileMaker. We'll start with the simplest.

Let's suppose you go into the Invoice table and you switch into Find mode. You enter "granola bars" into the first line of the portal, create a new find request, enter "tofu jerky," create one more find request, and enter "seaweed snacks." You might think that this is an AND find, or one that will only find invoices that contain all three of those items. You'd be wrong, though, because you'll find that a portal only allows you to do an OR search. That is, it will find all invoices that have any one of the Line Items you're looking for, but not necessarily all of them together.

The cleverest way we've heard of to get around this problem was created by Alejandro Rodriguez of Venezuela. Due to the nature of repeating fields, you can do an AND search in the field you're interested in just by formatting it as a repeating field. In our case, we'd go into field definitions in the Line Item table and format the Product ID field and/or the Product Name field with as many repetitions as you'd need for all of your search arguments. For example, if we knew that we'd never search for more than four items together, we'd just format it with four repetitions. If the file has a large number of records, keeping the number of repetitions to a minimum will help keep your file size down.

Once you have the field formatted, you can just add it to a search layout (as a related field) in the Invoice table. Format the field to display the appropriate number of repetitions, then switch into Find mode and enter your values (granola bars, tofu jerky, seaweed snacks) on separate lines in the repeating field in a single find request. It doesn't matter what order your values are in; the find will work the same regardless. Once they're entered, just click Find and you're done. You've performed a divide operation. Pretty easy, huh?

Okay, now here's the hard way. You would use the following technique if you wanted to end up with either a list of values in a global field or a summary report in the Line Item table. This example will require a separate table to use as your divisor. If this is the kind of functionality that you'd use a lot, you could also adapt the first technique to use a table to populate the search criteria values in the repeating field.

The Divisor file just needs to contain three fields. In this example, the Divisor file needs a Product ID field. In different scenarios, you would label the field as appropriate, or if you needed to make it work with multiple files, you can add an additional field called Field Name and then just have a value field. For this example, we're going to stick with a simple Product ID field. We also need two global fields and two calculation fields, so our final field list will be as follows:

```
ProductID [number]
gTest[global, number]
gResults[global, text]
Constant [calculation, number result] = 1
InvID_ProdID [calculation, text result] = gTest& "-" & ProductID
```

We're formatting gTest as a global number field because we're assuming your invoice IDs are number values. If your invoice IDs are text values, format this field as a global text field. The gResults field will be a global text field since it will be holding return-delimited data. You will also need to add fields to the Line Item file:

```
Constant [calculation, number result] = 1
InvID_ProdID [calculation, text result] = InvoiceID & "-" & ProductID
```

Once all of the fields are in place, the next thing we need to do is add two relationships in the Divisor table. The first will be called LineItem_by_Constant, matching from Constant in Divisor to Constant in Line Item. The second will be called LineItem_by_InvIDProdID, matching from InvID_ProdID in Divisor to InvID_ProdID in Line Item.

The last thing to do is create a script in Divisor that will cycle through all possible invoice ID values and see if each record in Divisor finds a corresponding match in Line Item. Let's call the script Build Result Set:

```
If ["Count (LineItem_by_Constant::Constant) "]
    Set Field ["gResults", """"]
```

```
          Set Field ["gTest", "Min (LineItem_by_Constant::InvoiceID"]
          Loop
               Go to Record/Request/Page [First]
               Loop
                    Exit Loop If ["not isValid (LineItem_by_
                                   InvIDProdID::InvoiceID) "]
                    If ["Status (CurrentRecordCount) = Status (CurrentRecord-
                                   Number) "]
                         Set Field ["gResults", "gResults& Case (not IsEmpty
                                   (gResults), "¶") & gTest"]
                    End If
                    Go to Record/Request/Page [Exit after last, Next]
               End Loop
               Exit Loop If ["gTest = Max (LineItem_by_Constant::InvoiceID)"]
               Set Field ["gTest", "gTest + 1"]
          Loop
     Else
          Show Message ["There are no records to divide."]
     End If
```

Note that we're relying on the Min and Max functions to control the start and end of our loop. If you're using text values for invoice IDs you may have to add leading zeros or strip out alphanumeric characters for Min and Max to work properly. For example, INV2 is greater than INV100 when sorted alphanumerically, but 2 is less than 100 when sorted numerically.

When we run this script, we'll end up with a list of invoice IDs in the gResults field, assuming that we get some matches. If that's all you wanted to find, you could stop there and do what you wanted with that information. If you want to get a corresponding found set in Invoice (and the first example is a far better method for doing this), you need to add a relationship to the Divisor table. The relationship will be called Invoice_by_Results_to_InvID, matching from gResults in Divisor to InvoiceID in Invoice. Next, you need to modify the last part of the above script as follows:

```
...
     Set Field ["gTest", "gTest + 1"]
     End Loop
     If ["not isEmpty (gResults) "]
          Go to Related Records [Show, "Invoice_by_Results_to_InvID"]
          Perform Script [Sub-scripts, External: "Invoice.FP5"]
     End If
```

```
Else
     Show Message ["There are no records to divide."]
End If
```

The Perform Script step calls a subscript in the Invoice table that switches the user to a list layout appropriate for viewing the resulting list of invoices. That takes care of showing the results in the Invoice table.

If you want to get your result list in the Line Item table, you first need to create a layout and script in the Line Item file. The layout is a simple list view that just contains the InvoiceID field. Change the layout body into a subsummary part that breaks on the InvoiceID field. Once your layout is ready, sort the database by the InvoiceID field so that your script will pick up that sort criteria. Create a script in the Line Item table called Sub:Invoice List with the following steps:

```
Go to Layout ["Invoice List"]
Sort [Restore, No dialog]
Enter Preview Mode [Pause]
```

The Restore option in the Sort step will lock in your InvoiceID sort. Once you have the Line Item file ready, switch back to the Divisor file and create a new relationship called LineItem_by_Results_to_InvID, matching from gResults in Divisor to InvoiceID in Line Item. Next, modify the end of the script as follows:

```
...
     Set Field ["gTest", "gTest + 1"]
     End Loop
     If ["not isEmpty (gResults)"]
          Go to Related Records [Show, "LineItem_by_Results_to_InvID"]
          Perform Script [Sub-scripts, External: "LineItem.FP5"]
     End If
Else
     Show Message ["There are no records to divide."]
End If
```

The Perform Script step calls your Sub:Invoice List subscript in the Line Item table. That takes care of showing the results in the Line Item table.

And there you have it. Three different methods for implementing the relational divide operator in your FileMaker systems.

Intersection

Imagine that you have a large sales force dealing with customers throughout the country, and that both the East territory and West territory have their own customer database. If you wanted to compare the sales territory databases to find out which customers salespeople have in common, you would need to use the Intersection operator. This operator requires you to have two tables that have identical field structure, which is not an issue in this scenario since we're just comparing two sets of customer data.

The easiest way to get an intersection between two files is to create a relationship from one table to the other. For the sake of this example, we'll say we have a CustomerA table and a CustomerB table. Both tables have a CustomerID field and a Customer Name field. In CustomerA, we'll create a relationship called CustomerB_by_CustomerID that matches from CustomerID in CustomerA to CustomerID in CustomerB.

Next, we'll switch into Layout mode (still in CustomerA) and add the related CustomerID field to the layout. To find the records that the two tables have in common, we just need to do a find for >0 in the related CustomerID field. The resulting found set of records, if any, will be the records that the two tables have in common.

Obviously, this quick and dirty solution won't work well if you're trying to find the intersection of several tables at once.

Union

Union is easy to implement, since before you can perform a union operation, the tables have to be union compatible, meaning they need to have identical sets of attributes. That being the case, all you need to do is import records from one table into another. The resulting collection is a union of the two tables.

Domains

A field's domain consists of the population of all permissible values. For instance, a Boolean field has a domain of 1 and 0. A planet field might have a domain of all planets in this solar system, or perhaps all planets in the universe. As we mentioned in Chapter 1, a domain is really a special data type. When a field is defined on a certain domain, data entered into that field has to be of that domain's type.

Enforcement of domains is possibly the biggest area where relational databases fall short of being true relational systems. Since domains can be quite large, validating a particular entry against a large domain makes for a big performance hit. If the domain is large enough, the performance may be unacceptably slow, in which case the decision comes down to enforcing the domain in an unusable system, or not enforcing the domain in a usable one. You make the call. Usually the answer is that you won't implement the domain — maybe next time.

Let's take a look at how we might enforce domains in FileMaker Pro. FileMaker already has some validation capabilities, so let's first review what we have. The validation dialog box is shown in Figure 2.3.

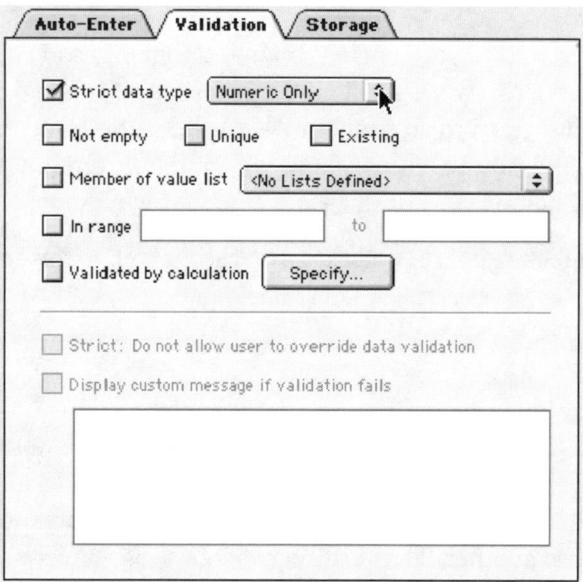

Figure 2.3 FileMaker has several validation options that can be used to implement domains.

With the first check box, FileMaker can validate that a field entry is in a number, date, or time format, depending on the format of the field in question. We need to consider each of these separately. If our domain consists of all possible times, we're all set, but if our domain consists of all possible dates, we have a problem.

Date Domains

FileMaker only supports dates from 1/1/0001 through 12/31/3000. Any dates outside of that range will not be accepted by FileMaker. This brings us to an important point. To a large extent, the scope of a domain is completely arbitrary. You, the database designer, get to determine how extensive your domain needs to be in order to meet the needs of the database system. If the date field in question is tracking invoice dates for the XYZ Corporation, you certainly don't need to store date values that predate the existence of the organization. You can also decide that the database system will have a definite life span, and will not be used for longer than 50 years. In this scenario, your domain for the invoice date field ranges from the company founding date to a date 50 years in the future. FileMaker's calculated validation feature can easily enforce this domain with a calculation such as the one shown in Figure 2.4.

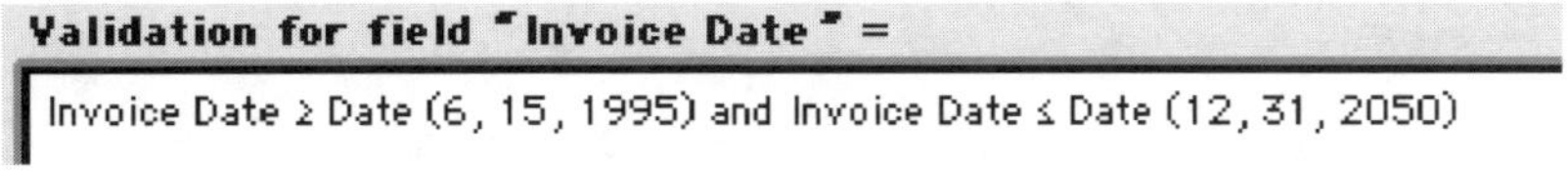

Validation for field "Invoice Date" =

```
Invoice Date ≥ Date (6, 15, 1995) and Invoice Date ≤ Date (12, 31, 2050)
```

Figure 2.4 This validation calculation will ensure that only dates from June 15, 1995, to December 31, 2050, will be accepted.

Since most databases deal with events happening in our lifetime, FileMaker can easily enforce proper date domains in most scenarios. You're unlikely to ever need dates outside of that range, but if you ever need to have a domain of all possible dates, perhaps for a museum collections database, you'll need to use a text field instead of a date field for data entry. Be warned that this can be problematic. For one thing, dates stored in a text field will be sorted as text values, not as date values, and that means that all dates in the same month (in the U.S.) will sort together, or that all dates on the same day (overseas) will sort together.

Enforcing Other Domain Types

While our domain could possibly include all number values, or all possible dates, we might need to validate that a field entry is in a city format, meaning that it's a valid U.S. city name. This is way beyond what we can do with the type validation. We really need to be able to define new data types on the fly, and we can't, although we can use another type of validation to get a close approximation of this capability.

For list-based domains like this, we can fall back on the member of a value list validation. With a short list like gender, we can just define the domain/value list in the value list dialog. For longer lists, it's better to store the domain member values in a separate table. By creating a separate table that contains every U.S. city, and by creating a value list based on that table, we could enforce a U.S. city domain.

It's nice that we can do that, but if you stop and think about how many fields you have in your average database solution, it's probably not practical to think that you can create domain tables for every field. You'd quickly run into FileMaker's limit of 50 open files unless you lumped all of your domain lists into a single file with lots of fields, which is actually a reasonable solution. The resulting "domain" table should not be considered as one of the base tables in the relational system. It's really just a utility component of the system.

Not all domains are defined by lists. We could have a domain as arbitrary as every other letter in the alphabet, four-letter words, or maybe odd whole numbers. While you could try to enforce these domains with a list, the last two would be a huge job to set up. All of these domains can be defined mathematically. By happy coincidence, FileMaker can validate by calculation. In FileMaker these domains would be enforced with the following calculations (assuming a data entry field called Value):

```
(Pattern Count ("acegikmoqsuwy",Value)) and (Length (Value) = 1)
Length (Value) = 4
(Mod (Value, 2) > 0) and (Mod (Value, 1) = 0)
```

There's one thing to keep in mind whenever you use FileMaker's built-in domain validation: If you import data or have a script set data, no validation takes place. In those cases, you'll need to encode your validation logic in a pre- or post-processing script.

Scalar Values

One of the first concepts of the relational model is that a field can contain only scalar values, meaning that you can only have one fact per field. This means that repeating fields and fields that are formatted as check boxes (since this creates multiple values in a single field) do not contain scalar values and that they can't be used to store table data without violating the relational model.

Consider that last sentence carefully. Given our notion of table fields and view fields, we maintain that they only really violate the relational model if they're being used as table fields. You can use repeating fields as an aid to data entry or to create charts with, but such uses really have nothing to do with the relational model. They're just mechanisms employed by a particular view. Similarly, a global field that's used as a variable for a script can't be considered a true field. Since its purpose is utilitarian and not as a container of table values, it doesn't matter if you load it up with a bunch of values.

What about check boxes, though? They're so useful as a data entry structure. What check boxes really represent is a set of related records. A check box field is a portal in disguise. If you use check boxes only as a data entry structure and parse the values out to separate portal rows, you can still claim compliance with the relational model.

Those special uses aside, though, you should avoid using repeating fields or other fields with multiple values at all costs. Storing field values this way makes it very difficult to do any kind of reporting on the data.

Aside from the obvious check box and repeating field problems, you need to watch out for more subtle ones. Suppose you had a product database that contained a piece of data like this: 8 oz. Veggie Dogs. If the domain of this field is a product, this is probably not a scalar value. It's actually three values:

Quantity	**Units**	**Product**
8	oz.	Veggie Dogs

Then again, it could be a scalar value if the domain of that field contained products packaged in various forms. Databases are all about representing meaning, and if you'll never report or sort by units of measure or quantity, then perhaps no additional meaning is gained by breaking these facts out into separate fields (with distinct domains). As we mentioned in Chapter 1, the complexity of the domain is completely arbitrary. A legitimate value might be a legal contract, even though it's comprised of various clauses and obviously has an internal structure. As long as the domain of the field consists of legal contracts, then it's okay. It's entirely up to the database designer how simple or complex the various data types can be, and domains are the enforcing mechanism of valid data types.

Before you get too hung up about this, remember that this is all supposed to make things simpler for you down the road. The relational model is designed to make it as easy as possible to work with data stored in databases. If you have more than one fact per field, you're going to have real difficulties when you need to report on components of a field's contents. You can break the rules, but realize that you'll probably run into problems when you do. Conforming to this rule isn't required in FileMaker Pro, but if you design your systems so that they can only contain scalar values, you'll have an easier time interfacing with other relational systems that conform to this rule.

Primary Keys

Most relational database systems have specific support for primary keys. By this, we mean that you can designate a field or fields as the primary key for the table, and in so doing, you ensure that nulls and duplicate values will be disallowed. There isn't anything like this in FileMaker, but there should be. Ease of use constraints not withstanding, a developer of a relational database system should know what a primary key is.

Since a primary key uniquely identifies a record, we can't allow duplicate values, and allowing blanks (nulls) opens the door for duplicate values (or lack thereof) if more than one record can contain a null. The easiest way to deal with this issue is to create an auto-entered serial number. This is what we would term the "brute force method," since you're actually adding a new field to your data structure instead of relying on the existing fields for a unique value or set of values.

On a related note, since foreign keys need to relate to a value (or values) that uniquely identifies a row in the related table, the Define Relationships dialog box should constrain the relationships so that only matches to primary keys are possible. This is not the case with FileMaker, and it's actually not the case with SQL either. You can create “improper” relationships between tables in other systems, so this problem isn’t unique to FileMaker. Actually, this flexibility is a real asset when it comes to creating “utility” relationships. (The example of a constant relationship comes to mind.) It just requires that the database designer knows what he’s doing, since the system will not try to protect him from creating unsound relationships.

We can’t leave the topic of primary keys without addressing compound primary keys. A *compound key* is one that is composed of more than one field. Compound primary keys are always found in join files that were created to break up many-to-many relationships. For example, in the invoice system diagram shown in Figure 2.5, the Line Item file contains two foreign keys, an Invoice ID field which relates to Invoice and a Product ID field which relates to Product.

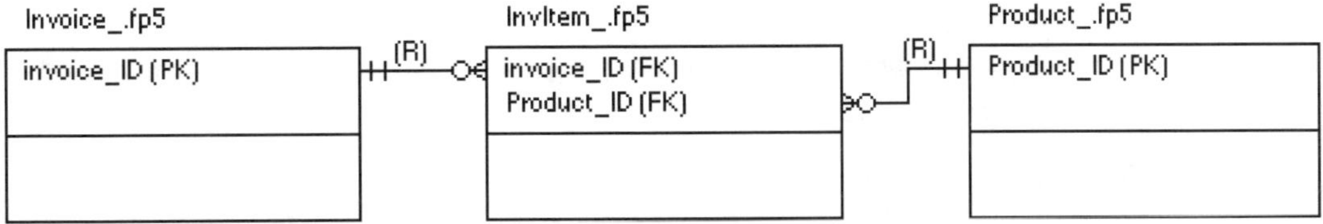

Figure 2-5

These two foreign keys together comprise the primary key of Line Item, thus making for a compound key. Since compound keys must be unique, we should validate that these two fields taken as a pair always form a unique pair. It’s easy enough to validate that a single field value is unique by checking a box in the validation dialog box. Validating that a combination of fields is unique is much trickier. This gets back to the whole issue of FileMaker’s lack of support for primary keys. If FileMaker supported this feature, we could just designate these two fields as the primary key and not worry about it anymore.

Complaining seldom gets you anywhere, though, so we need to take matters into our own hands. Given the two fields, Invoice ID and Product ID, we need to create a field called Primary Key:

Primary Key [text] = Invoice ID & "-" & Product ID

We always put some kind of delimiter between values when we do this kind of concatenation. If we don't, values of 11 and 1 will have the same result as 1 and 11, even though the starting values are completely different.

Okay, now that we have a single field, we can just go into the validation dialog box and check the box in front of Unique, right? Wrong. You don't get validation options on calculation fields. No, you have to perform the validation on the components of the compound key. Here's how:

1. Create a relationship called **Self by Primary Key**. Relate from Line Item to Line Item using Primary Key as your match field on both sides of the relationship.
2. Create a calculated validation for both Invoice ID and Product ID as follows:

   Count(Self by Primary Key::PrimaryKey) = 0

Don't forget to add a custom warning message that tells users they can't have the same product on an invoice twice.

This sort of solves the uniqueness problem, although it does so badly. Let's see why. If we go into the Invoice database and try to add an item to the invoice twice, we get a warning message. In the aftermath of that, we realize the error of our ways and we do... what? Suppose we click Revert Field. The result is what we have in Figure 2.6.

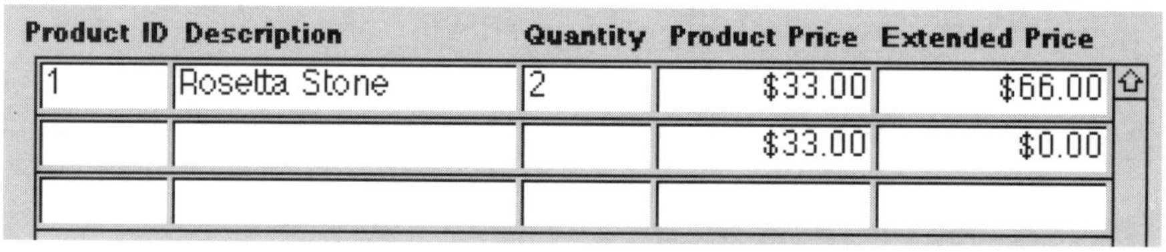

Product ID	Description	Quantity	Product Price	Extended Price
1	Rosetta Stone	2	$33.00	$66.00
			$33.00	$0.00

Figure 2.6 Even though the user has removed the Product ID code, the product price lookup information remains.

Even though the user hasn't technically exited the field, lookups trigger anyway. They still remain even after the trigger field (in this case the Product ID) has been blanked out. This is obviously a maintenance issue. We can't leave this data here because it might get counted in some report. It would be nice to have the record disappear, but if we have a blank record floating around, it won't summarize into any reports and it will be unlikely to get pulled into one via some find criteria. If it does, it will sort to the top and be immediately visible. This will likely make a user find and delete it.

So, we can possibly live with a blank record. To get a blank record, though, we need to get this lookup information to disappear if the Product ID reverts to a blank state. This is actually pretty easy to take care of. Just check the option to use a literal text string if there's no exact match, as shown in Figure 2.7.

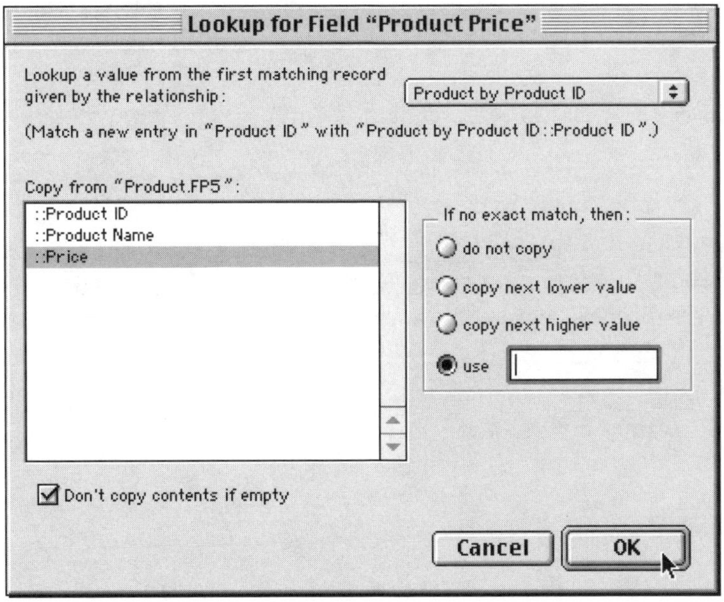

Figure 2.7

This way, when the Product ID code is blanked out, the lookup information will retrigger, find no match, and turn blank.

Referential Integrity

Referential integrity is an impressive way of saying that a foreign key in one table needs to be pointing at a primary key in another table that actually exists and is unique. There are a few different problem scenarios to watch out for. If an invoice references a certain customer, and that customer is deleted, the invoice has become "orphaned" (integrity compromised by delete). If another customer with the same ID is added, you have a problem in that it's unclear which customer should be referenced by the invoice.

Similar problems can occur if the customer ID is changed and the corresponding ID in the invoice is not also updated (integrity compromised by update).

Integrity constraints rely heavily on the uniqueness of the primary key, and the second scenario should be impossible if the customer ID is the primary key. The other two are problems arising from deletes or updates. There are two methods of preventing delete or update problems. One approach is to prevent the delete or update if any related records exist. This approach gives rise to restricted update and restricted delete integrity constraints. The other approach propagates the delete or update through all related records, and this gives rise to the cascading update and cascading delete integrity constraints.

There are a few ways to detect whether or not a given record in a FileMaker Pro database has any related records. You can use the Count function to count the related records, and you can use the IsValid function to detect any related record. You could also script a find in another file, but that gets into more trouble than it's worth. Other approaches are essentially variations on these. Using the IsValid method, let's see how we might implement the various constraints in FileMaker Pro.

Restricted Deletes

Since users can delete records using the Delete Record menu command, passwords obviously need to be a component of any scheme to implement restricted updates. You'll need to set up password access so that the menus are restricted to Edit Only. This will take away the Delete Record menu option and keyboard shortcut.

Taking away the menu option means that you need to replace it with a scripted delete that can be invoked by a button. The script would look something like this:

```
If (IsValid (Invoice by Customer ID::Customer ID))
     Show Message ("This customer has related invoice records and can't be
                   deleted.")
Else
     Delete Record/Request
End If
```

Restricted Updates

Typically, primary keys in FileMaker are serial numbers, and serial numbers can be set to prevent modification. If, for some reason, you need to allow users to modify the primary key, you'll have to set up a script to guide users through that process. You can't use a calculated validation in this case because the validation only checks the new value, not the old value.

You'll need to set up a script that makes the user enter the new value into a global field and then click an Update button. The script for that Update button would look something like this:

```
 If (IsValid (Invoice by Customer ID::Customer ID))
     Show Message ("This customer has related invoice records and can't be
                  updated."
Else
     Set Field (Customer ID, gCustomer ID)
End If
```

Cascading Deletes

Cascading deletes are very easy to implement in FileMaker. All you need to do is check a box, the one labeled When deleting a record in this file, also delete related records, in the Define Relationship dialog box.

Cascading Updates

Cascading updates have a similar mechanism to the restricted update. You need to have the user enter the new value into a global field and then check to see if there are related records. If so, jump to the related records and replace the old value with the new value. The script might look something like this:

```
If (IsValid (Invoice by Customer ID::Customer ID))
     Go to Related Records (Invoice by Customer ID, Show)
     Perform Script (External, Invoice.FP5)
End If
Set Field (Customer ID, gCustomer ID)
```

The external script in Invoice would switch to a utility layout that contained the Customer ID field, then replace the Customer ID with the gCustomer ID field using a constant match back to Customer.

Summary

No commercial relational database product is fully compliant with the relational model. FileMaker is not alone in that it does not fully comply with the model. The relational model addresses three main areas: objects, operators, and integrity. Objects such as FileMaker tables actually contain more information than just table data. They also contain views and scripts. Other database systems also have scripts (stored procedures) stored at the table level, which means that the tables don't strictly conform to the relational model. The concepts of table fields (text, number, date, time, container) and view fields (summary, calculation, global) were discussed. Table fields in FileMaker can meet the requirements of the relational model to a large extent. Field domains that can be defined mathematically can be implemented in FileMaker, and non-mathematical domains can be implemented to the extent that they can be stored in FileMaker tables. All of the traditional relational operators can be implemented in FileMaker by means of finds, layout changes, and scripts. Referential integrity can be implemented using field validation, relationship settings, and scripting.

Chapter 3

Normalization

Like a hammer, FileMaker is a versatile, easy to use tool that can be utilized to build lots of things. Also like a hammer, it's up to you to keep from hitting your thumb. With a hammer, you can build a sturdy house, or you can build a bad one. The same goes for constructing databases with FileMaker. With both tools, a little knowledge about sound design principles will take you a long way.

In the last two chapters, we've introduced you to the theory of relational databases and we've discussed implementing relational theory using FileMaker. The discussion wouldn't be complete, however, without covering normalization. Simply put, normalization provides you with a method for identifying potential problems in a database system and rules for correcting the problems. These rules were called the "Normal Forms" in the 1970 paper that first described the relational model, and have been known as such ever since. That paper discussed First, Second, and Third Normal Forms. In the years since, other papers have identified problems that couldn't be solved with these rules, and have offered additional rules to correct them. Boyce-Codd Normal Form is an extension of Third Normal Form, while Fourth and Fifth Normal Form address problems specific to multivalued dependencies.

While normalization is usually part of the design process, you'll find that after you've done it a few times, normalized structures just come to you intuitively.

As we discuss normal forms in this chapter, we'll also tell you about the problems that they were designed to avoid. But you should know from the start that there are, at times, very good reasons for having a denormalized data structure, such as performance, reporting, or connections to other systems. As a rule of thumb, it's a good idea to start with a fully normalized data model, and then make decisions about denormalizing as necessary. As you decide to denormalize, it will be important that you understand the potential problems that may arise and deal with them accordingly. Your denormalization should be by design rather than out of ignorance of the rules.

Our discussion of normal forms will necessarily involve a fair amount of theory. And while this theory applies to relational databases in general, we'll also try to show you considerations that are unique to FileMaker. By the end of this chapter our hope is that you'll understand the benefits that normalization provides.

Functional Dependence

The concept of functional dependence is fundamental to the rules of normalization. While we'll consider the concept theoretically, you should know that it's actually fairly intuitive. *Functional dependence* describes a relationship between two or more attributes (or sets of attributes) of a table, and is governed by the business logic of the particular system. An attribute A is said to be functionally dependent on another attribute B (or set of attributes) if you can uniquely determine the value of A given the value of B. Put differently, B functionally determines A.

An example will help clarify this. Suppose that we have an Invoice table with the following fields and values:

Invoice ID	Invoice Date	Customer Name	Invoice Total
1	11/17/2001	Dusty's Cleaners	$163.45
2	11/17/2001	Fred's Beds	$24.50
3	11/17/2001	Denis's Dentistry	$59.00
4	11/17/2001	Phil's Stones	$24.50
5	11/18/2001	Acme Widgets	$163.45

If you were given an Invoice ID, you would unambiguously be able to state the Invoice Date, the Customer Name, and the Invoice Total. We would therefore say that the Invoice Date, the Customer Name, and the Invoice Total are all functionally dependent of the Invoice ID. Represented symbolically, we would render this as:

Invoice ID → Invoice Date
Invoice ID → Customer Name
Invoice ID → Invoice Total

The set of attributes on the left side of this equation is called the *determinant*, and the set on the right side is called the *dependent*.

The reverse, of course, isn't true. Given an Invoice Date (such as 11/17/2001), there's no way to uniquely determine the Invoice Total, the Customer Name, nor the Invoice ID. What about the Customer Name? Based on the sample set above, it is possible that a Customer Name can determine the value of the three other attributes. Should we conclude from this that the Customer Name functionally determines the other attributes? Logic and experience tell us the answer is no. The reason, of course, is that the next entry in the table might be:

Invoice ID	Invoice Date	Customer Name	Invoice Total
6	11/18/2001	Fred's Beds	$81.43

At this point, the Customer Name no longer can be used to uniquely identify any of the other attributes. We bring this up to make it clear that functional dependencies reflect the business logic the system is designed to implement (as opposed to logic that apparently exists in a sample set of data). You can't know what the functional dependencies are without first knowing how the attributes should interact with each other. While in many cases, such as the one we've been discussing, the interactions are intuitive, it's always a good idea to acknowledge and check the assumptions about business logic that are inherent in your data structures. Look beyond what you see in a particular set of records and try to determine the interactions for all possible records. In the example above, you certainly wouldn't want to conclude that the Customer Name field would always be able to uniquely identify a record.

In Chapter 1, we presented a definition of primary key as an attribute or set of attributes that uniquely identifies a row in a table. Now, armed with the concept of functional dependence, we can offer another definition of primary key. An attribute (or group of attributes) is considered the primary key if all of the attributes in the table are functionally dependent on it.

When it comes to functional dependencies in FileMaker, keep in mind the discussion in Chapter 2 about the difference between table fields (text, number, date, time, and container fields) and view fields (calculations, summaries, and globals). View fields only exist in the database for data presentation, scripting, and validation purposes. For the purposes of functional dependency and normalizing databases in FileMaker, only Table fields need be considered.

First Normal Form (1NF)

The simplest definition of First Normal Form that we've come across is "one fact per field." In practice, this means two things. First, data must be atomic; second, and more importantly, the table cannot contain repeating groups of information.

We covered atomic values in Chapter 1, but we'll refresh your memory here so you don't need to go back and look it up. An atomic value is one that can't be broken into smaller parts without losing meaning. For example, a name field that contained "Jay Welshofer" would not necessarily be atomic, because it could be divided meaningfully into first name and last name. While the name "Welshofer" can be broken down into its constituent letters, doing so would destroy its meaning. Therefore, the value "Welshofer" can be considered to be atomic. As we've mentioned before, atomicity is subjective and can certainly vary from table to table.

Repeating groups of information can either mean one field that contains multiple values (think of FileMaker check boxes and repeating fields) or multiple fields that essentially refer to the same object (i.e., fields like Contact 1, Contact 2, Contact 3). The reason these should be avoided is that they cause problems with finding and reporting.

Let's look now at two examples of repeating groups of information in FileMaker and discuss the pros and cons of putting the database into 1NF.

For the first example, consider a simple table we'll call Registration that a school might make to track course enrollment:

Student ID	Student Name	Course ID	Course Name	Grade
123	Sandy	Sci200	Biology	B+
		Eng103	American Lit	A–
124	Jasper	Eng103	American Lit	B+
		Mat421	Calculus	C–
125	Felix	Soc126	Political Science	B
		Sci340	Chemistry	B–
		Mat313	Geometry	C

For now, let's say that Course ID, Course Name, and Grade were formatted as repeating fields. You'd be able to use this database quite well to collect large amounts of data. However, the flaws of this structure will quickly become apparent when you try to produce even the most basic reports.

For instance, while you could perform a find in the Course ID field to find all the students registered for a given course, you wouldn't be able to create a list containing the students' names and grade in that course. This is because the course grade might be found in any of the repetitions, and you won't be able to just display the one that corresponds to your query. Similarly, it would be impossible (without altering the data structure) to create a simple alphabetical listing of all the courses offered.

The bottom line here is that repeating fields and check boxes are fantastic user interfaces, but they severely limit the versatility of the data. They are a blatant violation of First Normal Form.

We often encounter the second example of a 1NF violation. Usually, the violation occurs as the database develops over time. Imagine that you have a database of client data with fields for Client_ID, Client_Name, and Contact_Name. Everything works just fine until you need to record the names of two contacts for a given client. What usually happens is that a new field is added to the table called Contact_Name2. Time passes, and eventually a Contact_Name3 field is added.

Again, the problem isn't data entry, it's data retrieval and display. When you want to find the client record for "Joe," which field do you do the search in? How can you produce labels for holiday cards for all of the contacts in the system? How can you tell how many contact names are in the database? There are, of course, workarounds to do all of these things. But that's not the point. Rather, know that a database that hasn't been normalized to 1NF contains numerous potential problems.

Let's return now to the first example and see how we'd put the data into First Normal Form. The Course ID, Course Name, and Grade form the repeating group of information. Each repetition needs to be split into a separate record, with non-repeating information (Student ID and Student Name) being extended through the set. So, the table from above would look like the following in 1NF:

Student ID	Student Name	Course ID	Course Name	Grade
123	Sandy	Sci200	Biology	B+
123	Sandy	Eng103	American Lit	A–
124	Jasper	Eng103	American Lit	B+
124	Jasper	Mat421	Calculus	C–
125	Felix	Soc126	Political Science	B
125	Felix	Sci340	Chemistry	B–
125	Felix	Mat313	Geometry	C

Notice that the Student ID is no longer unique in this normalized table. The new primary key is the combination of the Student ID and the Course ID. In general, as you eliminate repeating groups, the identifier of the repeating group (here, the Course ID) becomes part of the primary key.

The 1NF version of the table above still suffers from problems (which we'll address soon — fret not). But the reporting problems we mentioned earlier have all disappeared. It would be simple now to produce a list of students and grades for a given course. And, using a layout with a subsummary part, you could quickly produce an alphabetical listing of courses.

If you are ever asked to evaluate a FileMaker database, immediately check for violations of First Normal Form. It's easy to spot these by looking at the field definitions. If you see repeating fields or groups of fields with similar names, you'll know there are potential problems. But don't overreact if you see this. Let's say you're looking at a real estate database and see container fields for pictures of the property called Image 1, Image 2, and Image 3. This is a clear violation of First Normal Form, but one you might easily be able to live with, as the images certainly won't be involved in finds or reports. The only tangible problem here is the lack of extensibility; without adding more fields, you're limited to a maximum of three images per property. The benefits of the repeating group would be ease of display, ease of transferring data, and a simpler data model. On a case-by-case basis, you'll need to decide whether the benefits of denormalizing outweigh the problems and eventual workarounds you'll need to implement.

Second Normal Form (2NF)

Functional dependencies didn't come up at all in our discussion of 1NF, but they're central to an understanding of Second Normal Form. A table is said to be in 2NF if all of the non-key attributes are functionally dependent on the entire primary key. Right off, notice that you only have to worry about 2NF in tables that have compound primary keys.

Review again the 1NF version of the student and course table that we ended up with in the last section. A catalog of the functional dependencies would look something like this:

Student ID → Student Name
Course ID → Course Name
Student ID, Course ID → Grade

Let's put this in plain language. The Student Name is functionally dependent on the Student ID. Just to review, this means that if someone gives you a Student ID, you'll unambiguously be able to determine the Student Name. This holds here even though the Student ID is the same in multiple records. The same can be said of Course Name and Course ID: The Course Name is functionally dependent on the Course ID. The Grade attribute, however, can only be uniquely determined by a combination of the Student ID and the Course ID.

Thus, there are two violations of 2NF evidenced by these dependencies. The primary key here is the combination of the Student ID and the Course ID. But both the Student Name and Course Name fields are dependent on only a portion of the primary key.

The potential problems caused by violations of 2NF are usually referred to as update anomalies. Specifically, there are three situations you need to be aware of:

- When you update data, you must update it in multiple records. For instance, if the name of Course Eng103 changed to World Literature, several records would be affected, which is not only slow but could lead to inconsistent data if not done completely. If some of the records weren't changed, then the Course ID would no longer functionally determine the Course Name, and a piece of business logic would be lost (i.e., that piece of business logic that states that each course has a unique name).

- Imagine that there's a new course being offered, Mus100 — Music Theory. But there's no way to add a course to the table until there's a student who signs up for it. This would clearly be a major shortcoming of the denormalized table.
- There's a problem with deletion as well, namely that deleting a record in the table destroys too much information. If a student is only registered for one course and you delete this record, you've just destroyed not only the registration but also all evidence that the student exists.

The remedy for 2NF violations is to create a new table where the partial key is the primary key and move all of the attributes that are dependent on the partial key to the new table. Correcting the two violations in the Registration table would yield the following new table structure:

Student ID	Course ID	Grade
123	Sci200	B+
123	Eng103	A–
124	Eng103	B+
124	Mat421	C–
125	Soc126	B
125	Sci340	B–
125	Mat313	C

Student ID	Student Name
123	Sandy
124	Jasper
125	Felix

Course ID	Course Name
Sci200	Biology
Eng103	American Lit
Mat421	Calculus
Soc126	Political Science
Sci340	Chemistry
Mat313	Geometry

This structure is now in 2NF since within each table all of the non-key fields are functionally dependent on the entire primary key.

Importantly, no information is lost in this transformation. The original table can be reproduced at any time by performing a join operation on the new tables. Note, though, that this simple transformation has cured all of the update anomalies. Course names need only be updated in one place, and it's not possible to have inconsistent pairings. New course records can be added to the Course table independently of registering a student for a course. And finally, course registrations can be deleted without the risk of destroying information about a student.

We'll conclude this section on 2NF with some discussion about issues unique to FileMaker that you need to be aware of. A moment ago, we mentioned that the original table could be reproduced by performing a join operation. Say, for instance, that we wish to produce a list of students in a given course. We perform a find in the Registration table for the Course ID; the find returns a list of Student IDs (not names). Now, there are three ways to turn this into a list of names. All of them start with the creation of a relationship from the Registration table to the Student table based on the Student ID.

With that in place, the first option is to simply place the related Student Name field on a layout in the Registration table. The second is to create an unstored calculation field in the Registration table that returns the related Student Name. And the third way is to create a new text field in Registration that looks up the related Student Name field whenever a Student ID is modified.

From the standpoint of normalization, the second method (creating an unstored calculation) is probably the best option. This is because the Course Name can't be modified from the Registration table, and the data isn't stored redundantly (as with the lookup). The problem, of course, is that any finds or sorts you perform based on the unindexable calculation will be (painfully) slow in a table with a large number of records. Thus, a table is often denormalized by using lookups to boost performance. When you do this, just be sure to design in a process to retrigger lookups appropriately.

Just for clarification, there's another use of lookups that's unrelated to issues of normalization, and it's important not to confuse the two. Often, lookups are used to capture data at a particular time. The classic example is looking up the price of an item when generating an invoice. Here, you absolutely don't want relookups to occur because prices change over time and historical data would be destroyed. Be sure that you know which purpose your lookup fields serve; they must be treated differently.

Third Normal Form (3NF)

The difference between Second and Third Normal Form (3NF) is subtle and, in the end, not terribly important. 2NF saw the extraction of data that was dependent on only a portion of the primary key. 3NF, on the other hand, extracts any attributes that are dependent on fields other than the primary key. Another way of expressing this is that 3NF eliminates transitive dependency. An example will clarify what this means. Let's look at the 2NF Course table we ended up with in the previous section, but add some information about the instructor:

Course ID	Course Name	Teacher ID	Teacher Name
Sci200	Biology	T1	Mr. Jones
Eng103	American Lit	T2	Ms. Moore
Mat421	Calculus	T3	Mrs. Smith
Soc126	Political Science	T4	Ms. Brown
Sci340	Chemistry	T1	Mr. Jones
Mat313	Geometry	T3	Mrs. Smith

The primary key of this table is still the Course ID. As long as we have agreed on a business rule that a course is taught by one and only one instructor, then this table is in 1NF. And any table in 1NF whose key is a single attribute is automatically in 2NF. (Multiple instructors for a course would result in a violation of 1NF, and the remedy would contain violations of 2NF. For this example, the assumption is one instructor per course.)

Let's look at the dependencies in this table:

Course ID → Course Name
Course ID → Teacher ID
Course ID → Teacher Name
Teacher ID → Teacher Name

Notice that although the Teacher Name is dependent on the Course ID, it is also dependent on the Teacher ID. And since the Teacher ID is dependent on the Course ID, we have what's called a transitive dependency.

Course ID → Teacher ID → Teacher Name

The problems of a table not in 3NF are essentially the same as those of a table not in 2NF. Here, you would have the problem of needing to update the Teacher Name in multiple places; you wouldn't be able to create new teachers without assigning them to at least one course; and deleting a record from the Course table destroys too much information.

The strategy to correct these problems is also essentially the same. A new table is created whose primary key is the non-key determinant (here, the Teacher ID), and all the attributes dependent on this determinant are moved to the new table. Thus, putting the Course table into 3NF would result in the following new data structure:

Course ID	Course Name	Teacher ID
Sci200	Biology	T1
Eng103	American Lit	T2
Mat421	Calculus	T3
Soc126	Political Science	T4
Sci340	Chemistry	T1
Mat313	Geometry	T3

Teacher ID	Teacher Name
T1	Mr. Jones
T2	Ms. Moore
T3	Mrs. Smith
T4	Ms. Brown

The same comments about lookups and unstored calculations that applied to 2NF also apply to 3NF.

3NF was the highest form in the original definition of the relational model. In the years since, however, other possible structural problems have been identified, and additional Normal Forms have been defined to address those issues. The remainder of this chapter discusses briefly the problems and remedies identified by the higher forms.

Boyce-Codd Normal Form (BCNF)

Boyce-Codd Normal Form is a stronger version of 3NF. It addresses situations where the non-key determinants are also candidate keys. Recall from Chapter 1 that it's sometimes possible to have more than one field or set of fields qualify to be designated as the primary key of a table, and that these fields are all called candidate keys. As an example, consider if we added the social security number to the Student table we derived earlier:

Student ID	SSN	Student Name
123	123-12-3421	Sandy
124	533-56-4237	Jasper
125	652-46-4084	Felix

Both the Student ID and the SSN are candidate keys. (For the sticklers out there, the government doesn't guarantee that social security numbers are unique, but we'll assume it's unique enough for our example here.) Let's say that between these, we've chosen Student ID to be the primary key of this table. Now, let's look at the dependencies:

Student ID → SSN
Student ID → Student Name
SSN → Student ID
SSN → Student Name

Hopefully, you can see that this is technically a violation of 3NF; a key other than the primary key is a determinant. But the update anomalies inherent in 3NF violations wouldn't be issues here. All Boyce-Codd Normal Form does is alter the definition of 3NF to allow for non-key determinants that are candidate keys. While it's technically more rigorous than 3NF, in practice there's really not much you have to be concerned about.

Fourth Normal Form (4NF)

Fourth Normal Form deals with independent multivalued dependencies. This sounds complex because of the terminology, but it's really not that bad. A multivalued dependency is really just a repeating group of information like the one we encountered in the Registration table during the discussion of 1NF. The problem addressed in 4NF is when there are multiple, yet independent repeating groups of information. Under 4NF, these groups should not be allowed to be contained in the same table.

As an example, consider students who can register for multiple courses and can speak one or more languages. If there's no relationship between course enrollment and languages spoken, these attributes are independent. Any attempt to build a table with all three attributes will violate 4NF; the solution, as you might have anticipated, is to build two tables.

Let's look at the problems that arise when you put all of this data in one table. Imagine starting with the following data:

Student ID	Course ID	Language Spoken
1	A, B	English, German, French
2	B, C, D	English

To put this data in 1NF, we need to eliminate the repeating groups of information. In order to not imply a relationship between Course ID and Language Spoken, you'd end up with the following:

Student ID	Course ID	Language Spoken
1	A	English
1	A	German
1	A	French
1	B	English
1	B	German
1	B	French
2	B	English
2	C	English
2	D	English

Interestingly, this table is in 2NF and 3NF. Yet, the problems inherent in this structure are similar to the ones found in 2NF and 3NF. Updates would need to be done in multiple records, adding the fact that a student spoke a language would potentially require adding many records to the table (which is inefficient), and deletion of a language could lead to the deletion of course registration data. Similar problems would occur even if the complete cross product of the multivalued keys hasn't been generated, as it was above.

To convert this table to 4NF, we would replace the existing table with two new tables, each of which contained information about one of the multivalued attributes:

Student ID	Course ID
1	A
1	B
2	B
2	C
2	D

Student ID	Language Spoken
1	English
1	German
1	French
2	English

Notice that each table contains fewer attributes than the original, and that the total number of rows in the two new tables is also less than the number of rows in the original. Additionally, the original table can be reproduced by joining the two new tables; no information is lost. This is subtle but important. Both structures contain exactly the same information, but the 4NF version sidesteps the update, add, and delete problems that plague the 1NF version.

Chances are that if you were designing this system, you never would have attempted to put information about course enrollment and languages spoken into the same table in the first place. You would have immediately recognized that you needed two tables, both one-to-many relations from the Student table. The rules of 4NF formalize what we usually do intuitively, so you probably don't need to spend too much time worrying about whether your tables are in 4NF or not. The reason for the rule is precisely because of the possibility that a table can be in 3NF and still have update anomalies.

So, since the problem occurs when we have multivalued dependencies, let's say that a table is in Fourth Normal Form when it meets the criteria for the earlier normal forms, and that there are no multivalued dependencies.

Fifth Normal Form (5NF)

In our earlier examples, we've been decomposing tables into component tables. This act uses the project operator. This composition is valid because we can join the resulting tables to reproduce the original table. If we were unable to join the tables to reproduce the original table, we would lose meaning, so decomposing tables in a loss-less way is called non-loss decomposition.

There are special cases where a table can't be non-loss decomposed into two tables, but can be non-loss decomposed into three or more tables. These cases are called *n*-decomposable. It is for these cases that we need Fifth Normal Form. Because this kind of decomposability acts as a constraint on the table, it's called a *join dependency*. Just because you can non-loss decompose (project) a table into constituent pieces doesn't mean you need to, but in the case of *n*-decomposable tables, there are subtle update anomalies that can occur, so they do need to be decomposed. A table can thus be said to be in Fifth Normal Form if it meets the criteria for Fourth Normal Form and it is not *n*-decomposable.

Let's consider a scenario where Employees have multiple Skills (like FileMaker, HTML, and PHP) and work on multiple Projects. At first blush, you might notice that there are two multivalued dependencies here. Employee multidetermines Skill, and Employee also multidetermines Project. But if a certain project requires certain skills, then these attributes aren't independent, and 4NF wouldn't apply. Now, if the relationship between the multivalued attributes is ad hoc, we just have a table with a triple compound primary key:

Employee	**Skill**	**Project**
Bob	FileMaker	Web site redesign
Bob	FileMaker	Contact database
Bob	HTML	Web site redesign
Chris	FileMaker	Contact database
Chris	HTML	Web site redesign
Chris	PHP	Web site redesign

As it stands now, there are no functional dependencies in this table, and the multivalued attributes aren't independent, so this table is in 4NF, 3NF, 2NF, and 1NF. But, since there's no way to decompose this table into several smaller tables without losing information, it's also in 5NF.

A small change in business logic will reveal a case for 5NF. Let's add the constraint that if an Employee has a Skill and works on a Project that requires that Skill, then he uses that Skill on that Project. The table above doesn't adhere to this constraint: Notice that Chris has the FileMaker skill and works on the Web site redesign project (which requires that skill), but he doesn't use that skill on that project. In the absence of a rule like this, a table in 4NF is always in 5NF.

In light of this constraint, let's replace the data in our table with the following:

Employee	Skill	Project
Bob	FileMaker	Web site redesign
Bob	FileMaker	Contact database
Bob	HTML	Web site redesign
Bob	HTML	Contact database
Chris	FileMaker	Contact database
Chris	HTML	Contact database
Chris	PHP	Contact database
Chris	PHP	Numerology
Steve	FileMaker	Web site redesign
Steve	FileMaker	Contact database

This table can be decomposed into the following structure:

Employee	Skill
Bob	FileMaker
Bob	HTML
Chris	FileMaker
Chris	HTML
Chris	PHP
Steve	FileMaker

Skill	Project
FileMaker	Web site redesign
FileMaker	Contact database
HTML	Web site redesign
HTML	Contact database
PHP	Contact database
PHP	Numerology

Employee	Project
Bob	Web site redesign
Bob	Contact database
Chris	Contact database
Chris	Numerology
Steve	Web site redesign
Steve	Contact database

If you were to join these new tables together, the result would be exactly the original table, which means that there's no loss of information from the decomposition. We would now say that this structure is in 5NF.

It's rare to find real-world situations where the conditions are right for 5NF to be necessary. Think, though, of normalization as an effort to break tables into smaller tables with fewer elements, while preserving information. You know that information has been preserved as long as the smaller tables can be joined to form the original table. 5NF is necessary for completeness, but it's fairly esoteric. Know that it exists, but don't worry about it the same way you do 1NF, 2NF, and 3NF.

Summary

This chapter has covered the rules of normalization from a FileMaker developer's perspective. We feel strongly that knowing what the rules are and the problems they attempt to avoid will make you a better developer. First, Second, and Third Normal Form are by far the most important for most database systems, so be sure that you have a strong understanding of these, if nothing else. And finally, when you make decisions for reporting or performance reasons to denormalize your data structure, be sure that you have considered the potential problems that might arise and create routines to deal with them.

Chapter 4

Audit Trails

By now, you've probably noticed that the thrust of this book (so far) is that if you follow good design principles, you'll get "good" data in your database. After you've done a proper design and built a relational system, you can be assured that users can only enter data in an appropriate way. Even with all of these precautions, though, it's still possible for users to enter correct data in an incorrect way. By assigning an invoice to the wrong customer or changing a price on the wrong product, users can still compromise the data integrity of the system even though you've forced them to do it in a very specific way.

The bottom line is that even a perfect database has to operate in an imperfect world. That being the case, what's needed is a tool that allows you to identify and undo any mistakes that have been made. In database jargon, this kind of an undo operation is known as a *rollback*. In order to perform a rollback, you first need to have an audit trail.

An *audit trail* is nothing more than a list of changes that have been made to the database. Such a list has many potential uses. For example, if you have new users who are making data entry mistakes, you can look at an audit trail of their activities and find out what they did wrong so you can retrain them on that aspect of their work. Or, if you have sensitive data that should only be changed by authorized personnel, an audit trail can tell you who put what value into what field. It can also tell what value was in there before, so you can restore the original data if necessary. This restoration is the rollback we referred to, and it's the audit trail that makes a rollback possible. The act of writing a transaction to an audit trail is commonly known as *journaling*. Finally, audit trails and rollbacks are often a design requirement of database systems that track confidential information. Examples of these might be a disciplinary action database, a salary database, or a research project database.

This chapter will show you how to implement journaling in your own database systems. The methods we discuss require that you control the user's navigation from layout to layout as well as from record to record.

Capturing Changes to Fields

Creating audit trails is made more difficult by the fact that FileMaker doesn't have field modification triggers. That is, there's no way to trigger a script when a field is modified. There are plug-ins that allow you to do this, but as of the time of our writing, they exist only for the Macintosh platform.

The closest thing to a field modification trigger that FileMaker offers is a lookup. Fortunately, that's enough to allow us to capture changes made to fields. As far as we know, the method we'll show to do this was originally devised by our esteemed colleague Bob Cusick. We've made some significant modifications, but the basic mechanism is all Bob's.

In our examples, we'll use a very simple Contact database with four fields: Contact_ID, First_Name, Last_Name, and Birthdate. To add audit trail capabilities to this (or any other) table requires the creation of six new fields. The order in which these fields are created is somewhat important, so rather than just listing them, we'll present and discuss each in turn.

The first new field we'll add to the Contact database is a calculation called Audit_Existing Values that contains a simple array of the field names and values that you want to be included in your audit trail. You would typically include some subset of the table's text, number, date, and time fields. Global fields, summary fields, calculations, and container fields are not things that you can track changes to.

```
Audit_Existing Values = "First_Name::" & First_Name & "¶" &
     "Last_Name::" & Last_Name & "¶" &
     "Birthdate::" & DateToText(Birthdate) & "¶"
```

This field serves two purposes. First, it's where the audit log will look to find the new value of a field. Second, it will actually trigger the audit mechanism; anytime one of the fields it references changes, the calculation will be forced to reevaluate, setting off a chain reaction of calculations and lookups.

The second field you need is another calculation; we'll call this one Audit_Trigger.

```
Audit_Trigger = Case(Audit_Existing Values, Contact_ID, Contact_ID)
```

This field, as you might have guessed from its name, also forms part of the trigger mechanism. Any time Audit_Existing Values reevaluates, so will this calculation. So, anytime one of the fields referenced by Audit_Existing Values changes, Audit_Trigger will be set to the Contact_ID of the current record.

With these two fields in place, you next need to define a new self-relationship that matches Audit_Trigger to the Contact_ID, as shown in Figure 4.1.

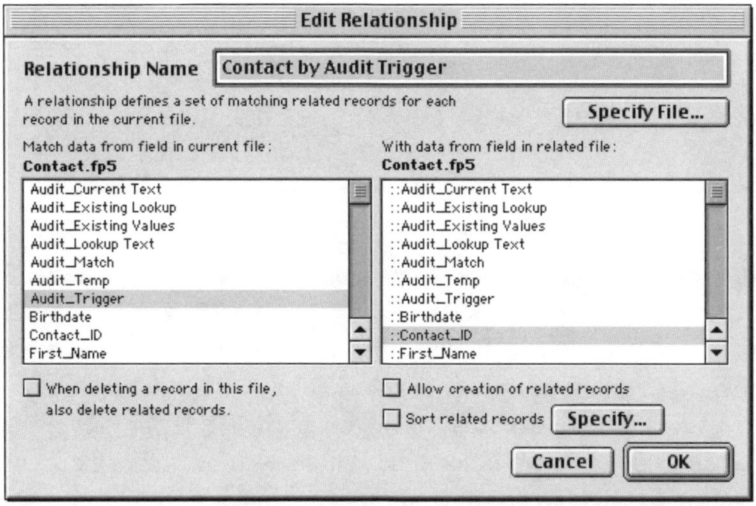

Figure 4.1

Now you can create a text field called Audit_Existing Lookup that is set to look up the Audit_Existing Values field through this relationship. The lookup dialog is shown in Figure 4.2.

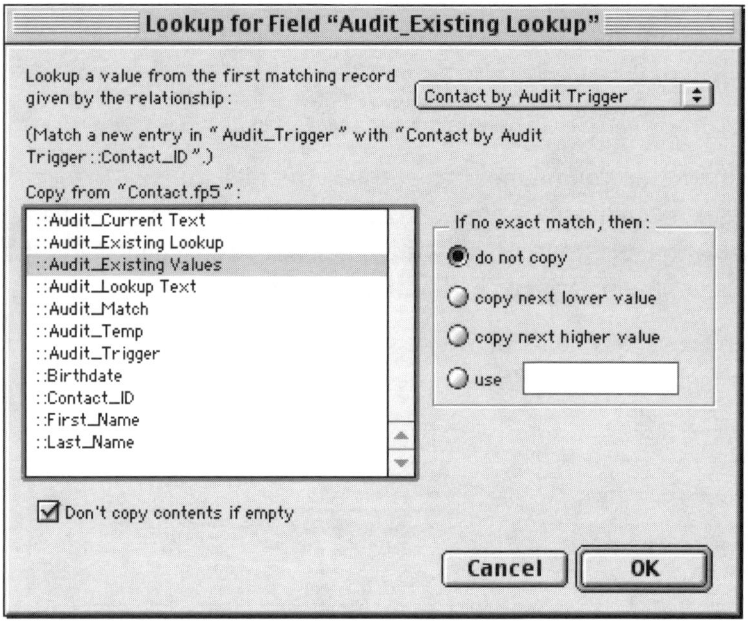

Figure 4.2

Let's review exactly how lookups work. A lookup involves two fields and a relationship. One field is known as the trigger, the other as the target. The target is the field you actually define as a lookup (here, Audit_Existing Lookup). It will be set to some value through the relationship you specify. The trigger field (here, Audit_Trigger) is the field that you've selected as the left-hand side of that relationship. Whenever the trigger field is modified, the target field is set to the value of the field you selected in the lookup dialog (here, Audit_Existing Values).

That's all probably stuff you know. What you might not know, however, is that calculations evaluate before lookups take place. This is crucial to understand. Say you change the First_Name field from "Fred" to "Joe." Since the value of this field is part of the definition of Audit_Existing Values, it changes immediately when you click or tab out of the First_Name field. This also causes Audit_Trigger to update, which then triggers the lookup. Audit_Existing Lookup will finally reflect that the first name is Joe. So, for some very brief instant, the contents of Audit_Existing Values and Audit_Existing Lookup will be different. The calculation will reflect the new value while the lookup field still contains the old.

This momentary difference can be captured in a new calculation called Audit_Current Text. This field uses several status functions to capture information such as the current date and time, the current field, the current layout, and the current user's name. By locating the name of the current field in the Audit_Existing Values and Audit_Existing Lookup arrays, you can also extract the old and new values of that field. The end result is that Audit_Current Text will contain a delimited list (we're using pipe characters as the delimiter) of information about the change that was made. In that brief instance between calculations updating and lookups being triggered, it will contain the field's name, the old and new values, and the layout, date, and time of the change.

Since this field contains status functions, you must explicitly set the storage options for this field to not store the calculation results (see Figure 4.3).

```
Audit_Current Text = "|" & Status(CurrentFieldName) & "|" &

Middle(Audit_Existing Lookup, Position(Audit_Existing Lookup, Status
        (CurrentFieldName) & "::",1,1) + Length(Status(CurrentFieldName) &
        "::"),
    Position(Audit_Existing Lookup, "¶", Position(Audit_Existing Lookup,
            Status(CurrentFieldName) & "::",1,1),1) - (Position(Audit_
            Existing Lookup, Status(CurrentFieldName) & "::",1,1) +
            Length(Status(CurrentFieldName) & "::"))) &

"|" &
Middle(Audit_Existing Values, Position(Audit_Existing Values, Status
        (CurrentFieldName) & "::",1,1) + Length(Status(CurrentFieldName) &
        "::"),
    Position(Audit_Existing Values, "¶", Position(Audit_Existing Values,
            Status(CurrentFieldName) & "::",1,1),1) - (Position(Audit_
            Existing Values, Status(CurrentFieldName) & "::",1,1) +
            Length(Status(CurrentFieldName) & "::"))) &

"|" & Status(CurrentLayoutName) &
"|" & DateToText(Status(CurrentDate)) &
"|" & TimeToText(Status(CurrentTime)) &
"|" & Status(CurrentUserName) & "|"
```

Chapter 4

NOTE If you've created a login system similar to the one we build in Chapter 7, you probably would want to replace the Status(CurrentUserName) with the user's ID.

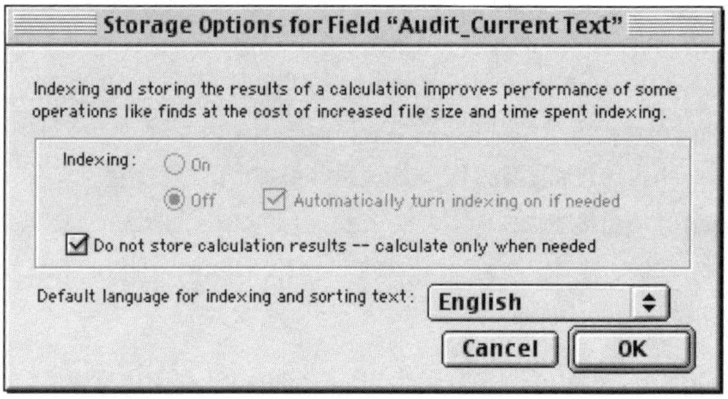

Figure 4.3

The calculation isn't as complex as it looks. Chapter 11 discusses text parsing functions like this in more detail. The Audit_Current Text field only contains the information we want in that instant between calculations updating and lookups triggering. We need to somehow capture that moment in a less ephemeral manner. Another lookup field can be used for this. This text field will be called Audit_Temp, and it will use the same trigger and relationship as the last lookup that we defined. If it is simply to look up the Audit_Current Text field, Audit_Temp will be overwritten every time a field changes, destroying the history of previous changes. The solution for this is to employ some circular logic.

First, define Audit_Temp as a plain old text field. Then, define a new calculation field called Audit_Lookup Text with the following definition:

```
Audit_Lookup Text = Audit_Current Text & "¶" & Audit_Temp
```

In that instant after calculations have been updated, this field contains exactly what we want to capture: the previous history for this record plus information about the change that's just been made. It's this field that we want the Audit_Temp field to look up. So, return to the options for Audit_Temp and specify the lookup as shown in Figure 4.4.

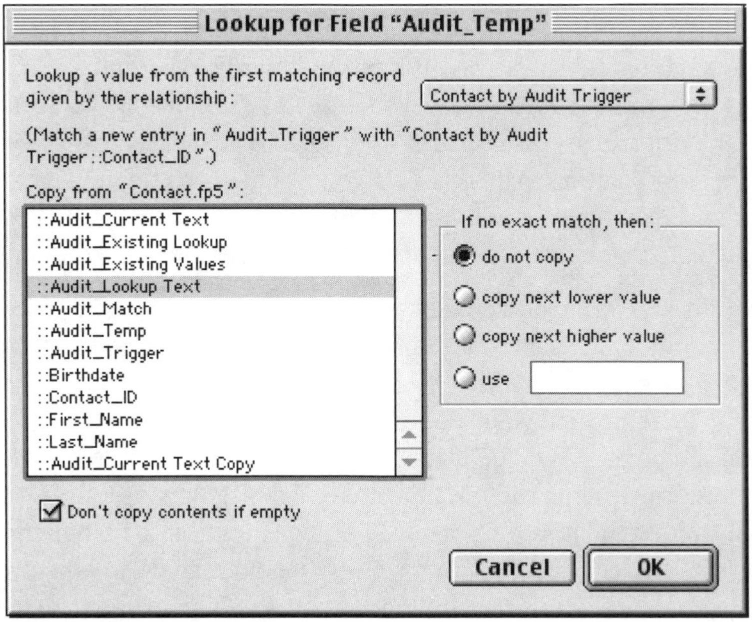

Figure 4.4

With that, the mechanism for capturing the changes to a field is complete. Now, anytime one of the fields referenced in Audit_Existing Values is changed, that change will be captured in Audit_Temp. Figure 4.5 shows an example of what the log ends up looking like. In this example, you can see that after the three fields were initially populated, the first name of the contact was changed from "Joe" to "Fred."

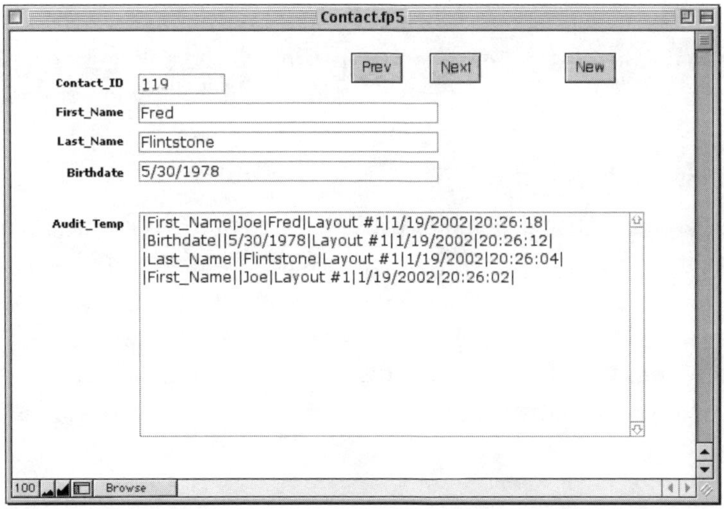

Figure 4.5

The audit mechanism is triggered even if the record is modified via a portal or as a related field from another table. It works whether you're viewing records in form view, list view, or table view, and doesn't require any special layouts or scripts. Just be sure to add the six fields described above to each file in your solution that has fields you want to include in your audit trail. The only real maintenance you need to do is make sure that you update the Audit_Existing Values calculation when you add, delete, or rename fields.

There is a caveat that we need to mention here. This audit process doesn't work properly during record imports or replace operations. During an import, no change is detected at all. During a replace, this mechanism is unable to determine which field was changed. The field name portion of the Audit_Temp entry will be blank, and the value of the first field in the calculation order will appear in both the old and new positions, but it will be the same value. About all you can do is recognize missing field names as cases where a replace occurred. There's nothing you can do to detect an import, although typically in a system that's protected like this, only a database administrator will even be allowed to perform an import, so it should be okay.

The Audit Log

There are a few drawbacks to holding a field's change history in the Audit_Temp field. First, over time this field may grow to be quite large for some records. It may even approach the 64,000-character limit for text fields in FileMaker Pro. Second, since each record contains its own history, it's difficult to do any sort of analysis, like finding all the changes that happened on a certain day or were made by a certain user. Third, when you delete a record, you destroy its change history as well, which defeats the concept of having an audit trail in the first place.

To get around these problems, you'll want to take the transactions from Audit_Temp and write each line out to a separate record in a separate file that we'll refer to as AuditLog.FP5. Breaking up the transactions in this way gives you great flexibility, and as we'll show later in this chapter, you can go so far as to roll back changes made to a certain field or certain record. A single AuditLog table can be used to record the changes from all of the tables in a solution.

Writing the contents of Audit_Temp out to the AuditLog table can only be accomplished by running a script, which we'll look at shortly. This script needs to be invoked as a subscript any time a user navigates from record to record, between layouts, or between files. Auditing functions need to be completely integrated into user navigation in order to be effective. This also means that if you have layouts with portals, you need to be sure to write out the audit trail for all of the related records each time you write out the parent record. It might help you to think of Audit_Temp as a place to temporarily cache or buffer change data. You need to make sure the buffer is "flushed" to the AuditLog before a user leaves a record.

Without further ado, let's look at the structure of the AuditLog table:

```
Audit ID [number, serial number]
Audit Match [text]
Date [date]
Time [time]
Field Name [text]
Layout [text]
Old Value [text]
New Value [text]
User [text]
Database [calculation, text result] = Left(Audit Match, Position(Audit
        Match, "-", 1, 1) - 1)
Record ID [calculation, text result] = Right(Audit Match, Length(Audit
        Match) - Position(Audit Match, "-", 1, 1))
```

Note that the Database and Record ID fields extract their values from the Audit Match field, with the database name on the left and the record ID on the right. Since the Record ID takes everything to the right of the first hyphen, this even works for compound primary keys.

Back in the Contact table, you'll also need to add an Audit_Match field:

```
Audit_Match [calculation, text result] = Status(CurrentFileName) & "-" &
        Contact_ID
```

Next, create a relationship from Contact to AuditLog called AuditLog by Audit_Match, as shown in Figure 4.6.

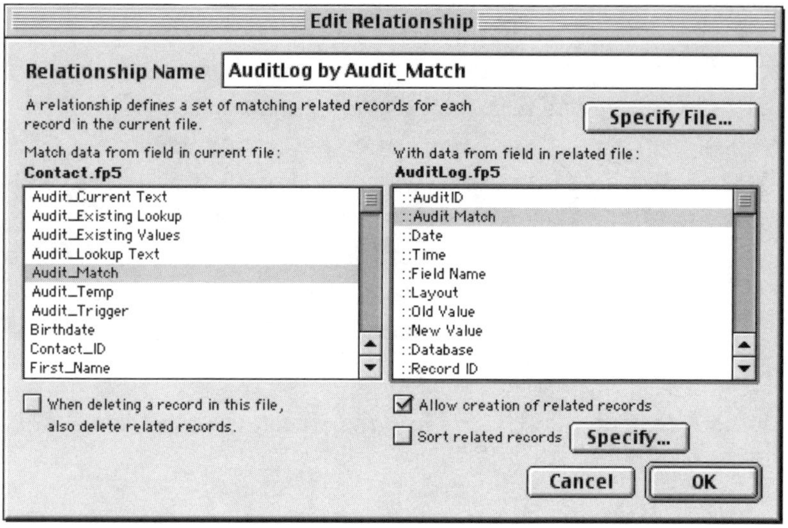

Figure 4.6

Make sure to set the relationship to allow creation of related records. As you create records via the relationship, the filename and record ID thus come over for free.

The next step is to create a new utility layout called Audit in the Contact table. The Audit layout, as you can see in Figure 4.7, needs to include a portal that uses the relationship defined above. This portal serves two purposes. First, it will be used by the script that follows for actually creating the audit trail. Second, it's a good interface to view all of the changes that have ever been made to the current record.

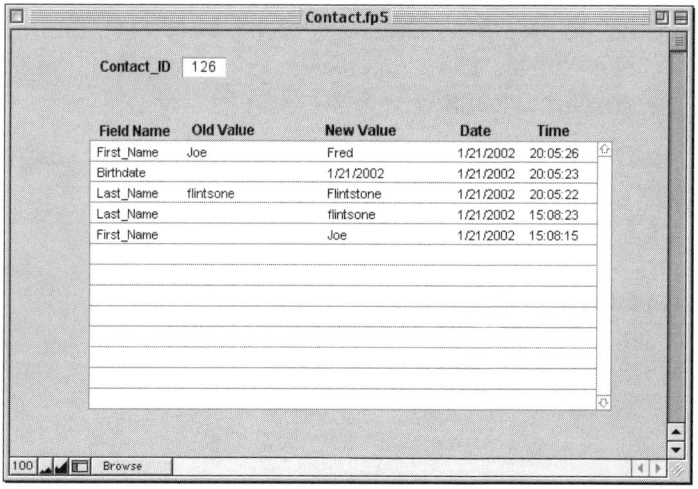

Figure 4.7

Let's now look at the auditing script, which we'll call Sub: Write Audit_Temp to Log.

```
Free e  indow
Exit Record/Request
If ["not IsEmpty (Audit Temp)"]
     Go to Layout ["Audit"]
     Loop
          Exit Loop If ["IsEmpty (Audit_Temp)"]
          Go to Portal Row [Select, Last]
          Set Field ["AuditLog by Audit_Match::Field Name", "Middle(Audit_
                 Temp, Position(Audit_Temp, "|", 1, 1) + 1, Position
                 (Audit_Temp, "|", 1,  ) - Position(Audit_Temp, "|", 1,
                  1) - 1)"]
          Set Field ["AuditLog by Audit_Match::Old Value", "Middle(Audit_
                 Temp, Position(Audit_Temp, "|", 1,  ) + 1, Position
                 (Audit_Temp, "|", 1,  ) - Position(Audit_Temp, "|", 1,
                   ) - 1)"]
          Set Field ["AuditLog by Audit_Match::New Value", "Middle(Audit_
                 Temp, Position(Audit_Temp, "|", 1,  ) + 1, Position
                 (Audit_Temp, "|", 1,  ) - Position(Audit_Temp, "|", 1,
                   ) - 1)"]
          Set Field ["AuditLog by Audit_Match::Layout", "Middle(Audit_Temp,
                 Position(Audit_Temp, "|", 1,  ) + 1, Position(Audit_
                 Temp, "|", 1, 5) - Position(Audit_Temp, "|", 1,  ) -
                 1)"]
          Set Field ["AuditLog by Audit_Match::Date", "TextToDate(Middle
                 (Audit_Temp, Position(Audit_Temp, "|", 1, 5) + 1,
                  Position(Audit_Temp, "|", 1,  ) - Position(Audit_Temp,
                  "|", 1, 5) - 1))"]
          Set Field ["AuditLog by Audit_Match::Time", "TextToTime(Middle
                 (Audit_Temp, Position(Audit_Temp, "|", 1,  ) + 1,
                  Position(Audit_Temp, "|", 1,  ) - Position(Audit_Temp,
                  "|", 1,  ) - 1))"]
          Set Field ["AuditLog by Audit_Match::User", "Middle(Audit_Temp,
                 Position(Audit_Temp, "|", 1,  ) + 1, Position(Audit_
                 Temp, "|", 1,  ) - Position(Audit_Temp, "|", 1,  ) -
                 1)"]
          Set Field ["Audit_Temp", "Right(Audit_Temp, Length(Audit_Temp) -
                 Position(Audit_Temp, "¶", 1, 1))"]
```

Chapter 4

```
        End Loop
    End If
    Go to Layout [Refresh window, original layout]
```

The script begins by checking if there are any changes that have been buffered in Audit_Temp. If not, the script just ends. If there are changes, it switches to the Audit layout, goes to the last portal row, and starts a loop that sets various fields in the AuditLog to the appropriate portion of the Audit_Temp field. Once these have been set, the top line of Audit_Temp is removed. The loop continues to chew up Audit_Temp line by line until finally exiting when there are no additional changes to process.

This script needs to be called as a subscript any time a user can navigate off a layout that contains fields that are audited. And as we mentioned before, if there are portals (in which the user can edit data), you'll also want this script to jump to related records and run a similar subscript in the child file. There, of course, you'll need to wrap an additional loop around the steps above to cycle through the records of the found set.

The basic audit trail is now complete. It's possible to extend this solution in a variety of directions. For example, if you wanted to set up a user probation period in the system, you could modify this auditing example so that users have their transactions audited until they achieve a "trusted" status within the system. To do that, you would modify the Audit_Trigger calculation so that if a user had a "trusted user" privilege, the calculation would return nothing. You could also just audit the most sensitive parts of the system, or even just the fact that someone moved through the system in a certain order, without even bothering to record specific value changes. With the addition of rollbacks (see the following section) you could even save and replay certain audit log sequences for training purposes.

One item we do need to touch on is how to handle record deletions. In many secure systems, you'll want to script record deletions anyway since you'll probably need to perform a privilege check to see if the user should be able to delete the record under those specific circumstances. Regardless, if you want to audit a record deletion, you'll need to script that process. We'd show you an example, but the script will need to be specific to various circumstances.

For example, if you were deleting a company record that had related company contacts, you'd probably be doing a cascading delete where the company record forced the deletion of the related company contact records. In that case, your delete script would first need to jump to the related records, create AuditLog records to record the deletion of each related record, delete the records, then return to the parent record. In the parent record, the script would need to create an AuditLog record to record the deletion of the parent record, then delete the record.

Obviously this gets even more complex if you have three or four levels of cascading deletes. In each case, the script will need to be specific to the logic of the files that are involved. Since the entire process is script-driven, you can choose whether or not to log the final values of the deleted record without relying on the Audit_Temp field.

You can also just leave the auditing process as it is and you'll have ample information any time you want to go back and check on what happened to a particular record or set of records. If you want to be able to "rewind" those transactions, though, then you'll want to proceed to the next part of this chapter: rollbacks.

Rollback Considerations

This particular rollback implementation is dependent on the AuditLog table described earlier in this chapter. If you skipped straight to this section, you'll need to at least look back to see how that table gets populated.

In other database systems, rollbacks are implemented in a variety of ways. When users log into the database system, they begin a session. They can then add, delete, or update records, and as long as they haven't committed those actions using a Commit command, the database management system, or DBMS, will allow them to use the Rollback command to undo those actions as if they had never happened.

It's also possible, though, that a database gets used in an auto-commit mode, which is similar to the way FileMaker works when a user exits a record. Changes are written to disk immediately. Exit Record/Request in FileMaker is tantamount to the Commit command in other systems.

Other systems also have temporary transaction logs, which are a bit different from what we described earlier in this chapter. A typical transaction log is similar to FileMaker Server's database cache. It contains transactions that haven't been written to disk yet. With a transaction log, you can either manually or automatically set checkpoints. A *checkpoint* is the earliest point in time that you can roll back to. Once you set a checkpoint, all transactions prior to that checkpoint are typically committed and then discarded from the transaction log.

For example, you might have a sequence of events that needs to happen every time you enter an order from a new customer. You would set a checkpoint at the beginning, then add the customer record, add the order and order item records, and only then commit the sequence of events as a whole transaction. If, at any point during that sequence, something goes wrong, you just roll back to the checkpoint.

If you have checkpoints that set automatically, say, every five minutes, it's possible that you might find yourself right in the middle of some incomplete user transactions. As an example, a user might have created a new record and started entering field values, but they haven't finished entering a complete record yet. That kind of half-finished transaction is called a *dirty transaction*, and it roughly corresponds to the situation FileMaker users have when they perform a replace operation and get a message that one or more records were in use by others.

Anyway, if you either manually or automatically set a checkpoint, any complete transactions are written to disk and discarded from the transaction log, and any dirty transactions are left in the log. If the system should go down before the dirty transactions are completed, the system will roll back to its prior state and the dirty transactions will be discarded. We haven't implemented checkpoint functionality in this example, but you could easily add that feature.

All of this discussion is to set up some considerations for how you might want to use the AuditLog table. Over time, it can become very large, and you'll need to prune it. You probably don't need to hang onto the information that five years ago a user who's no longer with the company changed a phone number field. Determine the rules for deleting or archiving the AuditLog table, and then either perform the necessary tasks manually as part of a periodic maintenance routine, or create scripts to automate the process.

Types of Rollbacks

Since each record in the AuditLog table contains a single value change for a single field in a single record, you have several options for performing rollbacks. You can look at the history for a single field for a particular record and roll that value back to a certain point in time, or you can roll an entire record back to a certain point, or you can roll an entire table back to a certain point, or you can even roll an entire system back to a certain point. Below we discuss various types of rollbacks and issues that you need to be aware of.

Rolling Back Updates to a Single Field

Imagine that you have a product database and you update the prices of your products each month. If for some reason you made some mistakes and wanted to restore the prices to their previous values, you could find all of the AuditLog records for that particular table and field and "undo" those modifications. Undoing changes to a field since a certain date and time is perhaps the easiest type of rollback to perform. The solution given at the end of this chapter will show you how to do just this.

Be aware, though, that performing this type of rollback without first examining the history of the entire record can be dangerous. Suppose the field in question is a price field on an invoice line item record. At one point in time, the record described a small bolt that sold for less than a dollar. It was later changed to a motor assembly that sold for several hundred dollars. Just rolling back the price field without rolling back the product description could be a very bad thing. Be careful and thorough when rolling back a field. It's safer to roll back a complete record.

Rolling Back a Record

It's possible also to undo all the changes made to a particular record since a certain date and time. You might find this type of rollback helpful if a user accidentally makes changes to the wrong record. And even if the user can't remember what record he actually changed, you can easily discover this by searching the AuditLog.

The only thing you might need to be concerned about is if the record you want to roll back had been deleted. Our AuditLog doesn't capture information about adds or deletes. It just tracks updates. It's potentially dangerous to your data integrity to simply say that if the record you want to roll back doesn't exist, then it should be recreated. If that record was deleted as part of a cascading delete and you restored the child record without restoring the parent record as well, you'd have orphaned records.

Rolling Back Changes Made by a Certain User

It's certainly possible to find and roll back all of the modifications made by a certain user, but unless you're absolutely sure that no other users have worked on the same records, we wouldn't advise engineering something like this. If person A changes a field from "X" to "Y," and then person B changes it from "Y" to "Z," undoing the modifications of person A will return the value to "X." It would be much safer to carefully review the records in question and undo changes made by a certain user manually.

Rolling Back a Table or System

For the reasons just mentioned, you probably wouldn't want to (or be able to) use just the AuditLog to roll back an entire table or system to reflect its state at a previous date and time. If you knew that no records had been created or deleted, then it would be easy. If you want to extend the solution we show you to be able to account for undoing adds and deletes, then you'll want to capture these events in some sort of transaction log. Deletes would be especially tricky, since you need to capture a snapshot of what the data looked like when you deleted the record.

In most cases, you'd be far better off going to a backup of your system if you ever needed to return it to a previous state. The AuditLog certainly isn't a replacement for a rigorous backup strategy.

Recreating Transactions Since the Last Backup

That said, the AuditLog can help supplement your backup strategy. Even if you have your server set to perform backups every hour, a crash will result in lost data and time as users try to remember all the changes they made since the last backup. If you have an AuditLog (and it hasn't been damaged by the crash), you can quickly bring up your last set of good files, find all of the modifications in the recovered AuditLog since that time, and run scripts to "replay" those modifications. Again, while updates are easy to replay, you'll need to think carefully about how to identify and deal with additions and deletions, especially if you have a complex system. Scripts to replay a set of modifications would require only minimal changes from the rollback routine we show below.

Constructing a Rollback Mechanism

In the remainder of this chapter, we'll show you how to build a system for rolling back modifications. The process starts by identifying a set of records in the AuditLog. You'll want to be able to find all changes to a field, record, database, or system since a specified date and time. Then, it's simply a matter of looping through the records in reverse chronological order and passing instructions to the appropriate database to "undo" the transaction. Finally, once the transactions have been undone, they need to be deleted from the AuditLog.

Before we begin, there are a few important caveats to cover. First, anytime you attempt a rollback, be sure that there are no other users logged into the system. If there are, you run the risk of having record-locking issues that might cause more headaches than you started with. Second, be sure that there are no unflushed modifications sitting in the Audit_Temp field. If there are, find those records and run some sort of looping script that writes them out to the AuditLog. Finally, the system we are about to show you handles modifications to records, but it doesn't have any logic for dealing with creation and deletion of records. As we discussed above, we feel such a system would be prohibitively fragile as a general tool. If you need this sort of capability for a specific system, you'll probably be able to modify the solution to account for your particular data integrity rules. In the implementation we show you here, if a record has been deleted from the main file, the rollback routine will simply skip those transactions that pertain to the deleted record.

The first step of implementing a rollback system is identifying the transactions that you want to roll back. This involves nothing more complicated than finding a set of records in AuditLog. You can either do this manually or build some sort of interface for it. This is simple enough that we won't go into the details of how to do this. In our sample files, we just take users to a layout where they can enter their search criteria (into global fields) and then run a script that performs the find based on these entries. This interface for this is shown in Figure 4.8.

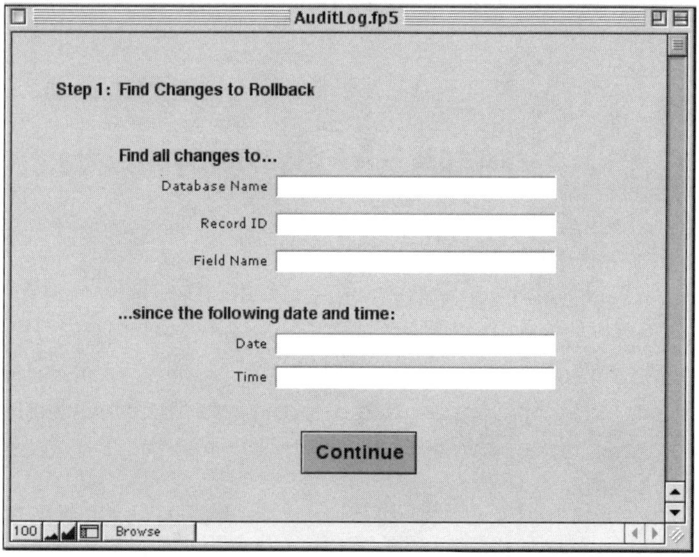

Figure 4.8

This interface allows you to easily find all the changes made to a field, a record, or a table (or some combination). You'll also want to sort the found set in reverse chronological order so that you can undo them in the proper order.

Figure 4.9 shows the results of finding all the changes that have been made to record 126 in the Contact database we've been using. As you can see, in the time period covered by these changes, the birthdate was given a value, a spelling and capitalization mistake was corrected in the Last_Name field, and the first name changed from "Joe" to "Frederick" to "Fred."

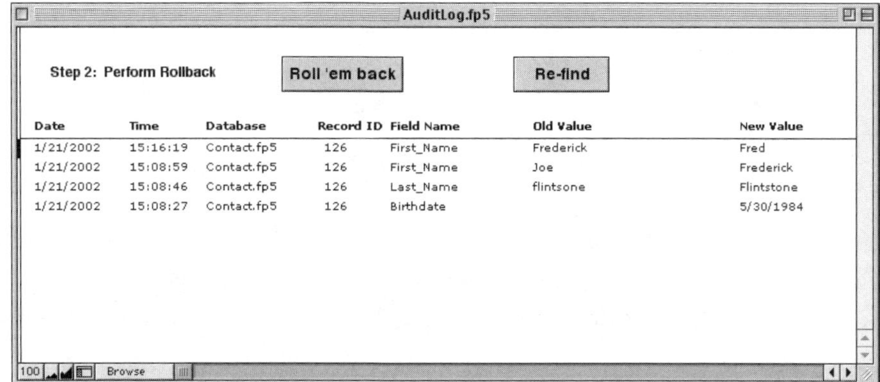

Figure 4.9

Once you've isolated the modifications you want to undo, it's just a matter of a few scripts to revert the record to its previous state. The main script is in the AuditLog table itself; we'll call it Rollback found set. You'll need to create four new global text fields (gPurge Flag, gRollback Record ID, gRollback Field Name, gRollback Field Value) in preparation for writing the script.

```
Go to Record/Request [First]
Loop
     Set Field [gPurge Flag, ""]
     Set Field [gRollback Record ID, Record ID]
     Set Field [gRollback Field Name, Field Name]
     Set Field [gRollback Field Value, Old Value]
     # you'll need an if statement like the one below to run the Rollback
          subscript
     # in the file specified in the "database" field
     If [Database = "Contact.fp5"]
          Perform Script [Sub-scripts, External: "Contact.fp5"] - calls
               "Sub: Rollback"
     End If
     #
     If [gPurge Flag = "OK"]
          Delete Record/Request [No dialog]
     Else
          Go to Record/Request/Page [Exit after last, Next]
     End If
     Exit Loop If [Status(CurrentFoundCount) = 0]
End Loop
If [Status(CurrentFoundCount) > 0]
```

```
          Show Message ["CAUTION: There were modifications that could not be
                         rolled back."]
     Else
          Show All Records
          Go to Layout["Main"]
     End If
```

This script is really not very complex. As it loops through the found set of records, it sets global fields with information the target table will need during the actual rollback subscript. The subscript, as we'll see momentarily, sets the gPurge Flag to "OK" if it has successfully rolled back the modification. If it has, the record is deleted from AuditLog. Ideally, the entire found set will be immolated. If there are records left over, that means the modifications could not be undone. Most likely this would result if you had renamed a field or deleted the record in question.

The subscript that you need to add to every file of your solution is slightly more complex. It begins simply enough by finding the correct record to update by pulling the gRollback Record ID field from the AuditLog. You could create a constant relationship to grab this value, but you can also just use the same relationship that we set up earlier, AuditLog by Audit_Match. The tricky part is next. The Set Field command requires that you explicitly state the field you want to set. Here, we would prefer to be able to set the field referenced by another field. In lieu of this, the best alternative is to create a simple utility layout with all of the data entry fields on it. You can then jump from field to field checking whether the name of the current field is the same value contained in the gRollback Field Name field. If it is, an Insert Calculated Result can be used (without specifying a field) to replace the current contents with gRollback Field Value. In order to avoid the possibility of an endless loop, we've added some logic to ensure that at most you'll loop once through all the fields on the layout. For this, a new global number field called gCounter is required.

```
Set Error Capture [On]
Enter Find Mode []
Set Field [Contact_ID, AuditLog by Audit_Match::gRollback Record ID]
Perform Find []
If [Status(CurrentFoundCount) = 1]
     Go to Layout ["All Fields"]
     Set Field [gCounter, PatternCount( FieldNames( Status
               (CurrentFieldName), Status(CurrentLayoutName)), "¶") + 1]
     Loop
          Go to Next Field
          If [Status(CurrentFieldName) = AuditLog by Audit_Match::gRollback
                    Field Name]
               Insert Calculated Result [Select, AuditLog by Audit_
                    Match::gRollback Field Value]
               Exit Record/Request
               Set Field [Audit_Temp, ""]
               Set Field [AuditLog by Audit_Match::gPurge Flag, "OK"]
               Exit Loop If [1]
          End If
          Set Field [gCounter, gCounter -1]
          Exit Loop If [gCounter = 0]
     End Loop
End If
Go to Layout [original layout]
```

Can you figure out why the script needs to clear out the Audit_Temp field after rolling back the transaction? When the script changes the field value, it triggers the audit process. If you don't clear it out, then you'll be capturing the rollback as a modification itself!

As we mentioned previously, the gCounter field is part of an error trap to make sure the script doesn't loop endlessly from field to field. It is initially set to the number of fields on the layout, and then counts down with each trip through the loop. If it equals zero, that means the correct field, for whatever reason, was never found. To find the number of fields on the layout, we use a design function called FieldNames, which returns a return-delimited list of fields on the layout and database specified in its arguments. Then, that function is wrapped with a PatternCount to determine how many return characters are in this list.

Summary

We began this chapter by teaching you how to capture changes made to fields and write them out to a log file. In and of itself, this can give you a lot of insight into how users are interacting with the database system. You'll find that if you implement an audit trail system like this, you'll do lots of ad hoc queries to find answers to all sorts of questions about why something was changed or who did what when.

The second half of the chapter extended the usefulness of an audit trail by showing you how to roll back sets of modifications. The actual rollback mechanism involves looping through the audit log and calling subscripts in the appropriate files. Before implementing rollbacks, be sure to think about how deletions should be handled in your system, and be aware of the other rollback considerations we discussed.

Chapter 7 tells you how to capture the User ID at login. The User ID is a more reliable identity indicator than Status(CurrentUserName), so once you learn the methods in Chapter 7, you should try modifying this example to audit with a User ID.

Chapter 5

Relational Design

We're mostly from the run and gun school of database development. That doesn't mean we don't like to be thorough; it just means we like to move through the process quickly. Like most FileMaker developers, we get the most enjoyment from actually building the system. The more we can minimize things like creating paperwork or reworking features, the better.

Our typical design process for a system of any complexity usually follows this trajectory:

1. Create a plain text process description.
2. Develop and review iterative ER diagram (data modeling).
3. Develop the logical database structure.
4. Modify the logical structure to arrive at the physical structure (denormalization).
5. Look for potential performance bottlenecks and, if necessary, conduct performance tests.
6. Prototype the interface and get feedback from the stakeholders.
7. Build and test the system.

Some might argue that we should have included training and deployment on this list, but that's a bit iffy as a relational design issue. Anyway, the above list seems simple, doesn't it? It is simple in an ideal world, because in an ideal world, your database project will have these features:

- The design effort has the full support of everyone within the organization in question.
- The person in control of the budget gives you unlimited time and money that you can use to conduct your interviews and design reviews.

- The busy people who have their regular jobs to do think nothing of spending countless hours with you describing the nuances of their business processes.
- Those same people remember to include every possible scenario and exception.
- You are an all-star interviewer who meticulously documents every conversation.
- Each business rule is thoroughly reviewed and signed off on by the appropriate person of authority.

This never happens. What does happen is usually something like this:

- The budget is too small to include an extensive data modeling effort. Often the key decision-maker thinks the modeling effort will make the project too expensive.
- People are too busy doing their jobs to devote much time to a modeling effort. You may be able to get some time with them, but not much.
- When you do get time with subject matter experts, you often find that they're not used to explaining their jobs and business processes to outsiders. Extracting process information is often like pulling teeth. They leave out important details and exceptions to their rules.
- Sometimes the database project is being used to implement a completely new way of doing things, and that often means that new processes haven't been completely thought through yet. They may not even work.

If you've been doing database work for any length of time, the above scenarios probably sound pretty familiar to you. We have to operate in a less than ideal environment, and we can't consume huge chunks of time on an exhaustive data modeling effort. We're going to show you how our design process works. It doesn't take too much time, there's a minimum of paperwork, and it results in a sound design.

To give you a better idea of how the whole process works, we'll go through an example from start to finish. Our example client will be a college coach who needs to create a system to manage recruiting activities.

You may have heard of XP — extreme programming. This is a style of programming originally described by Kent Beck in his book *Extreme Programming Explained*. It has an ethos of small releases, lots of feedback and testing, and a constantly changing specification, just like in the real world. XP programming doesn't completely lend itself to FileMaker development, especially with regard to testing processes, but there are some aspects that are very applicable. We like XP as a development philosophy and try to incorporate it into our FileMaker projects where it's practical. As we go through our methodology, we'll call out XP practices as we come to them.

Process Description

One thing we've always found helpful to the design process is the capturing of the business process in story form. This typically happens in a needs analysis stage, and it might be a consulting project unto itself.

After sitting down with a client to spec out the system, writing the process down as a narrative text description has several advantages. For one, it forces you to think through everything you covered, and you'll almost always come upon a concept that you're unclear about. It's also good for uncovering questions that you forgot to ask initially.

Once you've written the process description, you can then hand it back to the client for confirmation. You'll usually get some good feedback and clarification, and sometimes you'll even find that you misunderstood something. It's much less expensive to discover that at this stage of the process than it is after you start building the system.

Another advantage is that this exercise also forces the client to think through the process. Often this may highlight some problem that they've always noticed and wanted to fix. Sometimes they're coming up with a brand new process that has never been tested or even completely thought out. This exercise can make the ramifications of the new process more apparent, and it can be easily shared with others in the organization so they can give their feedback.

Yet another advantage is that when they say, “Yes, this is what we want the system to do,” you have documentation of what was originally agreed to. It’s a crude functional specification. This can be very helpful down the road with clients who change their minds a lot.

Let’s return to our college coach who needs to create a system to manage recruiting activities. After an initial consultation, the process description looks like this:

> High school juniors and seniors express interest in a particular college and request more information via the school’s web site, through their school guidance office, on standardized tests, or by responding to a mass mailing.
>
> Once they begin communicating with the admissions office, they indicate if they have any interest in any of the athletic programs. Those prospects are forwarded by the admissions office to the coach of that program. The coach gets this information in paper form, but can also get an electronic list of names with some basic information such as high school, year of graduation, GPA, and address. This list needs to be imported into the system so communication with the students can be tracked.
>
> There are various recruiting events at the school, and prospective students can come for a campus visit and even stay overnight with a student athlete in the sport that they’re interested in. Campus visits can be scheduled any time, but recruiting events have definite dates and times. The system needs to track a prospective student’s interest in these events and schedule them for the event if they decide to attend.
>
> Phone calls with the student and letters sent to and received from the student need to be tracked as well. When the student makes a final decision on attending a school or joining the sports team, that information needs to be tracked.

After reviewing this information, the designer (that would be you) has a few thoughts:

- It might be a good idea to keep track of existing and former athletes’ high schools so that if a student from that high school expresses an interest in the program, the student can be put in touch with the alumnus.

- The correspondence issue isn't very clear. We need more information on what sorts of letters or forms get sent back and forth.
- We need to get more information on what constitutes a desirable recruit.
- We don't have any information on what the minimum requirements are for admission to the school. There's no point in spending time and effort on a student who can't be admitted to the school.
- Are there any other ways that students get on the radar screen? What about referrals from alumni?
- It might be worth tracking what the most successful source and even the most successful process is for successful recruiting outcomes. It would be nice to know that a certain number of phone calls or contact at certain times of the year had more impact.
- If there are different sources for recruits, we need to be careful that we don't load the same student into the system more than once. We need to develop a method for screening out duplicates, while still making sure that we capture any new information from a duplicate prospect.

The next step in the process can happen in a variety of ways. If the client has the time to sit with you, you could write up your description with the client and ask questions as you compose it. Then the client can give immediate feedback and make corrections so that you work your way to a final description in one continuous process.

More typically, we return to our office after an initial consultation, write up the description from our notes, and perhaps call for a few clarifications or with questions like the ones listed above. We would then send the description to the client. Often they like to take some time to read it and think about not only if the description accurately describes the current process, but also if they want to change the process before implementing a new database system. Many times they don't have a single employee who is completely familiar with every step in the process, and they might want some extra time to have the various subject matter experts review their portion of the document.

We'll continue with our current example to give you an idea of how such a document can evolve over time. After reviewing our initial draft and our list of thoughts and questions, the client gives us this feedback that results in us changing our process description to read as follows:

> Prospects for the athletic program can be in any year in high school, and they come from a variety of sources:
>
> - Recruiting services
> - Web site inquiries
> - Unsolicited letters from prospects
> - Unsolicited e-mails from prospects
> - Scouting at games and tournaments
> - Club or high school coach recommendations
> - Admissions inquiries
>
> If a prospect comes from multiple sources, the first source will be used as the only source.
>
> Prospects that come from the admissions office come in the form of a weekly list of new inquiries. The format can be either a comma-delimited list or in Microsoft Excel. Once a prospect has applied for admission, the athletic department gets a weekly update of the prospect's status.
>
> For any given prospect, the athletic department needs to track:
>
> - GPA, SAT, ACT, PSAT, class rank, year of graduation
> - High school name or if transfer student, all colleges attended
> - Prospect's address, e-mail, phone
> - Sport, position, personal best times (where applicable), height, weight, statistics
> - Club team name and high school and club coaches' names and phone numbers or e-mail addresses
> - Any athletic awards or special status
> - Other schools the prospect is considering

Once a name has been obtained, that prospect is sent a letter or e-mail with a profile for that prospect to fill out and send back. Once the profile is returned, the prospect becomes an active file. If the coach determines that a prospect is a desirable candidate, their status is promoted to "varsity recruit." Otherwise, their status is "athletic interest."

There are various recruiting events at the school, and prospective students can come for a campus visit and even stay overnight with a student athlete in the sport that they're interested in. Campus visits can be scheduled any time, but recruiting events have definite dates and times. The system needs to track a prospective student's interest in these events and schedule them for the event if they decide to attend. Varsity recruit visits are arranged by the athletic department, while athletic interest prospect visits are arranged by the admissions office.

Phone calls with the student and letters sent to and received from the student need to be tracked as well. When the student makes a final decision on attending a school or joining the sports team, that information needs to be tracked.

There needs to be a method for combining duplicate prospect records.

It's worth pointing out that this is a relatively simple process description. If you need to write one for a large department or an entire organization, it's easy to get lost in all the detail. If you're creating a process description for multiple processes or a complex single process, things will go a lot smoother if you break the description up into pieces. You could write separate process descriptions for each department, or even from the point of view of different users. Having descriptions specific to different parts of an organization sometimes uncovers problems in the ways that people or departments are working together. Finding and resolving problems like those early in the process can be the difference between a project failing or succeeding.

The process description usually continues to evolve throughout the project, even after programming has begun. That's not cause for alarm. In fact, you should expect it. Just be sure that you have a description that everyone agrees on for now and a system for tracking changes as they occur.

For this example, we'll assume that the process description has been accepted by the client. Depending on how you've structured your project, at this point you may be in the middle of a needs analysis, or you may be refining an estimate. We'll be getting into more detail on XP practices later in this chapter, but starting with a rough estimate and then refining that estimate to gradually make it more accurate is an XP-style approach. With the process description in hand, you're now in a position to break the project down into smaller pieces.

Based on experience with projects of similar size and scope, you might have a rough idea of how long this project will take, but it will be very rough. In other words, it will be way off. Our experience has been that we're better at estimating small projects than we are at estimating large projects. That being the case, the obvious solution is to break this down into smaller and more detailed pieces. We'll estimate the pieces, add them all up, and arrive at a more accurate estimate.

You can go straight into breaking this process description up into smaller stories (and XP programming advocates doing just that), but we're much more comfortable with developing a structural diagram, known as an entity relationship diagram, or ERD, before we do anything else. That gives us an overall frame of reference when we look at small details.

Entity Relationship Diagramming

Even before we refined it with client feedback, the description was enough to allow us to draw a first draft of an entity relationship diagram (ERD) of the database system. Let's set the estimate issue aside for a moment and talk about how we move from a process description to an ERD. The simplest way to describe our method is that we hunt for nouns. We're looking for nouns that occur in multiples. For example, there are multiple prospects that need to be tracked, but there's only one athletic department, so we don't need to build a table to track the athletic department. Using this simple method, we'd develop the following list of candidate entities:

- Prospects
- Coaches
- Sources
- Events
- Colleges

- Clubs
- Test scores
- Phone calls
- Letters
- Visits
- Phone numbers
- Sports statistics

With this list, we have the building blocks of our ERD. The next step is to try to determine the relationships between the various entities. In doing so, you need to establish the cardinality of the relationships. For example, does a prospect only play for one coach, or can they play for more than one coach? A coach can obviously coach more than one player. In this particular case, keep in mind that a prospect's playing history usually extends back over a period of years, so it will be common for a prospect to play for multiple clubs under multiple coaches. Coaches could also move around in that time. It's also helpful to describe the relationship twice, once from the point of view of the first entity, and once from the point of view of the second entity. You'll see what we mean in the following list:

- Prospects can play for many coaches, and a coach can coach many players.
- Prospects can play for many clubs, and a club has many players.
- Clubs can have many coaches, and a coach can coach for many clubs.
- Sources list many prospects, and a prospect is only credited to one source.
- Prospects can have many phone numbers, but a phone number belongs to only one prospect.
- Prospects can attend many events, and each event can be attended by many prospects.
- Prospects can make many visits, and a visit is made by one prospect.
- Prospects can have many sports statistics, and each sport statistic belongs to one prospect.

- Prospects can have many test scores, and each test score belongs to one prospect.
- Prospects can receive many letters, and each letter is addressed to one prospect.
- Prospects can receive many phone calls, and each phone call is made to one prospect.
- Prospects consider many colleges, and each college can be considered by many prospects.
- Prospects can transfer from many colleges, and each college can produce many transfer students.

This last item may not sound quite right, but remember that a prospect could possibly attend one college, transfer to another, and then transfer to this one. It's not likely, but it's possible. The athletic department needs to know the college playing history of each prospect to determine eligibility, so even though a prospect only technically transfers from one school, all previous schools need to be tracked.

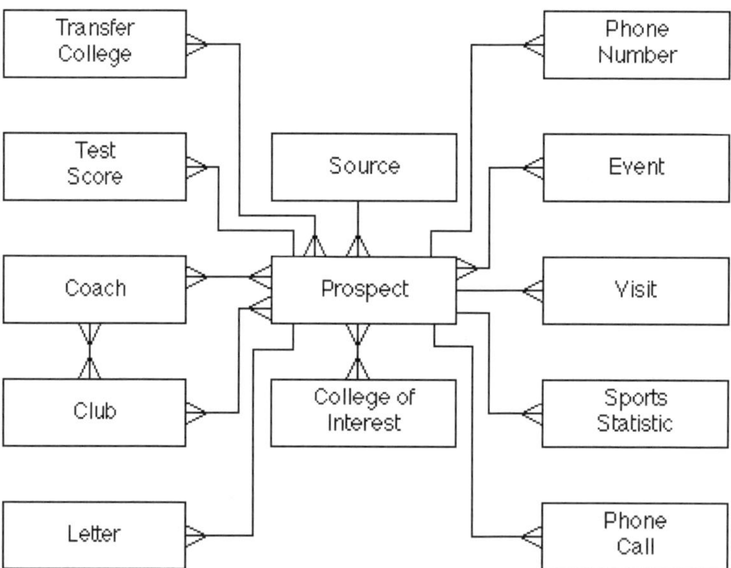

Figure 5.1 An entity relationship diagram graphically represents the relationships between entities.

It can be useful to go over a list like this with a client, but as you gain confidence in your ability to convert a process description into an ERD, you'll probably end up doing this step in your head and just drawing the relationships in the ERD. If you go straight to an ERD, you definitely want to confirm these relationships with the client. The above relationships can be represented by the ERD shown in Figure 5.1.

For those of you not familiar with an ERD, it's just a simple diagram listing the entities in boxes. The relationships are represented by the lines between the boxes and the symbols at the ends of the lines. Here's a quick explanation of the symbols:

——— Represents a one-to-one relationship

——< Represents a one-to-many relationship

>——< Represents a many-to-many relationship

While technically accurate, the structure shown in Figure 5.1 is less than ideal. For one thing, colleges appear twice in the diagram. We had to label them as Transfer College and College of Interest in order to distinguish between them. Also, this diagram is rife with many-to-many relationships. To explain why this is a bad thing, it's best to think through an example.

A prospect can play for more than one team, and a team can have many prospects playing for it. If we imagine a Prospect file with a Team field, that Team field can only hold one piece of information at a time (remember the one fact per field rule?). If a player plays for Team A, and then plays for Team B, B will overwrite the A information, and it will be lost. The way to solve the problem of needing to store more than one piece of information is to move it out into a related table, which we might call Team Member. If we store that information in the Team table, then every time we designate the fact that a player plays for a team, we're overwriting the fact that a different player also plays for that team. The solution is to create an intermediate Team Member table that shows one player playing for one team at a point in time. This decomposes the many-to-many relationship into two one-to-many relationships and solves the problem. Logically, it's impossible to implement a many-to-many relationship in FileMaker or any other database system without creating a structure that destroys data.

Since the many-to-many relationships in our list can't be implemented in a database system, they need to be resolved. The relationships between clubs, coaches, and prospects are especially messy. Let's deal with the many-to-many relationships first.

Since a prospect might have attended more than one college prior to transferring, and since each college can have more than one student prospect, we need to resolve the many-to-many relationship by creating a new entity: College History. Also, since a prospect might be interested in multiple colleges and since a college might have more than one prospect interested in it, we'll resolve the many-to-many relationship by creating a new entity called Prospect Interest.

A coach can coach multiple clubs, and a club can have multiple coaches, so we'll resolve the many-to-many relationship with an entity called Club Coach. A prospect can play for multiple clubs and each club can have more than one prospect playing for it, so we'll resolve that many-to-many relationship with an entity called Club Affiliation. The many-to-many relationship between prospects and coaches is resolved by the Club Coach to Club to Club Affiliation set of entities, as shown in Figure 5.2.

It's also worth noting that since a prospect could attend more than one event and since an event can be attended by multiple prospects, we have yet another many-to-many relationship that we'll resolve with Prospect Event.

There's one other issue we need to look at, and that's the issue of generalization. For example, coaches and prospects are both people. We want to track much of the same information for both entities: first name, last name, etc. If you find situations where two entities have very similar sets of fields, it might be worth considering generalizing the two subtypes into a supertype. In this case, we only need basic information about a coach, but we need detailed information about a prospect, so it doesn't make that much sense to combine them into a supertype entity called People, although that would be a valid approach.

Let's look at Letter and Phone Call. In both entities, we're just tracking a correspondence with the prospect. We're tracking the date and substance of the correspondence, and we could easily generalize the two subtypes into a supertype Correspondence entity. We can easily indicate that each record belongs to one subtype or another by using a type field. Since we want to track all correspondence in a similar fashion, generalizing these two entities also makes it easier for us to report on this information.

The resulting revised ERD is shown in Figure 5.2.

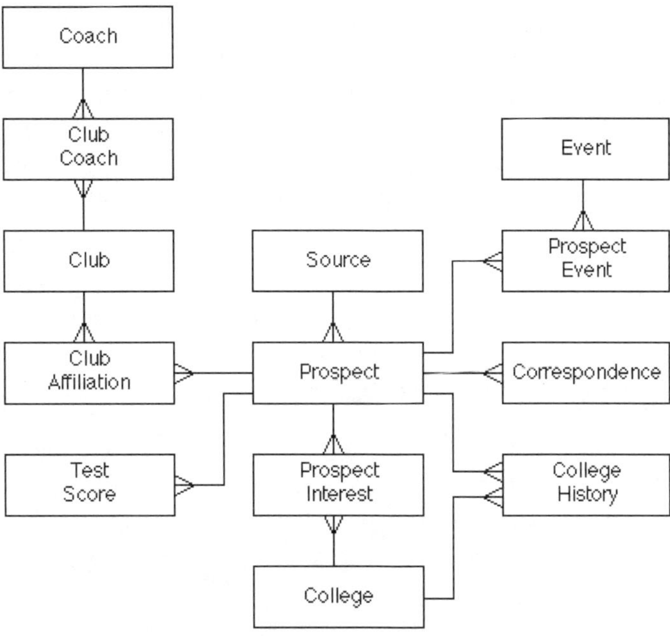

Figure 5.2 This ERD resolves all of the many-to-many relationships.

At this point, we have a good idea of the tables we're going to need for this project. If pressed, you can give a rough estimate from just this much information. One rule of thumb you can use is that you'll need an hour for each table (two if you anticipate a lot of fields in that table), plus two hours for every layout or report in the system. Some tables, like Club Affiliation, will probably only be used as line items in a portal. Most of the join tables that were created to resolve many-to-many relationships will be that way, although it's not uncommon to need to create reports in those files as well. It's not important now that you know which file a report will live in. You just need to know that you'll have a report somewhere and that, depending on its complexity and your development speed, you'll need to budget a certain number of hours for it.

You should adjust numbers up if you anticipate complexity. If you know that a specific report will draw information from several tables or if it will have several subsummaries or complicated grand totals, add hours to that particular report as you deem appropriate. The nice thing about this approach is that you can say that for a system with this structure and these layouts and reports, it will cost x to build it once. Emphasize that last part. Inevitably, you'll create a report and then begin several rounds of tweaking. Before you do, point out that you built the feature, and that the rounds of tweaking are now adding to the cost. A useful approach is to review previous projects and develop a ballpark number of hours per layout or table (depending on how fast you work) so that if features or reports are added that require additional tables or layouts, you can say that it will cost roughly x hours per layout. That gives the client some idea of the cost of future changes, and if the system becomes more complicated than what you originally envisioned (and it will), you've already given fair warning about how the costs are going to rise.

The next step is to figure out what fields will be needed in each table. You can collect forms and reports and identify several fields that way. That will give you a good start, but it probably won't identify them all. One technique that we've used with great results is an interface prototype.

Prototyping the Interface

While it may sound crazy to build an interface before you even have a database structure or a field list, this technique works really well. What we do is create a single FileMaker file with a single field. We draw all of the screens in that single file, using the one field as a placeholder for fields that will eventually inhabit the layouts. This has several benefits.

One benefit is that you can mock up different interface styles for the client very quickly. Everyone has a different aesthetic, and most people have difficulty articulating exactly what they want. Those same people are really good at recognizing what they want and don't want when they see it, though. By presenting them with some options, you can quickly get a feel for likes and dislikes. These may seem like little things, but the client is going to spend a lot of time looking at the system. They'll be a lot happier with that experience if they like what they're looking at. It's a mistake to impose your design ethic on them. Give them some choices and let them choose.

We like to use a tabbed interface for navigation. If you're not familiar with the term, go look at Amazon's web site. It has navigation tabs across the top of the site. Microsoft Excel uses a tabbed interface to navigate between the sheets in a workbook. It's a familiar device, and that means that users will have an easy time understanding and using it.

We typically present a few different styles of a tabbed layout (see Figure 5.3), and we get feedback on what colors they like. Some people prefer larger or smaller buttons and larger or smaller field labels. Show them a few different portal styles, and if you're planning on doing anything unusual like filtered portals or portal selection tools, make sure those interface elements are clear to the users before you take all the time and trouble to implement them for real. You may have to abandon them and try different approaches.

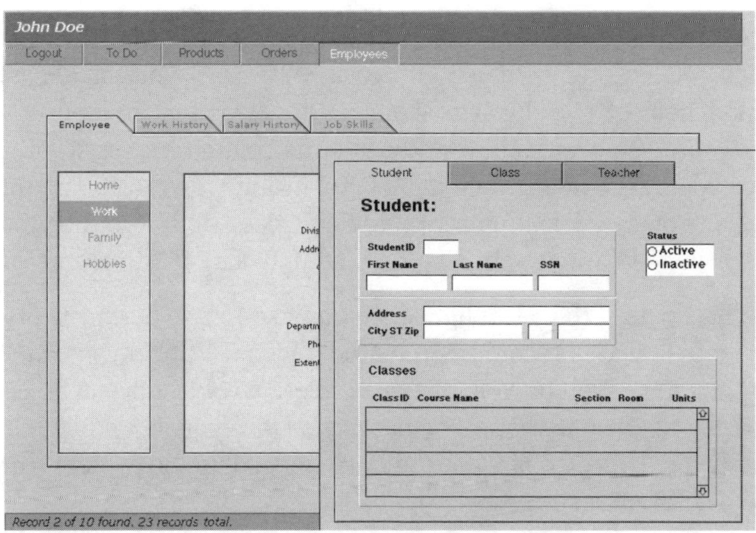

Figure 5.3 It's a good idea to give users a variety of interface styles to choose from.

Eventually we come up with a design. It's a good idea to present it to all the users to get feedback and buy-in. If everyone feels like they had a chance to be heard, they're going to be a lot more receptive to the system when it comes time for deployment.

Anyway, once we have an accepted interface style, we can then start mocking up the screens we think we're going to need. You can wire up navigation buttons that take the users from layout to layout so that they get a sense of the flow of the system. You'll get a lot of changes at this point, but it's much better to get them in now than after you've built the layouts into the structure.

Building the Structure

At this point, it's almost anticlimactic to build the database. Everything's been figured out, and you just have to build the structure. From your accepted interface prototype, you're going to have a list of all the fields that users are going to need to see on the layouts. The next step is to take that list and assign each field to the table that it describes.

Once you have the field lists categorized by table, you can begin building the tables themselves. The easiest way to do this is to just duplicate the interface prototype over and over. Rename the copies as appropriate, and then start adding the fields to the tables. By making the tables this way, you don't lose any of the navigation scripting that's been built into the prototype. You will have to go through the layouts and respecify the fields.

You'll also need to go through and modify scripts to perform sort operations or jump to related records as required. Since the prototype contained layouts for the entire system, you'll need to delete any layouts and associated scripts that don't belong in that particular table. Once you've implemented your system functionality for real, you're ready to load up the system with sample data and begin testing.

The XP Approach

As we mentioned earlier, we're still experimenting with applying XP approaches to FileMaker development, but that doesn't mean we should ignore the subject entirely. For those of you who aren't familiar with the ideas, we'll give you some of the basics, along with some encouragement to read up on the subject. We've listed some suggested reading in Appendix A. The first step in the XP approach is to break the system down into stories. Since we started with a process description, we'd need to break the process description into simpler pieces. Remember that the smaller the piece is, the more accurate the estimate will be.

Stories need to be testable, meaning that you can test whether or not the programmer fulfilled the requirements of the story. They also need to be in a form that you can apply an estimate to. The story "all backgrounds must be blue" isn't really a story, since you can't estimate that requirement until you know how many backgrounds you need to create. In this form it's just a constraint, or a rule that you need to follow when completing other stories.

Using the process description that we developed earlier in the chapter, we might come up with these stories:

- The system needs to be able to import either a comma-delimited text file or Microsoft Excel spreadsheet that contains a list of prospects from the Admissions office.
- Contacts, meaning visits, scouting trips, phone calls, letters, and forms sent to and received from the student, need to be tracked by date.
- If the prospect is a transfer student, we need to track all colleges attended.
- We need a way to detect duplicate prospects. If we find more than one record for a prospect, we need to combine all the information into one record and then delete the extra records.

There are more stories that need to be written, but these will give you an idea of the scope of a typical story. Each one of these stories is testable (more on that in a bit) and a programmer should be able to estimate how long it will take to complete each one. Let's take another look at these stories and think through the estimating process for each one.

The system needs to be able to import either a comma-delimited text file or Microsoft Excel spreadsheet that contains a list of prospects from the Admissions office.

We know that FileMaker already has the ability to import both text files and Excel spreadsheets, so that's not a problem. What might be a problem is if those formats will change over time. We could create an automated import script that prompts the user for the filename and then restores an import order. We'll need to verify the stability of the file format, but assuming it's stable, we should be able to review sample files, run some trial imports, set up the script, build an interface for the Import button, build a separate screen to view the imported results, and tie both of them into the rest of the system navigation in, say, four hours.

That's just the implementation part, though. Testing is just as important in XP. Later in the process, the client needs to come up with an acceptance test, and it will take time to implement and run that test. For now, we're just going to estimate the time for development. We need to keep in mind, and we need to remind the client, that we will need more time for testing.

Contacts, meaning visits, scouting trips, phone calls, letters and forms sent to and received from the student, need to be tracked by date.

Contacts will take place between someone in the athletic department and a prospect, so at the minimum, we need tables for system users, prospects, and contacts. We'll probably need portals in the User and Prospect tables so that we can view the related contact records. We might also need some kind of search facility so that a user can search for contact records by date, but the story doesn't specify this. Many FileMaker developers have a habit of intuiting future needs and requests of their clients. XP programming specifically prohibits this. The reason is that as small batches of features get released, the client gets a chance to see how they work, and they often change direction as the project progresses. Adding features not asked for not only might be a waste of time if the project changes direction, but it also hampers your ability to track your true estimate accuracy since you did more than what was specified in the estimate.

At any rate, we think we need three tables and two screens for data entry and/or review. Since we're doing no more than what's specified in the story, the tables will be very simple — maybe just a user and prospect name and record ID. For the sake of this example, let's say that building the three tables and two screens without any interface beautification should take only one hour.

If the prospect is a transfer student, we need to track all colleges attended.

In this story, we need tables for prospect and colleges attended. It's tempting to add a table for colleges so we can look at a college and see how many transfer students came from that college, but we could do that just as easily with a report in the colleges attended table. An even better reason to avoid temptation is that it's not specified in the story. After a few iterations of the client only getting just what was asked for, they'll learn that they only get what they ask for, and they also learn that they get charged for what they ask for, and they need to set priorities. It's a much healthier environment for everyone to operate in.

We need a way to detect duplicate prospects. If we find more than one record for a prospect, we need to combine all the information into one record and then delete the extra records.

This story requires a Prospect table, which is simple enough. Beyond that, though, it's a lot trickier to estimate than the other stories. The reason is that it's unclear how you detect a duplicate. Janet Doe and Jan Doe may be the same prospect, but checking for a duplicate first and last name wouldn't pick up this duplication. We could check social security numbers, but even that value isn't guaranteed to be unique (just ask the feds). Perhaps a combination of social security number and last name might work. Even so, we probably don't want to automatically do anything with prompting the user to verify a possible duplication. It's easy enough to create a concatenation field that combines social security and last name. It's also pretty easy to create an automated search that checks for duplicates in that field, and then presents the user with a sorted list of probable duplicates.

Once we do that though, and once the user says that yes, the records that are checked off are duplicates, how do we go about combining the data? This is especially tough because we don't yet know what related data there might be and how difficult it would be to consolidate it. To even find out if we can consolidate related data in other tables, we might want to run what's called a spike, or a quick test. In this case, we might build a few tables to see if we could randomly pick one of the duplicates, load its primary key into a global field, and then use that global value to replace all foreign keys in related records. That would probably work.

What about duplicate related records that are generated during consolidation, though? Suppose we have two prospect records for the same person, and both have related phone records with identical data. If we consolidate them, then we'll have duplicate phone records attached to one person.

When an estimate starts to get this complicated, it's probably a good idea to break the story down into smaller parts. For example, this story might be broken into identifying duplicate prospects, consolidating duplicate prospect records, consolidating related records, and removing duplicates from consolidated related records. Estimating each one of those stories is much simpler than trying to estimate them all at once.

Let's suppose we do that, and we come up with:

- We need a way to detect duplicate prospects.

  We already discussed this story. Let's say that the prospect file and a button and script that searches for duplicate social security number and last name combinations will take two hours, complete with a list view to present probable duplicates to the user.

- If we have duplicate prospect records , we need to combine all the prospect information into one record and then delete the extra records.

  Why don't we let the user decide which record is the one to keep? If we do that, we can loop through each field value in the surviving record to see if it's empty. If it is, we use a self-relationship to check the duplicate record(s) to see if there is a value for that field, and if so, pull that value into the surviving record. Once we have gathered all information into the surviving record, we can delete the others. This is a fairly complex looping script, and will probably take about two hours. The total time would thus be four hours.

- If we have duplicate prospect records, we need to combine all the related prospect information under one prospect ID and then delete any duplicate related records.

  This process will be similar to the last de-duplicating routine, except that we don't need the user to pick a surviving record. We'll just go with the scripting time of two hours.

So there you have an idea of the estimating process using XP programming. Once you have all your estimates, you add them up to get the estimate for the entire project. That number will be wrong. Don't be too hard on yourself, though. It's the nature of the beast. Here's the cool thing about XP programming, though: It's designed to make your estimates more accurate as you go through the project.

The way this happens is that you break your project into a series of small, fully functional releases of equal duration in terms of development time. In this system, the first release might only allow data entry of prospect information and tracking of letters and phone calls. You want to keep these releases small so that they're easy to estimate and the feedback on estimate accuracy comes back quickly. If you estimate a release that's supposed to take 30 hours and it takes 35, you know right away that you're over. You also know that you only did a few things, and it's easier to identify why you went over on time. Armed with that information, you're better prepared to be more accurate on the next release, which should contain 30 hours of work. Keep estimating 30 hours' worth of tasks, keep correcting for mistakes, and you get much more accurate about your estimates in a very short period of time.

Some of the stories won't fit neatly into small release cycles, so you'll need to break them up into even smaller pieces called tasks. For example, this story:

- If we have duplicate prospect records, we need to combine all the related prospect information under one prospect ID and then delete any duplicate related records.

...can be broken down into the following tasks:

- Identify duplicate prospect records.
- Combine all data from the duplicate records into one record.
- Combine all related records under one foreign key.
- De-duplicate all related records.

Each task then needs to be estimated. Don't be too surprised if the total of your task estimates is more than your estimate for the story. The inaccuracy is natural. What you're after is the steady improvement in accuracy over the course of the project.

You'll need to prioritize stories so that you can work on the high priorities first. As you get a clearer idea of what the actual estimate is going to be, you'll have some low-priority stories that you can drop from the project to keep the project under budget.

Summary

In this chapter we reviewed a methodology for creating process descriptions and entity relationship diagrams. We briefly discussed a method for rough estimates at the beginning of the process, and then took you through some of the interesting ideas in XP programming and how that process ultimately leads to more accurate estimates.

Chapter 6

Database Security Issues

There's an old joke about two guys getting chased by a bear in the woods. One guy stops to change into his running shoes. The other guy asks him why he's even bothering, since he still won't be able to outrun the bear. The shoe-changer replies that he doesn't need to outrun the bear, he just needs to outrun his companion.

The same holds true for database security. It's pointless to invest in extreme database security measures if someone can just open up a filing cabinet and get the same information on paper. Your goal in database security is to make it difficult enough so that would-be data stealers will be inclined to look for easier ways to get the information. If you can achieve that, then the data in your database will be secure. That doesn't mean that you shouldn't try to have great database security. We just want to make it clear that there is no such thing as (and probably little need for) absolute security. You also need to trade off between the often conflicting needs of good security and ease of use.

If you aren't yet familiar with the potential security issues you might face, it can be a depressing topic to cover. We're going to go over several areas where FileMaker databases can be compromised, and it might be tempting to think that FileMaker isn't a very secure database. We want to say at the outset that these security issues are common to all databases and all computer systems. Given enough time, a determined expert hacker can break into your systems.

The risk of such a hacker targeting you specifically is small. The most dangerous database security issues come from people who don't keep their passwords private. We've seen clients with good security implementations have them compromised when a user yells his password to the user on the other side of the cubicle wall can run a report that she doesn't ordinarily have access to. It's worth mentioning that if you spend some time making sure users get the privileges they need to perform their jobs properly so that sort of thing doesn't happen as much. Be careful you don't create an environment where security gets compromised because you frustrate users' legitimate need to access sensitive data.

Now that we have all of that said, let's get into our topic. We're going to start the discussion with single-user databases running on a computer that you control. We'll go over what the security risks and remedies are. From there, we'll move on to a scenario where your single-user databases run on computers that you don't control. Developers who use the FileMaker Developer Edition often create commercial products that they need to protect. We're aware that some commercial FileMaker-based products are run with FileMaker Server, but those security issues have extensive overlap with our last topic, which is securing FileMaker databases that are shared over networks.

We want to make a distinction between protecting against unauthorized access to data and controlling access by legitimate users. This chapter will cover protecting against unauthorized users, and the next chapter will go over controlling legitimate user access.

Another point we'd like to make: Regardless of whether your database systems are going to be used by one person or shared over a network, it's best if you can design security features in from the beginning rather than adding them later. Similar to installing a security system on a building, it's usually more difficult and time-consuming to apply security to a complete structure than to incorporate it during construction.

Guarding Against Physical File Access

Imagine that you've created a database system and you've deployed it on the computer that sits on your desk. Depending on your environment, it may be easy or difficult for someone to gain access to your computer's hard drive. If you have Internet access, it might be possible for someone to access your hard drive without ever entering your premises. The first scenario we're considering is one where a hacker has access to your hard drive and thus the database files that reside on your hard drive.

The first line of defense is to make use of FileMaker's access privileges. A casual snooper could be discouraged if you have simply added passwords to your databases. Even a casual snooper probably has a text editor, however.

By using something like Microsoft Word to open a FileMaker file as raw text in a word processing application, you can see the data inside the file. You may have opened a database file in this manner before, and seen something similar to Figure 6.1 below. This is just a small portion near the beginning of a file. We don't have room to show you a complete file here, but note that even with this small sample, you can clearly see some readable information.

```
□□□□□□¿ Copyright 1984-2001 FileMaker, Inc. □
.................................Column Break.................................
HBAM2016AUG95¡□H□Pro
□
□W□□¡□E□□X□□¿¡□¡□¡□B□¿¿¿¡□¡□¡□¡□A□
¿¡□@□ ¿¿¿¿P□□¡°@□□¿□ˇ ¸□□¿
□□ˮ
.................................Column Break.................................
HBAM3016AUG95@□□
¡□A□□□¡□¡□As□PHH□~□(ˇ·ˇ,□"□FP□(□¸□PHH□~□(d□'□□□□□d□□"r□□□□¸<□□ˇ□z¿¡□A□□□□□□.J□□
□d□□□□ˇ□□¿¿¡□¿D□□¿¿¡□¿□¿□¿□¿□¿□¿□¿□¿□¿□¿□¿¿□Q4
1st Quarter
2nd Quarter
3rd Quarter
4th Quarter□□□□, □ □, □□□Ì¡□X5*□
```

Figure 6.1 When viewing a FileMaker Pro file in text processor software, this portion of the text appears near the top of the file.

If you look around the file, you will see a lot of unintelligible characters which are ASCII representations of file components, but occasionally you will come across plaintext gems. These might include:

- Field names
- Script names
- Path names to files
- Layout names
- Layout text
- Relationship names
- Text constants from scripts (from Set Field, Show Message, or other commands)
- Field validation messages
- Field layout formats for numbers, dates, times
- Field data

Basically, anytime a developer or user types from the keyboard, that information is stored as unencrypted text. It almost completely undercuts any notion of protecting sensitive data when the file in which it is contained is publicly available. This is not the lightning strike of doom it appears to be, however. It just suggests that you must restrict disk access to your database system if it contains sensitive data.

Also, the data that can be viewed should be qualified as less than perfect for the hacker. It is interspersed with garbage characters that probably describe field delimiters, formatting options, etc. A lot of numbers in a block of text won't necessarily be discernable as either salaries or serial numbers or performance ratings, and the data is certainly not set up so the hacker can tab from field to field or run reports. However, an e-mail address does look a lot like an e-mail address, and a phone number will look a lot like a phone number, so it justifies being careful if the data is sensitive enough. The bottom line is that when the data security needs are significant, you must keep database files on a secure storage volume where they cannot be accessed and read as plaintext.

This can be problematic in environments that back up files over a network. If a backup process can't gain access to the FileMaker server, then you would think that the files can't be backed up. That's not the case, though. Just because other machines can't access the volume that the FileMaker files reside on doesn't mean that FileMaker Server can't back up those same files to a volume that is accessible to your backup process. The problem is that in doing this, you return to the physical file access vulnerability issue. A workaround in this case might be to have FileMaker Server back up the database files to an inaccessible volume on the same server and then have either compression or encryption software compact (with a password) or encrypt the data before it gets moved to a server that is accessible by the regular backup process. In a Windows environment, these post-processing steps can be managed by the Schedule Service/Task Scheduler, depending on your version of Windows. On the Mac OS you can use a utility like Cron or even AppleScript, and you can just use a shell script on Linux.

We've discussed how a casual hacker can use a word processor to get some access to the data stored in a FileMaker database. A better equipped hacker might be armed with password cracking software. This type of software has been around for years. You can get software that will break into Microsoft

Access or Quicken or just about anything else. It's just a reality that we need to acknowledge. Hacking software has been able to reveal FileMaker passwords in the past. The software is typically unable to break into brand new versions of FileMaker, but after the version has been out a while, your FileMaker databases should be considered vulnerable to password cracking software. One reason for this is that the password functionality travels with the files. The important thing to note here is that in order to use password cracking software, a hacker needs to have access to the file. A hacker usually can't use password cracking software if he only has network access to a FileMaker database.

The bottom line is that hacking access to the raw data or using password cracking software is relatively simple if there is not sufficient physical restriction to the volume on which the file is stored. If you can't secure access to your hard drive and you have sensitive data that needs protecting, you should move your database files to a machine that cannot be accessed by other machines on the network and serve them up as multiuser files. You could conceivably do this with a regular copy of FileMaker, but ideally, this machine will be running FileMaker Pro Server on a server running Windows or Linux or Mac OS X where it will be easy to restrict access to the files. This will also improve FileMaker Pro Server's performance, generally speaking. If the server is actually a desktop machine that is running FileMaker Pro, make sure that any peer-to-peer file sharing is turned off. FileMaker servers should not (file) share well with others!

Invisible Files

Even with storage volume access restrictions, it is still theoretically possible to use password hacking software to get at the files in a more traditional manner, using FileMaker Pro. This is due to the way FileMaker publishes its files to the network when sharing them. To avoid this completely, you need an island — a single-user version of the database system on hardware that cannot be accessed. We will consider single-user database systems to be rare for purposes of the rest of our discussion, so if you place your database files on a physically secure server, is there still a threat to your master passwords? The unfortunate answer is yes. We'll examine FileMaker Pro passwords more closely in a moment. Let's first briefly discuss the implications of hidden, or invisible, files in a shared environment.

When you set up the file for sharing and you select the Multi-User (Hidden) option shown in Figure 6.3, FileMaker Pro will hide that file from view in the Hosts dialog box.

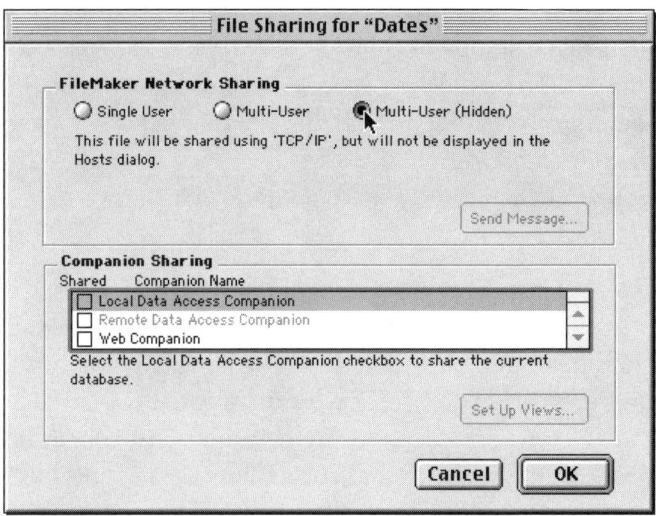

Figure 6.2 When you set a file as Multi-User (Hidden), it will not appear in the File|Open|Hosts dialog box.

Files shared in this manner will not appear in the File|Open|Hosts dialog. Making files invisible is useful and convenient for users who would rather not search through long lists of files to find what they need. Therefore, sharing files in this way is generally a good practice. From the database security standpoint, invisible files can seem useful as well. If the developer exposes only one file or just a few files to users over the network, he can reduce the variables involved with users entering the database system. Obviously, this seems like it would improve the security picture. Don't assume, however, that sharing files in this way makes them invisible to a potential hacker. It only applies to the File|Open|Hosts button dialog. You can still see "invisible" files over the network when you do the following:

- Define relationships
- Define value lists (based on a field value)
- Call an external file while scripting
- Import

- Use an Open Script step in a script

The reason for this behavior is fairly simple. Any Open File dialog that's required for linking files in the act of database development will reveal all available files after clicking the Hosts button. This is one of those paradoxical issues with FileMaker Pro. Since it's both a development tool and a user tool, it can't properly address each role. Any user with FileMaker Pro 5.5 becomes a developer with the mere effort of creating a new file. All new files start you off with full master password access. Since users then have complete "developer access" to the new file, they also have access to view all files on the network, regardless of how they've been shared. Because there is no restricted "client" version of FileMaker, this presents a risk we must account for.

So the moral of the story is: Use the Multi-User (Hidden) feature to improve the user login experience, but don't rely on this trick for database security. Of course, all of the dialogs that allow you to open files over a network will trigger the password dialog box if that file has a password. So now you may be thinking that if the FileMaker passwords are secure, then the files are secure. That notion brings us to our next topic.

Protecting FileMaker Pro Master Password Access

Considering the discussion thus far, it might seem reasonable to give up on FileMaker passwords. However, the password privileges in FileMaker are tools of empowerment for the developer as much as they are tools of access restriction. Regardless of other methods for restricting access to files and controlling user activities, password and group privileges remain convenient for managing procedural flow inside an open database.

The best possible method for protecting your master passwords (here come the groans) is to change them frequently. It's practically a law and at least a rule in many business organizations that computer users change their passwords regularly. In a business solution where the system is managed by a database administrator, it's a simple policy to implement. Even in the most complex systems, a database administrator can change the master password in an hour or less. Granted, this may need to be done when no users are accessing the system. Even so, this should still be done monthly, weekly, or randomly (but frequently), depending on the degree of security risk. Users hate this, of course, but we'll leave it up to you to balance the unpleasantness of taking flak from your user community against taking flak for having someone break into your database system.

When you're distributing software, you can't change the master password once it leaves your sphere of control. But you might change it during upgrades and updates. If you're distributing trial software, consider changing master passwords regularly along with time bomb seeds, if you implement them. Trial software solutions are more likely to be improperly shared between users than licensed (paid for) versions. It's a general truism that the more customers pay for a solution, the less likely they are to illegally copy and share it.

Here's another tip: Don't be obvious. Some examples of bad passwords include: administrator, root, god, master, filemaker, <your name>, etc. Curiously, recent research has shown that "root" and "god" are the most popular passwords among database and network administrators. Definitely avoid using these passwords.

Binder to the Rescue

Starting with the release of FileMaker Pro 5.0 Developer Edition, FileMaker Inc. has included a feature in the FileMaker Pro Binder which is important to the security discussion. In Figure 6.3, you can see an option called Permanently prevent modification of database structure. This option removes most of the capabilities that a user with a master password would uniquely possess. Contrary to popular belief, this option does not remove the master password itself. The password is still in the file with the rest of the non-master passwords. But regardless of whether or not a password was at one time a master password, after running the file through the FileMaker Pro 5.5 Binder, the password will no longer have access to the file editing capabilities of FileMaker because the functions themselves are removed from the file.

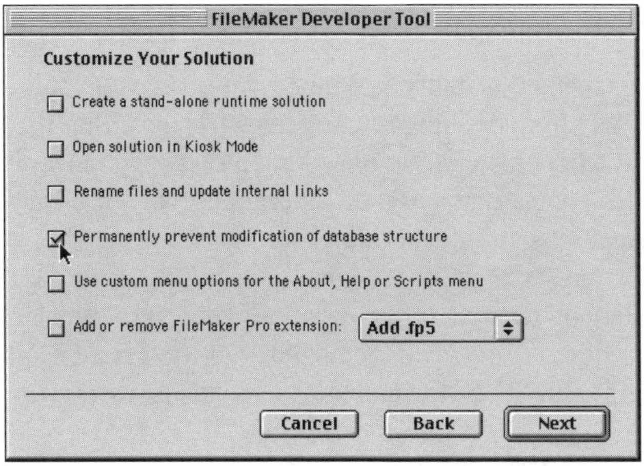

Figure 6.3 By preventing modifications to the database structure, you can protect the inner workings of your database solution against someone who has obtained the "master" password.

Removing these capabilities also seems to have an effect on password cracking software. These programs currently seem to fail consistently when analyzing a file that has been bound with this option. This does not mean that hacking software will always fail. In fact, since the passwords still exist in the file, it is feasible that someone may find a way to access them. Finding those passwords, however, will enable the hacker to access only the features that you program for your users. The hacker can thus be contained, and restricted from evading scripts, buttons, and validations or avoiding other internal security systems that you create by means of scripts and validations.

One downside regarding bound FileMaker files from a security standpoint is that you can still view the file as text. As we mentioned before, this allows anyone to peek at the data in the file, if not the structure of the file. But it would appear that the combination of bound files and a secure file server will deliver the best physical file security profile we could currently hope for. Are you getting excited yet?

But wait! FileMaker Pro 5.5 Binder's run-time engine doesn't allow multiuser sharing, does it? That may be true, but bound files can still be run with FileMaker Pro 5.5 Server, which does allow for sharing. Let's explore the capabilities of bound files, with the master access removed, that are being hosted by FileMaker Pro 5.5 Server on a network.

No New Relationships

Once Binder removes the ability to define relationships in a file, you are restricted not only from defining relationships locally within that file, but also from defining relationships to that file. From a security standpoint, this is great news. This means that a hacker cannot merely create a new file and then define a relationship to your bound solution in order to open it without triggering a startup script. It also means that a hacker cannot use new destructive relationships to alter your data. If you try to create a relationship to a bound file with master access removed, you will get a dialog saying, "Your Password to file 'File.fp5' does not allow you to edit this relationship."

ScriptMaker Issues

ScriptMaker continues to offer complications, however. Even though Binder can remove ScriptMaker access from the bound files, it still allows for new files to call existing scripts in bound files via the script step Perform Script [External: "File.fp5"]. The good news, however, is that although a hacker can run scripts that exist in the bound files, he cannot modify them. Therefore, you can contain the activities of a hacker by building proper controls in your scripts. For example, you might include something like this among the first steps of every script:

```
Allow User Abort [Off]
If [<some security test>]
     <allow entry to file>
Else
     Quit Application
     <or perhaps force the user through an authorization script>
End If
```

During database development you might create a single basic script skeleton that includes steps like these. It's a simple matter to duplicate that skeleton script to create new scripts. In this way, you can force the hacker to trigger the startup script for the file, even if he tries to bypass it. This may seem like a difficult solution to implement in very complex systems, but when you are creating a file from scratch, it's very easy to implement. Even in existing complex systems, the "gatekeeper" script above could be added to other scripts as a subscript command, and so implementation would be relatively quick.

Of course, if a hacker does not possess any passwords that allow access to a file, then he can't call any scripts from that file at all. But for the purposes of this discussion we will continue assuming that FileMaker's passwords are obtainable.

Those Pesky Value Lists

Is there any other way to bypass the startup scripts without triggering any script? Once again, the answer is, unfortunately, yes. This is one of the least obvious entry points to any FileMaker file, but now that you know the secret you will never forget it. If you want to open any file in which you have some level of password access, all you have to do is create a value list from a field in that file. Figure 6.4 shows the value list definition dialog as generated from a hacker's file to look into a restricted file.

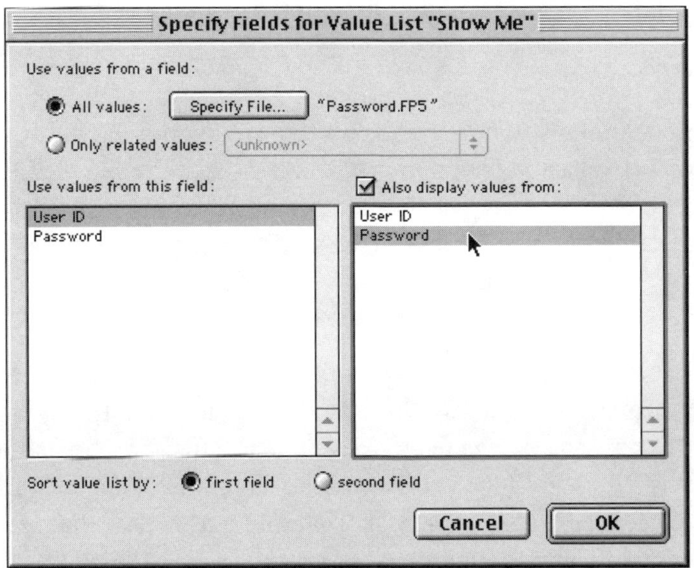

Figure 6.4 If there are any indexed fields in a file, a hacker can use a value list to examine every value in a field.

Here we selected the Use values from a field option to open a bound file without triggering any scripts.

You might think that passwords that restrict the creation of value lists would stop this sort of thing, but restricting the defining of value lists only stops you from creating new value lists in the file where you set the password. Again, if the hacker creates a new file, he automatically carries master access in that new file and can use Define Value Lists to open your files. The only way a hacker can be stopped from opening your file with Define Value Lists is by keeping all the passwords in your database secret from him or her.

Assuming that a hacker possesses FileMaker Pro 5.5 and knows one of your file's passwords, it's impossible to keep him out of your file. But it's not time to lose heart yet. The hacker that opens your file as such is still restricted to the interface you provide, since he's in a bound file without master access. If the default layout that appears contains no data and he's forced to use buttons to navigate the file, once again you have succeeded in forcing the hacker to trigger your startup scripts. This can admittedly take some extra development effort, but developing a fully button-driven interface is within reason at the high end of risk management for complex systems.

Binder Review

So far, Binder seems to be a great way to lock up your database. Running master access disabled bound files with FileMaker Pro 5.5 enables the system to keep even hackers with a valid password within the confines of a scripted interface. Over a network, this offers the possibility of completely protecting the file structure and sensitive data. If this doesn't justify the purchase of FileMaker Pro 5.5 Developer Edition, what does?

When a database solution is distributed, bound files can keep the file structure away from the prying eyes of almost any hacker. In these cases, though, there still exists the issue of data risk since the files will be on the local disk of the user and accessible to text editing software. Fortunately, this data risk can also be reduced. Using FileMaker plug-in extensions that are available today, you can encrypt sensitive data in your file. We'll explain how to do this later in the chapter.

It's also possible to bind only a portion of your database. You might want to do this so that you can continue development work on portions of a system, but beware of this practice if security is important. If a hacker gets master access to a non-bound file that contains previously defined relationships to your bound files, then he can use ScriptMaker in the non-bound file to start performing Set Field commands on data inside the bound files. This could be extremely damaging. Regardless, using a mix of bound and non-bound files is usually more of a nuisance than it's worth. More likely, you'd elect to use Binder in an all-or-none fashion.

Which leads us to a last caveat about bound files. Obviously, after removing Define Fields, Define Relationships, ScriptMaker, and Access Privileges, you can't do much to improve on or maintain your database. In other words, you had better get it right before deploying a system in this manner. This is the "Birth of Athena" style of deployment, akin to the solution leaping from the head of Zeus in a complete fashion. In other words, there is no "growing up" for your child. She had better arrive complete and ready for action. There is no real modification to the system after this. The only way to deploy revised versions of the system is to keep an unbound copy. When you've modified that version, you'll need to import the data from each file in the bound deployed version. You can then bind your new version and replace the version you already have in production. Needless to say, this could be a long, dull job. All the more reason to make sure you get things right before turning your creation loose.

You might still attempt a combination of bound and non-bound files in your solution. The maintenance implications of having bound files in your solutions should reinforce and elevate the importance of thorough planning, design, and testing before deployment. In most other database development environments such strict implementation procedures are standard practice. For many FileMaker developers and clients, however, these precautions may seem like foreign concepts. Used to the amazing flexibility of the FileMaker platform, it is sometimes hard to distinguish between development usage and production usage.

Zen and the Art of Annoyance

Organizational environments today seem to be changing faster than they ever have in the past, and perhaps the best feature of FileMaker is its ability to undergo change after it's been deployed, even with users in the system. Sacrificing that flexibility and an organization's ability to quickly respond to change is a lot to ask, and for many people, the locked-down nature of Binder security just isn't an option. One of our clients would not allow us to eliminate layout and script editing access to his database system. Even though this access severely threatened security measures we built into the system, ad hoc report generation was more important than good security. We settled on a compromise, giving layout and scripting access to only a small group of trained and trusted users, but given the client's goals, we clearly could not remove master access with FileMaker Pro 5.5 Binder.

Based on the security picture we've drawn so far, FileMaker's master password access remains at risk. In fact, there is little more that can be done to improve the sanctity of the master passwords. But there are some methods of at least discouraging unwanted users. We will discuss these techniques in the next chapter, so let's just mention them here. They're not so much a hacker deterrent as an annoyance, although in the age of immediate gratification, annoyance and tedium can be powerful deterrents.

If you implement some sort of login authorization scheme in your system, you can make any database exceptionally annoying for any user who accesses the files without a proper login. Merely the combination of the script commands Allow User Abort[Off] and Quit Application in the same script can spell disaster for any script that doesn't satisfy a proper Boolean evaluation (If… statement). Any time a user triggers any script, that action can trigger land mines.

Furthermore, such Boolean evaluations don't need to be based on login authorization. A clever client of ours rigged his scripts so that they could only be called by another script if it was "blessed." In other words, Script B could only be called by Script A. He made this happen by having Script A set a global field to a specific value. For instance, perhaps Script A sets the global field gScript_Authorization to a number value like 127. Then Script B can start like this:

```
Allow User Abort [Off]
If ["gScript_Authorization = 127"]
     <do rest of script>
Else
     Quit Application
End If
```

At the end of the script sequence, control should return to Script A so that gScript_Authorization can be set to a blank or some other value that will prevent other scripts from being run improperly. Scripts are not the only tools that can perform Boolean evaluations either. Field Validation by Calculation is another extremely powerful tool that allows you to determine whether a user can add or edit data in your fields. It goes without saying that these techniques require you to think through all possible permutations of script combinations, lest you inadvertently block access to users who are supposed to be there.

Protecting Your Intellectual Property with Easter Eggs

We just wanted to briefly mention some ideas that seem to be rarely used, but that can help you protect your intellectual property if you're a developer who distributes commercial solutions. Specifically, you might embed "Easter eggs" inside your FileMaker Pro files that identify you as the developer. Easter eggs can be any kind of hidden (thus the "Easter egg" moniker) quirk that's not part of the regular program logic. The idea is that if the authorship of a particular work comes into question, only the real developer would know about the hidden Easter egg or eggs. Easter eggs are not foolproof, but they are sneaky (and thus kind of fun on that basis alone), and therefore may elude all but the most thorough thief who might try to steal your database files and claim your work as his own. If you think we're making this up, we refer you to the following web site: http://www.eeggs.com.

Let's say you add the text, "AwesomeDatabase version 1.3, July 2002, by Molly Thorsen" to your layout. You might next change the text color to white, set the fill and line patterns to invisible, send the text to back, reduce its point size to 2 pts, move it to the edge of the layout, group it with a text field that's essential to the layout, and lock it. If it is unlikely that someone will stumble across this, and that you will be able to identify it later, this might be useful hard evidence if someone steals your database. Layouts are reasonably volatile, though, so perhaps this isn't perfect for identifying your file. You may prefer to use script steps, calculations, field validations, or value lists, as shown in the following examples.

Script Step Example

```
If["(Boolean_Eval = 1) or ("ID" = "AwesomeDatabase version 1.3, July
      ...")"]
     <do something>
End If
```

Calculation Example

```
calc_Field = If (1, <proper result>, "AwesomeDatabase version 1.3,
            July ...")
```

Note that this calculation will always be true, since "1" is the test parameter. Therefore, the Easter egg test will never interfere with the display of the data.

Field Validation Example

See Figure 6.5 for one example of using field validation to hide your identity. Here the egg is located in the validation calculation, much like the previous calculation example. The validation calculation always returns "1" so that it always evaluates to true.

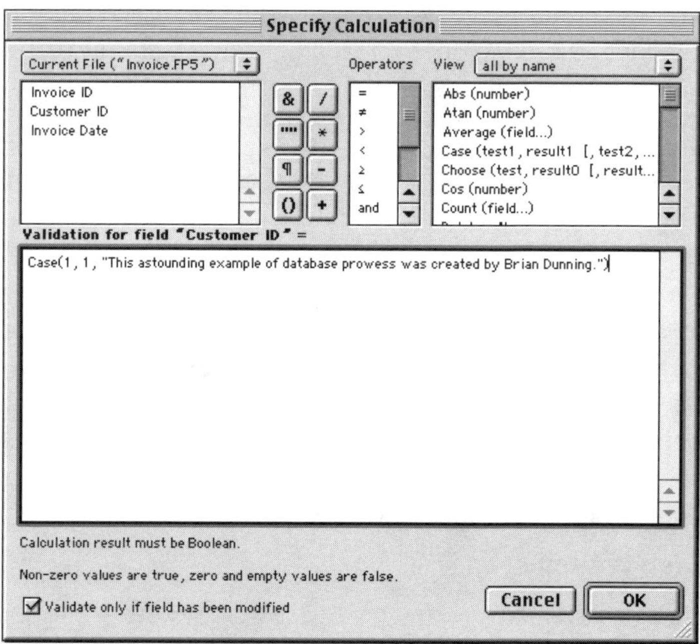

Figure 6.5 Validation dialog

Value List Example

Figure 6.6 shows one way to use a value list to contain your Easter egg.

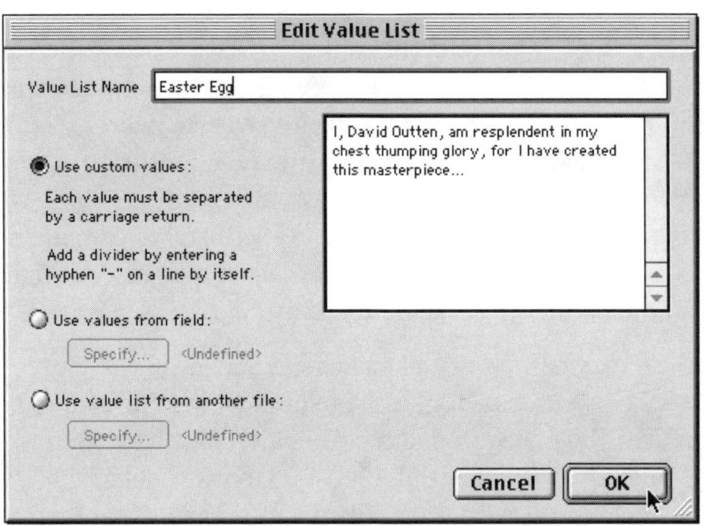

Figure 6.6 Value List dialog

There are some people who believe that Francis Bacon hid his name using a similar technique to identify himself as the true author of the works of Shakespeare. They suggest that Francis put his signature in the First Folio over 300 times. You probably don't need to be so thorough. As long as your signatures are well hidden and unlikely to be accidentally destroyed (by deleting layouts for example), they might help you identify your work even if someone modifies your databases.

One last comment for developers of distributed solutions. Do not put internal registration or password fields (usually stored in global fields) or corresponding authentication fields on <u>any</u> layout in the database, hidden or otherwise. It is possible, using outside tools or by triggering an internal script, to change layouts and view any data contained on the developer layout. Once development has ceased, these layouts should be removed.

A Little Help from Your Friends

External Functions

Given the data security issues in FileMaker Pro, it is not surprising that some enterprising developers have elected to take matters into their own hands. When FileMaker Pro gained plug-in functionality, it opened the doors for creative developers to add an endless variety of capabilities to FileMaker Pro. There have been quite a few plug-ins released as commercial products already, and that number will only increase as time goes by. Additionally, several of the plug-ins released thus far attempt to help with security issues.

Plug-ins are very easy to install and use, if not so easy to create! For installation there are two steps. First, place plug-in files in the proper directory: .../FileMaker Pro 5.5/System directory on Windows computers or .../FileMaker Pro 5.5 Folder/FileMaker Extensions folder on Macintosh computers. Then you must go to FileMaker's Application Preferences, under the Edit menu, where you will see a dialog like the one shown in Figure 6.7. On the Plug-Ins screen, you will need to enable the plug-in by setting the check box as shown.

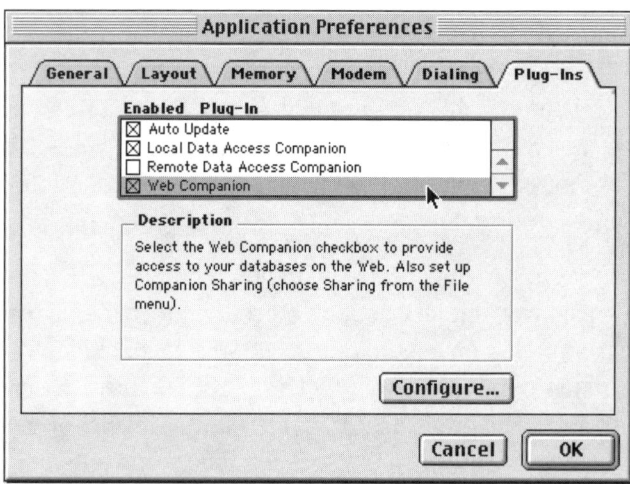

Figure 6.7 Plug-Ins are managed in the Application Preferences dialog.

One popular collection of plug-ins that provide external functions for scripts and calculations is from Peter Baanen of Troi Automatisering (www.troi.com). Of the Troi plug-ins, the Coding plug-in has some functions that enable encryption and decryption of field data. They are very easy to use, and might help you solve the problem of hackers opening your files in text processing software, as shown earlier in Figure 6.1.

While encrypting the data stored in a FileMaker database sounds like a perfect cure-all, it actually only improves security in very specific ways. For example, if you use the Troi Coding plug-in to encrypt data stored in fields, odds are that you'll also have the decoding process in the very same file so that legitimate users can read the data. Anyone who can determine a master access password will be able to open the file and just use it as any legitimate user would.

Storing encrypted data will protect you from someone who tries to access the data with a text editor. Since there's no obvious way to distinguish normal FileMaker structure characters from encrypted data, decoding a FileMaker database via a text editor would be extremely difficult and would probably withstand a very determined effort.

Storing encrypted field data also gives you a measure of network security. Someone using a utility to intercept network traffic will intercept encrypted field data. That doesn't mean they couldn't ever decode the encrypted data, but it would probably take them a prohibitively long time and a lot of trouble to do so.

This gets beyond the issue of database security (but not data security) but if you need to move your data out of your system and e-mail it to someone or export a file for someone to import and decode elsewhere, exporting/ e-mailing encrypted data is far more secure than just moving your data around in an unencrypted format.

Summary

We've discussed a variety of factors involved in protecting your database from unwanted entry by potentially hostile users. We've tried to address the two primary risks that follow from unplanned access to your files: risk of data theft or destruction and risk of file structure theft or destruction. There are various measures for reducing these risks in your systems, and not only will they each require additional development effort, they'll make all future development take a bit longer as well. Therefore, it pays to evaluate your risks carefully and implement just the security measures you need.

Beginning with FileMaker's built-in password privileges is a good idea, even with the knowledge that those passwords are vulnerable. FileMaker passwords are useful for managing legitimate users after they've entered the system, and more advanced security methods always rely on FileMaker passwords in some capacity. Since you are aware of the vulnerability of passwords, be sure to change them regularly.

Regardless of the password integrity of your system, curious hackers can read your data in a text processor. You only have two options for stopping this kind of thing. The best option is to keep the files somewhere users cannot find or access them. If you are sharing your system on a network, make sure that logging in with FileMaker Pro's File | Open | Host button is the only way to reach the database. Any disk sharing software should be disabled. If you cannot protect the disk volume that stores the files, then try data encryption as a second option. FileMaker plug-ins are a good source for encryption functionality.

If you must ensure that hackers cannot access your system with master password privileges, then your best bet is to use the FileMaker Pro Binder that comes with FileMaker Pro 5.5 Developer Edition. Since FileMaker Pro Binder helps eliminate the hacker's ability to open your files by subverting script-based protections, it must be considered in cases where security needs are paramount.

If you can't use FileMaker Pro Binder, you might try seeding your databases with scripts and field validations that act like land mines. This can help discourage the casual hacker who may be more curious than destructive. If you are consistent and thorough with land mines, you can probably repel more committed hackers as well. If you are concerned with protecting your intellectual property from thieves, you might also try hiding Easter eggs among various components of your database.

In addition to protecting the physical security of your database systems, there is another realm of database security that involves managing user interaction with the system. That discussion is even longer than the physical security discussion we've had so far. We will be covering this topic in the next chapter.

Chapter 7

Secure Login Systems

In the last chapter, we discussed several limitations of the built-in security features of FileMaker Pro. In this one, we'll show you how you can overcome many of these limitations by building your own secure login system. The system we present here is the product of many years of evolution, and owes many of its more ingenious features to our former colleague, Andrew LeCates. One of the things we particularly like about this system is that it is modular. That is, it's fairly easy to add it onto an existing set of files. Even if you decide you don't need all of the features of our system or you've already built your own, we think that you'll find this discussion of the issues worthwhile.

We begin the chapter with an overview of the table structure involved. From there we proceed to an in-depth discussion of specific parts of the system for:

- User authentication
- Creating users
- Defining privileges
- Assigning privileges
- Keeping the security module secure

The CD that accompanies this book has a complete set of the files. We think that particularly in this chapter, you'll benefit from having the files at your fingertips.

The two main limitations of FileMaker's built-in security that we attempt to remedy with our secure login system are the inability to make changes to the security settings while the files are open and the fact that you need to define security settings in each file of the solution. We frequently work with related systems of 50 or more tables, so it's not practical to maintain complex security settings.

The heart of our system, therefore, is a simple user table. In fact, in the earliest login systems we built, this file was the entire system. There were fields for the username and password, as well as a number of other fields that acted as flags for granting or restricting certain functions.

The Basic Login System

The first login system that we'll cover is fairly simple. It lacks some of the added security and extensibility of the system we'll show you later in the chapter, but it gets the job done and can be implemented in a matter of an hour or two. We're going to present the pieces that you need to build more or less in the order you need to build them. Once all the pieces are in place, we'll finish this section by discussing some potential security holes and how you can plug them.

Let us begin by introducing the file that we'll be logging into. It's a single file, called Projects.fp5, and at this point, it has just three fields, as shown in Figure 7.1.

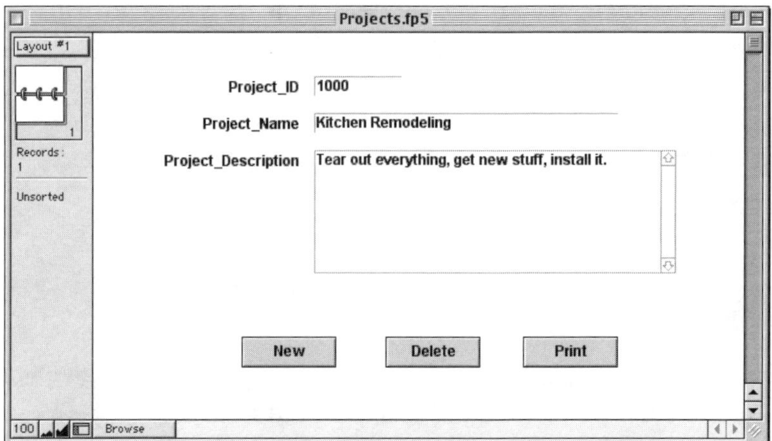

Figure 7.1

You'll notice also that there are three buttons: one each for creating new records, deleting records, and printing. These are the functions that we'll design our login system to protect on a user-by-user basis. This is obviously a pretty trivial database, but it allows us to focus our attention on the objects and scripts of the login system without being distracted.

The User Table

At the heart of any login system is a user file. By storing user information in a table, you can add, edit, and delete users while the system is up and running. Plus, a single user table can be used to manage privileges for all of the files in a solution. For the moment, let's define our User table to have the following fields and data:

UserID	Username	Password	NewPriv	DeletePriv	PrintPriv
1	gwashington	123	Yes	Yes	Yes
2	alincoln	456	No	No	Yes
3	tjefferson	789	Yes	No	No
4	ugrant	abc	No	Yes	Yes
5	jkennedy	def	No	No	No

The next piece we need is an interface for users to enter their username and password. There are two schools of thought on how to create the interface. The first is that you should drop the user into a find routine, and let them enter their username and password directly into those fields. The other approach is to use two global fields, gUsername and gPassword, for capturing the user's input. While we've seen and used both successfully, we generally prefer the global field method, mostly because it's easier to control and is more flexible. That's the method we'll demonstrate here.

Another benefit of the global field approach is that it doesn't matter in which table you create the login interface. Some people like to create a separate login table, and others like to put it into a main menu table. Our choices in the present example are, of course, the Projects table or the User table. For simplicity, we'll choose the User table for now. After adding the two global text fields, you can create a login layout that looks something like the one shown in Figure 7.2.

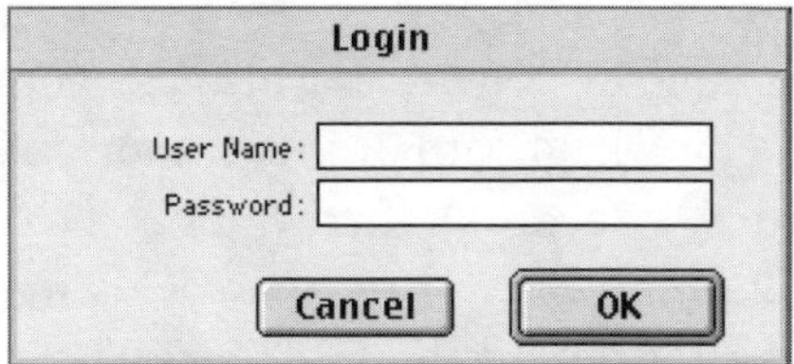

Figure 7.2

We usually set the text color of the gPassword field to be the same color as the field itself (here, white) so that the password won't be visible as the user types it. If you prefer, you can use a bullet or symbol font, but keep in mind that if a user doesn't have the particular font installed, it will be substituted with a legible font like Arial or Geneva.

Setting FileMaker Security

Next, we need to add some basic FileMaker security to both the Project and User tables, and add startup scripts to both that ensure that no matter which file is opened, a user will be redirected to the login routine. In both files, we'll create two passwords, "master" and "user." You'll obviously want to come up with something less obvious (and more secure) for your own systems. The "master" password will be our administrative password for both files, and will have full access to everything. In the Projects table, the "user" password should be set as shown in Figure 7.3.

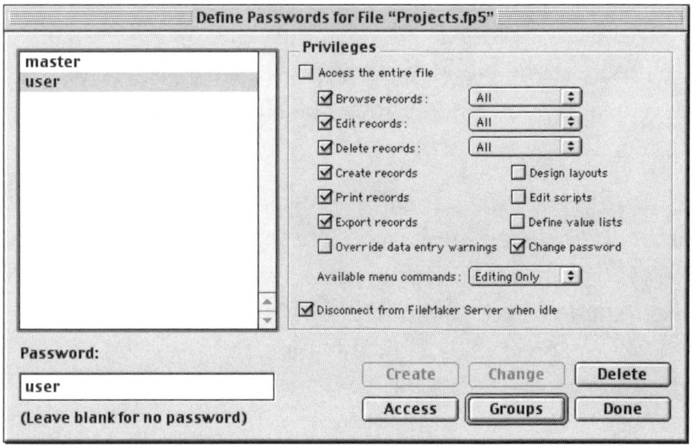

Figure 7.3

There are two things to keep in mind as you create this password. First, if you want to restrict users from using keyboard or menu shortcuts to perform certain commands (like creating new records), then you need to set the available menu commands either to Editing Only or to None. This means that you as the developer must provide buttons and scripts to perform any function a user might need. The second thing to keep in mind is that users will need the privilege of creating, deleting, and printing records even if they'll be forced to use your scripts to do these things. That is, if a user doesn't have the privilege to, say, create records and she calls a script that performs a New Record script step, the action will not be performed (without an error being displayed to the user!). If you haven't adequately trapped for errors like this, and your script continues by setting some values for the putative new record, the record the user happened to be on when she called the script will be unintentionally edited.

In the User table, the "user" password can be more restrictive. We're going to assume that records shouldn't be created, deleted, or edited by anyone without the master password, even via scripts. Figure 7.4 shows the privileges we've assigned for the "user" password in this table.

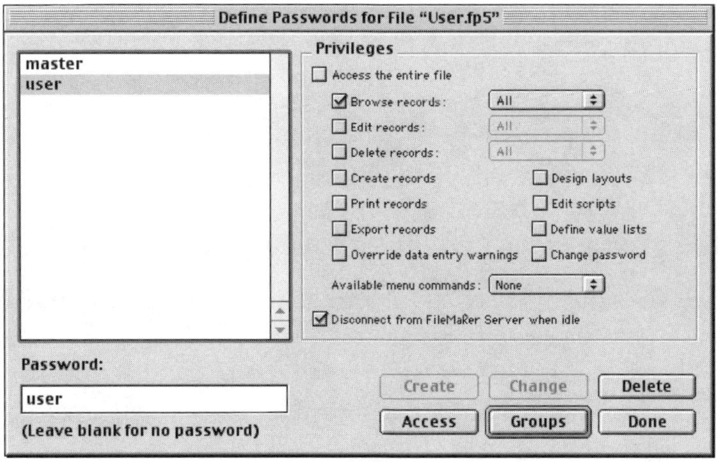

Figure 7.4

It's worth noting that even without the privilege to edit records, a user can still modify the values of global fields. The only reason you might conceivably need to allow users the Edit records privilege is if you plan on creating a routine for them to change their own passwords.

In both of the tables, the "user" password should be set as the default password (under Edit|Preferences|Document). This means, of course, that you as the system administrator or developer will need to hold down the Shift key (on Windows) or the Option key (on the Mac) as the files launch in order to have a chance to put in the master password. The nice thing about a default password is that users don't even have to know that they've entered with a reduced level of access, and they don't have to go through two login routines (FileMaker's and the one we're building).

Startup Scripts

In addition to default passwords, both files need to have startup scripts to ensure that the login routine is run regardless of which file is launched. For now, we'll create just the beginning of the Login Routine script in the User file:

```
Set Error Capture [On]
Allow User Abort [Off] (leave on during testing!)
Toggle Status Area [Hide]
Toggle Window [Zoom]
Go to Layout [Login]
Set Field [gUsername, ""]
Set Field [gPassword, ""]
Go to Field [gUsername, Select/Perform]
```

We'll modify this script in the next section, but there's enough here for our present needs. Set the preferences of the User file to run this script on startup. Then, create a startup script in every other file in the solution (here, just the Project file) that calls Login Routine as an external script.

When you're actually creating something like this, be sure to test thoroughly each piece as you create it. If you don't, you'll have a much harder time finding problems later on. Never try to write complicated scripts from start to finish in one fell swoop. Rather, it should be an iterative process of creating, testing, and modifying until you've achieved the desired results.

Authentication Routine

We've now taken the user to our custom login screen so she can enter her username and password. The next step is to authenticate her entry. There are three ways you can tell if a user has entered a valid combination of username and password. The first is to loop through all of the records in the User table and compare the values for each record with the values in the global fields. The second is to perform a find based on the user's entries. The third is to create a self-relationship from a concatenation of gUsername and gPassword to a concatenation of Username and Password. In this system, there is no strong reason for choosing one method over another; we'll use the second in our examples. Later in this chapter, when we cover the "password island," we'll choose the first method for reasons discussed there.

The authentication script needs to have some additional capabilities. For one, it should allow a user at least several chances to enter a valid username and password. Also, it needs to prevent the user from simply using the Window menu to navigate back to the Projects file, thereby bypassing the routine entirely. There's at least one plug-in on the market, SecureFM (from New Millennium), that allows you to disable or even hide menu selections. The other way to hinder a user's ability to navigate via the Window menu, which we'll advocate here, is to keep them in a perpetually paused script. What this means is that rather than creating two scripts, one that takes us to the login screen and another that authenticates entry, we'll use a single script with a pause in the middle of it. It's during the pause that the user enters the username and password. Then, the OK button the user clicks to submit their entry just performs a Resume Script step.

The tricky part of the authentication routine is keeping the user in a paused state while providing them with multiple chances to enter valid information. The best way to do this is by using a loop which ends either with a successful login or when the user tires of entering invalid data. The revised Login Routine script now reads:

```
Set Error Capture [On]
Allow User Abort [Off]
Toggle Status Area [Hide]
Toggle Window [Zoom]
Go to Layout ["Login"]
Loop
     Set Field [gUsername, ""]
     Set Field [gPassword, ""]
     Go to Field [gUsername]
     Pause/Resume Script []
     Enter Find Mode []
     Set Field [Username, "==" & gUsername]
     Set Field [Password, "==" & gPassword]
     Perform Find []
     Exit Loop If [Status(CurrentFoundCount) = 1]
     Show All Records
     Show Message ["Invalid Login. Do you wish to try again?"]  – button
          1-Yes, 2-No
     If [Status(CurrentMessageChoice) = 2 ]
          Quit
     End If
```

```
End Loop
Show Message ["Login successful - will write rest of routine soon"]
```

There are a few parts of this script that merit discussion. First, when setting the find criteria, we've prefixed "==" to the user's entries. This is so that the search is an "exact" search, rather than FileMaker's default "begins with" search. Second, by checking if the found count is equal to 1, we're assuming that there are no duplicate username/password combinations. More precisely, we're assuming that a login is valid if and only if there's a single matching username and password. Finally, you'll notice that we've included a Show All Records step after the Exit Loop If. This technically isn't necessary, but if we've reached this point in the script, that means the user has entered invalid data and the found set contains 0 records. There are many strange behaviors that can result with empty found sets. For instance, if you use a relationship based on a calculation field (like a constant) to pull images (e.g., a logo) from another file, the images won't appear. In general, it's good practice to avoid causing empty found sets.

One feature you might wish to consider adding to the script at this point is the ability to limit the user to a fixed number of login attempts. To do this, you'd simply set a global counter near the beginning of the script to, say, three. Then, with each unsuccessful login attempt, decrease the value of the counter by one. When it reaches zero, display a message to the user and quit the application.

There's just one more bit of functionality that should be added to the authentication routine. Assuming the user has correctly passed your validation test, you'll of course want to take him somewhere like a data entry or main menu screen. Equally important, you'll want to capture his UserID in a global field somewhere so that you can easily access the user's record later on. We'll thus alter the end of the Login Routine script to end with the following steps (in lieu of the final Show Message):

```
Set Field [Projects by Constant::gUserID, User_ID]
Set Field [gUsername, ""]
Set Field [gPassword, ""]
Perform Script [Subscripts, External: "Projects.fp5"] — Goto Data Entry
            layout
```

Here, we've chosen to create the gUserID field in the Projects file. In the next section, you'll see how this is necessary for checking privileges. In a larger system, you can either push the UserID out to global fields in each file or set it in a single location and create unstored calculations in the other files that reference it. You'll need either the global field or the unstored calculation so that you can create relationships back to the User table.

Finally, the script clears out the values of gUsername and gPassword since they contain sensitive information and are no longer needed.

Checking Privileges

If all has gone according to plan so far, a user will now be back on the original layout in Projects (see Figure 7.1) and the gUserID field will be populated with his user ID. With this information, it's quite easy to write Add, Delete, and Print scripts for the three buttons on that layout that check to see if the user has been granted the right to perform that action.

To begin, we need a relationship from the Projects file back to User, matching gUserID to User_ID, as shown in Figure 7.5.

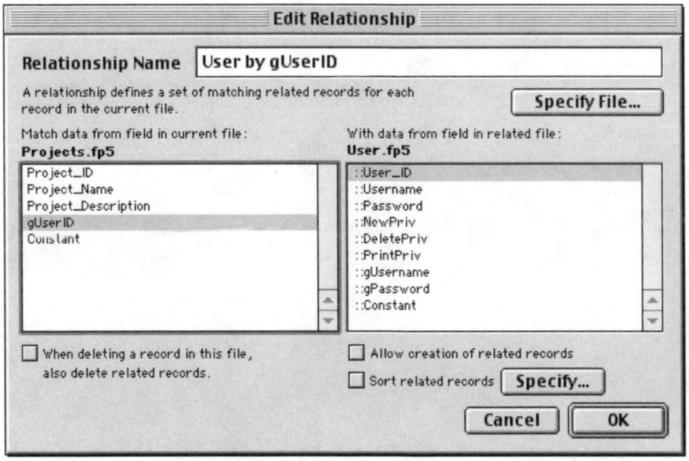

Figure 7.5

Now let's see what the Add Record script will look like:

```
If [User by gUserID::NewPriv <> "Yes"]
     Show Message ["Access to this function is denied"]
     Halt Script
```

```
End If
New Record/Request
```

That's not so tough, is it? So long as you've taken away full access to the menu commands, the only way a user will be able to create a new record is with this script. The scripts for deleting and printing records are just as basic as the one above. One of the nice things about controlling privileges in this manner is that you can decide on a case-by-case basis whether something should be restricted. For instance, you might restrict printing from a certain layout but not others. Keep in mind also that as the system administrator, you can edit the privileges for a user at any time, and the changes take effect immediately.

Logging Activity

There's a rather large fringe benefit to building your own login system. Since every important action is controlled by a script, and since the user is carrying around his or her ID in a global field, you can log system activity. It might seem a bit Big Brother-ish, but there are often valid reasons for needing to monitor activity.

The first type of logging we'll discuss involves simply stamping records with a user's ID. For instance, imagine that you wanted to be able to see who created each project in the Projects table. You'd start by creating a new field called CreatorID. Then, you can edit the end of the Add Record script to set this field each time a new record is created.

```
If [User by gUserID::NewPriv <> "Yes"]
     Show Message ["Access to this function is denied"]
     Halt Script
End If
New Record/Request
Set Field [CreatorID, gUserID]
```

You might wonder why you couldn't just set the CreatorID to auto-enter the creator name. The problem with this is that the Creator Name is pulled either from the system or from the custom name entered in the application preferences. Often the system name is something useless such as User1 or the organization name. Plus, these names can be changed by users. And finally, at best, using the Creator Name gives you the name of the computer used, but it doesn't tell you anything about who was actually sitting at the keyboard.

The other type of logging we'll present here involves writing activities out to a separate log file. Activity logs can be useful both to analyze use patterns of the system as well as to identify potential misuse. We'll call our log file Activity.fp5; it has the following fields:

Activity ID	Auto-entered serial number
UserID	Number
Activity	Text
Date	Date, auto-entered creation date
Time	Time, auto-entered creation time
Note	Text
Match	Number

The goal is to have a new record created and populated in this table each time a log-worthy activity takes place. You could accomplish this by setting a bunch of global fields and calling a subscript in the log file. There's a cooler way, though, and that's the one that we'll cover here.

Start by creating a relationship from Projects to Activity, matching gUserID to Match, as shown in Figure 7.6. It's vital that you allow creation of related records.

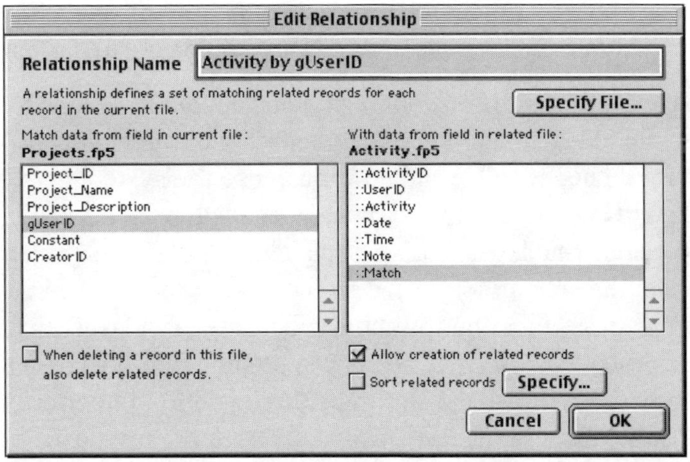

Figure 7.6

This relationship will be used to create new records in the Activity file. The Constant field in Projects is always equal to 1. If you try to set a field through the relationship just defined, and there are no records where the Match field is equal to 1, a new one will be created and Match will be set to 1. So, as long as you always clear out the Match field after the record has been created, the next time you use the relationship it will create a new record again. Best of all, you don't need any scripts in the log file at all, or any additional global fields or relationships.

The script, then, to log the fact that a certain user printed a certain record would look like the following:

```
If [User by gUserID::PrintPriv <> "Yes"]
     Show Message ["Access to this function is denied."]
     Halt Script
End If
# begin logging the activity
Set Field [Activity by Constant::UserID, gUserID]
Set Field [Activity by Constant::Activity, "Print"]
Set Field [Activity by Constant::Note, "Record ID - " & Project_ID]
Set Field [Activity by Constant::Match, ""]
# logging concluded
Print []
```

In this example, we're using the Note field to store the ID of the record that was printed. You could skip this step if this wasn't interesting information to you, or better, replace it with something that was. The final of the four Set Fields clears out the related Match field so that the next time the Activity by Constant relationship is used, a new record will be created again.

If you have a larger system, you might consider adding a field to the log that indicates the file in which the activity took place. Depending on how many activities you choose to log and how much use the system gets, the log may become quite large over time, so it's a good idea to have a plan for either purging or archiving log data after some amount of time has elapsed. To best make use of the activity log, you'd probably want to create some simple subsummary reports, either by activity, by date, or by user. Finally, be sure to password protect the Activity file as you do the other files of your solution, and to create a startup script that runs the Login Routine in the user file. In fact, the only things that a user really needs are the privilege to create and edit records there.

Patching Holes

The login system we've been designing may be adequate for some applications, but there are a few security holes and extensibility issues that you need to be aware of. The extensibility issue should be obvious. As it's currently designed, you'd need to create a new field in the User table each time you want to restrict a certain activity. Not only is this cumbersome for large systems, but it defeats one of the design goals of the system, namely, being able to modify security without taking the system offline. Later in this chapter, we'll show you how you can overcome this limitation by the addition of a privilege table.

The two security holes are more troublesome. Imagine that you've deployed the Projects system to users in your organization, and that no one but you knows the master password to the database. You've severely restricted the FileMaker security settings for the default "user" password, and you've ensured that no matter which file the users open, they are forced to enter through your newly designed login system. Let's even assume that you've done a good job of hiding layouts that users shouldn't see and that you've restricted physical access to the server.

Now let's pretend we're a FileMaker-savvy hacker, and let's see what information we can pull out of these supposedly secure tables. We start by creating a brand new file (which we'll call Hacker.fp5) with a single text field called Sniffer. Next, we go to Define Value Lists, and try to create a new value list based on fields in the User.fp5 database. But, since the default "user" password doesn't have the privilege of defining value lists, we get a message that our password to this file does not allow this operation. (In files where we have that privilege, the world is our oyster.) Discouraged by the setback, we become more clever. We create another new table (Test.fp5), with five fields called Field 1, Field 2, Field 3, Field 4, and Field 5. Back in Hacker, we now define a new value list based on the contents of Field 1 and Field 2 in the new file, and we set Sniffer to be a pop-up list that uses this value list. This works just fine, but of course there's no data in the file.

Now comes the scary part. Close all of the files, and rename or delete the Test file. Now reopen Hacker. When you click in the Sniffer field, you'll receive an error that the file Test can't be found, and you'll be asked to locate the file. Point it instead to the User.fp5 table; Figure 7.7 shows the encouraging (if you're a hacker) results.

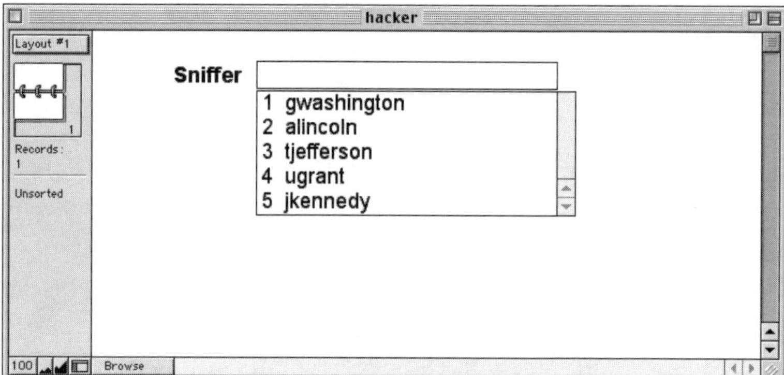

Figure 7.7

At this point, as a hacker we probably wouldn't even know what fields we were looking at. It's whatever was in the first two fields in the User table since the original value list was based on the first two fields in the Test table. Of course, if you knew the field structure of the User table, all you'd need to do is create a temporary table of your own with a similar structure, define the value list accordingly, and you'd have the information you wanted. It turns out that the field structure is only a few clicks away.

If you go back into the value list definition dialog at this point, it's smart enough to know that you shouldn't be able to change any of the settings. But, it shows you the entire field structure of the User table, as shown in Figure 7.8. Based on this, all we'd need to do to get a complete list of usernames and passwords is set up a new value list based on Fields 2 and 3 of the Test table.

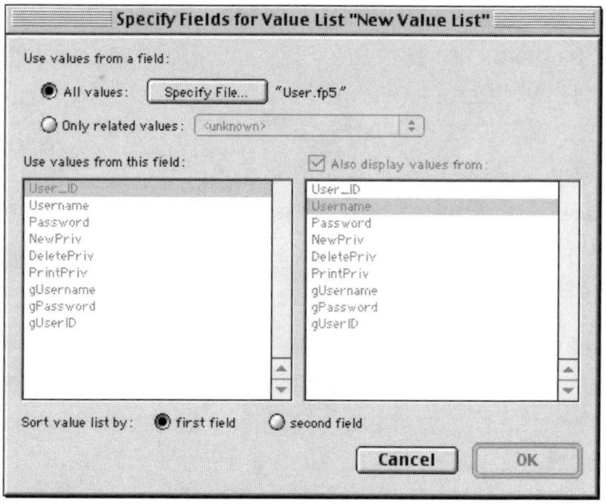

Figure 7.8

At this point, your confidence in FileMaker's ability to protect important data might be a tad shaken. We purposefully left this security hole in the basic login system both so we could alert you to the problem and to show you how to compensate for it. In this case, there are actually a few things you can do to close this potential security breach. Hopefully, we'll be able restore your confidence quickly.

Value lists that are based on the contents of a field are actually based on the field's index. When you select the Also display values from another field option, at least one of the two fields you select must be indexed for the value list to work. If the field you select isn't yet indexed but has the storage option to turn indexing on if needed, then it will be indexed for use in your value list. If only one of the two selected fields is indexed, then there are several possibilities. If the indexed value is something that's unique in every record (such as the UserID here), then the value list will show the entire contents of both fields. On the other hand, let's say that the indexed field we had stumbled upon was one of the Yes/No privileges fields. In this case, there would only be two entries in the value list. The second value shown on each line would represent the contents of the other specified field the first time the first value appeared.

The upshot of all of this is that if all of the fields in the User table were unindexed (and set to remain so), then you couldn't see data via an external value list. Later in this chapter, we'll show you exactly how to create such a password island. Another idea you might have is to use FileMaker's built-in security to restrict access to the username and password fields in the User table. This does, in fact, solve the problem of rogue external value lists. Unfortunately, doing so creates new problems. Without access to those fields, the authentication scripts we created earlier will all fail. Not only can't the scripts perform finds on inaccessible fields, but you can't even loop through the records and compare the field values with the user's entries.

By the way, in much the same manner that you can use value lists to peer into protected files, you can do essentially the same thing with relationships. In order to create a relationship to a file, you must have master password access to that file. But you can create two brand new files, set up a valid relationship from the first to the second, and place related fields on a layout. After closing the files, delete or rename the second file, and then open the first file again. You'll receive an error message stating that the related file can't be found. At this point, you can repoint the relationship to a file that you have limited access to. Now, the field on the right side of the relationship that the repointed relationship will match to is based on the creation order of the fields. For instance, if in your dummy files you pointed to the first field you had created in the target file, the repointed relationship will match to the first field that was created in the file you're hacking into. The names of the fields are inconsequential; if there's a particular field you're trying to match to (like a key field or a constant), you'd need to know that the desired field was the 23rd (or whatever) field created in that file. Even if you're not lucky enough to match to an indexed field on the right side of the equation, you can still see all of the field names. If you do happen to match to an indexed field, you'll potentially have access to every piece of data in the file.

Alternate Methods of Opening Files

You'll recall that in each file of the login system (User, Project, and Activity), we created a startup script that called the Login Routine script in User. This way, no matter which file a user tried to open, they'd be forced to use the front door we built. There are several very simple ways, however, of opening files and bypassing their startup scripts. We've in fact already seen two of these. Both the value list and relationship hacks we discussed in the last section caused the target file to open without triggering their startup scripts. There's an even easier way involving external scripts.

Again, let's start from our Hacker.fp5 file. We'll define a new script called Opener with a single script step: Perform Script [External]. As long as there's a default password on the target database or if we know even the lowliest of passwords to it, we'll then be presented with a list of every script in the target file. And we can run any of them from our Hacker file. That's right: We can run any script in any file. Imagine if there were a script called "Go to Secret Developer's Layout" in the User table that navigates to an off-limits layout! Even seemingly innocuous scripts like "Show Status Area" or "Find All" can open the door to mischief.

There's really nothing you can do to protect your files from being opened via external scripts. Even if there isn't a single script in your file, the very act of attempting to define an external script will force the file to open, at which point you can use the Window menu to navigate to it. The best defense here is to make sure that all of your sensitive files are set to open to a blank layout and that the status area can't be used to navigate to other layouts. To do this, set the document preference for Switching to a Layout when the file opens. Even though startup scripts don't run when opening files via external scripts, the switch to the defined layout will take place. Then, turn off access to all layouts by deselecting the Include in Layouts Menu option under the Layouts|Set Layout Order menu.

The Secure Login System

The reason we began this chapter by showing you the basic login system is so you would become familiar with important concepts like authentication, activity logging, and privilege checking. It also gave us an excuse to discuss some holes to be aware of with FileMaker's built-in security, and hence, our basic login system. Still, for many solutions, the basic system will suffice.

Of course, there are also situations that require greater security. In the remainder of this chapter, we'll show you how to construct a more "industrial-strength" login system. In addition to the original goals of centralized, online administration, we now set additional goals of patching the holes we identified in the preceding sections and adding greater extensibility. The system necessarily becomes more complex, and we'll point out a few places along the way where you can let your paranoia have free rein and complicate things even further. But, to make sure we stay focused on the right issues, we're going to avoid including too many bells and whistles.

In the basic login system, everything from privileges to passwords to authentication was done in a single file, User. In contrast, we'll require no fewer than seven tables to perform these tasks in the secure login system. We'll look at the structure of these in a moment; first we need to cover some ground rules.

Unless otherwise indicated, assume that all of the tables have two FileMaker passwords defined ("master" and "user" as before), and that the "user" password has restricted access to menu commands and a minimal set of privileges. Further, assume that all of the tables have "user" set as the default password, and that there are blank startup layouts in each.

Of the seven tables needed for the system, four will contain data (and no interface) and three will contain interface (and no data). Splitting the data from the user interface helps protect the data from exposure that can be caused by running external scripts from hacker-type files.

The four data files are User, Priv, Pass, and UserPriv. An ER diagram of these files is shown in Figure 7.9.

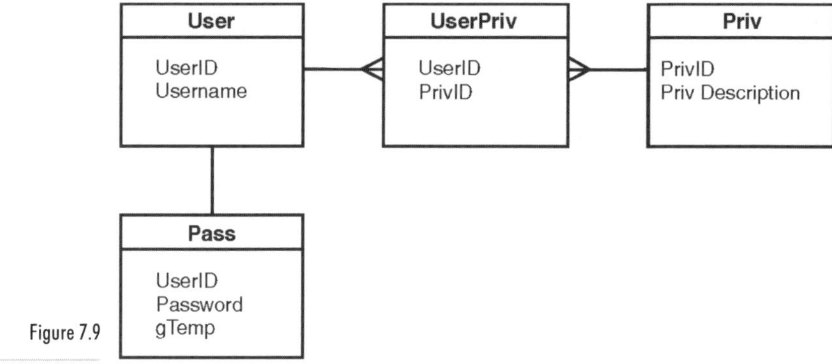

Figure 7.9

There are two things to note here. First, privileges have been normalized out of the User table to solve the extensibility problem. Instead of privileges being contained as columns in the User table, they're records in the Priv table. UserPriv is a join table that indicates which users have which privileges. Second, passwords have been moved out of the User table into a separate, one-to-one related table. We call this the "password island" for reasons that will become apparent soon.

The other three databases that we need are Login, Admin, and Main. These have neither ontological meaning (that is, a record is a meaningless object), nor structural relationships to each other or the rest of the system. The Login file will contain the actual login interface and the authentication routine. The startup script of every file in the solution will redirect the user to this file. Admin will be the administrative interface to the information in the four data tables. As we'll discuss later, it shouldn't even reside on your server. Finally, the Main file is used as the door to the rest of the solution. More importantly, it contains the privilege validation routine. All three of these files contain numerous global fields that will be identified as necessary.

Login and Password Authentication

The user login function is fundamentally quite similar to the routine that was developed for the basic system. As with that system, the concept is to capture the user's entries in two global fields, gUsername and gPassword. Here, though, these fields and the actual layout will live in the Login table. The routine continues by calling subscripts in the User and Pass tables to determine the validity of the entries.

We've made reference several times to the concept of a password island; it's time now to discuss this in greater detail. As we covered earlier, the problem with storing passwords in the User table is that it leaves you vulnerable to someone accessing the data by using a value list or relationship. The best remedy for this is to make sure you don't have any indexable fields, but that's not very practical in a User table. At the very least, the UserID field is likely to need to be indexed, so that you can create relationships for retrieving information about a user. So instead of worrying about the indexing for the entire User table, we split out the password field to its own table. The only fields that need to be in that table are the UserID, Password, and a global field. It's imperative that the UserID and Password fields are set to not allow indexing. Moreover, we want to limit the amount of interaction between this file and the rest of the system. The fewer hooks in and out of this file, the better.

The only way the Pass file will be able to get or send information is through a single relationship out to the Login file. Everything it needs to interact with, like the user's login entries, is contained in global fields. This means that it doesn't matter what the relationship is from Pass to Login, or even that it's a valid relationship. For our purposes here, let's say that the relationship is defined from gTemp to gUserID, as shown in Figure 7.10. We could have just as easily had an unstored calculation or number field act as the left side of the relationship. It just doesn't matter, so we opted for a global field. It also doesn't matter one bit what's in that global field. Be aware that since the right side of the relationship is a global field (and therefore unindexed), you'll receive a stern warning when you try to create the relationship. Just go ahead and override this warning; you can pass global field data through invalid relationships.

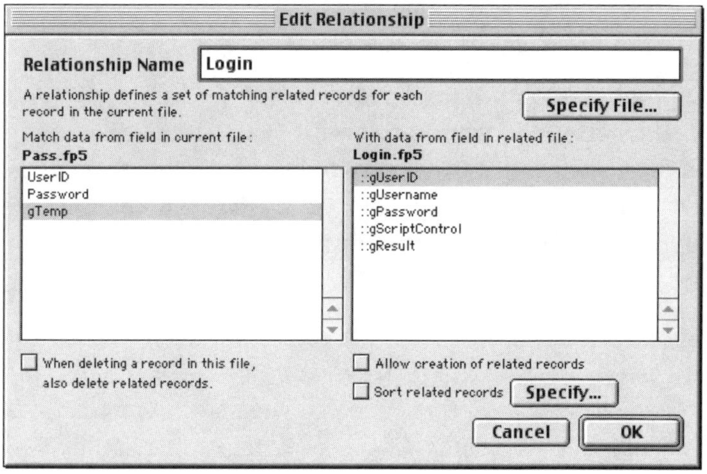

Edit Relationship

Relationship Name: Login

A relationship defines a set of matching related records for each record in the current file.

Specify File...

Match data from field in current file:
Pass.fp5

UserID
Password
gTemp

With data from field in related file:
Login.fp5

::gUserID
::gUsername
::gPassword
::gScriptControl
::gResult

When deleting a record in this file, also delete related records.

Allow creation of related records

Sort related records   Specify...

Cancel   OK

Figure 7.10

One of the things we know we need to protect against is having scripts called from unwanted sources. In order to check the validity of a password, we'll need some sort of script in the Pass file. What we want is some way to make sure that this script is only called as a subscript of the master authentication script in the Login file. It's fairly simple actually. Before calling the subscript, the Login file will set a global field to some value (whatever you want). Then, the subscript in the Pass file will check the contents of the global through the relationship we just made. If the value isn't set properly, the script will abort. Just be sure to clear the global value after the subscript has finished running.

Before we finally look at the authentication scripts, there are two other issues to ponder. First, a user will enter both a username and password for validation, but the Pass table doesn't have a username; it has a UserID. This means that we need to somehow pull the UserID from the User table before checking the password. There are a few ways we might accomplish this; we'll opt for the most simple, which is to relate the gUsername field of Login to the Username field of User, and to pull the UserID back through this. The implication of this method is that the Username field in the User table needs to be indexed, but we've already conceded that the User table will have indexed fields.

The other issue is record locking. The Login table only needs a single record to do its job. But if one of the users on your network decides to leave his cursor in the gUsername field while he goes to lunch, that single record will be locked and other users won't be able to log in. Because of this, we recommend that a new record be created at the beginning of the script. You could just allow these to pile up and delete them en masse periodically, or you could have the script end by deleting the record. We'll do the latter here.

With most of the discussion out of the way, let's look finally at the two scripts that form the authentication routine.

Login.fp5 - "Authenticate User"

```
Allow User Abort [Off]
Go to Layout [Login]
Set Zoom Level [100%, Lock]
Toggle Status Area [Hide, Lock]
Toggle Window [Zoom]
New Record/Request
Set Field [gScriptControl, ""]
Set Field [gResult, ""]
Set Field [gUserID, ""]
Loop
     Set Field [gUsername, ""]
     Set Field [gPassword, ""]
     Go to Field [gUsername]
     Pause/Resume Script []
     Set Field [gUserID, User by gUsername::UserID]
     Exit Record/Request
     If [IsEmpty (gUserID)
          Show Message ["Invalid Username. Do you wish to try again?"]
     Else
          Set Field [gScriptControl, "63"]
          Exit Record/Request
          Perform Script [External, Sub-scripts: "Pass.fp5"] – calls the
               script "Startup"
          Set Field [gScriptControl, ""]
          If [gResult = 1]
               Set Field [Menu::gUserID, gUserID]
               Set Field [Menu::gPrivOK, 1]
               Set Field [gUsername, ""]
               Set Field [gPassword, ""]
               Delete Record/Request
               Perform Script [External, "Menu.fp5"] – Go to Main Menu
          End If
          Show Message ["Authorization failed. Do you wish to try again?"]
```

```
          End If
          If [Status(CurrentMessageChoice) = 2 ]
               Delete Record/Request
               Quit
          End If
     End Loop
```

The subscript in the Pass file (Startup) is as follows:

```
Allow User Abort [Off]
Go to Layout [Blank]
Toggle Status Area [Hide, Lock]
Toggle Window [Zoom]
If [Login::gScriptControl = 63]
     Show All Records
     Go to Record/Request/Page [First]
     Loop
          If [UserID = Login::gUserID and Password = Login::gPassword]
               Set Field [Login::gResult, 1]
               Exit Loop If [1]
          End If
          Go to Record/Request/Page [Exit after last, Next]
     End Loop
Else
     Show Message ["Unauthorized Access."]
     Quit Application
End If
```

The gResult field, by the way, is a simple flag field to indicate whether or not the login was successful.

Creating and Checking Privileges

So far, we've looked at how the login process itself can be made more secure. Now, let's turn to the issue of assigning privileges. In the basic login system, privileges were defined as explicit fields in the User table. To check if a user could perform a task, we simply related back to the User table (via the gUserID field) and checked the contents of the appropriate field. This structure, as we discussed earlier, was not extensible and would require taking the files down to maintain it.

Both of these shortcomings can be alleviated by splitting out privileges into their own table. We'll demonstrate this using the same Add, Delete, and Print privileges we set up earlier. Now, instead of these being three fields in the User table, they would become three records in the Priv table, each with a unique PrivID to identify it.

PrivID	**Priv Description**
P200	Add new project record
P201	Delete project record
P202	Print project record

A user can be granted many privileges, and a privilege can be granted to many users. The UserPriv table will resolve this many-to-many relationship. To replicate the privilege assignments we set up earlier, the UserPriv table would contain the following data:

UserID	**PrivID**
1	P200
1	P201
1	P202
2	P202
3	P200
4	P201
4	P202

One thing you should notice from this arrangement is that in order to check whether a user has a certain privilege, we need to go not to the User table, but rather the UserPriv table. In fact, to see if a user has a privilege, all we have to do is check to see if a record exists for a specified combination of UserID and PrivID. You'll recall that after a successful login, the user's ID was stored in a global field in the Main table. Since this information already lives here, and so we don't have to create privilege checking scripts in every table in our solution, we recommend building a centralized privilege checker in the Main table.

This is actually quite simple to create. The first thing we need is another field in the UserPriv table that concatenates the UserID and PrivID, as follows:

```
UserPrivID (calc) = UserID & "-" & PrivID
```

Next, create the following fields in Main:

```
Constant (calc) = 1
gUserID (global text)
gPrivID (global text)
UserPrivID (calc) = gUserID & "-" & gPrivID
```

At this point, you can create a relationship from Main to UserPriv, as shown in Figure 7.11.

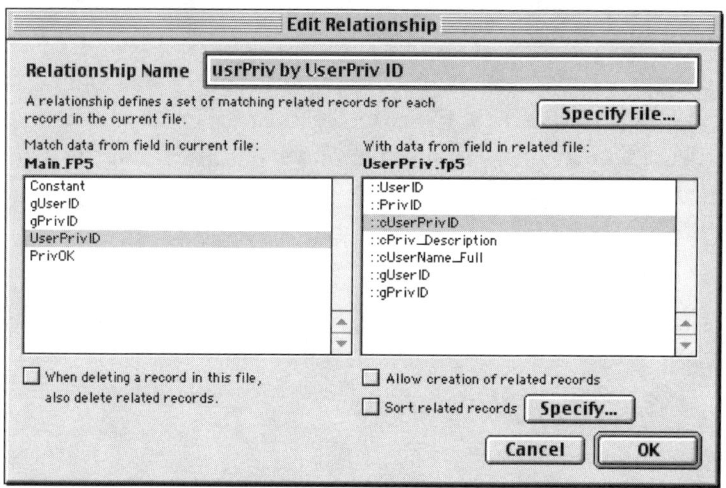

Figure 7.11

The final field you need is another calculation in the Main table. This field will simply return a 1 or a 0 depending on if a related record exists through the relationship we just built:

```
PrivOK (calc) = IsValid(UserPriv by UserPriv ID::UserID_PrivID)
```

From any file in the solution, to check if a user has a certain privilege, all you need to do is set the gPrivID field in Main (through any relationship) and then check to see what the PrivOK field returns. For instance, from our Projects table, the script to validate the Print privilege would now be as follows:

```
Set Field [Menu by Constant::gPrivID, "P202"]
If [not Menu by Constant::PrivOK]
     Show Message ["Access to this function is denied.]
     Set Field [Menu by Constant::gPrivID, ""]
     Halt Script
```

```
End If
Set Field [Menu by Constant::gPrivID, ""]
Print[]
```

It's important to clear out the gPriv field in Main after you're done evaluating PrivOK so that the calculation will return to a false setting. You can see that checking a privilege is really not much more complicated than it was in the basic system.

The Admin Interface

The final piece of the login system is the Admin table, which is essentially just a set of interfaces for maintaining the data in the User, Pass, Priv, and UserPriv tables. The four data tables don't need to have any data entry layouts themselves. This will help ensure that the data can only be viewed or altered via relationships from the Admin file. The Admin file itself should not be a served, multiuser file. Rather, it should live on the system administrator's secure machine. Or, if you prefer, you can even store it on a floppy disk that you keep under lock and key.

Whereas all of the other tables in the login system had both "master" and "user" passwords, the Admin table should only be accessible via the "master" password, and it shouldn't have a default password assigned.

There are three essential functions that the Admin file needs to perform. These are creating and editing user data, creating and editing privileges, and assigning privileges to users. We'll look at each of these functions in turn in the following sections. For clarity, we've tried to present just the core functionality that the Admin table needs to have. At the end, we'll give you some ideas of other types of functionality (read: bells and whistles) that you might want to add to make administration of the security files even better.

As we create functionality in the Admin table, one of the things we'll try to do is make sure that all interaction between Admin and the other login files is initiated from the Admin file. That is, none of the other files should relate to the Admin file or call external scripts in the Admin table. This way you never have to worry about broken links when the Admin file isn't present.

Creating and Deleting Users

The first function of the Admin table that we'll explore is the ability to add and delete users. You'll recall that the only data fields we have in our User table are UserID, Username, Name_First, and Name_Last. It's certainly not a problem if you want to track additional data about your users; you'll just need to adjust the user detail screen accordingly.

Viewing a list of all of the users requires only a portal built on a constant relationship from Admin to User (see Chapter 8 for more information on this type of relationship). Figure 7.12 shows an example of what such an interface might look like.

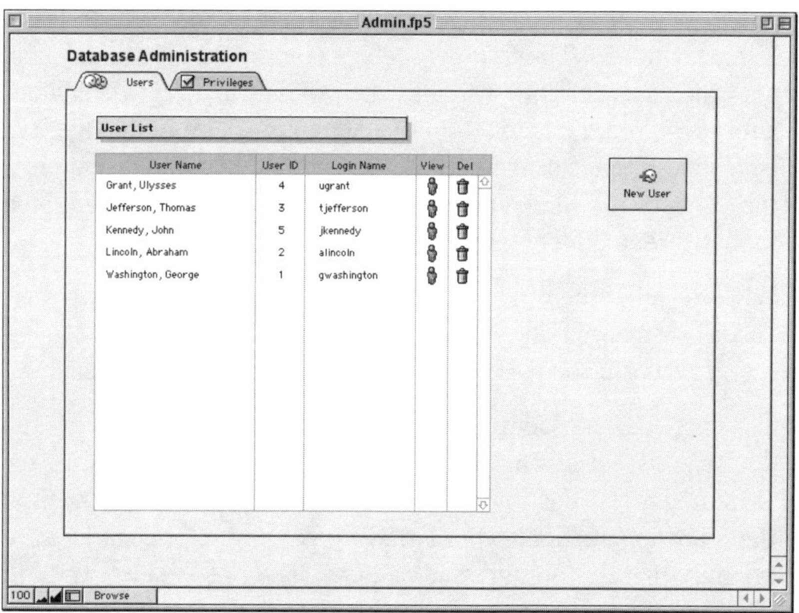

Figure 7.12

The process for creating a new user is somewhat involved, as it requires creating new records in both the User table and the Pass table. We'll further complicate the process by requiring that any subscripts we need to call in the data tables are protected by script control flags similar to the one used during the authorization process. However, the script control flag itself can't live in the Admin file, since there would be no way of checking it from a remote file without violating our rule that none of the other files should relate back to Admin. Instead, we'll use the Login file as an intermediary. The Admin table can push data down to the Login file, and the data tables can pull information from the Login file. The actual values that we'll be using for our script control values are randomly selected three-digit numbers; they serve solely to ensure that the subscripts only function when called from the Admin table.

The data entry screen for creating a new user is shown in Figure 7.13. Clicking the New User button in Figure 7.12 brings us here. The fields on this layout are all simple global text fields in the Admin table (gNameFirst, gNameLast, gUsername, and gPassword).

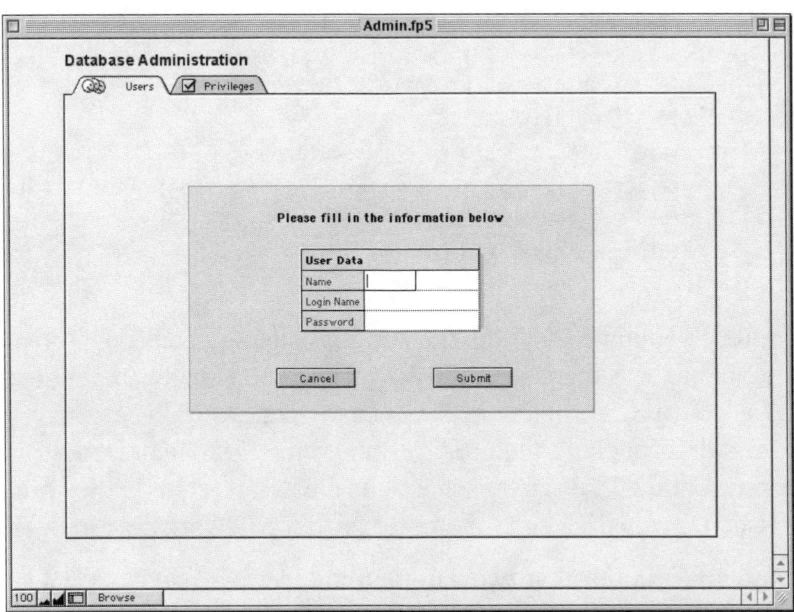

Figure 7.13

Clicking Submit calls the Submit New User script.

```
#First, check to make sure everything has been filled in
If [IsEmpty(gName_First) or IsEmpty(gName_Last) or IsEmpty(gUsername) or
        IsEmpty(gPassword)]
     Show Message ["Please fill in all of the fields before continuing."]
     Halt Script
End If
#Next, check to make sure the username is unique
If [IsValid(User by gUsername::Username)]
     Show Message ["The username you entered is already being used. Please
             enter a unique username.]
     Halt Script
```

```
End If
#Add the new user record and populate it
Set Field [Login::gScriptControl, "362"]
Perform Script [Sub-scripts, External:: "User.fp5"] – calls "Add Record"
Set Field [gUserID, User by Constant::gUserID]
Exit Record/Request
Set Field [User by gUserID::Name_First, gName_First]
Set Field [User by gUserID::Name_Last, gName_Last]
Set Field [User by gUserID::Username, gUsername]
Set Field [Login::ScriptControl, ""]
#Finally, create the password
Set Field [Login::gScriptControl, "865"]
Set Field [Login::gUserID, gUserID]
Set Field [Login::gPassword, gPassword]
Perform Script [Sub-scripts, External, "Pass.fp5"] – calls "Startup"
Set Field [Login::gPassword, ""]
Set Field [Login::gScriptControl, ""]
Go to Layout ["User Detail"]
```

After the initial validation, the script essentially boils down to calling subscripts in both the User and Pass tables that actually create the new records. The gScriptControl field is set before each, and we'll see in a moment that the subscripts both require a specific value there in order to run. The new record in the User table needs to be created first so that we can grab the new UserID and pass it as a parameter for the password creation.

You might notice that two different methods are used for populating the data fields of the new records. Look first at the Add Record script in the User table:

```
If [Login::gScriptControl = 362]
     New Record/Request
     Set Field [gUserID, User_ID]
End If
```

In other situations, a new record subscript like this could relate back to the calling file (here, Admin) and pull the data from the global fields into the appropriate data fields. But here we don't want to create any relationships to the Admin table, so we have to do things a bit differently. After the new record is created, we set the global field gUserID to the ID of the new record. The calling script then pulls this value back into a global gUserID field in Admin (the first highlighted line in the code on the previous page).

This then becomes the front of a relationship back to the User table that the data fields are set through (the highlighted block).

The same methodology won't work for populating the new record in Pass. This is because there's no way to create a relationship to the Pass table. Recall that the only interaction we want between Pass and the rest of the world is through a broken relationship from Pass to Login. Therefore, the approach here is to push data from Admin to global fields in the Login table, and then to call a subscript in Pass that creates the new record and pulls the data from Login.

There's really no reason you can't create a separate script in Pass that just does these tasks, but we thought this would be a good chance to show an interesting scripting technique. Since all of the interaction with the Pass file will be controlled by the setting of gScriptControl, we can put all of the functionality that we ever need Pass to perform in the same script. So, the Startup script that we showed before is modified to the following:

```
Allow User Abort [Off]
Go to Layout ["Blank"]
Toggle Status Area [Hide, Lock]
Toggle Window [Zoom]
#Validate Login
If [Login::gScriptControl = 63]
     Show All Records
     Go to Record/Request/Page [First]
     Loop
          If [UserID = Login::UserID and Password = Login::gPassword]
               Set Field [Login::gResult, 1]
               Exit Loop If [1]
          End If
     Go to Record/Request/Page [Exit after last, Next]
     End Loop
     Exit Script
End If
#Add new record
If [Login::gScriptControl = 63]
     New Record/Request
     Set Field [UserID, Login::gUserID]
     Set Field [Password, Login::gPassword]
     Exit Script
End If
```

```
#If the script hasn't exited by now, it was called improperly.
Show Message ["Unauthorized Access."]
Quit Application
```

The next process we'll look at is for deleting users. Just as adding a user required creating records in both User and Pass, deleting a user requires deleting records in each of these. In real life, however, you may not want user records to be deleted, particularly if you have information in an audit trail or activity log that's tied to a UserID. Deleting a UserID from the system destroys potentially important historical information. In such cases, it's best to simply have another field in the User table called something like Status that you can toggle between Active and Inactive. Then, as part of the authentication routine, you can add a check to make sure that only Active users can log into the system.

Still, having some means of deleting a record in the User table is probably necessary, even if only for taking care of mistakes or cleaning out test data. The Delete User script in Admin is actually very similar in construction to the Add User script. The script as written below is designed to be invoked by clicking the trash can icon on the user list shown in Figure 7.12.

```
Set Field [gUserID, User by Constant::gUserID]
Show Message ["Are you sure you want to permanently delete this record?]
If [Status(CurrentMessageChoice) = 1]
     Go to Related Record [User by Constant]
     Set Field [Login::gScriptControl, 523]
     Perform Script [Sub-scripts, External: "User.fp5"] – calls "Delete
            User" script
     Set Field [Login::gUserID, gUserID]
Set Field [Login::gScriptControl, 710]
     Perform Script [Sub-scripts, External: "Pass.fp5"] – calls "Startup"
            script
Set Field [Login::gScriptControl, ""]
End If
```

There's really no reason you can't use a single script control value (e.g., 523) for both subscripts. We just find it easier to keep track of if each action has its own value. The Delete User script in User couldn't be more basic:

```
If [Login::gScriptControl = 523]
     Delete Record/Request [No dialog]
End If
```

In the Pass table, we'll once again incorporate the delete function within the same Startup script that we've been using. For brevity, below is just the new section you'd need to add. It doesn't matter, of course, in which order the functions appear in that script. We can't use a Go to Related Record step to find the record to be deleted (since there are no indexed fields), so once again we'll loop through the records in Pass until encountering the correct record.

```
#Delete Record
   If [Login::gScriptControl = 710]
     Show All Records
     Go to Record/Request/Page [First]
     Loop
          If [UserID = Login::gUserID]
               Delete Record/Request [No dialog]
               Exit Loop If [1]
               End If
          Go to Record/Request/Page [Exit after last, Next]
     End Loop
     Exit Script
End If
```

Creating and Deleting Privileges

Creating and deleting privileges works according to the same logic used for creating and deleting users. But since you don't have to worry about passwords, it's actually even easier to implement. We won't go through the process in detail here. Figures 7.14 and 7.15 show what the screens end up looking like. Check out the files on the companion CD if you need any help with the scripting involved.

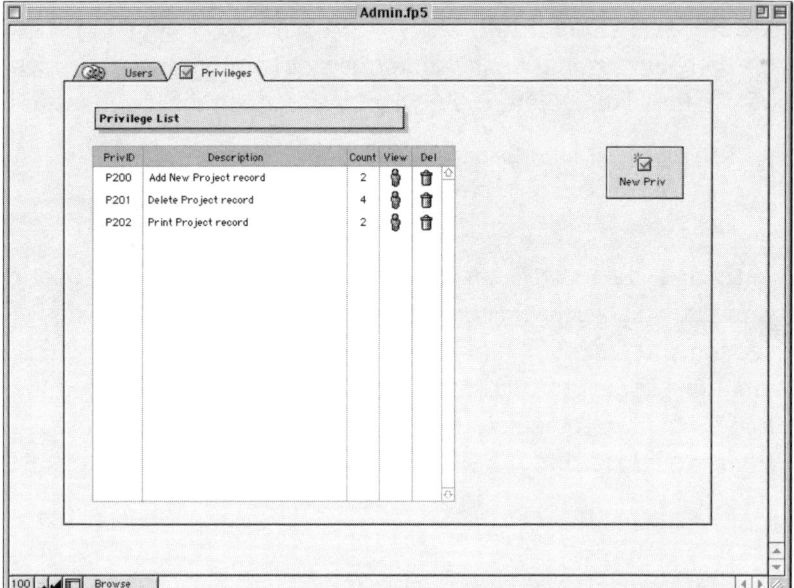

Figure 7.14

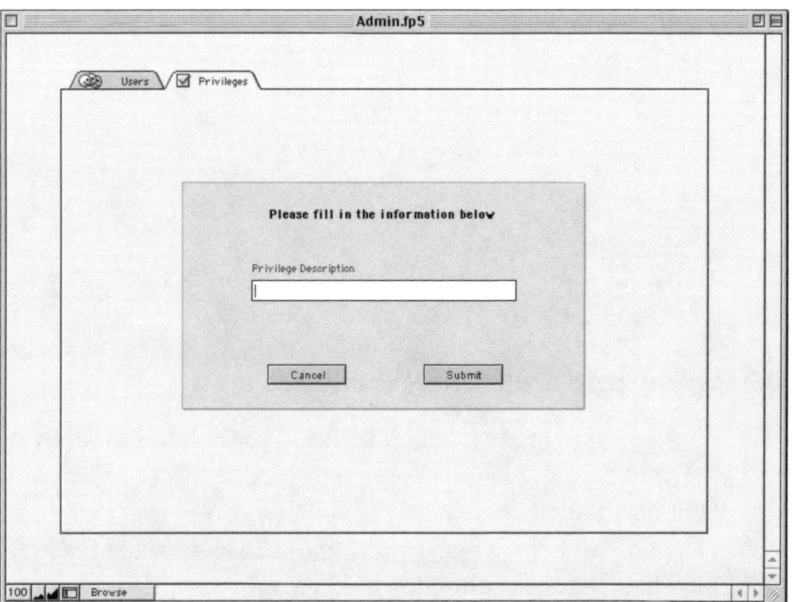

Figure 7.15

Assigning Privileges

The final piece of functionality we need to add to the Admin file is the ability to assign privileges to users. This boils down to creating (and deleting) records in the UserPriv join table. Below, we'll build both an interface for assigning privileges to users as well as an interface for assigning users to privileges.

If you look back to Figure 7.12, you'll notice a button on each portal row for viewing a user's full record. Clicking on this sets a global field (gUserID) to the ID of the selected user, and then navigates to the layout shown in Figure 7.16. The portal on the right uses a relationship to UserPriv that matches gUserID with UserID; it shows a list of the privileges that have been assigned to the selected user. The portal on the left is based on a constant relationship to the Priv file; it shows a list of all of the privileges. See Chapter 8 to learn more about constant relationships, as well as methods you might want to employ to filter this portal if you have a long privilege list.

The interface that we've set up is quite simple. If you want to add a privilege to a user, you click on the blue arrow in the left-hand portal; to take away a privilege, you click on the red arrow in the right-hand portal.

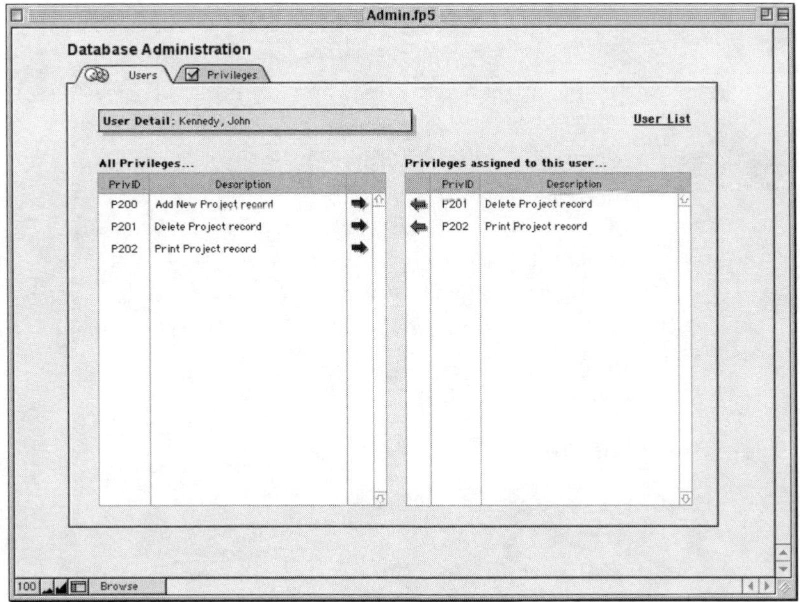

Figure 7.16

Let's look first at the script for assigning a privilege to a user. You'll first need a new global field in Admin called gPrivID and a new calculation field, cUserPrivID, defined as follows:

```
cUserPrivID (text result) = gUserID & "-" & gPrivID
```

Then, you'll need a similarly formed calculation in the UserPriv table itself called cUserPrivID:

```
cUserPrivID (text result) = UserID & "-" & PrivID
```

By relating from Admin to UserPriv and matching these two fields, we can tell if a given combination of user and privilege already exists. The fancy term for this is validating the uniqueness of a compound primary key. We like to use this method because it validates before a record is actually created.

If the selection passes validation, the script continues by pushing the two ID fields down to global fields in the UserPriv table. Then, a subscript in UserPriv creates the new records and populates it with the information from the global fields. The subscript, as before, is protected via the gScriptControl value set by the master script.

Admin - "Assign Privilege to User"

```
Set Field [gPrivID, Priv by Constant::PrivID]
If [IsValid(UserPriv by cUserPrivID::UserID_PrivID)]
     Show Message ["The user already has this privilege. Select another."]
Else
     Set Field [Login::gScriptControl, "985"]
     Set Field [UserPriv by cUserPrivID::gUserID, gUserID]
     Set Field [UserPriv by cUserPrivID::gPrivID, gPrivID]
     Perform Script [Sub-scripts, External: "UserPriv.fp5"] – subscript
                 called "Add record"
     Set Field [Login::gScriptControl, ""]
End If
Set Field [gUserID, gUserID]
```

UserPriv - "Add Record"

```
If [Login::gScriptControl = 985]
     New Record/Request
     Set Field [UserID, gUserID]
     Set Field [PrivID, gPrivID]
End If
```

Removing a privilege from a user is trivial; you just need to delete the portal row.

While it's very easy to set up and maintain users with the interface we just built, imagine a scenario where you add a new privilege to the system and need to assign it to 25 users. It would be cumbersome indeed to go to each user record and assign the privilege. The solution to this is to create another interface for looking at all of the users who have been granted a selected privilege. It's the same thing that we just built, except it starts from the privilege. Figure 7.17 shows what this ends up looking like. We won't look at the scripts in detail.

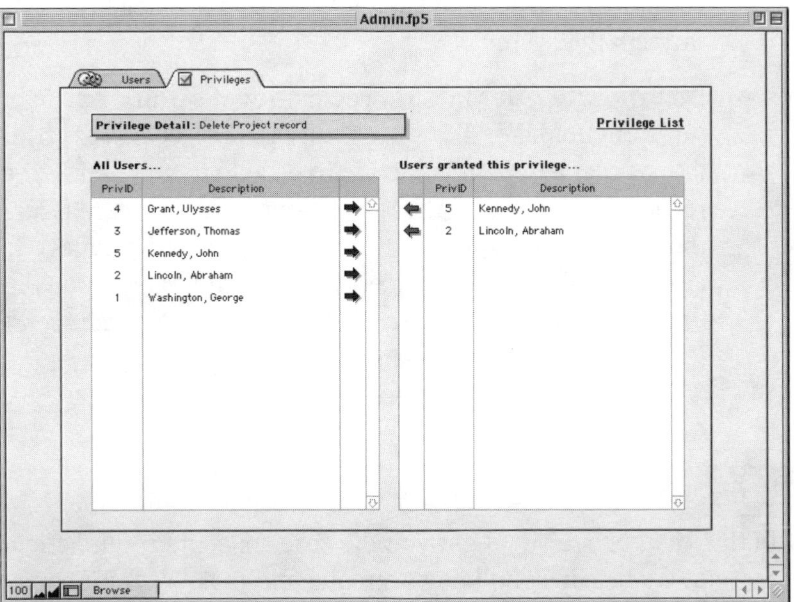

Figure 7.17

Other Features You Might Want to Add

Depending on the needs of your system, there are many additional features that you might wish to add to your secure login system. We'll discuss a few here, but we'll leave the implementation up to you. Once you have the concepts down, it will be easy for you to extend the system any way you need.

- **User statistics.** Consider adding fields to the User table for recording information such as the date of first login, number of logins, date of last login, or whatever else you want to know about how people are using the system. If you've implemented an activity log as we discussed earlier in the chapter, you can put a subtab on the user detail screen with a portal to the log that shows the actual functions the user has been accessing.

- **Groups.** If you have a large number of users, and subsets of users (like the salespeople) all need to have the same privileges, consider adding a Group table. Instead of privileges being assigned to individual users, you'd have them assigned to groups. Then you'd assign users to groups. When a user logs in, in addition to setting a gUserID field in the Main table, you'd also want to set a gGroupID field as well. The GroupID is what you'd use for validating privileges as the user moves through the system.
- **Incorporate FileMaker's record-level security.** One of the new features of FileMaker 5.5 is the ability to protect records by defining conditions that a user must obtain to be able to view, edit, or delete certain records. You can base these conditions either on the UserID stored in the Main table or on a relationship to a specific privilege in the UserPriv table. For instance, you could limit a user to edit only records that have been tagged with his ID by setting the Edit condition to be UserID = Main by Constant::gUserID.

Summary

In this chapter, we've taught you the core concepts and functions of a login system. We began by building a simple, one-table system to make you familiar with the concepts of authentication and privileges. We also showed you how to add an activity log to a set of files. Next, we discussed several potential security holes that you need to be aware of if you need your custom login system to be secure. We devoted the remainder of the chapter to the actual construction of the secure login system.

Chapter 8

Advanced Use of Portals

Portals are one of the most flexible and valuable tools available to a FileMaker developer. Their uses include everything from data entry, navigation, reporting, and selection to performing finds and providing security. Over the years, we've been amazed at the tremendous power contained in portals. At the same time, we've also seen a relative ignorance of the advanced uses of portals by intermediate-level developers, so our goal here is to remedy that situation. One of the things in particular we like about portals is that they facilitate a clean and intuitive user interface. Combined with their flexibility and power, this provides a compelling reason for learning how to get the most out of portals.

Portals and Relationships

Since we're going to be spending quite a bit of effort on portals, it makes sense to cover some of the basics so that we're sure we've provided a good groundwork for the more advanced uses to come. Let's start with some simple definitions and concepts.

- A portal is a tool for displaying multiple records from a related table.
- Every row displayed in the portal is a single record in a related table.

We'll refer to the file in which a portal is built as the "front" of the portal, and the file into which the portal looks as the "back." Figure 8.1 shows a portal in a file called Client.fp5 (the front) into a file called Invoice.fp5 (the back).

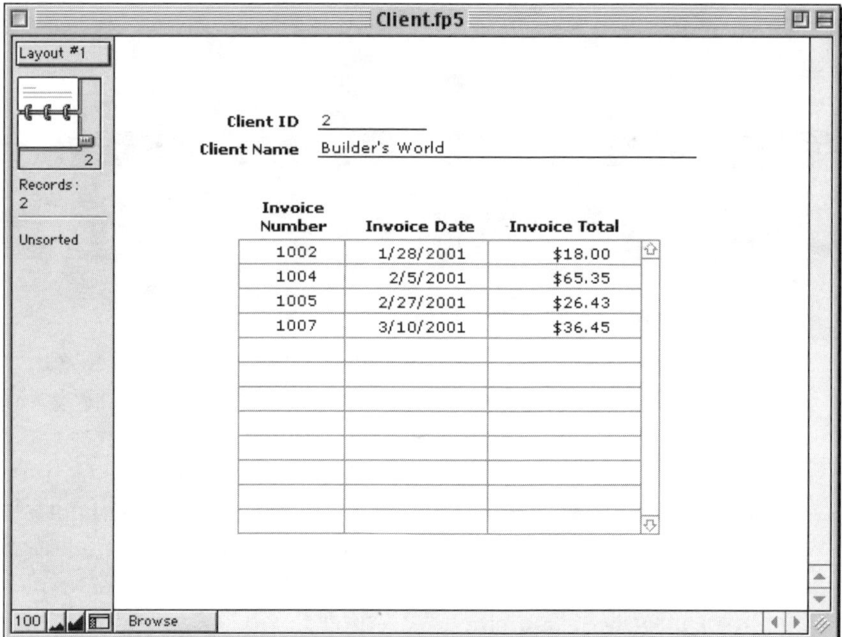

Figure 8.1

Every portal you create must be based on one (and only one) relationship, and this one is no exception. The relationship between these two files, and upon which this portal is based, is shown in Figure 8.2.

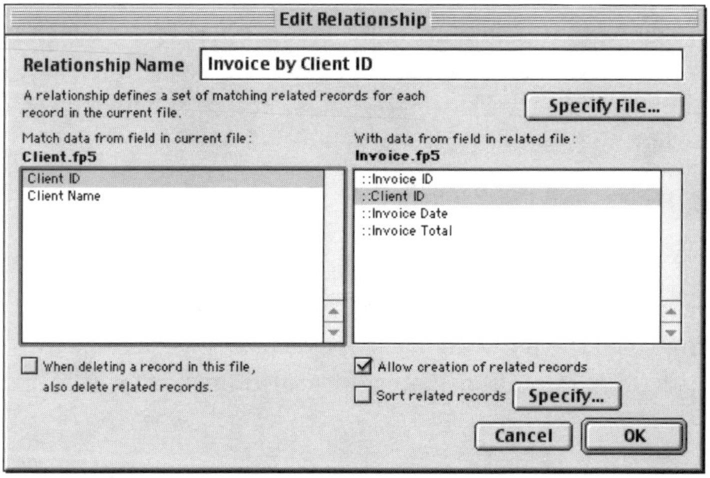

Edit Relationship

Relationship Name: Invoice by Client ID

A relationship defines a set of matching related records for each record in the current file.

Specify File...

Match data from field in current file: **Client.fp5**

Client ID
Client Name

With data from field in related file: **Invoice.fp5**

::Invoice ID
::Client ID
::Invoice Date
::Invoice Total

When deleting a record in this file, also delete related records.

Allow creation of related records

Sort related records Specify...

Cancel OK

Figure 8.2

A good way to understand what records will show up in a portal is to think about it in the following manner. Start by asking yourself, "on the record I'm viewing in the front end of the portal, what is the value of the field on the left-hand side of the relationship upon which the portal is based?" In our example above, it's easy: The Client ID of the current record is 2. The portal will, in essence, do a find (not case sensitive) for all the records in the back-end file where the field on the right-hand side of the relationship equals this value. In this case, it's going to show all the records in the Invoice table where the Client ID equals 2. Figure 8.3 shows a table view of the records in the Invoice.fp5 file. You'll spot immediately that the invoices that show up in the portal in Figure 8.1 are indeed those where the Client ID is 2.

Invoice.fp5

Invoice ID	Client ID	Invoice Date	Invoice Total
1001	1	1/15/2001	$25.98
1002	2	1/28/2001	$18.00
1003	1	2/4/2001	$49.50
1004	2	2/5/2001	$65.35
1005	2	2/27/2001	$26.43
1006	1	3/1/2001	$18.54
1007	2	3/10/2001	$36.45

100 Browse

Figure 8.3

The contents of the portal will change any time the value of the field on the left-hand side of the relationship changes, whether that change is the result of switching records, running a script, or some other user action. It may seem like these are trivial observations to make, but keep them in mind as you read on about more complicated portals.

Now's as good a time as any to digress for a moment and talk about some of the rules for defining relationships and their implications on building portals. First of all, for a relationship to be valid, the field on the right-hand side of the relationship must be indexed. You may know of, or have heard of, a few tricks you can do with invalid relationships, but let's leave those for later. When you build a relationship, FileMaker will try to index the field (if it isn't already indexed), so usually you don't need to think about this.

The index for a field is basically the set of all the unique entries found in that field. So, if you have a field called Status which contains either "Active" or "Inactive" in each record, no matter how many records you have in your table, your index will only have those two unique values. As you've likely discovered, you can perform finds and sorts on indexed fields much quicker than you can on unindexed fields.

So why doesn't FileMaker just index every field? Well, there are a few types of fields that can't be indexed. Specifically, container fields, global fields, summary fields, and calculations that reference related fields or other unindexed fields can't be indexed, and therefore can't be used as the right-hand side of a relationship. They're fine and actually quite useful on the front end (left-hand side) of relationships.

There are two important implications of this for our study of portals. First, when you build a relationship, you're actually building a link to the index of the field rather than to the field itself. This subtle distinction will soon become important when we discuss multivalued keys later in this chapter. Second, if the field on the right-hand side of the relationship is a calculation field, then you can't use the Allow creation of related records option when you define your relationship. This is because when you add a new row to a portal, you're actually adding a record to the related table, and FileMaker ensures referential integrity by automatically setting the value of the field on the right-hand side of the relationship so that it's equal to the value of the field on the left-hand side for the current record. However, just as a user can't manually edit the contents of a calculation field, neither can FileMaker itself, and you'll get an error if you try.

We've noticed over the years of teaching FileMaker that people tend to misconstrue this, so let's end this digression with a recap to make sure there's no confusion. It's fine to use a calculation field on the right side of a relationship, but it must be an indexed calculation. And, if you are using an indexed calculation as the right-hand side, then in any portal you build upon this relationship, you can't allow creation of related records.

The other important implication of the relationship settings to portals is the sort order of the records displayed in a portal. In the absence of any explicit sort order defined by the relationship, related records will appear in their creation order. No amount of manually sorting the records in the related file will change their order, though this is a common misconception. The ability to define a sort order for a relationship, and therefore for a portal, was one of the new features of FileMaker Pro 4.0. In FileMaker 3.0, where portals were first introduced, the workarounds were tedious and fragile, as they involved recreating the related records in the order you wanted them to appear in the portal.

Portal Setup Options

Now that we've covered some of the meaty theoretical issues, let's turn to the more mundane subject of actually setting up portals on your layouts. Even if you've done this a thousand times, we think there are one or two things you might not know, so read on.

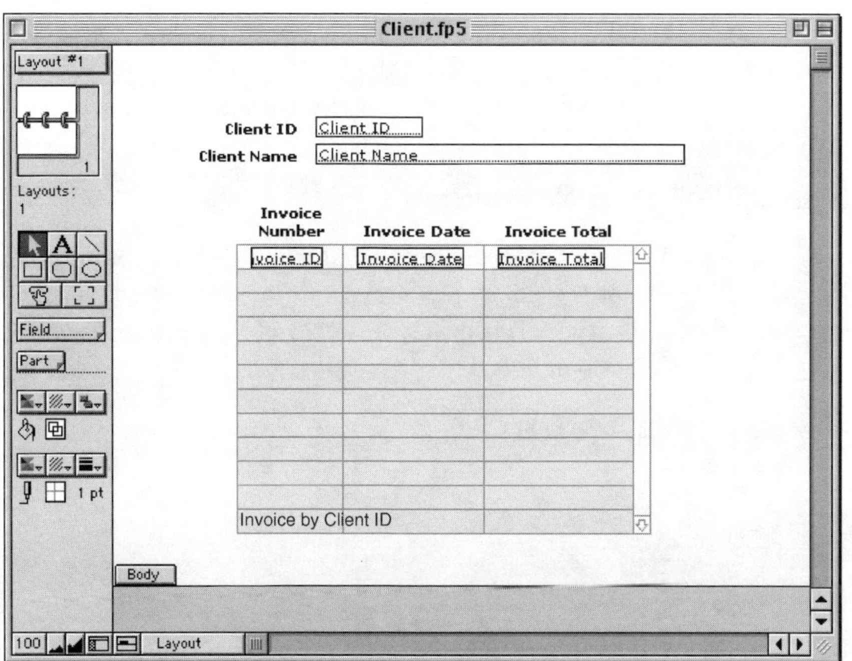

Figure 8.4

When you add a portal to a layout, the name of the relationship upon which the portal is built shows up in the lower left-hand corner of the portal. Any field you add to the portal must be a related field that uses this same relationship. Again, it may sound trivial, but we've often run into people who were confused about which relationship to use (especially when there's more than one into the same file) when adding fields to a portal. Just keep this rule in mind and you'll have no trouble. If your portal doesn't appear to be showing you the information you think it should, and particularly if every row in the portal displays the same data, then the most likely culprit is that the fields in your portal are not using the same relationship as the portal itself.

Be sure that if you duplicate a portal or swap out the relationship that it's built on, you also change the specification of the fields in the portal. It's also easy for the portal relationship and the field relationships to get out of whack when you copy portals from one file to another.

When you built your first portal, you likely discovered that you had to place the fields you wanted to display in the topmost row of the portal. Fields and objects can, however, cross the boundaries of this top line, so it's important to keep the following in mind: It's only the top-leftmost pixel of the object you wish to place in your portal that must be contained in the top row. The other corners don't matter, and can extend outside the borders of the portal.

Deletion of Related Records

Figure 8.5 shows the Portal Setup dialog with which you're probably familiar. Whether or not you choose to alternate the background color (yuck!) or to use a scroll bar (yeah!) is purely a matter of personal preference. The choice to Allow deletion of portal records, however, is important to consider.

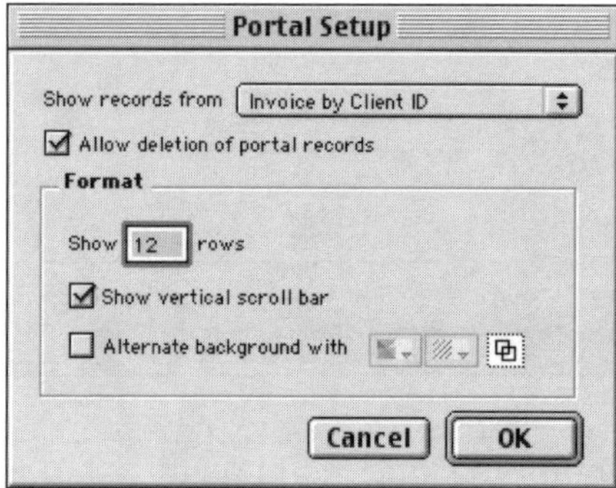

Figure 8.5

If you've checked this option, and a user has her cursor in a field in the portal, and she tries to delete a record (via the menu or keyboard shortcut), the following dialog will appear:

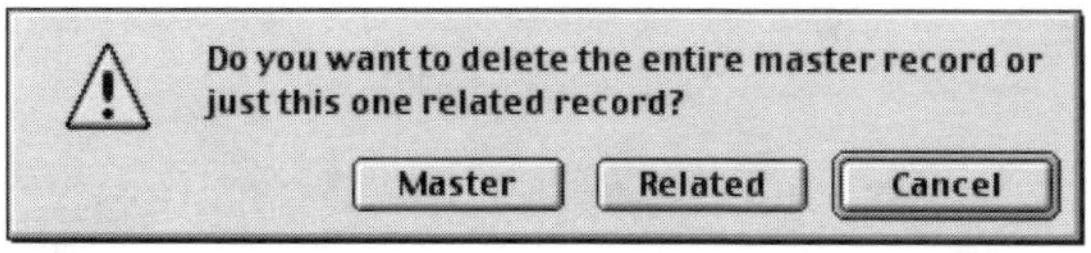

Do you want to delete the entire master record or just this one related record?

Master | Related | Cancel

Figure 8.6

It's possible though, to select a row in a portal without clicking into a field, either by clicking in the free space around the field or by clicking on a field that doesn't allow entry. If the entire portal row is selected and a user tries to delete a record (or hits the backspace key), then the dialog changes a bit to the following:

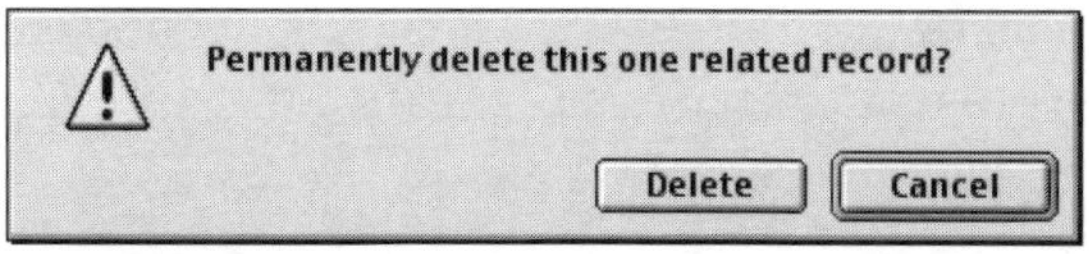

Permanently delete this one related record?

Delete | Cancel

Figure 8.7

This is more just an interesting thing to know about portals than something truly to be wary of, but there's one thing that's vital to know: If you place a button in a portal that tries to run a script to Delete Portal Row, the script will fail unless you've allowed deletion of portal records in the Portal Setup dialog box. Even worse, no error message is automatically shown to the user, and the script continues as if the deletion has taken place.

The important point is that if you want to be able to use the Delete Portal Row script step, then you have to allow deletion of portal rows, which then opens up the possibility of a user manually deleting rows of a portal. Nor can you restrict a user's ability to delete a portal row manually by setting their access privileges. If a user doesn't have the privilege to delete records, then neither can a script delete records. Even if you change menu access to None, the backspace key will delete a portal row if the entire row is selected.

What we recommend in these instances is that you leave the Allow deletion of portal records option unchecked, and instead of writing scripts that use the Delete Portal Row step, have them call subscripts in the related file that perform a Delete Record instead.

Selection Portals

Now that you have the basics under your belt, we'll turn to several examples of different types and functions of portals. The first is what we'll refer to as a selection portal. These are mainly used in place of pop-up lists or menus when you need to give the user more information about the item being selected, or when you simply want to have more control of what happens when the item is selected.

Figure 8.8 shows an ER diagram of the file structure we'll be looking at for this example, and Figure 8.9 shows a layout in Student with a portal into Registration that lists all of the courses for which the given student is registered. The goal of the present exercise is to create a user-friendly way to register a student for additional courses.

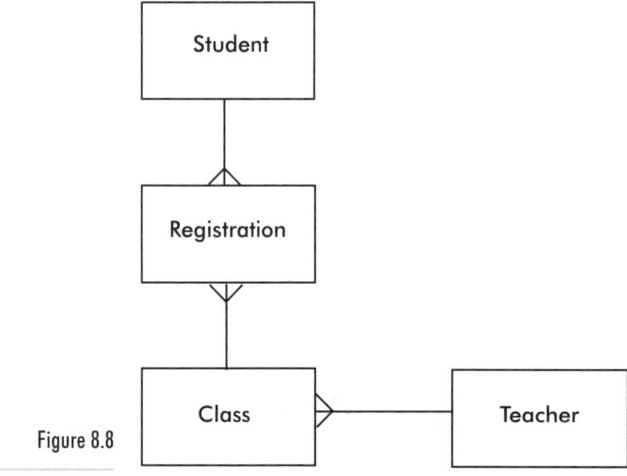

Figure 8.8

The first thought you might have is to simply allow creation of related records in the portal and let the user select the desired course ID from a pop-up list built from the Class table. This would indeed work, but there are at least a couple of drawbacks to this method you should be aware of. First, when creating value lists using the contents of a file, you're limited to displaying at most two fields from that table. You can circumvent this limitation by using a calculation to append multiple fields together so you can see them in the value list, but this isn't a great solution if you have a lot of data." In this case, a pop-up list that showed the Course ID and Course Name

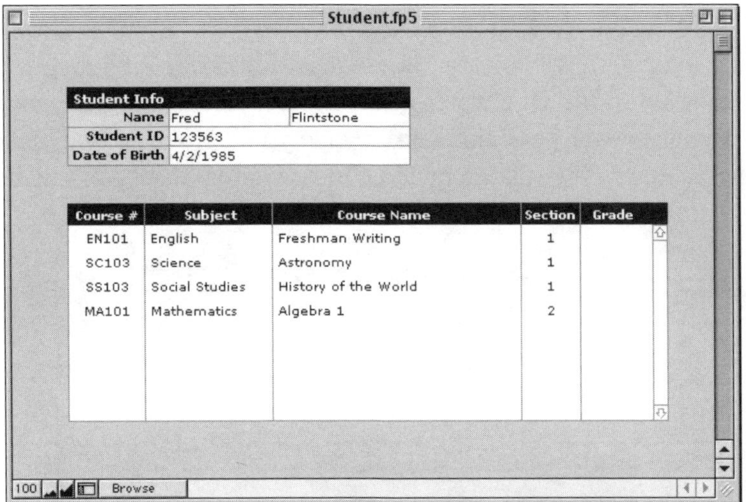

Figure 8.9

wouldn't be sufficient to allow a user to easily distinguish between multiple sections of the same course. Second, it would be difficult to effectively validate the user's selection. For instance, you might want to make sure a student met certain course prerequisites or didn't have a scheduling conflict before you allowed the course to be added. Using a pop-up list, something as simple as ensuring a student isn't double-registered for a course is mildly difficult. While you can indeed add validation to the Registration database to check if the combination of Student ID and Course ID already exists, validation isn't performed until after the new record has been added to the database. If a record doesn't pass validation, you can easily end up with blank (or worse, semiblank) records that can come back to haunt you later.

In this case, a much better interface is a selection portal. What we essentially want is a portal from Student into Class that shows all of the courses in the entire course catalog. As with any portal, such a selection portal needs to be based on a relationship, but as you can see from the ER diagram, there's no structural relationship between Student and Class. To build this portal, therefore, you'll need to build what's commonly referred to as a constant relationship. Constant relationships are not structural (that is, they aren't something that you'd ever model on your ER diagram), but rather are utilitarian.

To build a constant relationship, you start by creating a calculation field in each file that is simply equal to 1, and then create a relationship matching these fields. Figure 8.10 shows the calculation for Constant in the Student table, and Figure 8.11 shows the relationship dialog for the new relationship, Class by Constant. One word of caution: Be careful to never enable cascading delete in a constant relationship, or else you'll probably end up deleting every record in the related table sooner or later. Trust us — it's not fun.

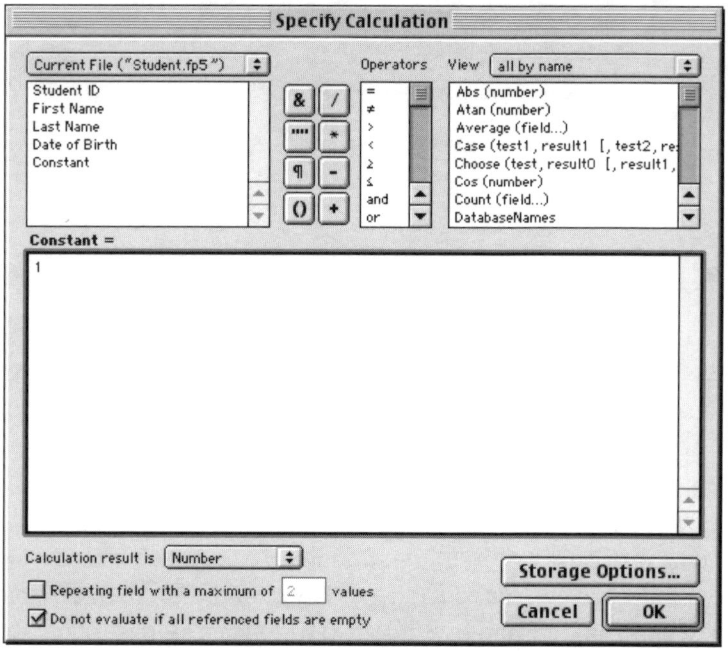

Figure 8.10

Many people prefer to create their constant fields as regular number fields with an auto-entered calculation of 1. In some cases, it's preferable to have the constant be a number field instead of a a calculation. When it's a number field, there's a remote possibility that the data could somehow be changed to something other than a 1. For this reason, we generally prefer to use constants that are calculations.

Constant relationships allow you to create a link between any two tables in a solution, regardless of the structural distance of the two tables. They come in handy for moving variables around and, of course, for building selection portals.

In Figure 8.12, we've added a selection portal built on a constant relationship to the bottom of the Student layout. In real life, we probably would have put the selection portal on its own layout and would have placed a button on the Student layout to get there, but for our purposes here, it's easier to show what's happening if everything is on the same layout.

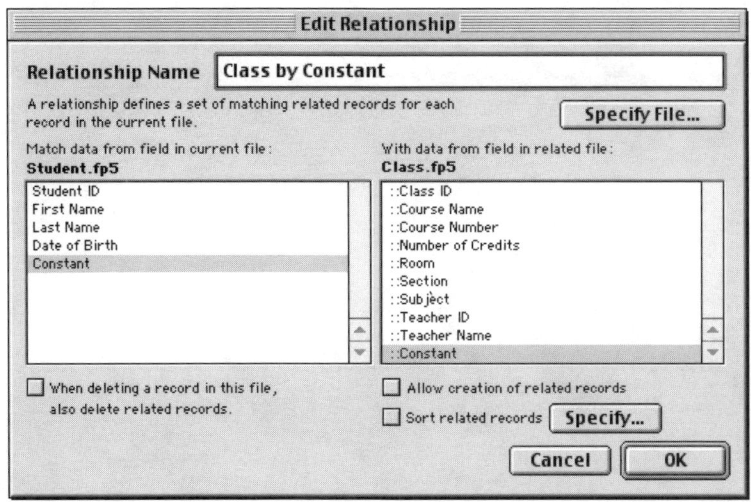

Figure 8.11

The contents of the selection portal will remain the same, no matter what student record you're viewing. This is because the front end of the relationship, the Constant field built above, is the same for every record in the Student database. And any new courses added to the Class table automatically show up in the selection portal. You can include in your selection portal whatever fields make it easy and intuitive for a user to identify the record they're looking for.

With the portal in placc, you'll want to put an invisible button over the entire portal row, so that a user can simply click whatever row he wants and have it added to the student's roster. Or, if you prefer, you can simply select all of the fields in the portal and designate these as your button. This works well when the fields in the portal are right next to one another, and saves you the creation of one more object. However, it can make resizing or changing the appearance of an individual field difficult, so we usually prefer to use an invisible button.

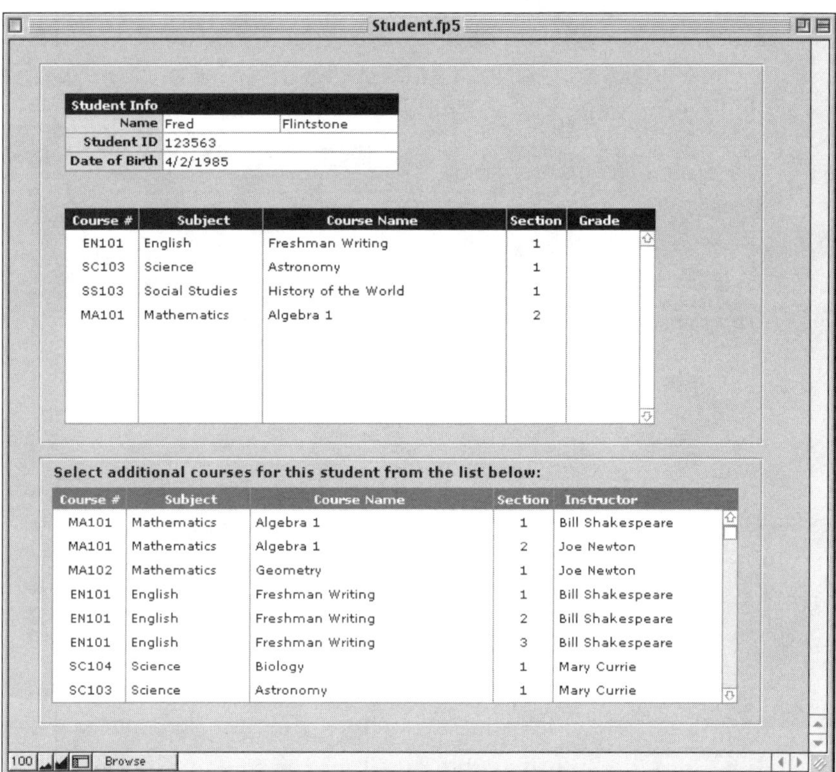

Figure 8.12

When writing a script like this, we find it helpful to start by stating the essential functionality in prose. Something like this: "When a user clicks this button, we need to grab the Course ID of the item they've clicked on, and we need to remember the Student ID of the current student. Then we need to create a new record in the Registration table and populate it with these two pieces of information. We should make sure the user ends up back in the Student table, and give them some sort of dialog confirming the record has been successfully added." The important thing is to get the basic script working, and then you can go back and add validation or error trapping as needed. Below is the necessary script in the Student table, as well as the subscript it calls in the Registration table.

Select additional class (in the Student table)

```
Set Field [gClass ID, Class by Constant::Class ID]
Set Field [gStudent ID, Student ID]
Perform Script [Sub-scripts, External: "Registration.fp5"]
```

```
    Sub: create new registration record
Show Message ["The course you selected has been added."]
```

Sub: create new registration record (in the Registration table)

```
New Record/Request
Set Field [Student ID, Student by Student ID::gStudent ID]
Set Field [Class ID, Student by Student ID::gClass ID]
```

It's quite a simple script, actually. It begins by setting a global field called gClass ID equal to the Class ID of the course the user has selected. As long as the portal is still active, the script knows what row the user clicked and the ID of that row. This value is put into a global field so it can be easily retrieved later. Remember, global fields are nothing more than variables. Similarly, the Student ID of the current record is put into a global gStudent ID field.

Next, the script calls the Sub: Create New Registration Record script in the Registration table. This subscript creates a new record and then sets the Student ID and Course ID to the values in the two global fields set before in the Student file. There are a couple of observations we should make about this. First, it doesn't matter what relationship is used from Registration into Student, since all you're grabbing through it are global fields. We happen to be using a relationship called Student by Student ID, but a constant relationship would have worked just as well. In fact, the relationship you use doesn't even have to be a valid one! Second, there's no reason we couldn't have created the gStudent ID and gClass ID fields in the Registration table instead of the Student table. Had we done this, we simply would have needed to change the Set Field steps in the first script to set related fields. It's really a matter of personal preference and what makes the most intuitive sense.

Finally, since the Perform External Script step in the first script is not the last line of the script, the rest of the steps will be performed once the subscript is completed. This ensures that the user ends up back in the Student table and not stranded on some layout in Registration.

We've seen people write scripts like this with several copy/paste functions, and we'd like to lobby against you doing it this way. The problem is that copy and paste require that the fields you're copying from and pasting into are on the active layout. If they aren't, the scripts don't work. Your script becomes quite fragile and will stop working if you remove the fields. Plus, it's a more complicated script to write and slower to execute. There are very few cases where a Set Field can't be used in place of copy/paste.

Hopefully you can start to see the advantages of the selection portal over the simple pop-up list. While it takes up a lot of real estate on the layout, it conveys much more information to the user and gives you as the programmer greater control over the functionality. To drive this point home, let's add validation to the script to prevent a user from registering a student to a class more than once. The primary key of the Registration table is a compound primary key that consists of the Student ID and Class ID. To ensure the integrity of our data, this combination must be unique.

One thought you might have is to loop through all of a student's records in Registration during the Create Record subscript, looking for a record that matches the values in the two global fields. If no match was found, the new record could be safely created. Another thought you might have would be to perform a find that looks for records with the values in the two global fields in the Registration table. No records found would mean that the combination under consideration was unique and could be added without problem. Again, this would work — probably better than the looping idea, in fact — but there's a more elegant and simple solution that we'll show you here.

We discussed this technique in Chapter 2, but let's review it again here. To begin, you'll need a new calculation field in Registration that concatenates Student ID and Class ID. We'll call this field Student\Class and give it the following definition:

```
Student ID & "-" & Class ID
```

We use the dash as a separator mostly out of habit. You could use a space or a pipe character or another delimiter as long as it doesn't confuse the meaning. For example, using a number as delimiter between numbers would confuse the meaning of the result.

Since there's no way to add validation to a calculation field, you need to be a bit more clever. Back in the Student table, you'll create another calculation field that concatenates the gStudent ID and gClass ID fields. We'll call this field gStudent\gClass and give it the following definition:

```
gStudent ID & "-" & gClass ID
```

Again, it doesn't matter what you use as a separator, but it does need to be consistent with what was used in the field in Registration.

Next, a new relationship is created from Student to Registration, matching the two fields just defined; the relationship dialog is shown in Figure 8.13.

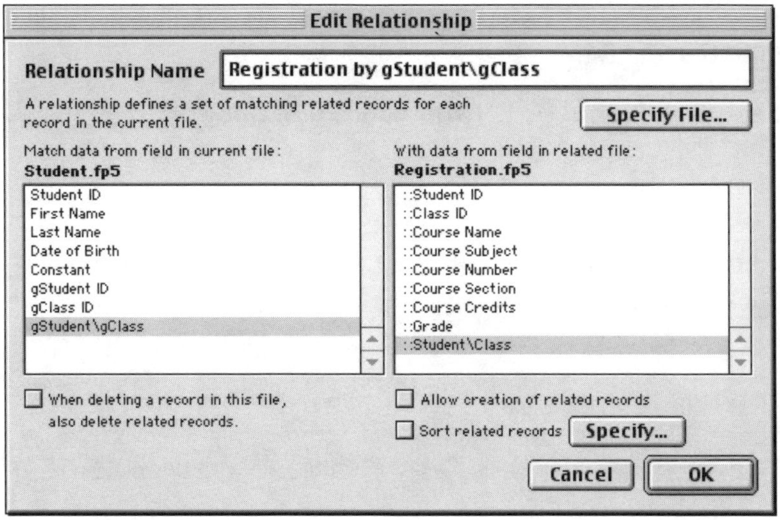

Figure 8.13

Once gStudent ID and gClass ID have been given values in the first part of the selection script, this relationship can be used to see whether the selected pair already exists in the Registration file. There are two ways to determine this. The first would be to use the Count function to count the number of related records. If it returns 0, the pair is unique; if it returns anything higher, it's been used before. The other way, which we think is both faster and a trifle more elegant, would be to use the IsValid function. IsValid returns a 0 if a relationship isn't valid (i.e., has no related records) and a 1 if it is. A quick note of caution when using the Count function: Be sure that the field you choose to count in the related file won't possibly contain nulls, as Count doesn't actually count the number of related records but rather the number of records that have data in the selected field. For that reason, whenever we use the Count function, we always count something like the key field or a constant field, which are guaranteed to never be empty.

Below is the first half of the selection script again, with the validation for uniqueness added. It's very fast, and also happens before a new record is added to Registration, both of which make this our favorite way to check for uniqueness of a compound primary key. Note that we've added an Exit Record/Request step before doing our validation check. We've found over the years that when you set global fields that are then used in relationships, you can sometimes get some strange behavior if the record isn't committed first. Exit Record/Request is a very innocuous script step that solves many problems like this. It's the equivalent of clicking on the background of your layout or hitting the Enter key.

Select additional class (with validation added)

```
Set Field [gClass ID, Class by Constant::Class ID]
Set Field [gStudent ID, Student ID]
Exit Record/Request
If [IsValid (Registration by gStudent\gClass::Student\Class)]
Show Message ["This student is already registered for this course. Please
              select another."]
Else
Perform Script [Sub-scripts, External: "Registration.fp5"]
     Sub: create new registration record
Show Message ["The course you selected has been added."]
End If
```

Selection Portal Variation

There's a variation on the basic selection portal that we've used countless times over the years. It can be used most any time you have a portal that starts to get overcrowded with fields. For this example, there are just two tables, Event and Attendee, and there's a one-to-many relationship between them. There's a portal from Event into Attendee for adding and editing attendee data, shown in Figure 8.14.

The problem with this portal is that the amount of information you'd like to display won't fit, and there is no way (unfortunately) to have a horizontal scroll bar in your portal! The portal in Figure 8.14 only contains the basic attendee data. There's clearly not enough room for other fields from the Attendee table such phone, fax, and e-mail address. Additionally, it isn't a very nice interface for users to enter or edit data.

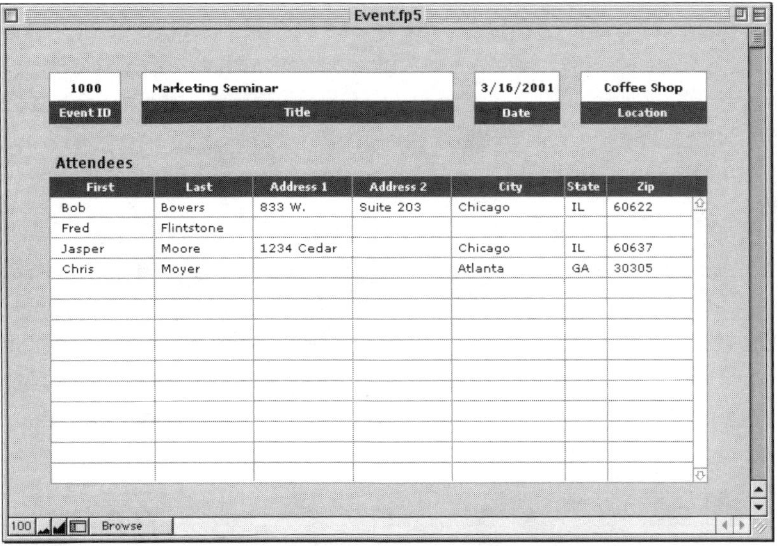

Figure 8.14

As a better alternative, we suggest shrinking the portal until it only shows the very minimum of information and putting a button on the portal to select one attendee at a time. Figure 8.15 shows what you might end up with.

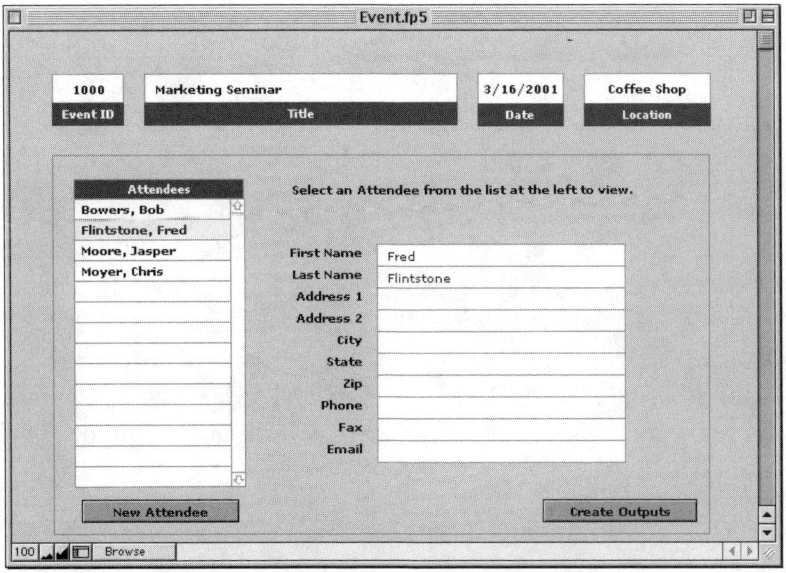

Figure 8.15

The portal on the left-hand side of the layout is no longer used for data entry; it's a selection tool. When you click a row in that portal, a script sets a number field called Selected Attendee ID equal to the ID of the particular person you've clicked on. All the fields on the right side of the layout are related fields through a one-to-one relationship from Selected Attendee ID to Attendee ID.

It will clarify things a bit to look at the relationships in the Event table; they're shown in Figure 8.16. The first relationship is the structural one, and is used by the portal to display all of the attendees related to this particular event. The second relationship is a utility relationship, and is used to display information about the particular attendee whose ID has been placed in Selected Attendee ID.

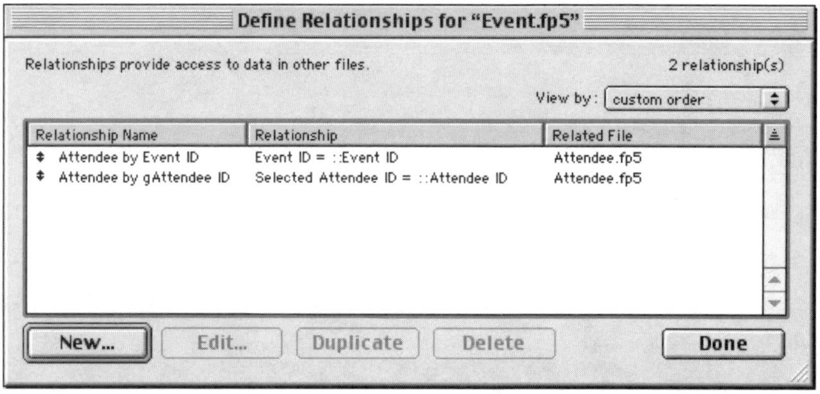

Define Relationships for "Event.fp5"

Relationships provide access to data in other files.

2 relationship(s)

View by: custom order

Relationship Name	Relationship	Related File
Attendee by Event ID	Event ID = ::Event ID	Attendee.fp5
Attendee by gAttendee ID	Selected Attendee ID = ::Attendee ID	Attendee.fp5

New... Edit... Duplicate Delete Done

Figure 8.16

The new layout allows you to display (and edit) a much richer set of information about a particular attendee without having to navigate over to the Attendee file itself. And you get more control over addition of new attendees than you would simply by letting users type in the last row of the portal. Imagine, for instance, that you wanted to ensure that new attendees weren't added to events that had already happened or had been cancelled. You could easily test for this early in a Create New Attendee script by checking the event date and status before proceeding.

You may be wondering why the Selected Attendee ID field is a number field rather than a global field. It can work as a global field, but then you will have problems with navigation between records. Think about what would happen if it were a global. When you switch from record to record, the content in the portal on the left changes because the Event ID is different for each record. But the global Selected Attendee ID wouldn't change. The same detail record would still be displayed, which would be quite confusing. By storing the Selected Attendee ID in a number field in each event record, you also ensure that when you return to an event record, the selection is automatically "restored." Be aware, however, that in a multiuser environment, if two or more people are working on the same event record, you might have some troubles. They couldn't each have different attendees selected, as they could if Selected Attendee ID were a global field (since globals, you'll recall, are local to individual users).

The bottom line is that this use of a portal as a selection tool for viewing more information about a particular item in the portal is a good tool to have at your disposal. It's not the best solution in every case, but quite often can be employed to reduce layout clutter and add control.

Portal Filters

We'll return to the student registration system to begin a discussion of portal filters. First, a definition: A *portal filter* is a tool which allows a user to narrow down the number of records displayed in a portal, so as to make it easier to find a particular item or set of items. The number of uses you can find for portal filters is virtually limitless. We'll start by looking at an example of a simple filter, and then work our way up to some more complicated flavors of filters. Once you have the concept down, you'll undoubtedly find dozens of uses in your solutions for portal filters.

Certain types of portals are more likely candidates for filters than others. In general, they'll be portals that contain a potentially large number of items that can be grouped into some sort of logical subcategories. For instance, if you had a portal from a Customer database into an Invoice database, you might have dozens or hundreds of related items, all of which have a Status field that contains either "Paid" or "Not Paid." In this case, it might be useful to filter the portal by status.

Similarly, the selection portal that we built earlier to display all available classes will probably contain quite a large number of items. Let's look first at how that portal can be filtered by subject.

Begin by creating a global text field called gSubject in the Student database. This field will contain the filter instructions. Add it to the layout above the selection portal, and format it as a pop-up menu using a value list built from the Subject field of the Class database. The value list definition is shown in Figure 8.17. The values could be hard-coded instead, but basing it on the contents of the subject field ensures that if ever a new subject is added, the pop-up menu will contain it automatically.

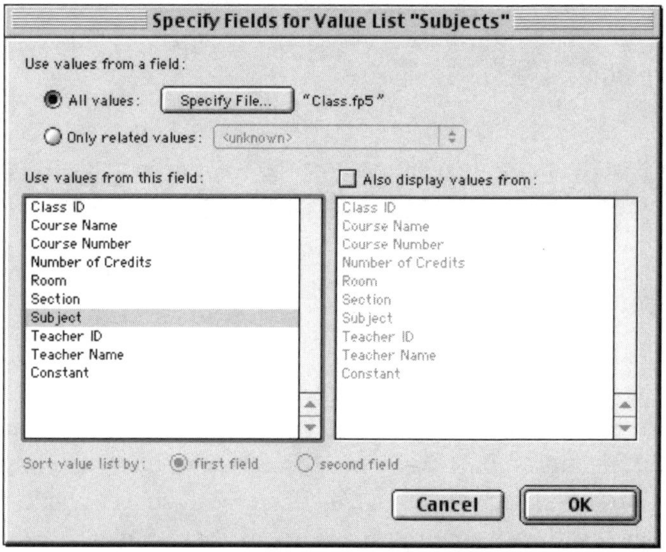

Specify Fields for Value List "Subjects"

Use values from a field:
All values: Specify File... "Class.fp5"
Only related values: <unknown>
Use values from this field:
Class ID
Course Name
Course Number
Number of Credits
Room
Section
Subject
Teacher ID
Teacher Name
Constant
Also display values from:
Class ID
Course Name
Course Number
Number of Credits
Room
Section
Subject
Teacher ID
Teacher Name
Constant
Sort value list by: first field second field
Cancel OK

Figure 8.17

Again, this field, gSubject, will allow the user to select which subcategory of the Class database to display in the portal. Completing the filter requires only a small adjustment to the relationship definition. Instead of a constant match, the classes you want displayed are those where the Subject matches the user's choice for gSubject.

The revised relationship is shown in Figure 8.18. Note that a new relationship hasn't been created. The existing one was revised and renamed, which means that you don't need to edit the layout or selection script at all.

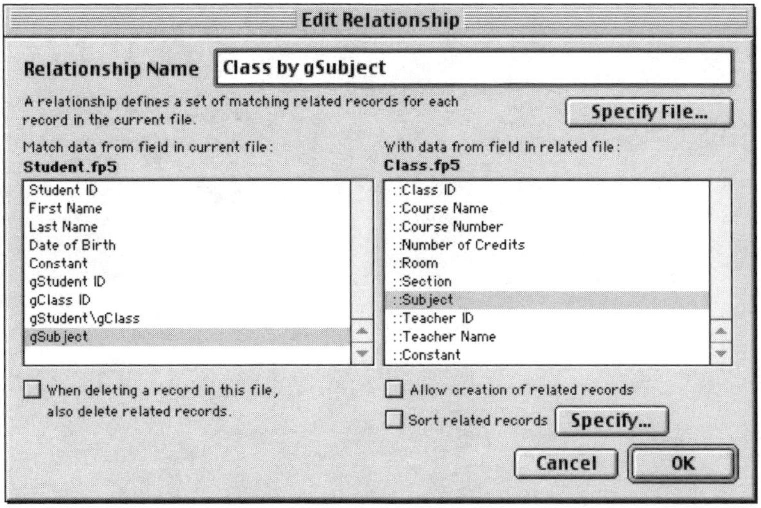

Edit Relationship

Relationship Name: Class by gSubject

A relationship defines a set of matching related records for each record in the current file.

Specify File...

Match data from field in current file: **Student.fp5**

Student ID
First Name
Last Name
Date of Birth
Constant
gStudent ID
gClass ID
gStudent\gClass
gSubject

With data from field in related file: **Class.fp5**

::Class ID
::Course Name
::Course Number
::Number of Credits
::Room
::Section
::Subject
::Teacher ID
::Teacher Name
::Constant

When deleting a record in this file, also delete related records.

Allow creation of related records

Sort related records Specify...

Cancel OK

Figure 8.18

If gSubject is left empty, the portal won't show any records. But, as soon as you select something like Science, the portal will display only those classes where the subject is Science, as illustrated in Figure 8.19.

That's it. The portal filter is now complete, and the selection script built earlier still works. Notice also that since the contents of the portal display one and only one subject, it's redundant to have the Subject field display in the portal. It can be taken out to free up space for another field.

There's no reason, by the way, that filters can't be used on portals other than selection portals. Imagine, for instance, that the first portal we looked at (the one that shows all of the classes a student is registered for) contained data for multiple years or semesters. A filter might be added to display only one time period at a time. The key thing to remember is that filters work best when the contents of the portal can be categorized into meaningful, discrete subgroups.

Let's look now at some variations that can add even more control and flexibility to your portals.

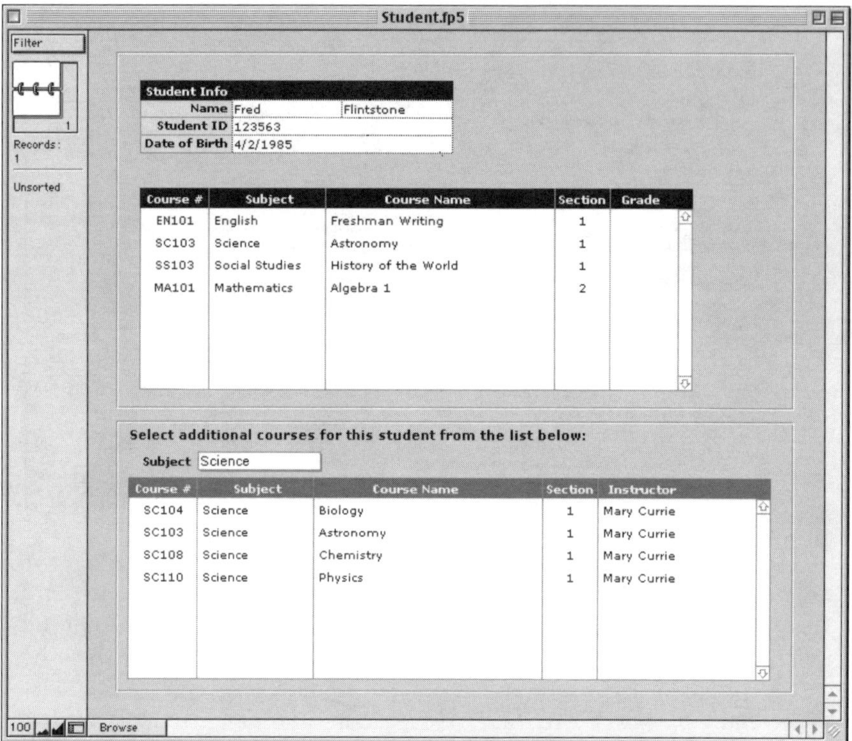

Figure 8.19

First, how can you give the user the ability to see either all of the courses (like before), or only those in a selected subject? One solution might be to have two selection portals, but we hope you'll agree with us that this would not only be a maintenance hassle but that it's also not very elegant or extensible. A far better solution would be to have the existing portal do double duty. It means a bit more work on our part as developers but results in a much cleaner, easier to use interface.

What we're trying to do, in essence, is to have the portal do an "or" search of the Class database. It might be helpful to think about it this way — there are two conditions under which a record from Class should be displayed in the portal: 1) if the user sets gSubject to the Subject of the record, and 2) if the user indicates that they would like to see all records. You need, of course, to establish exactly how the user will indicate the latter. If the Subject value list had been built manually, you could simply add another option for All Subjects to the bottom of the list. Since it's not, though, the best solution is to have a small button next to the pop-up menu that says something like Show All. When clicked, it runs a very simple script that sets gSubject to All Subjects.

There is, of course, no class whose subject is All Subjects, so unless you do something else, the portal will be empty when gSubject says All Subjects. To solve this, you need to modify the back end of the relationship. Over in the Class table, create a new calculation field (with text result) called Subject Match with the following definition:

```
Subject & "¶" & "All Subjects"
```

For each record in the Class table, this field will contain the contents of the subject field, a carriage return, and the literal text string "All Subjects." On a record where the Subject was Science, for instance, the Subject Match field would contain:

Science
All Subjects

What should be obvious are that these are the two conditions established a moment ago for deciding whether a record should be displayed in the portal. You can finish the exercise now simply by changing the relationship the portal is based on, so that it uses Subject Match rather than Subject on the right side. The revised relationship dialog is shown in Figure 8.20.

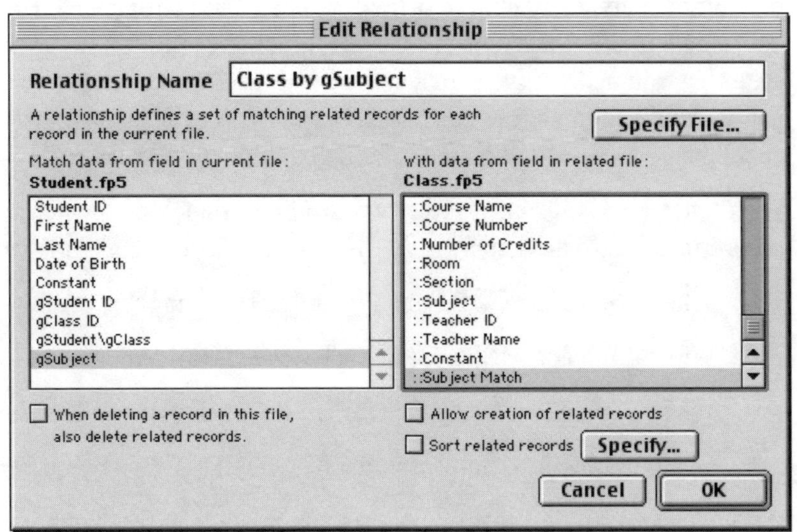

Figure 8.20

Okay, but why does this work? To understand this, you might need to adjust your thinking about how portals work. Remember at the beginning of the chapter when we said that the relationship was actually built on the index of a field rather than the field itself? Well, the carriage return in the Subject Match calculation causes the two values it separates to be indexed separately. It becomes what's called a *multivalued key*. Believe us when we say these are quite useful. It might help to understand this if you go back to our earlier suggestion that you think of a portal as displaying the results of a find. Here, it's like you're performing a find in Subject Match for the value that gSubject is set to. If gSubject is set to something like Science, those records that contain "Science" in their index will be displayed. When gSubject is "All Subjects," those records that contain "All Subjects" in their index (which is all of them!) will be displayed.

Multiple Portal Filters

Another variation on the basic portal filter is to add multiple filters. Again, you gain control and flexibility for the user at the cost of a little work by the developer. For this example, imagine that you wanted users not only to be able to filter classes by Subject, but also by Teacher. It starts simply enough by providing the user with another pop-up menu where he can select an instructor. The new global text field will be called gTeacher ID, and its value list will be built off the contents of the Teacher table. It's important in this case that you use both the Teacher ID and the Teacher Name for the value list, as you'll see in a few moments. Similar to the Subject filter, users will also be able to select all instructors by clicking a button.

With two filters, there are actually four conditions under which you'll want a record in Class to be displayed in the portal. These are as follows:

- When gSubject = "All Subjects" and gTeacher ID = "All"
- When gSubject = Subject and gTeacher ID = "All"
- When gSubject = "All Subjects" and gTeacher ID = Teacher ID
- When gSubject = Subject and gTeacher ID = Teacher ID

If you've ever studied set theory this will make intuitive sense. When you have a collection of two things (A and B), there are four possible subsets of the collection: AB, A, B, and the null set. In fact, any set with n elements will have 2^n subsets.

Before we continue, it's important to know why we're using Teacher ID here rather than Teacher Name. It comes down to the fact that in the Class database, Teacher ID is indexed and Teacher Name isn't; it's just an unstored calculation. In a moment we'll need to redefine the calculation on the right side of the relationship again so that it reflects the four conditions above, but as always, the right side of a relationship needs to be indexable.

Let's first deal with the left side of the relationship. Since you can only designate one match field on each side of a relationship, and since we now want two criteria selected by the user to be the basis for the portal, you're going to need to create a new calculation field in Student that concatenates the two selections the user has made. We'll call this field cClass Filter and define it as follows:

```
gSubject &"-" & gTeacher ID
```

As before, the choice of a delimiter is not important, but be sure you're consistent in your use on both sides of the relationship.

On the right side of the relationship, the Subject Match field needs to be edited to include the four conditions for display, all separated by returns so they're indexed separately. The order in which the conditions appear is irrelevant. The new definition for this field will be as follows:

```
"All Subjects-All¶" &
Subject & "-All¶" &
"All Subjects-" & Teacher ID &"¶" &
Subject &"-" & Teacher ID
```

Finally, the relationship needs to be modified yet again, this time changing the left side to be the new cClass Filter field, as shown in Figure 8.21.

By editing the existing relationship rather than creating a new one, you ensure that you don't have to respecify all of the fields in the portal or edit any scripts that may use Set Fields through that relationship. In general, it's good practice to proceed as we did here, first adding one filter, then the other. This way, if something doesn't quite work, it will be easier to troubleshoot. Always get the basics working first, then go back and add new functionality or validation, testing as you go. It's very rare indeed that you'll design a

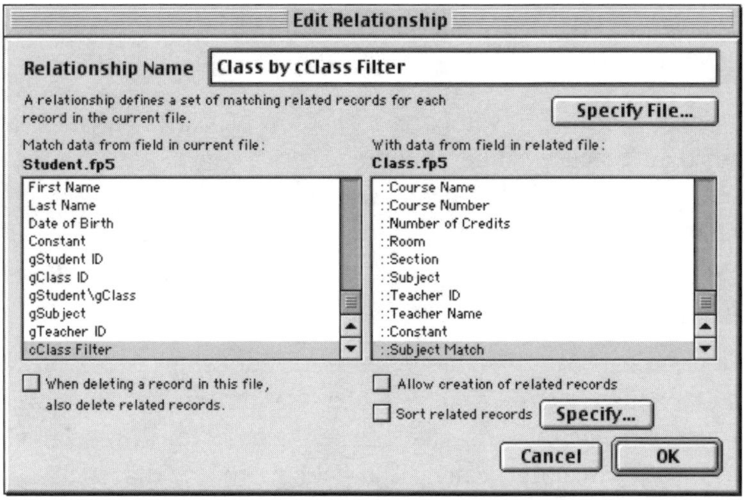

Figure 8.21

complicated layout or write a complicated script in a single pass, nor should this be your goal.

Once you've mastered adding a second filter to a portal, adding a third or fourth is no problem. Keep in mind, though, that with four filters there will be 16 conditions under which a record should be displayed, so the calculation on the right side of your relationship will get a bit complicated!

Type-Ahead Portals

There's one other variation on the basic portal filter that we'll cover here, and that's what's commonly referred to as a type-ahead portal. It's different than the standard portal filter in that we're not interested in broad subsections of the related file (like those defined by Subject in our earlier example), but rather in honing in on a particular record based on information supplied by the user. In this way, it behaves much like a find in the related file.

The most common use we've discovered for the type-ahead portal is to filter a large file of names. The concept is fairly simple. If the user types an "R" into the filter field, you want the portal to display only those people whose last names begin with "R." And if the user types in "Ro," the portal should discriminate further and only display those people whose names begin with "Ro." And so on.

In this example, you'll turn a simple selection portal for assigning sales reps to an order into a type-ahead portal. There is a one-to-many relationship from the SalesRep table to Order, and you'll be doing all of your layout work in the Order table.

The scenario for the example is as follows. Your client is concerned because when new orders are created, users sometimes forget to populate the Sales Rep field, and there have been complaints that it's hard to find the sales rep to assign using the existing pop-up list. Your proposed solution is to make a special layout for assigning the sales rep, and to make navigation to this layout part of the routine for creating a new order. So far, you've got your navigation scripts working and a layout built that looks something like Figure 8.22. The portal is built on a constant relationship from Order to SalesRep (and therefore lists all sales reps), and is defined to sort alphabetically.

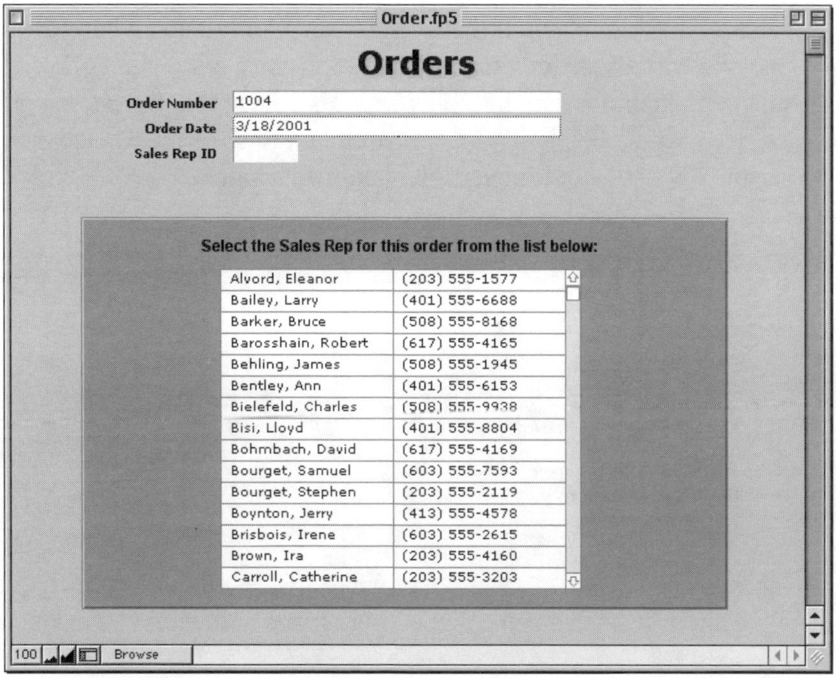

Figure 8.22

Some of the key benefits of the selection portal over a pop-up list, you'll recall, are the ability to display multiple pieces of information (like the phone number here), and the control you gain by scripting the actual selection. One of the drawbacks, however, is that in a pop-up list you can type a few letters and the list will jump to the items that begin with those letters. In a constant portal, on the other hand, you're forced to scroll until you find the item you want. If the Sales Reps could be divided by region or something like that, you might consider building a simple filter. Since they're not, a type-ahead filter is the best tool to reduce or eliminate scrolling.

Just as with the basic filter, you need to start with the creation of a global text field in the front-end table; we'll call it gNameFilter. This will eventually become the new left side of the relationship, but before doing this, let's do some work on the back end. Think a moment about the conditions under which a record should be displayed in the portal. When a user types one or more letters into gNameFilter, you want the records where the last name begins with these letters to display. You can't just match gNameFilter to the name field in SalesRep, as only records whose index contains gNameFilter exactly would be displayed. So, you need to construct a calculation that will explicitly list all of the possible values for matches.

```
cFilter Match = Left(Name LF, 1) & "¶" &
Left(Name LF, 2) & "¶" &
Left(Name LF, 3) & "¶" &
Left(Name LF, 4) & "¶" &
Left(Name LF, 5) & "¶" &
Left(Name LF, 6) & "¶" &
Left(Name LF, 7) & "¶" &
Left(Name LF, 8) & "¶" &
Name LF & "¶" &
"-ALL-"
```

It helps to look at an example of what this results in rather than try to explain it. If a sales rep's name is "Richard Sullivan," the calculation will contain:

```
S
Su
Sul
Sull
Sulli
```

```
Sulliv
Sulliva
Sullivan
Sullivan, Richard
-ALL-
```

Do you see how this works? What's listed here are all the conditions under which this record will appear in the portal. If the user types "S" (or "s" — relationships aren't case sensitive) into gNameFilter, this record will show up. If the user types "Sul" it will also show up. But if gNameFilter contains "Sal," it won't. You'll notice that in addition to the explicit first eight characters of the name (you can, of course, have more or less), we've added the entire Name LF field and the literal string "-ALL-." The latter allows you to still be able to list every SalesRep by setting gNameFilter to "-ALL-." The dashes simply help avoid confusion in the event the user has typed "All" into gNameFilter in hopes of seeing all the Allens, Allerbys, Allergists, and so on.

With the calculation created, all that's left to complete the solution is to modify the relationship from Order to SalesReps, as shown in Figure 8.23.

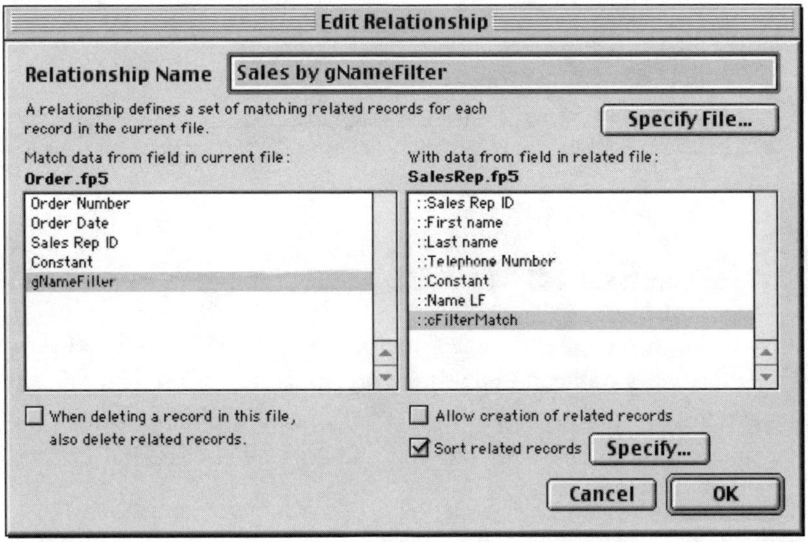

Figure 8.23

The finished layout is shown in Figure 8.24. However, there is one important thing to note still. The contents of the portal won't change as the user is typing. They must first exit the field, either by hitting the Enter key, tabbing to another field, or clicking somewhere on the background of the layout. The

Search button shown in Figure 8.24 isn't really a button at all. It's simply a colored rectangle with some text on it, designed to get the user to click out of the field so the portal can refresh. The Show All button does actually run a script. It sets gNameFilter to "-ALL-" and then runs Exit Record/Request.

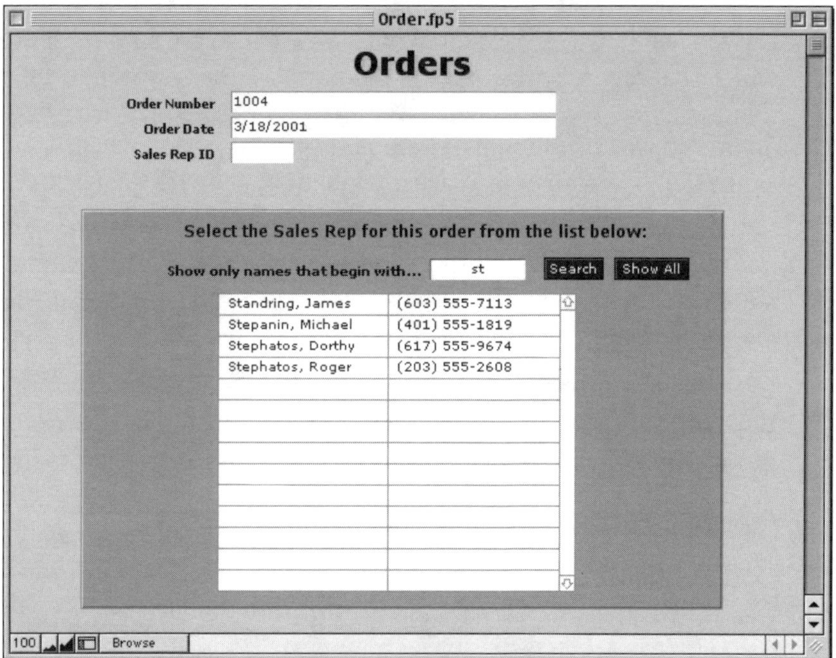

Figure 8.24

Highlighting Portal Rows

Now that we've spent some time building different types of portals, let's turn to some easy bells and whistles you can add to almost any portal. The first is the ability to highlight a selected portal row. We'll begin with highlighting a single row and then continue with an example of highlighting multiple rows.

For the first example in this section, we're going to return to the earlier example involving events and attendees. Recall that we built a selection portal for getting more information about a particular attendee. The goal of the current example will be to expand on that solution by having the selected attendee's name be highlighted in the portal.

Anytime you want to add a highlight (or other graphic element, like a check mark) to a portal, you need three things:

- A field to hold the ID of the selected record.
- A global container field that contains the graphic element.
- A calculation field that determines whether or not the graphic element should be displayed for any given record.

There's a certain amount of flexibility you have as to where the first two of these fields live. In many cases, you'll build them in the back-end table, but not always. The third field, the calculation, must live in the back-end table, as that's the field you'll end up displaying in the portal. The first field will sometimes be a global field and other times be a text or number field, depending on the situation.

In the previous exercise using these files, a field was created in Event called Selected Attendee ID to hold the ID of the selected record. So the only new fields needed now are for the second and third required elements. We'll create both of them in the back end, the Attendee file. The first will be called gHighlight; it's a global container field. This field must be populated with the graphic element that you want displayed. In the case of a simple highlight, the easiest way to do this is to go into Layout mode and draw a small yellow or light gray rectangle (without a border). Then, select the rectangle and cut or copy it to the clipboard. Return to Browse mode, click into the gHighlight field, and paste in the rectangle. Don't worry about the size of the rectangle; you can deal with that later on. The mistake many people make at this stage is that they simply go into Layout mode and give the gHighlight field a background color. Remember, you're trying to put a graphic object in the field itself, rather than merely changing the field's appearance on the current layout.

The other field you need will be called cHighlight (a calculation with container result), and it will have the following formula:

```
Case(Attendee ID = Event by Event ID::Selected Attendee ID, gHighlight)
```

What this says is that if the Attendee ID of the current record is the same as the Selected Attendee ID for this event, then result in gHighlight; else don't. To illustrate, look at Figure 8.25, which shows the contents of pertinent fields from Attendee when Selected Attendee ID in Event contains 2.

Naturally, the contents of cHighlight will change depending on the value of Selected Attendee ID.

Attendee.fp5

Event ID	Attendee ID	Last Name	First Name	gHighlight	cHighlight
1000	1	Bowers	Bob		
1000	2	Moyer	Chris		
1000	3	Moore	Jasper		
1000	4	Flintstone	Fred		

150 Browse

Figure 8.25

Next, you need to return to the Event file and put the cHighlight field (not gHighlight — be careful) in the portal behind the Name LF field. When you do this, be sure to stretch cHighlight so that it covers the entire top row of the portal and to set the Name LF field to be transparent. Also, go into the Graphic Format dialog for cHighlight and set it to reduce or enlarge the image to fit the frame, and uncheck the Maintain original proportions option. This allows the rectangle of color you built earlier to expand to the edges of the field.

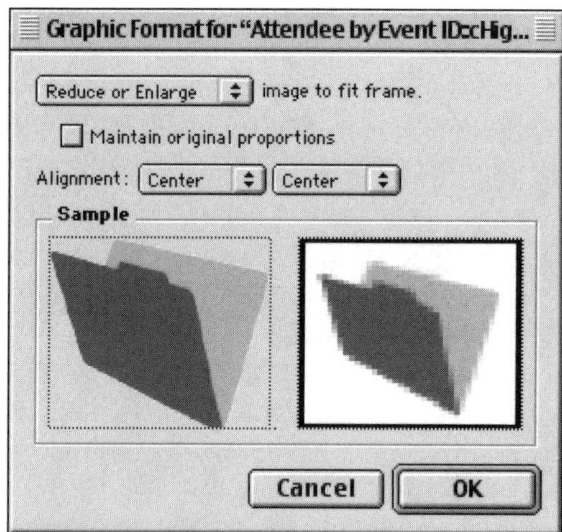

Figure 8.26

It may take you a few tries to get the fields aligned how you want them, but after you've done it a dozen times, it goes fairly quickly. The results of the portal highlighting are shown in Figure 8.27.

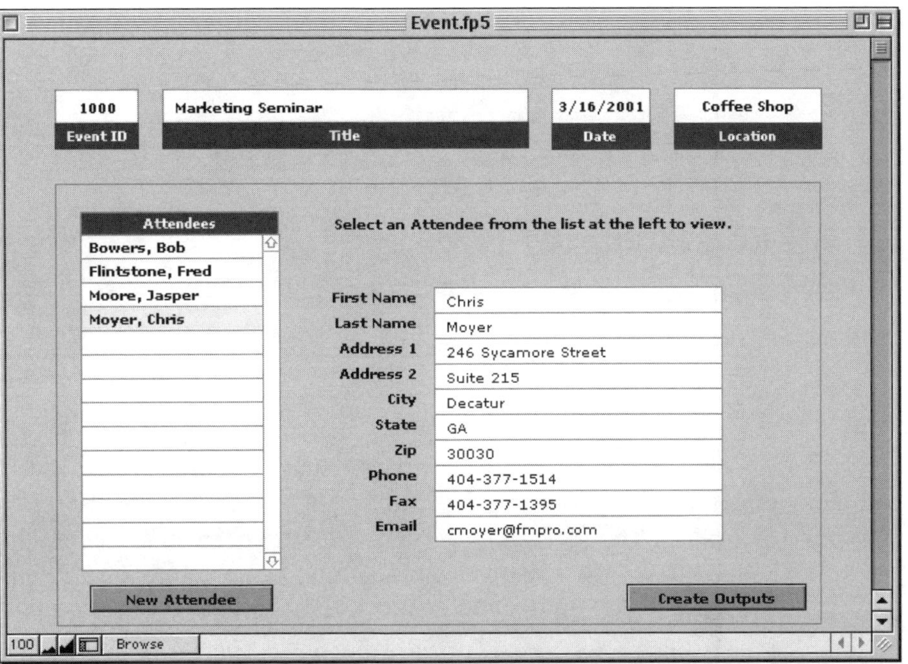

Figure 8.27

At this point, if you tried to select various attendees, you'd likely find that the highlight doesn't change properly. This is because of what we affectionately refer to as a "screen refresh issue." Even though the contents of Selected Attendee ID have changed and the right side of the screen correctly displays information about the selected attendee, the portal hasn't been redrawn. It won't, unless you explicitly make it refresh in your selection script. One way is to have the script switch briefly to Preview mode and then back to Browse mode, but the screen flickers a bit when you do this. Don't even consider using the Refresh Window script step, by the way. For whatever reason, it's fairly worthless in this and most circumstances when you want to refresh the window. A bit more clever and effective way to cause the portal to refresh is to set the field defined as the left side of the relationship equal to itself. Remember, the contents of a portal change anytime the value of the left-hand field changes. By setting it equal to itself, you force the portal to be redrawn. The only time you won't want to use this method for refreshing a portal is when the field on the left acts as a trigger for lookups or, of course, when it's a calculation field. In this case it doesn't and it's not, so you're safe. The revised Select Attendee script is as follows:

Select Attendee

```
Set Field [Selected Attendee ID, Attendee by Event ID::Attendee ID]
Set Field [Event ID, Event ID]
Exit Record/Request
```

Highlighting Multiple Portal Rows

There are many times when you'll want to highlight multiple portal rows. While the basic elements you'll need are quite similar to those for highlighting a single portal row, there are enough differences that it will be helpful to look at an example.

Consider the following scenario, based again on the Event and Attendee tables. At times during the planning for an event, there are numerous things that need to be created for each of the attendees such as mailing labels, name badges, evaluation forms, and thank you letters. Users would like the ability to produce these things for either one, several, or all attendees, as occasionally people register late or need things reproduced. The goal of the present exercise will be to allow the user to pick and choose which attendees to print materials for. And, since multiple users may need to produce different types of outputs at the same time, the solution should be as multiuser friendly as possible.

As before, there are three fields you'll need to create. The first, again, is a place to store the IDs of the selected records. To do this, you'll use an array, which is nothing more than a delimited list of items. There are, unfortunately, no built-in array functions in FileMaker. Repeating fields can sometimes be used as arrays, but the functions available for setting and retrieving items in repeating fields are too limiting for most applications. For this solution, you'll build your own array in a global field. As a user selects attendees by clicking on portal rows, those attendees' IDs will simply be added to the array.

Rather than create an array to store the user's selections, you may be tempted to actually set a flag field in the related attendee's record, and then simply go find the records which have been flagged. While this would indeed work, we caution you against it, as your solution will not be multiuser friendly. If more than one user tried to make selections at the same time, they'd be setting and unsetting each other's flags. So, instead of flagging individual records on the back end, we advocate using a global array on the front end.

With this as background, let's proceed with the solution. Begin by creating a layout that will be used explicitly for selecting attendees, as shown in Figure 8.28.

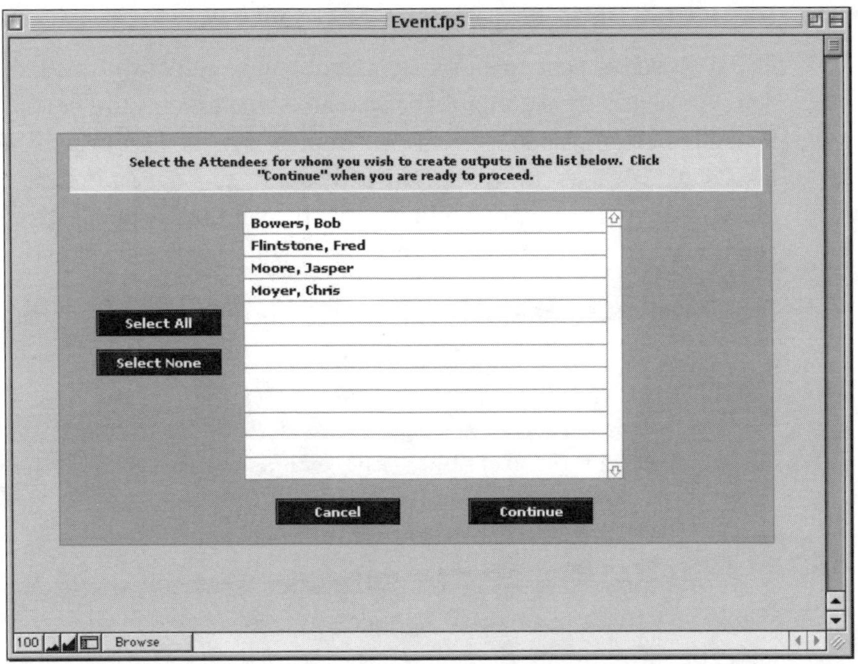

Figure 8.28

The portal on this layout uses the same relationship as the portal on the layout built earlier (Attendees by Event ID); it simply shows all of the attendees registered for this event.

Next, you need a field in Event for the array, a global text field called gSelected Attendee Array. You'll probably find it helpful to place this field on the layout (format it to be several rows high) while you're creating and testing the selection routine. Not only will this help you troubleshoot any bugs, but it will also help you understand exactly what the scripts are doing.

Before building the highlight field itself, let's do a bit of scripting and make sure the selection routine works as planned. The first script needed, shown here, is for a button on the main layout to take the user to the output selection layout.

Go to Select Attendees for Outputs

```
Go to Layout [Select Attendees]
Set Field [gSelected Attendee Array, ""]
```

Nothing fancy here. Just clearing out the selection array so that by default no attendees will be highlighted. It would be very easy, as you'll see shortly, to have all attendees selected by default if you'd prefer.

The next script needed is for selecting (and deselecting!) an individual attendee. You can tie this script either to the Name field in the portal, or to an invisible button placed over the entire first row of the portal. It doesn't really matter which. If an attendee is already selected (that is, if their ID is found in the array), you'll want to remove their ID from the array. If it's not found, you'll want to add it. For now, this script will consist of a single set field:

Toggle Attendee Selection

```
Set Field [gSelectionArray,
     Case( PatternCount("¶" & gSelected Attendee Array, "¶" & Attendee
          by Event ID::Attendee ID &"¶"),
     Substitute(gSelected Attendee Array, Attendee by Event ID::Attendee
          ID &"¶", ""),
     gSelected Attendee Array & Attendee by Event ID::Attendee ID & "¶")]
```

What this complex-looking calculation does is actually quite simple. First, it checks to see if the selected attendee's ID is already in the array by using the PatternCount function. Note that return characters are concatenated on either side of the ID (we're using returns as the delimiters of our array), just in case you've got something like ID "14" in the array and you try looking for ID "4." Including the delimiters ensures that we won't find an ID that happens to be a substring of another ID. If the Case statement evaluates as true, then the ID in question, along with the delimiter which follows it, is substituted out of the array by replacing it with "", and if it's not found, it's simply concatenated to the end of the array.

It usually doesn't matter much what you use as a delimiter when you construct arrays. We often use a pipe character ("|"), as it makes the array easy to visualize. In this case, though, we used a return character ("¶") for an important reason. Shortly, this array will be used as the front end of a relationship, and just as a return-separated multivalued key on the back end of a relationship acts as an "or" search (refer back to the multiple portal filter examples), a multivalued key on the front end will produce similar results. Whatever you choose as your array delimiter, make sure it's not something that will ever be used within the data itself, and make sure the array is balanced with at least the same number of delimiters and values. For instance, "Fred|Barney" is a poorly constructed array, while "Fred|Barney|" or "|Fred|Barney|" are well constructed.

Test the selection and deselection of attendees thoroughly before scripting any further. We can't emphasize enough that the best development practice is to work in small chunks rather than swinging for the fences and wasting a lot of time figuring out where even to begin troubleshooting if something doesn't work.

Once you're sure that the array is successfully being manipulated by the toggle script, turn your attention for a moment to the back end (that is, the Attendee file). Just as before, two fields are needed here to produce a highlight. The first is a global container field with a swatch of color, and the second is a calculation that actually displays the highlight. You can use the same global container, gHighlight, that you used in the last exercise. You'll need a brand new calculation field, though. It's not enough to simply check as before whether the ID of the current record is equal to the selected ID. Instead, you must check to see whether the ID of the current record is contained within the array of selected IDs. The PatternCount function, which returns the number of times one string is found within another, can be used as a Boolean function (one which returns True/1 or False/0) to perform this check. You don't care how many times the string is found, merely that it is found. Any result for the PatternCount other than "0" will yield a True statement. The new calculation (with container result) called cMulti Highlight, will therefore have the following definition:

```
Case(
    PatternCount("¶" & Event by Event ID::gSelected Attendee Array,
       "¶" & Attendee ID &"¶"),
       gHighlight
        )
```

The reason for including the delimiters in the search string is the same as before. Since the Attendee ID string can have a variable length (i.e., "5," "25," "5425"), you need to ensure when searching for ID "5" that you don't incorrectly find the "5" within "25." To this end, you search for the ID surrounded by delimiters. Since the selection array as constructed doesn't begin with a delimiter, a delimiter is prefixed onto the string being searched so that the first item in the array has the same structure (delimiter-value-delimiter) as the *n*th value.

Don't worry, it's downhill from here to the end of the exercise! Back in the Event file, place the new highlight calculation behind the name field in the portal, and as before, set its graphic format to reduce/enlarge and not maintain proportions. You'll have the same screen refresh "issue" highlighting multiple items as you did when highlighting a single item. To correct it, you again simply add a step to the Toggle Attendee Selection script that sets the Event ID equal to itself. Back in Browse mode, you should now be able to highlight multiple attendees in the portal, as shown in Figure 8.29.

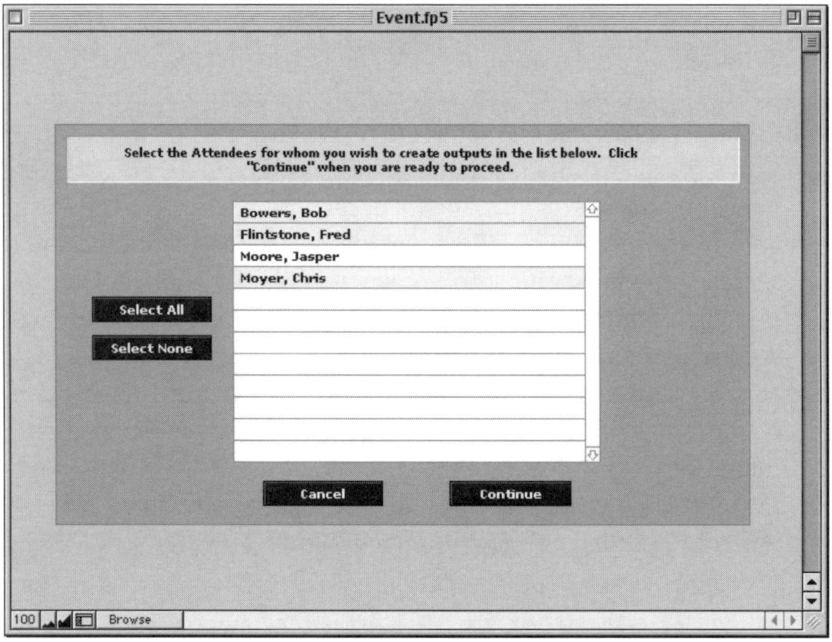

Event.fp5

Select the Attendees for whom you wish to create outputs in the list below. Click "Continue" when you are ready to proceed.

Bowers, Bob
Flintstone, Fred
Moore, Jasper
Moyer, Chris

Select All
Select None
Cancel
Continue

100 Browse

Figure 8.29

You'll notice there are two buttons on the left side of the layout labeled Select All and Select None. Users will appreciate these shortcuts immensely, and they're very simple scripts to write. The Select None script, in fact, merely needs to clear out the global selection array. The highlights will all disappear as the calculation in the back end reevaluates to False for each attendee.

Select None

```
Set Field [gSelected Attendee Array, ""]
Set Field [Event ID, Event ID]
```

The Select All script is only marginally more difficult. Start by clearing out the array, and then systematically loop through the items, collecting IDs as you go. The script for this is shown below.

Select All

```
Set Field [gSelected Attendee Array, ""]
Go to Portal Row [Select, First]
Loop
     Set Field [gSelected Attendee Array, gSelected Attendee Array &
               Attendee by Event ID::Attendee ID & "¶"]
     Go to Portal Row [Select, Exit after last, Next]
End Loop
Exit Record/Request
Set Field [Event ID, Event ID]
```

Now that you're able to select and highlight multiple attendees from a portal, you need to know how to put this information to use. Recall that the goal of the exercise is to select a subset of attendees and produce things like mailing labels or name badges. The layouts for these would live in the Attendee table. Thus, the Continue button on the selection layout needs to run a script that isolates the selected set of Attendee records and navigates to an Output menu in the Attendee table.

The trick for finding the selected set of attendees it to create yet another relationship (this is the third) from Event to Attendee. This time you'll relate from gSelected Attendee Array (a multivalued key) to Attendee ID, as shown in Figure 8.30.

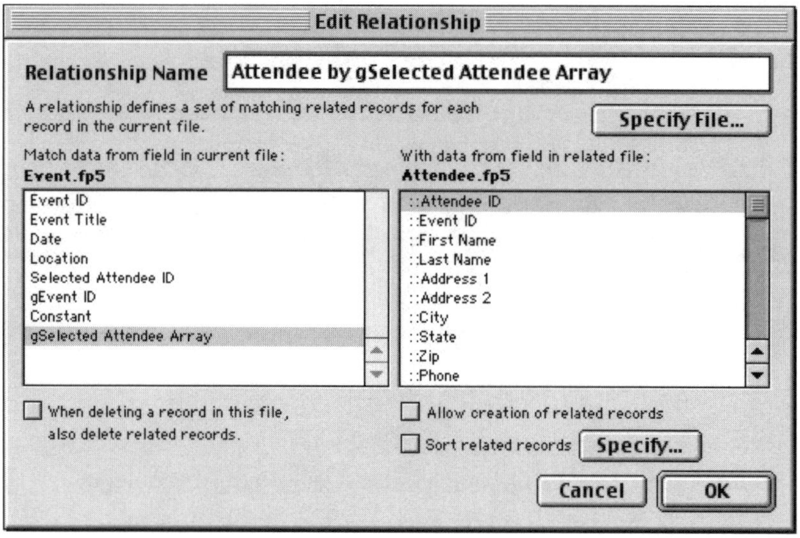

Edit Relationship

Relationship Name: Attendee by gSelected Attendee Array

A relationship defines a set of matching related records for each record in the current file.

Specify File...

Match data from field in current file:
Event.fp5

Event ID
Event Title
Date
Location
Selected Attendee ID
gEvent ID
Constant
gSelected Attendee Array

With data from field in related file:
Attendee.fp5

::Attendee ID
::Event ID
::First Name
::Last Name
::Address 1
::Address 2
::City
::State
::Zip
::Phone

When deleting a record in this file, also delete related records.

Allow creation of related records

Sort related records Specify...

Cancel OK

Figure 8.30

Again, this is very similar to the earlier use of a multivalued key for complex filtering. Most often, multivalued keys in the front end will be global fields, while in the back end, they will usually be calculation fields. This new relationship will match to all of the records where the Attendee ID is contained in the selection array. Keep in mind that multivalued keys require that the individual keys be separated by returns, so plan accordingly when building arrays.

If you go to related records through this relationship, showing only related records, you're in effect performing a find in the back end for those IDs contained in the array. But going to related records is much faster and easier to create than a find. So much so, in fact, that anytime we can, we'll use a relationship to find records rather than having a script perform an actual find. The only limitations to the use of front-end multi-value keys are the time it takes to create the array and the maximum size of the array. The maximum number of characters you can put in a text field is 64,000, so if your IDs are five characters in length and you need a delimiter between IDs, the total number of items you could put in the array would be just over 10,000. This is more than adequate in most situations, but can cause occasional headaches in large files.

Returning to the task at hand, the script tied to the Continue button is shown below. The subscript called in the Attendee file simply navigates to the Output menu.

Go to Output Menu

```
Exit Record/Request
Go to Related Records [Show, "Attendee by gSelected AttendeeID"]
Perform Script [Sub-scripts, External: "Attendee.fp5"]
```

Portal Sorting

Earlier in this chapter, we mentioned that records in a portal are displayed based on their creation order in the related file, but that the order can be changed by selecting the Sort Related Records option in the relationship setup. The sort feature, introduced in FileMaker 4.0, certainly provides more control over the portal display, but it's not very flexible.

Consider, for instance, how limited your options are for having users decide how they want the portal sorted. One solution we've encountered is to have multiple copies of the same relationship, differing only in how they're set to sort, and then to have multiple copies of the layout, each with a portal based on a different flavor of the relationship. While this works, it's a maintenance and scripting nightmare!

In this exercise, we'll show you a workaround for adding dynamic sorting to any portal you create. The overhead and upkeep are minimal, and after you've done it a few times, you'll find you can add dynamic sorting to just about any portal in about 15 minutes. To be sure, it's a "bell and whistle" that you might not always have the time or budget to implement, but one that users will greatly appreciate for the control it gives them.

Figure 8.31 shows a portal in a database called Client into a database called Policy. It's a basic one-to-many relationship for showing all of the insurance policies that are related to a given client's record. We purposefully wanted a portal that had text, number, and date fields in it, as field types will create some difficulties discussed later in this section. The goal of this exercise is to allow users to click on one of the column headings and have the portal then sort by the values in the selected column. The names of the fields in the portal are Policy Number, Policy Type, Effective Date, Termination Date, and Coverage Amount.

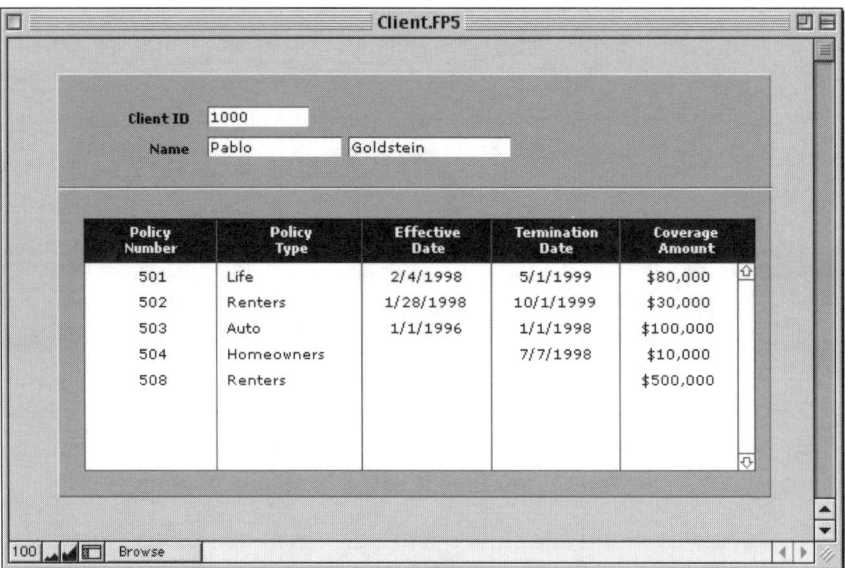

Figure 8.31

To accomplish this goal, you'll need two new fields and a handful of scripts. Start with the fields. The first one is a global text field, and it really doesn't matter whether you create it in the Client table or in the Policy table. This field will be used to hold the instructions for sorting the portal, and will be set by the scripts you'll write shortly. For this exercise, create this field, called gSort, in the Policy table.

The other field you need is a calculation field. This field will take on the appearance of one of the fields in our portal, based on the instructions contained in gSort. Because of its shifting appearance, we often refer to this field as a "chameleon field." The definition for this field will be built in a couple of passes. For now, cSortCalc is defined as follows:

```
Case(
gSort = "Policy Number", Policy Number,
gSort = "Policy Type", Policy Type,
gSort = "Effective Date", Effective Date,
gSort = "Termination Date", Termination Date,
gSort = "Coverage Amount", Coverage Amount)
```

From this, you can see that changing the value of gSort will indeed change the results of the calculation. Before getting into data type issues, let's return to the front end (the Client database) and see how this calculation can drive the sort order of the portal.

In the relationship definition for the portal, you can now instruct the relationship to sort by cSortCalc. Stick to ascending order for now. Whatever field cSortCalc takes the appearance of (as determined by gSort), the portal will appear sorted in the order of that field's value. The relationship itself never needs to be edited.

This is a good time to test the sorting. Do so by placing gSort somewhere on the layout, and manually typing into it something like "Policy Type" and see if the portal changes order. You may need to force the screen to refresh by toggling between modes, but that's something that can be taken care of by scripts and is not a concern at the moment.

Of far greater concern is what happens if you set gSort to "Coverage Amount." The resulting portal is shown in Figure 8.32.

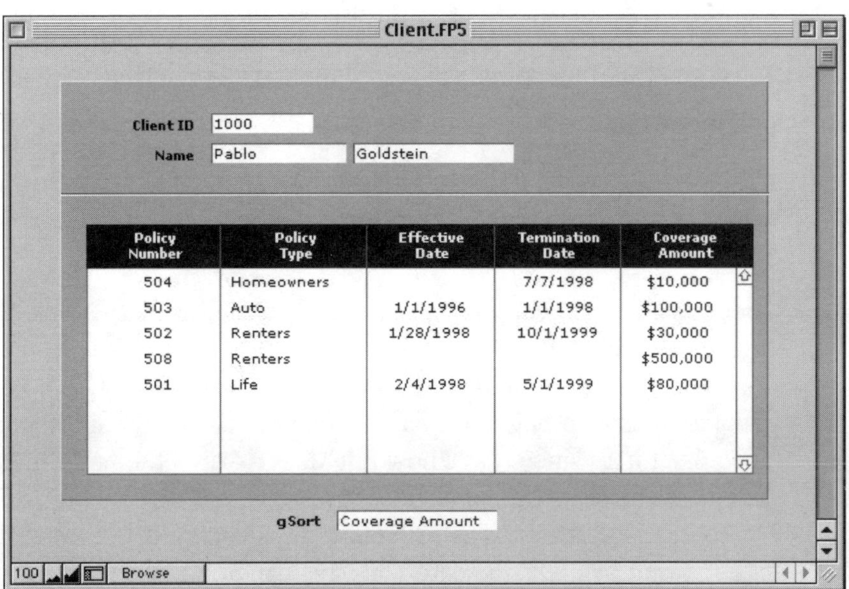

Figure 8.32

The portal is indeed sorted by coverage amount, but it's sorted alphabetically rather than numerically! This is because cSortCalc was defined to have a text result. When numbers are sorted alphabetically, their leftmost digit is the most significant, resulting in sort orders like 1, 10, 11, 2, 23, 200, 3, 345. The only time that alphabetic order and numeric order are the same is when all of the numbers being sorted have the same number of digits, which provides the clue you need to solve this dilemma. If you can pad the Coverage Amount field with leading zeros within cSortCalc, the portal will sort properly. The user never needs to view cSortCalc; it's strictly used for sorting so it doesn't matter what you do to it so long as it furnishes a proper sort order for the portal.

There's a very simple way to pad leading characters onto a string. Let's say in this case that you want to pad all of the Coverage Amounts to eight digits. The following formula is all you need:

```
Right ( "00000000" & Coverage Amount, 8)
```

Let's look at an example to see how this works. Say that Coverage Amount = "123." The first thing the formula above does is concatenate a string of eight zeros and the Coverage Amount string, yielding the following:

00000000123

Then, the Right function takes eight digits from the right end of the string:

000<u>00000123</u>

Using this approach, it doesn't matter how many digits the Coverage Amount field contains in the first place, so long as the largest number it will ever potentially contain is at most an eight-digit number.

There will be a similar data type issue with the two date fields. Since cSortCalc is defined to have a text result, the date fields will sort alphabetically, which means that 10/1/1998 will sort ahead of 4/1/1996! The best way to solve the sort problem for date fields is to coerce them into numbers, which isn't hard since that's how FileMaker stores them in the first place. Dates are stored as the number of days since January 1, 0001. So a date like March 25, 2001 is stored as 730569. Unless you've got some really far-out dates in your system, any date you have can be represented as a six-digit number, meaning that you don't have to also worry about padding leading characters onto the number.

But how do you coerce a date into its numeric equivalent? Oddly enough, the easiest way is to use it as a string in a trivial formula. The one we usually use is myDateField & "". If you don't want blank records floating to the top of your sorts, you can also do something like myDate & "x" and the blanks will fall to the bottom.

When you're done making these adjustments to the cSortCalc field, its definition will have become the following:

```
Case(
gSort = "Policy Number", Policy Number,
gSort = "Policy Type", Policy Type,
gSort = "Effective Date", Effective Date & "",
gSort = "Termination Date", Termination Date & "",
gSort = "Coverage Amount", Right("00000000" & Coverage Amount,8))
```

At this point in the game, we would usually return to the front end and manually test each value of gSort to make sure it led to the sort order we wanted. It's helpful sometimes to temporarily put cSortCalc itself in the portal to better see what's happening.

Assuming you haven't found any more issues to troubleshoot and are happy with the calculation formula, you can proceed to scripting. Since there are five columns in the portal, there need to be five separate scripts, each of which will be tied to an invisible button placed on top of the column heading. Each script simply sets gSort to the appropriate text, and then forces the screen to refresh to avoid the dreaded "screen refresh issues" that would otherwise cause headaches. It doesn't matter, by the way, if the text put into gSort is the actual name of a field or not. The only important thing is consistency between how it's set by the script and how it's decoded in cSortCalc. We've used the actual field names here for simplicity, but realize that might be misleading.

The script to cause the portal to sort by Coverage Amount is shown below:

Portal Sort: Coverage

```
Set Field [Policy by Client ID::gSort, "Coverage Amount"]
Set Field [Client ID, Client ID]
```

The other four scripts are identical save for the value assigned to gSort. Spelling counts since these are literal text strings, not field names, so be careful and test thoroughly.

Now a user can simply click on a column heading and dynamically sort the portal. One of the nicest things about this routine, though, is that it's very multiuser friendly. Two users can each be looking at the same portal at the same time, sorted two different ways. Of course, that's because the instructions for how to sort the portal are contained in a global field, and global fields act like session variables in a networked environment.

If all of the fields in your portal are of the same type (i.e., all text, all number, or all date), then you can also use a new FileMaker 5.5 function called GetField in cSortCalc in place of the Case function. The GetField function gets the contents of the field defined by the parameter, which in this case would simply be gSort. So, the entire formula for cSortCalc could just be GetField (gSort). Again, this would assume a homogeneous mix of data types. Just as important, it would also require that gSort be set to contain the actual name of the field whose value you wanted to retrieve.

Extra Credit

If you're up for bells and whistles on top of your bells and whistles, then consider trying either of the following two extensions to dynamic portal sorting.

First, wouldn't it be nice to give the user some sort of visual indication as to which column is being used as the sort field? Think, for example, of the Define Fields dialog in FileMaker, and how clicking on a column heading causes the heading itself and the entire column below it to change colors. To accomplish this, you'd need some of the same tools used earlier for highlighting portal rows. To highlight the column heading, you'd need a global container with your swatch of highlight color, just as before. Then, you'd need five calculation fields (in the front end, since that's where the layout is built) that resulted in the highlight when gSort was equal to the column name. Check out the demo files on the companion CD if you want to see this in action.

Second, you'll notice that the solution above only sorts in ascending order. The relationship is hard-coded to sort in ascending order, and you can't script changing that. To get the option of a descending order, you have to find some way to have cSortCalc itself turn things around.

For the number fields and date fields, there are a couple of options. The first is to subtract the number or date (as number) from a large number. The other would be to take the reciprocals of the numbers. Recall from high school math that if $x > y$, then $1/x < 1/y$. So, if you sort ascending by either of these derived values, the numbers or dates themselves will appear in descending order. Consider the following chart:

x	**999999-x**	**1/x**
5	999994	.2
4	999995	.25
3	999996	.333
2	999997	.5
1	999998	1

Notice that while the second and third columns are in increasing order, x itself decreases. There are, alas, a few things you need to worry about. First, whatever calculation you use will eventually make its way into the formula for cSortCalc, and you'll recall this field is defined to have a text result. That means that you'll have the same sorting problem as before, particularly for values of 999999–x when the number of digits in x varies. This problem all but disappears, however, using 1/x, as decimal values "pad" leading zeros already. The problem with using 1/x is that if x is 0, 1/x is undefined, and if x is 1, then 1/x is just 1, and it won't sort properly with other decimal values. Negative values of x will also cause problems, but assume for right now that x won't be negative. Changing the formula slightly to 1/(x+2) instead of 1/x will solve the problems of x=0 and x=1.

Taking these issues into consideration, we usually use 999999–x as the method for sorting dates in descending order, and 1/(x+2) as the method for numbers. Accordingly, cSortCalc needs to be modified to the following:

```
Case(
gSort = "Policy Number", Policy Number,
gSort = "Policy Type", Policy Type,
gSort = "Effective Date", Effective Date & "",
gSort = "Termination Date", Termination Date & "",
gSort = "Coverage Amount", Right("00000000" & Coverage Amount,8),

gSort = "Effective Date descending", 999999-Effective Date,
gSort = "Termination Date descending", 999999-Termination Date,
gSort = "Coverage Amount descending", 1 / (Coverage Amount + 2))
```

To finish this off, the users just need some way to indicate whether they want the portal sorted in ascending or descending order. Having two buttons works well, as does having the order toggle between ascending and descending as you repeatedly click the column heading. Another way we especially like is to have the user hold down a modifer key, like the Control key, when clicking the column heading to indicate a descending order.

The thing to remember with this method is that the same button will be used for both ascending and descending sorts; the only difference will be whether or not the user is holding down the Control key at the time the button is clicked. In a script, you can test for this using the Status(CurrentModifier-Keys) function. The table below shows the various values that this function can return.

Modifier Key	Value
Shift	1
Caps Lock	2
Control (Mac) Ctrl (Windows)	4
Option (Mac) Alt (Windows)	8
Command (Mac)	16

The ingenious reason for having these values be powers of 2 is that combinations of keys can be represented uniquely by a single number. For instance, if a user is holding down both the Option and Shift keys, the function will return a 9 (8+1). With five modifier keys, there are $2^5 = 32$ unique combinations of keys possible.

The revised script for the button over the Effective Date column is shown next. All of the scripts that can result in either ascending or descending sorts need to be modified similarly. Note that we're checking for both Status(CurrentModifierKeys) = 4 and Status(CurrentModifierKeys) = 6, just in case the user has the Caps Lock on.

Portal Sort: Effective Date

```
If [Status(CurrentModifierKeys) = 4 or Status(CurrentModifierKeys) = 6]
     Set Field [Policy by Client ID::gSort, "Effective Date descending"]
Else
     Set Field [Policy by Client ID::gSort, "Effective Date"]
End If
Set Field [Client ID, Client ID]
```

We've solved the ascending/descending issue for number and date fields, but what about plain old text fields? How do you take the inverse or reciprocal of a text string? The best way we've come up with for this is to change the order of the alphabet. The calculation we'll show you in a minute looks quite complex, but it's quite simple in theory. Basically, you want a "z" to appear every place that there's an "a" in the text string. Similarly, you want a "y" to replace each instance of a "b," and so on. The very strange-looking text string that results will be the alphabetic inverse of the original text string. So, an ascending sort of the inverted string results in a descending order for the original string. Piece of cake.

It's easy to nest substitute functions within one another to build this inverse function. For a text field called myText, you'd start out simply with:

```
Substitute (myText, "a", "z")
```

This function then becomes the string argument for the next substitution:

```
Substitute (Substitute (myText, "a", "z"), "b", "y")
```

You encounter a strange sort of problem as you continue to nest substitution functions. Namely, when you get to the end and want to turn z's into a's, all of the a's that you've already turned into z's will be turned back into a's! The astute reader will recall that the Substitute function is case sensitive; this provides you with the solution to the tail-chasing phenomena. If you first map the entire string to, say, uppercase, then replace uppercase A's with lowercase z's (and so on), when you get to the end of the line, you're replacing uppercase Z's with lowercase a's.

Since the calculation is so long, and to make it reuseable for different text strings, we'll create a new field in the Policy table called Inverted Text with the following definition:

```
Substitute( Substitute( Substitute( Substitute( Substitute( Substitute(
     Substitute( Substitute( Substitute( Substitute( Substitute( Substitute(
     Substitute( Substitute( Substitute( Substitute( Substitute( Substitute(
     Substitute( Substitute( Substitute( Substitute( Substitute( Substitute(
     Substitute( Substitute(Upper(Policy Type), "A", "z"), "B", "y"), "C",
     "x"), "D", "w"), "E", "v"), "F", "u"), "G", "t"), "H", "s"), "I", "r"),
     "J", "q"), "K", "p"), "L", "o"), "M", "n"), "N", "m"), "O", "l"), "P",
     "k"), "Q", "j"), "R", "i"), "S", "h"), "T", "g"), "U", "f"), "V", "e"),
     "W", "d"), "X", "c"), "Y", "b"), "Z", "a")
```

If you had multiple text strings you wanted to invert, you could place a Case statement in the middle of this formula to choose a certain field based on the value of gSort. To finally finish the exercise, you need to modify cSortCalc one last time:

```
Case(
gSort = "Policy Number", Policy Number,
gSort = "Policy Type", Policy Type,
gSort = "Effective Date", Effective Date & "",
gSort = "Termination Date", Termination Date & "",
gSort = "Coverage Amount", Right("00000000" & Coverage Amount,8),

gSort = "Effective Date descending", 999999-Effective Date,
gSort = "Termination Date descending", 999999-Termination Date,
gSort = "Coverage Amount descending", 1 / (Coverage Amount + 2),

gSort = "Policy type descending", Inverted Text)
```

As you can see, enabling the option to sort the portal either in ascending or descending order entails a fair bit of extra work. But once you're familiar with the concept and have done it a few times, it goes quite quickly. To save time, you can even copy and paste the field definition for cSortCalc and import scripts from previous solution. Soon, the biggest problem you'll have is that your users will begin to expect every portal to be sortable. There are worse problems to have!

Hidden Portals

There's one final use of portals that we'll cover here. This is a trick that we first learned of several years ago at a FileMaker Developers Conference in a presentation by John Mark Osborne, though he credits others with its first use. Since then, we've found it an invaluable addition to our toolbox, and hope that you will as well.

Essentially, the trick involves using a portal to hide things on a layout. In this example, we'll return yet again to the Event and Attendee tables used in the portal selection and highlighting sections earlier. You'll recall that at the bottom of the main layout (see Figure 8.27), there's a button called New Attendee. Imagine that you want to limit access to this function to certain users. Imagine also that you've built some sort of login system, so that by the time a user gets to this screen, a global field called gAccess Level has been set to either Admin or User. Your task is to make the New Attendee button disappear off the layout for any user whose access level is User.

Now, in many cases making the button disappear is overkill. You can certainly just add a test to the beginning of the New Attendee script that checks the value of gAccess Level and conditionally shows a dialog like "You don't have the proper authorization to do this task." Another option might be to have two nearly identical layouts, one for users and one for administrators, and to leave off the button on the user layout. However, not only is it a navigation nightmare to ensure that a given user is always taken to the proper screen, but it's a maintenance headache as well. Any modifications you make to either layout in the future need to be made to the other layout as well.

Hiding the button in a portal is nice because users won't waste their time trying to do things they don't have authorization to do, and it's fairly easy to build and maintain. To begin, you need a relationship that will conditionally be either valid or invalid. The easiest way to do this is to have a calculation field on the front end of the relationship that evaluates either to a 1 or a 0 depending on some condition, and a constant (=1) on the back end. It makes absolutely no difference what file you relate to, and consequently we frequently make this a self-relationship.

Call the calculation field cAdmin Access and define it as follows:

```
gAccess Level = "Admin"
```

This, of course, is a Boolean calculation, which means that the statement is either true or false, and therefore returns a 1 or a 0. You could have just as easily used Case (gAcess Level = "Admin", 1,0), but the Boolean is a bit more economical to use.

In either case, the next move is to relate cAdmin Access to Constant, as shown in Figure 8.33.

You should easily see that if gAccess Level is anything other than Admin, there won't be any related records.

Edit Relationship

Relationship Name: Event by cAdmin Access

A relationship defines a set of matching related records for each record in the current file.

Specify File...

Match data from field in current file:
Event.fp5

Event ID
Event Title
Date
Location
Selected Attendee ID
gEvent ID
Constant
gSelected Attendee Array
gAccess Level
cAdmin Access

With data from field in related file:
Event.fp5

::Event ID
::Event Title
::Date
::Location
::Selected Attendee ID
::gEvent ID
::Constant
::gSelected Attendee Array
::gAccess Level
::cAdmin Access

When deleting a record in this file, also delete related records.

Allow creation of related records

Sort related records Specify...

Cancel OK

Figure 8.33

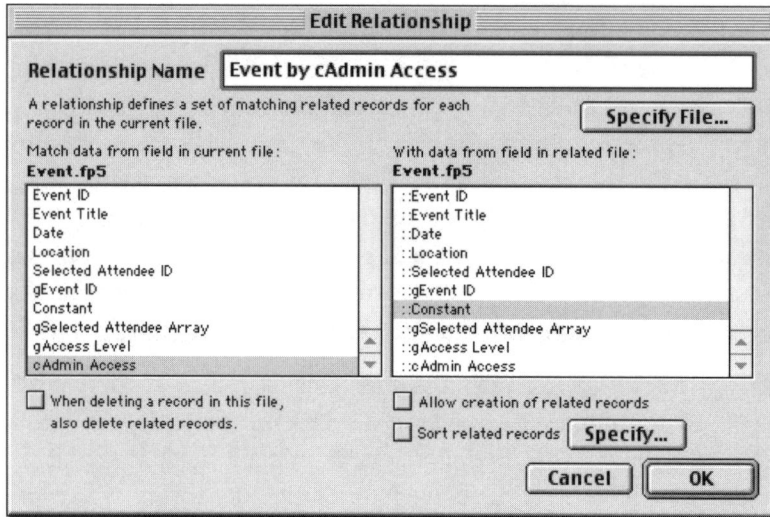

Back in Layout mode on the Event detail layout, create a new portal through this relationship and define it to show only one related record. Further, set the line width of the portal to 0 pt and select Transparent for the pattern, so that the portal is invisible except for its four selection points. Next, size the portal row so that it's just slightly larger than the New Attendee button and move it directly behind the button. The first few times you do this, it's helpful to leave the border on the portal and to oversize it a bit so you can easily troubleshoot any problems. When done, the layout will now look something like the close-up in Figure 8.34.

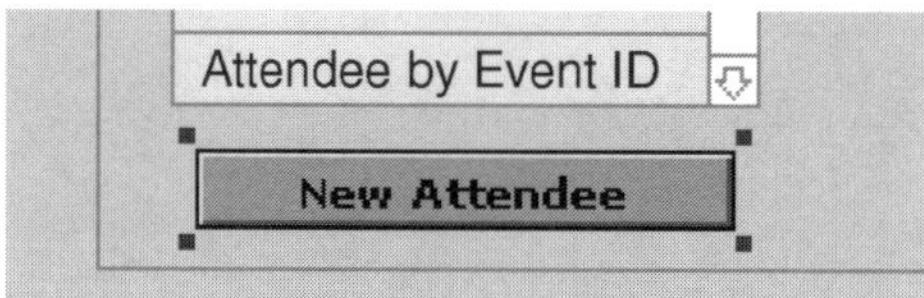

Figure 8.34

Note in this figure that the selection points aren't those of the button, but rather those of the "invisible" portal that's directly behind the button.

To test the solution, temporarily place gAccess Level on the layout, and manually change it from "Admin" to "User." As soon as the value of gAccess Level is anything in the world other than "Admin," there are then no matching related records and the portal literally disappears, taking with it any objects that had the misfortune to be contained therein. Figures 8.35 and 8.36 show the fruits of this labor.

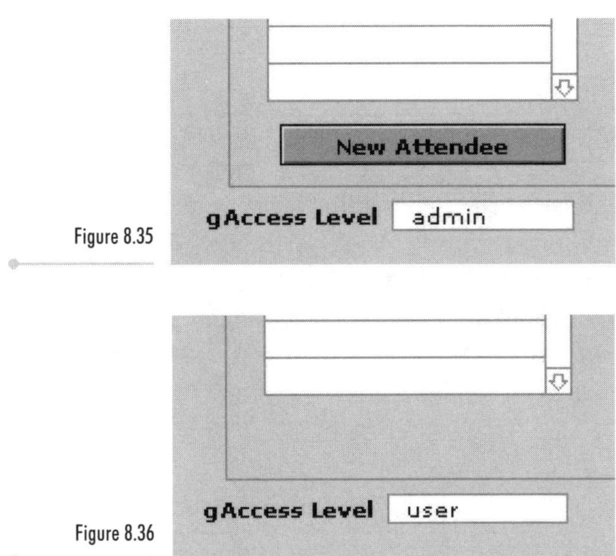

Figure 8.35

Figure 8.36

There are a few particularly nice things about this solution that are worth mentioning. First, the hidden objects leave no trace. That is, if you click on the space where the button was, you don't see any remnants of the button, as you would if, say, you tried to mask the button by having an alternate graphic appear in its place. Second, since it's based on a global field, it's entirely multiuser safe.

There are really only two downsides to using hidden portals. If you don't size the portal a mere pixel larger on each side than the object you want to hide or if you're trying to hide multiple objects with some space in between them, then there is a bit of dead space that's in the portal but outside the object. If the user clicks in this space instead of your button, the portal row itself will highlight, and this doesn't look very nice. Also, it's quite easy to forget there's a hidden portal behind an object. You'll find you move a button a few pixels to make room for something else and forget to move the portal with it. While this is usually something easy to find and fix, it can be a bit painful getting everything to line up just right.

Summary

We've tried to teach you a tremendous amount of portals in this chapter. To get the most out of it, you really need to look at the files on the companion CD and try creating some of these portals yourself. Concepts like selection portals, portal filters, portal highlighting, and portal sorting are not something you learn overnight. Just as a craftsman requires time and practice to master each tool he uses, so too does the FileMaker developer. Over time, we think that advanced portal tools like those contained in this chapter will become some of the favorites in your toolbox.

Chapter 9

Reporting

In this chapter, we will present several methods that we've used over the years for generating and enhancing reports. We're assuming that as a reader of this book, you're already familiar with and able to create simple columnar reports (aka lists) and subsummary reports. Plus, there are plenty of resources that cover these topics already. Instead of walking through the steps of the layout wizard, we'll jump immediately into some more advanced real-world reporting scenarios.

Creating a solid table structure and an intuitive user interface are only half the battle when it comes to making database systems. The other half is extracting meaningful data from the system. All too often, the desired outputs of a system are the least well-defined part of the initial specification. There's a certain amount of inevitability in this, as decisions made when constructing the tables and interface impact the way reports can be generated. Hopefully you'll have at least a rough idea of the core reporting features when you start, but it shouldn't be a surprise if the reporting requirements grow and change more than any other part of the system specifications.

The best thing to do when you're asked to create a new report is to ask the client (or your boss) to draw an example of the report he or she wants. We always pull out a blank pad of paper and say, "Draw a picture of what you want the finished report to look like." After they've jotted down a few column headings, that's when you can start asking questions: "How should this be sorted?" "Who's going to be running this report?" "What are you going to use this report for?" Ask lots of questions. Ask the same question multiple ways and make sure you get the same answer each time. The more you know about the report up front, the less time and energy you'll need to spend reworking it later on.

Now, there are two things you can do after collecting this information. One, of course, is to build the report. The other is to push back a bit. "Mr. Customer, I can build this report you've just described, but it's going to take about 10 hours to build, 3 minutes to process, and it won't provide you with the answers to your questions. What if we did something like this instead?" Furious scribbling ensues. "That gives you the data you need, answers these two other questions as well, takes about 5 seconds to run, and will only take 2 hours to build."

Try this sometime and see the reaction you get. The point is that as a developer, your job isn't necessarily to blindly build whatever's asked of you. The more you understand about the users' needs and the strengths and limitations of your tool, the better you'll be able to provide valuable solutions.

Year-Over-Year Reporting

Ask any small business owner for a list of his reporting needs and sooner or later he'll mention the ability to compare one period's data with another. For instance, the company might want to compare how the members of the sales team are performing this quarter compared to last quarter. Or perhaps the company wants to see total advertising revenue by type for the last several years to identify market trends. Such period-over-period reporting presents some interesting challenges and obstacles for the FileMaker Pro developer, which we'll explore in depth below.

Throughout this chapter, you're going to produce a number of reports for a fictional company that has a FileMaker database system containing customer and invoice records going back to the beginning of 1999. An ER diagram of the file system is shown in Figure 9.1.

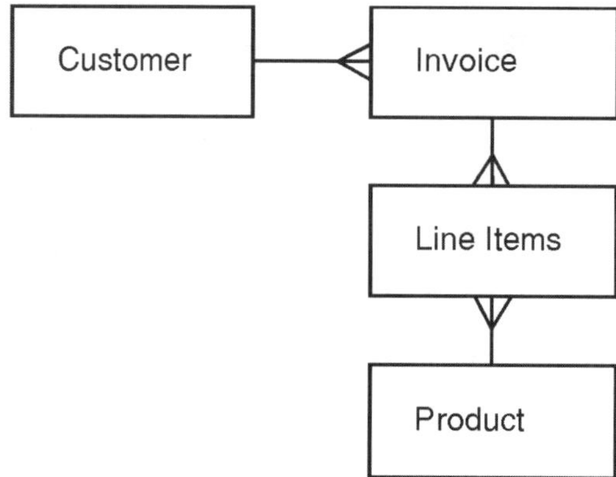

Figure 9.1

Imagine this company has hired you to add reporting capabilities to their system. The first report your new boss wants is something that will tell her the percent change in sales by customer from one year to the next. She's hoping to identify those customers whose sales have dropped from one period to the next so she can have her sales force target accounts to win back. She scribbles out on a pad of paper the way she'd like the report to look:

Customer	1999 Sales	2000 Sales	$ Change	% Change

Rather than just presenting a step-by-step solution for building this report, we're going to try also to take you through the thought process involved, so you can better see the choices open to you when developing your own solutions.

One of the first things you need to determine is how extensible this report needs to be. For instance, if you build the report to just compare 1999 sales to 2000 sales, will you then later need to create a report that compares 2001 sales with 2000 sales? Do you need the flexibility of sorting from biggest change to smallest, or is alphabetically by customer good enough? Don't turn molehills into mountains, though. Keep it as simple as you can while still fulfilling the requirements.

The other thing you always need to think about with FileMaker Pro reports is what file to build them in. If you were writing for the Web or most other programming languages, this would be an absurd consideration, but in FileMaker, there's no way to build a layout that's not in one particular database. The usual answer is to build the report where the data is at the proper level of granularity. In most cases, this means that given two files in a one-to-many relationship, most reports will end up being in the "many" file. It's far easier to bring related information from the parent file into the child file than to build reports in the parent file with portals on them. Portals not only don't print well (page break issues), but you have to define the number of rows to view. This is fine on-screen where a user can scroll, but doesn't work well on a printed report.

In this case, the choice is whether to build the report in the Customer table or in the Invoice table. Without actually building both, it's tough to tell the pros and cons of each. If you were to build this report in the Customer file, your final report would be some sort of list view with aggregate calculations summing up the 1999 invoices and 2000 invoices through a pair of utility relationships. The dollar and percent changes would be relatively easy to calculate, and there would be no problem sorting the report a variety of ways. It might be difficult, however, to limit the report to only a subset of each customer's invoices, since relationships are not dependent on the found set. Moreover, you'd be out of luck if you ever needed to change the report to summarize not by customer, but by something like salesperson or market segment.

On the other hand, building this report in the Invoice file would entail creating a subsummary report by Customer. The dollar and percent changes then become more complex calculations (as they're using summary data), but since subsummaries are found-set dependent, it would be fairly easy to find whatever set of records you were interested in and then report on those. And, it would be fairly easy to modify the report to summarize by something other than Customer down the road.

So what's the right answer? If that's what you're thinking then we haven't quite made our point yet. There is no right answer. Either could be used to solve the immediate problem, but both have pros and cons you'll want to consider carefully before selecting a method. In part, it probably also comes down to whether you're more comfortable working with summary fields or relationships, and if someone other than yourself will need to maintain the system. We'll show you how to build it both ways, since there are times you'll undoubtedly use elements of each.

Method 1 — Customer Table

In order to build the year-over-year report in the Customer table, you'll need a few new fields and relationships. First, create two global text fields called gYear1 and gYear2. These are for the user to enter which two years they want to compare and give the report an element of extensibility. The alternative would be to hard-code a couple of calculation fields with "1999" and "2000" as constants. The added flexibility the globals provide is well worth the effort.

Next, you need calculation fields in both the Customer and Invoice tables that concatenate the Customer ID and the year. In the Customer table, the two new fields have the following definitions:

```
Year 1 Match (calc, text result) = Customer ID & "-" & gYear1
Year 2 Match (calc, text result) = Customer ID & "-" & gYear2
```

In the Invoice database, the new field's definition is similar:

```
Customer ID \ Year (calc, text result) = Customer ID & "-" & Year
      (Invoice Date)
```

It doesn't matter what you use as a separator (we use the hyphen mostly out of habit) or in what order you concatenate the elements. Just be consistent in both files.

You might be able to guess what the next move is. You need to create two new relationships from Customer to Invoice:

Relationship Name	Field in Customer	Field in Invoice
Invoice by Year 1 Match	Year 1 Match	Customer ID \ Year
Invoice by Year 2 Match	Year 2 Match	Customer ID \ Year

Neither of these relationships is structural. That is, they wouldn't be modeled on an ER diagram. The structural relationship between these files is simply that which matches Customer ID to Customer ID. By tacking on the year, you're filtering this relationship (in much the same way a portal filter would) to match only to that subset of Invoice records where the year of the invoice date is the same as the value in the global field.

It's downhill from here. With the relationships in place, create two more calculation fields in Customer, as follows:

```
Year 1 Inv Total (calc, number result) = Sum(Invoice by Year 1
      Match::Invoice Amount)
Year 2 Inv Total (calc, number result) = Sum(Invoice by Year 2
      Match::Invoice Amount)
```

These fields will contain the total sales for a given customer for the years specified by the global fields. Two final calculations will yield the change in sales in dollars and as a percent:

```
Change in Dollars (calc, number result) = Year 2 Inv Total - Year 1
     Inv Total
Change in Percent (calc, number result) = (Year 2 Inv Total - Year 1
     Inv Total) / Year 1 Inv Total
```

Be aware anytime you're doing division in a calculation that if the denominator is zero you're going to end up with a "?" in your field since division by zero is undefined. To purge the question marks from your report, the easiest thing to do is wrap the calculation above in a case statement.

```
Change in Percent (calc, number result) = Case(not IsEmpty(Year 1 Inv
      Total), (Year 2 Inv Total - Year 1 Inv Total) / Year 1 Inv Total, "")
```

Finally, create a simple list layout with the Customer Name, Year 1 Inv Total, Year 2 Inv Total, Change in Dollars, and Change in Percent, as shown in Figure 9.2. For the column headings showing the years, we've simply placed the two global fields, gYear1 and gYear2, on the layout as merge fields.

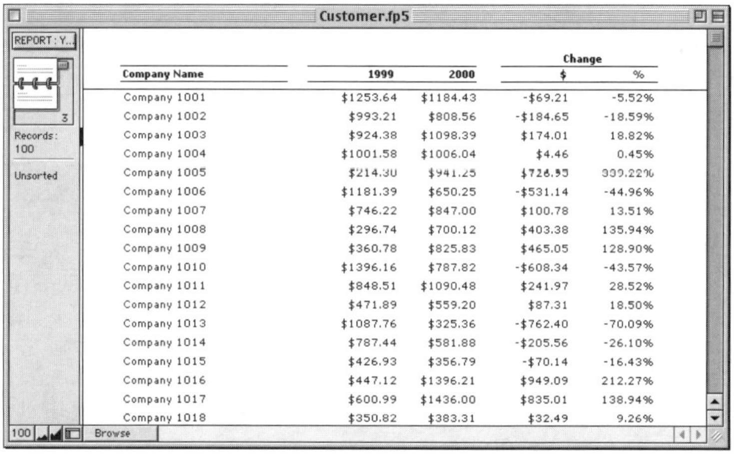

Customer.fp5

REPORT: Y...
Records: 100
Unsorted

Company Name	1999	2000	Change $	Change %
Company 1001	$1253.64	$1184.43	-$69.21	-5.52%
Company 1002	$993.21	$808.56	-$184.65	-18.59%
Company 1003	$924.38	$1098.39	$174.01	18.82%
Company 1004	$1001.58	$1006.04	$4.46	0.45%
Company 1005	$214.30	$941.25	$726.95	339.22%
Company 1006	$1181.39	$650.25	-$531.14	-44.96%
Company 1007	$746.22	$847.00	$100.78	13.51%
Company 1008	$296.74	$700.12	$403.38	135.94%
Company 1009	$360.78	$825.83	$465.05	128.90%
Company 1010	$1396.16	$787.82	-$608.34	-43.57%
Company 1011	$848.51	$1090.48	$241.97	28.52%
Company 1012	$471.89	$559.20	$87.31	18.50%
Company 1013	$1087.76	$325.36	-$762.40	-70.09%
Company 1014	$787.44	$581.88	-$205.56	-26.10%
Company 1015	$426.93	$356.79	-$70.14	-16.43%
Company 1016	$447.12	$1396.21	$949.09	212.27%
Company 1017	$600.99	$1436.00	$835.01	138.94%
Company 1018	$350.82	$383.31	$32.49	9.26%

100 Browse

Figure 9.2

Since this report can be viewed in Browse mode, you can easily add user-friendly features such as the ability to sort the records by clicking on the column headings. Anytime you can add low-cost extensibility like this to a report, it's probably a good idea to do so. Making one report that does several things, especially things a user can control, is better than several reports that each do one thing.

Method 2 — Invoice Table

Now let's see how you can create nearly the same report in the Invoice table. As before, it starts with the creation of a number of new fields, but in this case you won't need any new relationships.

Just as you created global fields above for the user to designate the years to compare, you'll start off again with a pair of globals, gYear1 and gYear2 (in the Invoice table this time, though). These will be used in a pair of calculations that stratify the Invoice Amount into two mutually exclusive fields:

```
Amount Year 1 (calculation, number result) = Case(gYear1 = Year(Invoice
      Date), Invoice Amount)
Amount Year 2 (calculation, number result) = Case(gYear2 = Year(Invoice
      Date), Invoice Amount)
```

It will help you understand what's going on here to look at a few records. If gYear1 is set to "1999" and gYear2 is set to "2000," then observe how the Invoice Amount field ends up split into columns appropriate to each year. We'll explore this useful technique more when we look at bucket reports later in this chapter.

Invoice Date	Invoice Amount	Amount Year 1	Amount Year 2
6/25/1999	136.06	136.06	
9/6/2000	50.48		50.48
1/31/2000	196.66		196.66
8/25/2000	150.58		150.58
7/25/1999	198.25	198.25	
12/3/1999	88.11	88.11	
8/14/2000	210.05		210.05
10/22/1999	130.99	130.99	
12/12/2000	112.16		112.16

The next move is to create two summary fields that total up each of these split-out columns:

```
Total Year 1 (Summary) = Total of Amount Year 1
Total Year 2 (Summary) = Total of Amount Year 2
```

You have sufficient information at this point to create a subsummary report by Customer that shows the total invoiced for each year. Or, if you wanted, you could subsummarize by some other element, such as Market Segment or Salesperson. This added flexibility is one of the nice things about building the report in the Invoice table.

Getting the amount and percent change from year to year, however, is slightly more difficult than it was using the first method. In order to do math with summary fields, you need to use the GetSummary function. If you've never used this function before, it can be a bit confusing at first. Let's review the syntax of GetSummary:

GetSummary (summary field, break field)

The first argument is easy enough; it's where you'll specify the summary field you want to use. The second argument, the break field, is where you'll specify how you're subsummarizing your report. For this report, we're subsummarizing by Customer ID, so that's what you'll use as your break field. The downside of this syntax is that if you have a report with multiple subsummary parts, you'll need separate calculations for each part. Also, it's important to know that if your found set isn't sorted by the break field, then GetSummary won't evaluate.

Using this function, you can create the two fields for dollar and percent change:

```
Change cust dollars (calculation, number result) = GetSummary(Total Year 2,
      Customer ID) - GetSummary(Total Year 1, Customer ID)
Change cust percent (calculation, number result) = (GetSummary(Total Year 2,
      Customer ID) - GetSummary(Total Year 1, Customer ID)) /
      GetSummary(Total Year 1, Customer ID)
```

To construct the report, you'll need a subsummary part (when sorted by Customer ID). You don't, however, need a Body part, since the goal is a report with one line per customer, not one line per invoice. The easiest way to do this, is to create a simple list report with the fields you want, then double-click on the Body part label and respecify the part to be a subsummary when sorted by Customer ID. In this case, the fields you'll want on your layout are Customer by Invoice ID::Customer Name, Total Year 1, Total Year 2, Change cust dollars, and Change cust percent.

Figure 9.3 shows the results of building the year-over-year report in the Invoice table. You can see that, indeed, it's virtually the same as the report generated from the Customer table (see Figure 9.2).

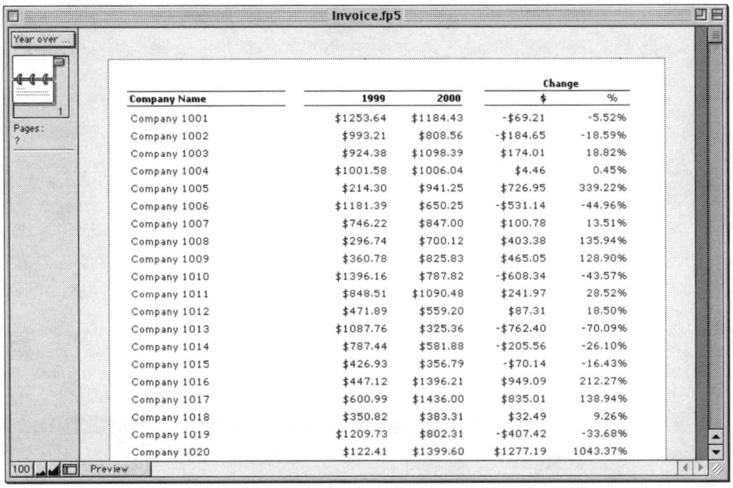

Invoice.fp5

Year over ...

Pages:
?

Company Name	1999	2000	Change	
			$	%
Company 1001	$1253.64	$1184.43	-$69.21	-5.52%
Company 1002	$993.21	$808.56	-$184.65	-18.59%
Company 1003	$924.38	$1098.39	$174.01	18.82%
Company 1004	$1001.58	$1006.04	$4.46	0.45%
Company 1005	$214.30	$941.25	$726.95	339.22%
Company 1006	$1181.39	$650.25	-$531.14	-44.96%
Company 1007	$746.22	$847.00	$100.78	13.51%
Company 1008	$296.74	$700.12	$403.38	135.94%
Company 1009	$360.78	$825.83	$465.05	128.90%
Company 1010	$1396.16	$787.82	-$608.34	-43.57%
Company 1011	$848.51	$1090.48	$241.97	28.52%
Company 1012	$471.89	$559.20	$87.31	18.50%
Company 1013	$1087.76	$325.36	-$762.40	-70.09%
Company 1014	$787.44	$581.88	-$205.56	-26.10%
Company 1015	$426.93	$356.79	-$70.14	-16.43%
Company 1016	$447.12	$1396.21	$949.09	212.27%
Company 1017	$600.99	$1436.00	$835.01	138.94%
Company 1018	$350.82	$383.31	$32.49	9.26%
Company 1019	$1209.73	$802.31	-$407.42	-33.68%
Company 1020	$122.41	$1399.60	$1277.19	1043.37%

100 Preview

Figure 9.3

Remember, though, that when working with subsummary reports, you have to be sorted by the field you're summarizing by, and you have to be in Preview mode to see subsummary parts.

Using the same techniques covered above, it's easy to modify either version of the basic period-over-period report. For instance, you could add a third global field (gYear3) to allow comparison of three years worth of data at a time. Or, you could turn them into quarter-over-quarter reports by modifying the calculations that compare the invoice date to the values in the global fields. Instead of using Year(Invoice Date) as the basis for comparison, you would use something that returned the quarter and year of the invoice date (see Chapter 11, "Complex Calculations" for some suggestions on how to do this).

Data Warehousing with Utility Files

The next reporting technique we'll explore is the use of utility tables to simulate a sort of data warehouse. By utility table, we mean a separate database that doesn't play a structural role in your data model. The main benefit of warehousing data in utility tables is speeding up access to historical data. They can also reduce the reporting load on tables that are used heavily for daily transactions.

Typically, a data warehouse will store data at low levels of granularity. That is, the data will already be summarized, often in multiple ways or at multiple levels. You probably won't build utility tables in brand new systems. Typically they'll be added at later stages of a project as the amount of data accumulates past the point where it can be summarized quickly.

The creation of a data warehouse in FileMaker Pro can be broken down into three essential steps.

1. Creating a utility table to serve as the warehouse.
2. Writing routines to get data into the warehouse.
3. Writing routines to access the data in the warehouse.

In the example that follows, you'll continue using the Customer and Invoice files that were used in the previous section. The scenario is that sales reps want to be able to pull up a snapshot of sales activity by month for a given customer. Now, such a report could be created in the Invoice table as a subsummary by year and month. But some customers have hundreds and even thousands of invoices. Over the network, a subsummary report like this might take 10 or 20 seconds to display. That's acceptable for certain things, but not when you're a sales rep on the phone with a customer.

Step 1 — Creating the Utility Table

The first step in creating a data warehouse is building a new database table to store the data. For the current example, you'll want a table where each record represents a single customer for a single month. As such, you'll need fields for customer ID, month, and year; the combination of all three of these will be the primary key of this table. Besides these, what you'll store in this table is aggregate data pertaining to the sales of a given customer. As examples, you might want to store the total number of invoices for the customer/month and the total amount invoiced. Basically, anything for which you would normally have a summary field in the Invoice database is a likely candidate for inclusion in the warehouse. Again, keep in mind that the concept is to summarize historical data once and store them in the warehouse as raw number fields.

Call this new table CustomerMonthly.fp5. If you did want to include this table on your ER diagram, you could show a one-to-many relationship from Customer to CustomerMonthly. The fields you'll start out with, then, are as follows:

Field Name	Type
Customer ID	Number
Month	Text
Year	Text
Invoice Count	Number
Total Invoiced	Number

Step 2 — Getting Data into the Warehouse

With the new table in place, the next step is to create the process for adding data to the warehouse. The first decision you'll need to make is how automated you want to make the process. While automation is a good thing, we recommend you don't go overboard, as the costs often don't exceed the benefits. Automating a process that needs to be performed daily or even weekly makes a lot of sense, but something that needs to be run monthly or quarterly might be better off as a manual process.

Let's begin by running through the big picture of what needs to happen. Since the CustomerMonthly table stores monthly data, it makes sense that the data be warehoused monthly as well. At some point when all the invoices have been generated for a month, you'll want to find all that month's invoices, summarize them by customer (so there's one record per customer), and move this data to the warehouse.

First, you'll want to give the user an easy way of finding all of the invoices for a particular month. There are a few ways to do this. You could, for instance, just put users in Find mode and let them type in a date range like "3/1/2000…3/31/2000." While there's nothing wrong with this, let's look at another way using globals and self-relationships. We think it makes for a more intuitive user experience, is faster, and is less likely to result in errors.

Create two global text fields in the Invoice table called gMonth and gYear, and place them on a layout like that shown in Figure 9.4. The gMonth field is formatted as a pop-up menu with choices 01 through 12 (the leading zero will help with sorting later on), and gYear is formatted similarly with choices 1999, 2000, and 2001.

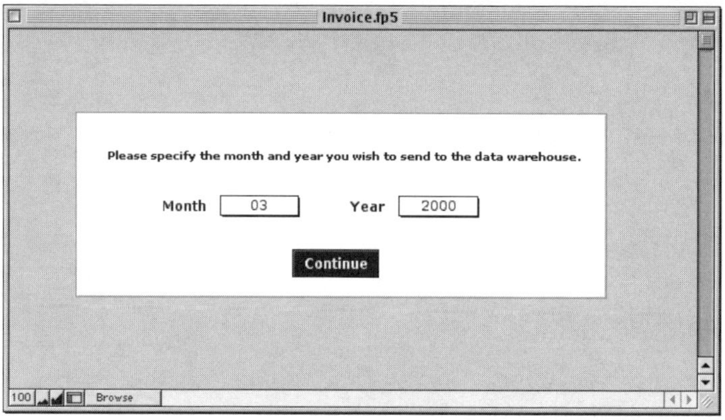

Figure 9.4

When a user clicks the Continue button, he'll kick off a script we'll call Create CustomerMonthly records. The script will check three things before actually summarizing and moving the data. First, it will check that the user made a selection for both the Month and Year. Second, it will check that there are indeed invoice records in the system for the specified Month and Year. And third, it will check the warehouse to see if it already contains data for the specified Month and Year and prompt the user whether or not he wishes to proceed.

For the second and third of these, you'll need a few new fields and relationships. In the Invoice database, create two new calculations that concatenate the global Month and Year fields, and another that extracts and combines the year and month from the invoice date.

```
gYear\Month (calculation, text result) = gYear & "-" & gMonth
Year\Month calc (calculation, text result) = Year(Invoice Date) &"-"& Right
      ("00" & Month(Invoice Date),2)
```

As always, the order (month/year or year/month) and delimiter don't matter; you just have to be consistent. Now, create a self-relationship in Invoice from gYear\Month to Year\Month calc (called Invoice by gYear\Month). You'll be able to use this relationship both to determine if there are records for a given combination of gMonth and gYear and to find that set.

Next, in the CustomerMonthly file, create a calculation similar to the two above that puts together the year and month fields from that file:

```
Year\Month (calculation, text result) = Year &"-"& Month
```

Back in the Invoice table again, create another new relationship, this time matching gYear\Month with the Year\Month field in CustomerMonthly (called CustomerMonthly by gYear\Month).

After all that preparation, you're finally ready to write the beginning of the script:

```
If [IsEmpty(gMonth) or IsEmpty(gYear)]
Show Message [Please specify both a month and year to summarize before
        clicking "Continue"]
    Halt Script
End If
If [not IsValid(Invoice by gYear\Month::Customer ID)]
Show Message [There are no invoice records for the month and year you've
        specified.]
    Halt Script
End If
If [IsValid(Customer Monthly by gYear\Month::Year\Month)]
Show Message [There are already records in the warehouse for the month and
        year you've specified. If you proceed, they will be replaced
        by the current data.]
If [Status(CurrentMessageChoice) = 2]
    Halt Script
Else
Go to Related Record [Show, "Customer Monthly by gYear\Month"]
Perform Script [Sub-scripts, External "CustomerMonthly.fp5"]
    Sub: Delete Found Set
End If
End If
```

A brief note about the third check, which tests if there are already records in the warehouse for the specified month and year: If the user decides to proceed, the Go to Related Record step isolates that set of records in the CustomerMonthly file that should be replaced. The Perform Script step that follows calls a one-line subscript in the CustomerMonthly file that simply deletes the found set (without dialog).

With the checks complete, the rest of the script is actually quite simple:

```
Go to Related Record [Show, "Invoice by gYear\Month"]
Sort [Restore, No dialog]
Export [Restore, No dialog, "CustTemp.txt"]
Perform Script [Sub-scripts, External "CustomerMonthly.fp5"]
     Sub: Import Customer Monthly
Show Message [Data has been successfully summarized in the warehouse.]
```

As mentioned above, the Go to Related Record through the self-relationship isolates that set of records you want to summarize and move. The Sort that follows (by Customer ID) is crucial for the summarized export to work. The Export is the only tricky part of the script, and since summarized exports aren't something you do every day, we'll look at this a bit more closely.

As with any export you want a script to perform, you need to do it once manually so that the export parameters can be stored in the script. To export data from the Invoice file, summarized by Customer ID, you'll need to do the following:

1. Sort the found set by Customer ID.
2. Choose **File|Export Records**.
3. Specify a filename for the export (something like CustTemp.txt will do nicely).

4. Select the fields Customer ID, gMonth, gYear, Invoice Count, and Total Invoice Amount, as shown in Figure 9.5. The reason for exporting the global fields is that these will import nicely into the Month and Year fields in CustomerMonthly, saving you the trouble of having to do a calculated replace or looping script after they're imported.

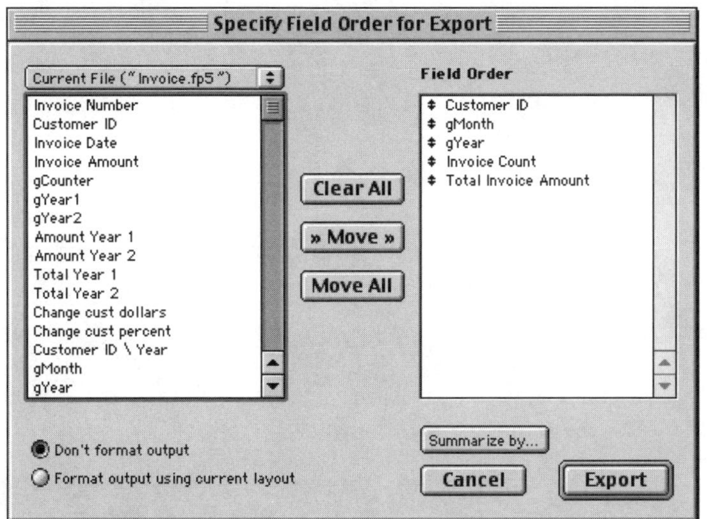

Figure 9.5

5. Click the **Summarize by** button on the Export specification dialog, and click **Customer ID** on the dialog that comes up. If you've forgotten to sort your records before exporting, you won't see any choices for summarizing. After you've clicked **OK**, the Export dialog will look like Figure 9.6, with the summarized fields in italics.

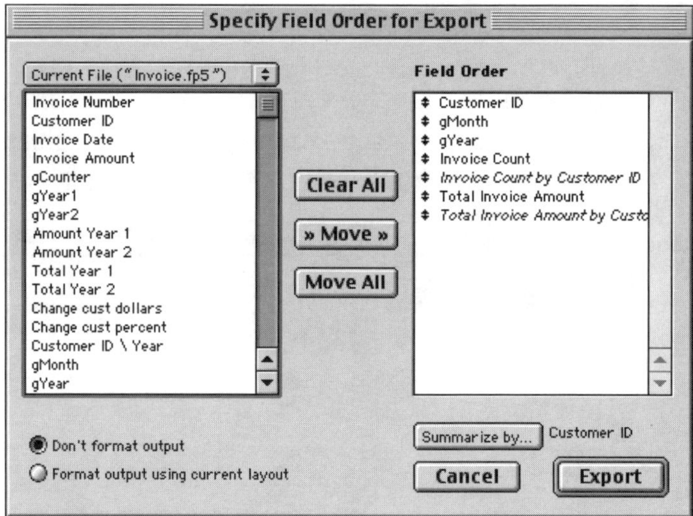

Figure 9.6

6. Now here's the crucial part. Remove the original summary fields from the list of fields to export, leaving behind the fields in italics, so that the dialog looks like Figure 9.7.

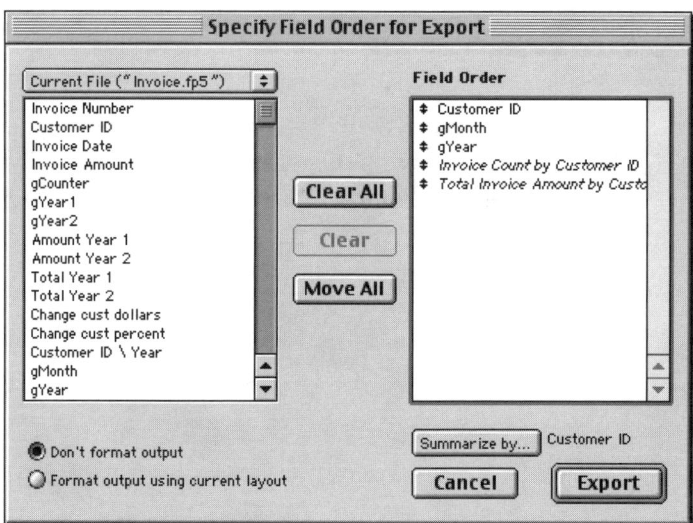

Figure 9.7

7. Click **Export**.

All that remains is to write a subscript in Customer Monthly that will import the CustTemp.txt file that's just been exported from the Invoice table. As with the export, you'll want to do it once yourself manually, and then set up the import to run without dialog. Be sure to test all possible scenarios (selecting the same month/year twice, selecting a month/year that doesn't have invoice data, etc.) before declaring the job done. Then, assign someone the responsibility of running the routine each month and teach that person how to do it. There's much more to creating a process than just writing scripts after all!

Step 3 — Accessing the Data in the Warehouse

After all the work of creating the warehouse and loading it with data, what's the payoff? Well, let's look at how quick and easy it is to pull up sales history for a given customer. Imagine you've got a basic data entry screen in the Customer table that looks something like Figure 9.8. There's a button to view invoice history but it doesn't do anything yet. What you'd like is for this button to pull up the monthly totals for this customer from the warehouse.

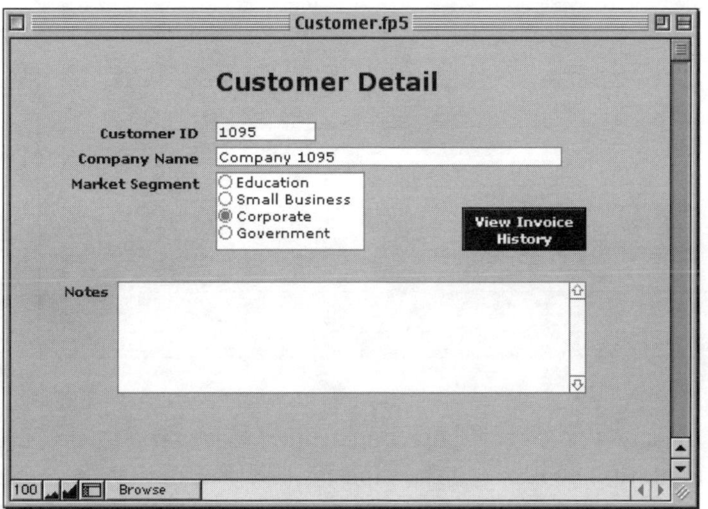

Figure 9.8

To begin, create a relationship from Customer to CustomerMonthly by Customer ID. You could use this relationship to build a portal that displays the invoice history for a customer, but for the sake of something different, let's actually build the display for the invoice history as a list layout in CustomerMonthly.

The script that runs when a user clicks View Invoice History really only needs to do two things: go to related records and perform an external script that sorts and displays the set of records. Figure 9.9 shows an example of what the resulting display of the invoice history looks like for Customer 1095.

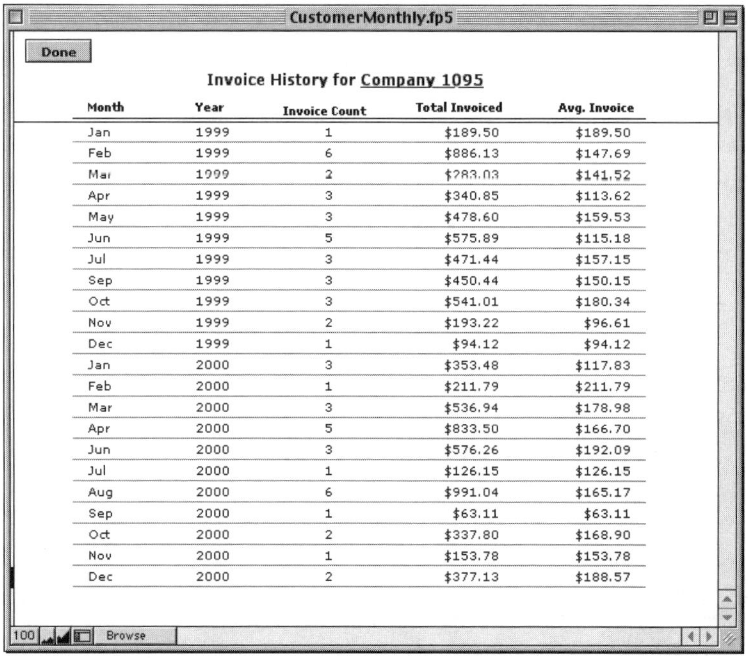

CustomerMonthly.fp5

Done

Invoice History for Company 1095

Month	Year	Invoice Count	Total Invoiced	Avg. Invoice
Jan	1999	1	$189.50	$189.50
Feb	1999	6	$886.13	$147.69
Mar	1999	2	$283.03	$141.52
Apr	1999	3	$340.85	$113.62
May	1999	3	$478.60	$159.53
Jun	1999	5	$575.89	$115.18
Jul	1999	3	$471.44	$157.15
Sep	1999	3	$450.44	$150.15
Oct	1999	3	$541.01	$180.34
Nov	1999	2	$193.22	$96.61
Dec	1999	1	$94.12	$94.12
Jan	2000	3	$353.48	$117.83
Feb	2000	1	$211.79	$211.79
Mar	2000	3	$536.94	$178.98
Apr	2000	5	$833.50	$166.70
Jun	2000	3	$576.26	$192.09
Jul	2000	1	$126.15	$126.15
Aug	2000	6	$991.04	$165.17
Sep	2000	1	$63.11	$63.11
Oct	2000	2	$337.80	$168.90
Nov	2000	1	$153.78	$153.78
Dec	2000	2	$377.13	$188.57

100 Browse

Figure 9.9

There are a few fields that have been added to this report that are worth noting. The first is the name of the month itself. Recall that the month is stored as a number. To turn it into the name of the month (or the abbreviation, as done here), the best tool is the Choose function. The calculation is as follows:

```
Month Name (calculation, text result) = Choose(Month-1, "Jan", "Feb", "Mar",
     "Apr", "May", "Jun", "Jul", "Aug", "Sep", "Oct", "Nov", "Dec")
```

The other field that was added is a calculation for the Average Invoice amount, which is simply Total Invoiced divided by Invoice Count.

The report as shown here is a simple list. It would require only minor tweaking to become a subsummary by year. However, if you leave it as a list, you don't need to be in Preview mode to view it. There's one big potential benefit to being in Browse mode, and that's that you can allow the user to click on a row and, say, drill down to the list of invoices that make up the monthly total. All that you would need is a relationship from Customer Monthly to Invoice built on a combination of Customer ID, Year, and Month.

Beyond showing you the invoice history for a selected customer, there are a number of other questions that could easily and quickly be answered using the summarized data from the warehouse. For instance, you could add summary fields to the warehouse to get total invoice counts and amounts by month. Given the number of records, it would be much quicker to summarize this data here rather than the Invoice table. You could also store different types of summary data in the warehouse along with the customer data, though this can get tricky. You might, for example, want to store invoice totals by Salesperson or Market Segment. Instead of creating new utility tables for those, you could simply add a Type field to the warehouse and store all of these in the same file. As long as you're careful and consistent, using utility files to store aggregate data can really be a powerful tool to add to your arsenal.

Bucket Reports

You've already seen a type of bucket report back when you were creating the year-over-year report in the Invoice table. Perhaps the name "bucket report" is uninspiring, but it's somehow aptly descriptive of the process involved. Of all the reporting methods we discuss here, you'll probably find bucket reports to be the most useful.

Essentially, the bucket approach can be used anytime you have a column of data that you want to split into multiple columns (aka "buckets") based on some categorical data element. An example will clarify this; don't worry.

Imagine that your new boss, impressed with your reporting capabilities so far, scribbles out a new invoice report she wants, showing the breakdown of sales for the year 2000 by both Market Segment and Month.

Market Segment	**Jan**	**Feb**	**Mar**	**Apr**	**May**	**Jun**	**Jul etc.**
Corporate	x	x	x	x	x	x	x
Education	y	y	y	y	y	y	y
Government							
Small Business							

You're not quite sure how to do this, but tell her you'll see what you can come up with. So, you start by identifying the relevant fields in the Invoice database and/or related tables that contain the data you'll likely need to use, and you jot down a few sample records:

Customer by Customer ID

Market Segment	**Invoice Date**	**Invoice Amount**
Small Business	10/30/2000	150.66
Corporate	10/28/2000	183.77
Government	1/31/2000	54.65
Education	8/13/2000	135.94
Government	2/21/2000	63.47
Small Business	4/26/2000	176.36
Education	7/2/2000	103.95
Corporate	4/1/2000	144.64
Small Business	6/6/2000	105.55
Government	2/13/2000	131.98

Your first thought is to create a subsummary report, sorting first by Market Segment and then by Month. A reasonable thought, but you soon realize this would result in a report that looked as follows:

Corporate

Jan x
Feb x
Mar x
Apr x
etc.

Education
Jan x
Feb x
Mar x
etc.

The numbers would be right, but the format just won't do. Think as you might, there's just no way you can figure out how to get a subsummary part to display horizontally rather than vertically.

Enter the bucket concept. The idea is that you want to set up 12 buckets, one for each column on the report you're trying to generate. Each record's data gets tossed into one (and only one) of the buckets, depending on some rule that you set up. Looking at the sample data above, for instance, the first record has an invoice date of 10/30/2000. You'd want to toss its invoice amount of $150.66 into bucket 10, since it's a month 10 invoice.

Each bucket will be a new calculation field in your table. Their definitions in this case are as follows:

```
Jan Amount (calculation, number result) = Case( Month(Invoice Date) = 1,
          Invoice Amount)
Feb Amount (calculation, number result) = Case( Month(Invoice Date) = 2,
          Invoice Amount)
Mar Amount (calculation, number result) = Case( Month(Invoice Date) = 3,
          Invoice Amount
Apr Amount (calculation, number result) = Case( Month(Invoice Date) = 4,
          Invoice Amount)
May Amount (calculation, number result) = Case( Month(Invoice Date) = 5,
          Invoice Amount)
Jun Amount (calculation, number result) = Case( Month(Invoice Date) = 6,
          Invoice Amount)
Jul Amount (calculation, number result) = Case( Month(Invoice Date) = 7,
          Invoice Amount)
Aug Amount (calculation, number result) = Case( Month(Invoice Date) = 8,
          Invoice Amount)
Sep Amount (calculation, number result) = Case( Month(Invoice Date) = 9,
          Invoice Amount)
Oct Amount (calculation, number result) = Case( Month(Invoice Date) = 10,
          Invoice Amount)
Nov Amount (calculation, number result) = Case( Month(Invoice Date) = 11,
          Invoice Amount)
```

```
Dec Amount (calculation, number result) = Case( Month(Invoice Date) = 12,
Invoice Amount)
```

Figure 9.10 illustrates how the data above is split into the 12 buckets.

::Market Segment	Invoice Date	Invoice Am...	Jan am...	Feb am...	Mar am...	Apr am...	May a...	Jun am...	Jul amo...	Aug am...	Sep am...	Oct am...	Nov amo...	Dec amo...
Small Business	10/30/2000	150.66										150.66		
Corporate	10/28/2000	183.77										183.77		
Government	1/31/2000	54.65	54.65											
Education	8/13/2000	135.94								135.94				
Government	2/21/2000	63.47		63.47										
Small Business	4/26/2000	176.36				176.36								
Education	7/2/2000	103.95							103.95					
Corporate	4/1/2000	144.64				144.64								
Small Business	6/6/2000	105.55						105.55						
Government	2/13/2000	131.98		131.98										

Figure 9.10

None of these calculations needs to be stored or indexed, so beyond cluttering up your field definitions, they don't take up much space in your table. Once the data have been split into separate buckets, all that remains is to summarize them by Market Segment. Unfortunately, this means adding some more clutter to your field definitions, since each bucket needs a summary field.

```
Total Jan (summary) = Total of Jan Amount
Total Feb (summary) = Total of Feb Amount
Total Mar (summary) = Total of Mar Amount
Total Apr (summary) = Total of Apr Amount
Total May (summary) = Total of May Amount
Total Jun (summary) = Total of Jun Amount
Total Jul (summary) = Total of Jul Amount
Total Aug (summary) = Total of Aug Amount
Total Sep (summary) = Total of Sep Amount
Total Oct (summary) = Total of Oct Amount
Total Nov (summary) = Total of Nov Amount
Total Dec (summary) = Total of Dec Amount
```

The good news, though, is that you now have everything you need to build your report. The layout will be a simple subsummary when sorted by Market Segment, with the Body part deleted, as shown in Figure 9.11. The summary fields can, of course, also be used in a Trailing Grand Summary part to generate column totals. Figure 9.12 shows the finished report. Be sure to do a find for a particular year's worth of data before running this report.

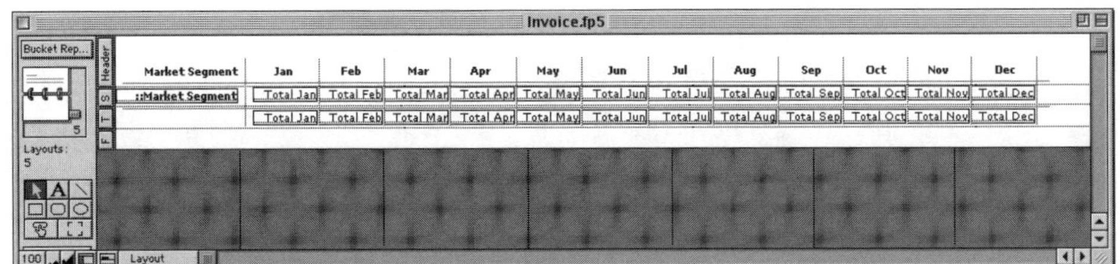

Figure 9.11

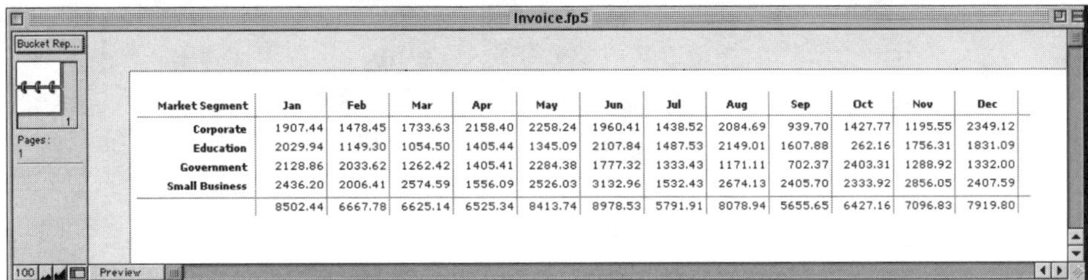

Figure 9.12

Because of the number of fields you need to create, bucket reports work best when the number of columns won't change. Beyond that, though, they're actually quite flexible in that you can easily summarize by different fields to create entirely new reports without defining more fields. For instance, the report above could be summarized by Salesperson or Customer. The only downsides, really, are that summary reports can be frustratingly slow with large amounts of data and that the report has to be viewed in Preview mode, which means you can't allow the user to click on a row or column to "drill down" to a more granular look at the data. We'll look next at an alternative way of creating a bucket report that attempts to remedy both of these shortcomings.

Another Approach to Bucket Reports

As much as we like bucket reports, the method described above is not always the best way to create them. Reviewing, the three things we don't like about the previous method are the number of new fields that need to be created, the speed (or lack thereof) with large sets of data, and the inability to drill down. There's an alternate method for creating bucket reports that solves all of these, though it's admittedly a bit more complex to create.

The concept, at least, is simple. Rather than sort and summarize, a script will loop through the records and build the entire report as an array in a single global field. Then, this global field will be passed to a utility file that will parse and display the data as a simple list. The only new field needed in the Invoice database is a global text field that we'll call gReportArray.

An array can be thought of simply as a delimited list of items. Unfortunately, FileMaker doesn't have very good tools for working with arrays, but with basic text parsing, you can still do quite a lot. For the current report, you need a two-dimensional array (which you can think of as a spreadsheet, if it helps). Each piece of data in the array can be located uniquely by a pair of ordinal numbers representing its position (row and column). Again, there's no array feature in FileMaker (alas), so you need to construct the array yourself. We'll use pipe characters (|) to delimit values within a row, and return characters (¶) to delimit rows. Figure 9.13 shows the initial state of the global array before adding values to it.

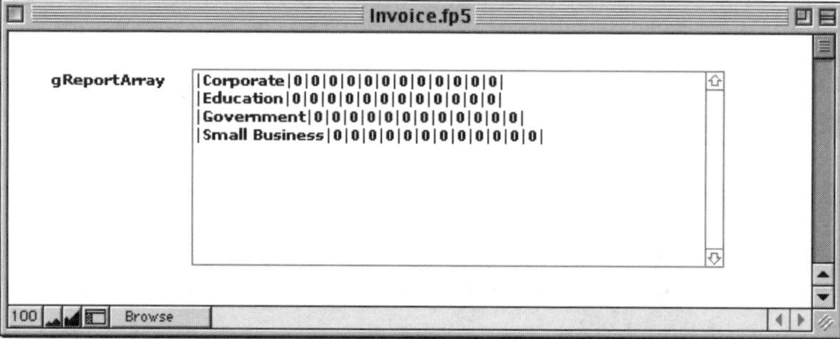

Figure 9.13

Eventually, all those zeros will turn into the numbers for your report. Let's look first, though, at the script that was used to initialize the array:

```
Set Field [gReport Array, ""]
Go to Record/Request/Page [First]
Loop
     If [not PatternCount (gReportArray, "|" & Customer by Customer
         ID::Market Segment &"|"]
          Set Field [gReportArray, gReportArray & "|" & Customer by Customer
                 ID::Market Segment &"|" & "0|0|0|0|0|0|0|0|0|0|0|0|¶"]
     End If
     Go to Record/Request/Page [Exit after last, Next]
End Loop
```

The script begins by clearing out the global text field gReportArray. Then, it loops through the found set of records in the Invoice table. The records don't need to be sorted, by the way. For each record it comes to, it asks the question, "Is there a row in the array for this Market Segment?" Notice that the search string argument in the PatternCount function is surrounded by delimiters; without them, if one of the Market Segments happened to be a subset of another (i.e., "Business" and "Small Business") there would be problems. If the Market Segment isn't found in the array, the next line of the script adds a new row to the array and initializes 12 columns with zeros.

Believe it or not, adding actual values to the array requires only one more script step. It's a doozie, though: a Set Field that replaces the existing value from the proper place in the array with itself plus the invoice amount of the current record. Let's briefly review the syntax of the Replace script step before looking at the calculation:

```
Replace (text, start, size, replacement text)
```

- text — the string of data to work with
- start — the character position to begin cutting
- size — the number of characters to cut
- replacement text — the text to drop into the cut-out part

For example,

```
Replace ("This is a test", 6, 2, "was")
```

would yield

```
"This was a test"
```

For the bucket array, the text attribute is just the gReportArray field itself. The start character can be found first by finding the position of the Market Segment within the array, and then finding the (month+1)th pipe character after that, and adding 1. The size attribute is the position of the next pipe character after this, minus the start position.

An example will help clarify this.

Let's assume that gReportArray contained the following string:

```
|Corporate|10|20|30|40|50|60|70|80|90|100|110|120|
1   5    10   15   20   25   30   35   40   45   50
```

and the current record contained:

Market Segment = "Corporate"
Invoice Date = "4/2/2000"
Invoice Amount = "123.45"

The start value would be the position of the fifth pipe character from the position of "|Corporate|", plus 1, which in this case is 21.

The size would be the position of the sixth pipe character following "|Corporate|" (which is 23), minus the start position (21), which results in 2.

The replacement text for these two characters is simply the sum of the value of those two characters (found using the Middle function and the same position logic as above) and the Invoice Amount. After processing the current record, gReportArray would contain the new string:

|Corporate|10|20|30|163.45|50|60|70|80|90|100|110|120|

The calculation that does all of this at once is the following:

```
Replace(
gReportArray,

Position(gReportArray, "|", Position(gReportArray, "|"& Customer by Customer
     ID::Market Segment & "|",1,1) , Month(Invoice Date) + 1)+ 1,

Position(gReportArray, "|", Position(gReportArray, "|"& Customer by Customer
     ID::Market Segment & "|",1,1) , Month(Invoice Date) + 2) -
     (Position(gReportArray, "|", Position(gReportArray, "|"& Customer by
     Customer ID::Market Segment & "|",1,1) , Month(Invoice Date) + 1)+ 1),

Middle(gReportArray,
Position(gReportArray, "|", Position(gReportArray, "|"& Customer by Customer
     ID::Market Segment & "|",1,1) , Month(Invoice Date) + 1)+ 1,
Position(gReportArray, "|", Position(gReportArray, "|"& Customer by Customer
     ID::Market Segment & "|",1,1) , Month(Invoice Date) + 2) -
     (Position(gReportArray, "|", Position(gReportArray, "|"& Customer by
     Customer ID::Market Segment & "|",1,1) , Month(Invoice Date) + 1)+ 1))
     + Invoice Amount)
```

The entire script, then, consists of the following:

```
Set Field [gReport Array, ""]
Go to Record/Request/Page [First]
Loop
If [not PatternCount (gReportArray, "|" & Customer by Customer ID::Market
     Segment &"|"]
Set Field [gReportArray, gReportArray & "|" & Customer by Customer
     ID::Market Segment &"|" & "0|0|0|0|0|0|0|0|0|0|0|0|¶"]
     End If
     Set Field [gReportArray,  – the big calculation above –  ]
     Go to Record/Request/Page [Exit after last, Next]
End Loop
```

The contents of the array after running the script are shown in Figure 9.14.

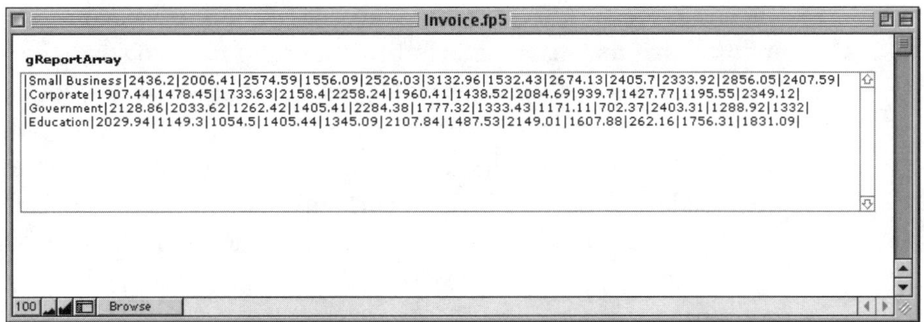

Figure 9.14

With the array built and populated with data, all that remains is to parse it into records in a utility file. If you were doing a lot of this sort of reporting, you could build the utility file to be flexible enough to parse different data sets, but for now, we'll build one suited to the task at hand.

The fields in the new table, which we'll call MarketReport are as follows:

Field Name	**Type**
Market Segment	text
Jan	number
Feb	number
Mar	number
Apr	number
May	number
Jun	number
Jul	number

Aug	number
Sep	number
Oct	number
Nov	number
Dec	number
Constant	calculation = 1
gTempString1	Global, text
gTempString2	Global, text

You'll also need a constant relationship from MarketReport to Invoice, so you can move data from one table to the other. The script below to parse the report array looks more complicated than it is. It's a basic parsing routine where the top line of the array gets sliced off and parsed into various fields, continuing until there's nothing left in the array.

The script opens with Show All Records / Delete All Records to clear out anything that may have been left in the utility file. However, be warned that this could cause serious issues in a multiuser setting. Imagine one person is viewing a report and someone else runs a new report. The new report will completely replace the first user's report, which will likely alarm that user. The simple workaround in a network environment is to stamp all records in the utility file with either a User ID or a Session ID. Then, instead of deleting all records, just delete any records belonging to the current user before parsing a new set of data.

Finally, then, the parsing script is as follows:

```
Show All Records
Delete All Records [No dialog]
Set Field [gTempString1, Invoice by Constant::gReportArray]
Loop
     Exit Loop If [IsEmpty(gTempString1)]
     New Record/Request
Set Field [gTempString2, Left(gTempString1,
Position(gTempString1,"¶",1,1)-1)]
Set Field [Market Segment, Middle(gTempString2, Position(gTempString2,
     "|",1,1)+ 1, Position(gTempString2,"|",1,2) -
(Position(gTempString2,"|",1,1) + 1))]
Set Field [Jan , Middle(gTempString2, Position(gTempString2, "|",1,2)+
     1, Position(gTempString2,"|",1,3) -
     (Position(gTempString2,"|",1,2) + 1))]
```

```
Set Field [Feb, Middle(gTempString2, Position(gTempString2, "|",1,3)+ 1,
     Position(gTempString2,"|",1,4) - (Position(gTempString2,"|",1,3) + 1))]
Set Field [Mar, Middle(gTempString2, Position(gTempString2, "|",1,4)+ 1,
     Position(gTempString2,"|",1,5) - (Position(gTempString2,"|",1,4) + 1))]
Set Field [Apr, Middle(gTempString2, Position(gTempString2, "|",1,5)+ 1,
     Position(gTempString2,"|",1,6) - (Position(gTempString2,"|",1,5) + 1))]
Set Field [May, Middle(gTempString2, Position(gTempString2, "|",1,6)+ 1,
     Position(gTempString2,"|",1,7) - (Position(gTempString2,"|",1,6) + 1))]
Set Field [Jun, Middle(gTempString2, Position(gTempString2, "|",1,7)+ 1,
     Position(gTempString2,"|",1,8) - (Position(gTempString2,"|",1,7) + 1))]
Set Field [Jul, Middle(gTempString2, Position(gTempString2, "|",1,8)+ 1,
     Position(gTempString2,"|",1,9) - (Position(gTempString2,"|",1,8) + 1))]
Set Field [Aug, Middle(gTempString2, Position(gTempString2, "|",1,9)+ 1,
     Position(gTempString2,"|",1,10) - (Position(gTempString2,"|",1,9) + 1))]
Set Field [Sep, Middle(gTempString2, Position(gTempString2, "|",1,10)+ 1,
     Position(gTempString2,"|",1,11) - (Position(gTempString2,"|",1,10) +
     1))]
Set Field [Oct, Middle(gTempString2, Position(gTempString2, "|",1,11)+ 1,
     Position(gTempString2,"|",1,12) - (Position(gTempString2,"|",1,11) +
     1))]
Set Field [Nov, Middle(gTempString2, Position(gTempString2, "|",1,12)+ 1,
     Position(gTempString2,"|",1,13) - (Position(gTempString2,"|",1,12) +
     1))]
Set Field [Dec, Middle(gTempString2, Position(gTempString2, "|",1,13)+ 1,
     Position(gTempString2,"|",1,14) - (Position(gTempString2,"|",1,13) +
     1))]
Set Field [gTempString1, Right(gTempString1, Length(gTempString1) -
     Position(gTempString1,"¶",1,1))]
End Loop
Go to Layout [Market Report]
```

You would call this script as a subscript at the end of the Alternate Bucket Report script in the Invoice table. Even though it looks like there's a whole lot going on, all of the string functions are lightning fast, so the whole array creation and parsing don't take long at all. In fact, the slowest part of the script above is the creation of the new record, and in the previous script, the slowest step was movement from record to record.

Figure 9.15 shows the finished report as it appears in MarketReport. Let's review some of the benefits of this method of creating bucket reports:

- Faster with large sets of data and/or over a network
- Doesn't clutter Invoice table with dozens of new fields
- Report viewable in Browse mode

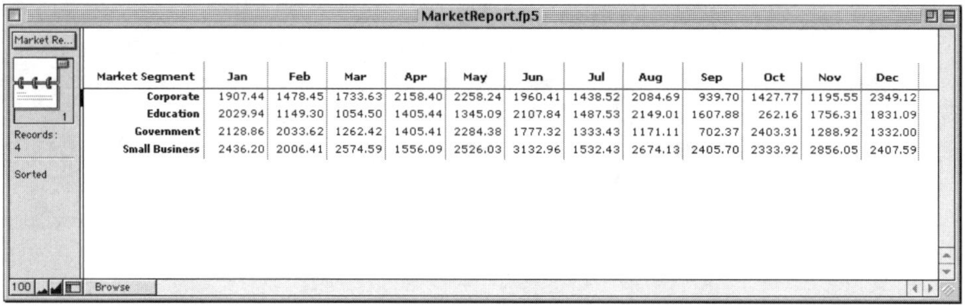

MarketReport.fp5

Market Segment	Jan	Feb	Mar	Apr	May	Jun	Jul	Aug	Sep	Oct	Nov	Dec
Corporate	1907.44	1478.45	1733.63	2158.40	2258.24	1960.41	1438.52	2084.69	939.70	1427.77	1195.55	2349.12
Education	2029.94	1149.30	1054.50	1405.44	1345.09	2107.84	1487.53	2149.01	1607.88	262.16	1756.31	1831.09
Government	2128.86	2033.62	1262.42	1405.41	2284.38	1777.32	1333.43	1171.11	702.37	2403.31	1288.92	1332.00
Small Business	2436.20	2006.41	2574.59	1556.09	2526.03	3132.96	1532.43	2674.13	2405.70	2333.92	2856.05	2407.59

Market Re...
Records: 4
Sorted
100 Browse

Figure 9.15

And since it's mostly script based, this method is easier to modify and troubleshoot, especially over a network.

We should mention that there are several methods other than using arrays that could have been used to move data into the MarketReport table. For instance, you might create a relationship from Invoice to MarketReport based on Market Segment, and then push data into the appropriate bucket during a looping script.

There are always multiple ways to accomplish a given task, especially when it comes to scripting. You need to evaluate the pros and cons of various methods and pick the one that best suits your purpose. The array approach, for instance, requires a minimum of new fields and relationships in the Invoice table, yet offers a great deal of flexibility to summarize by other parameters if necessary (i.e., Salesperson or Customer). When you're not sure which approach will be the fastest, you probably need to build some test tables to compare them. Or work on backups until you're confident you've got a good approach. Think of yourself as an artist making sketches before working on the final piece. The sketches themselves are a good learning exercise and may solve other, yet unasked questions.

Charting

Before the invention of plug-ins, creating high-quality charts and graphs with FileMaker was nearly impossible. A few brave souls did come up with workarounds that involved stacking underscores or pipe characters. But on the whole, producing charts meant exporting to something like Excel.

There are currently two charting plug-ins in the market that we know of. One is øAzium Chart from Waves in Motion (www.wmotion.com) and the other is xmChart from X2max (www.x2max.com). Both come with terrific examples and instructions, are affordable, work cross platform, and produce high-quality charts.

Charting is a great example of why plug-ins were developed in the first place. Rather than FileMaker, Inc. attempting to build in all the features that everyone requested, they opened up the program to allow people to write their own "features" as needed. Now, quite a few developers are earning a good living doing nothing other than creating and selling plug-ins.

In this section, we'll show you some basic ways you can add charting to your report repertoire. Your users will love these. We'll use the xmChart plug-in in the examples that follow, but all of the charts we show could easily be produced by øAzium Chart as well.

In order to try any of the example files on the CD or build these yourself, you'll obviously have to download, install, and enable the plug-in. On Windows, place the plug-in in your FileMaker System folder, and on Macintosh, place it in the FileMaker Extensions folder. You can confirm that the plug-in is active by launching FileMaker and going to Edit|Preferences|Application, and clicking on the Plug-Ins tab.

The xmChart plug-in has literally hundreds of variables you can specify, but it's really not complicated to use. Essentially, you build a list of instructions in a field (usually a global) and pass it to the plug-in via the external function xmCH-DrawChart. The plug-in creates the chart and places it on the clipboard. From there, you can simply paste into a container field to view the chart.

The final bucket report built in the last section will act as the source for the chart examples that follow (see Figure 9.15). Your two tasks this time are to turn the column headings into buttons that create pie charts showing the distribution of revenue for the selected month, and to turn the row headings into buttons that create line charts showing the monthly sales for the selected market. Figures 9.16 and 9.17 illustrate the end goals of your tasks.

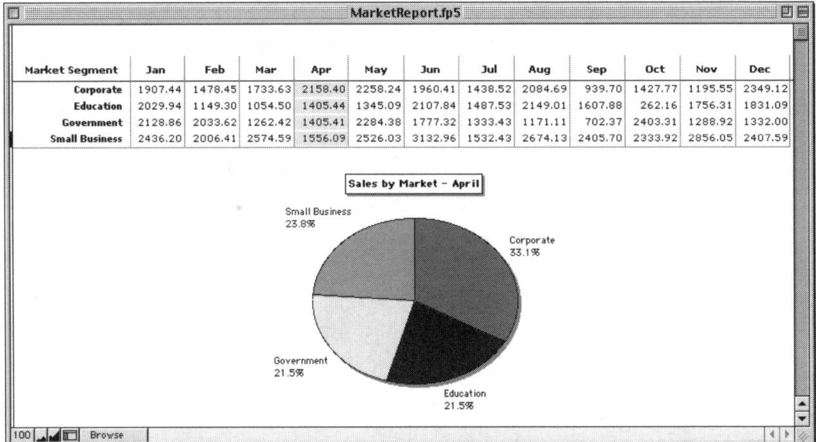

MarketReport.fp5

Market Segment	Jan	Feb	Mar	Apr	May	Jun	Jul	Aug	Sep	Oct	Nov	Dec
Corporate	1907.44	1478.45	1733.63	2158.40	2258.24	1960.41	1438.52	2084.69	939.70	1427.77	1195.55	2349.12
Education	2029.94	1149.30	1054.50	1405.44	1345.09	2107.84	1487.53	2149.01	1607.88	262.16	1756.31	1831.09
Government	2128.86	2033.62	1262.42	1405.41	2284.38	1777.32	1333.43	1171.11	702.37	2403.31	1288.92	1332.00
Small Business	2436.20	2006.41	2574.59	1556.09	2526.03	3132.96	1532.43	2674.13	2405.70	2333.92	2856.05	2407.59

Figure 9.16

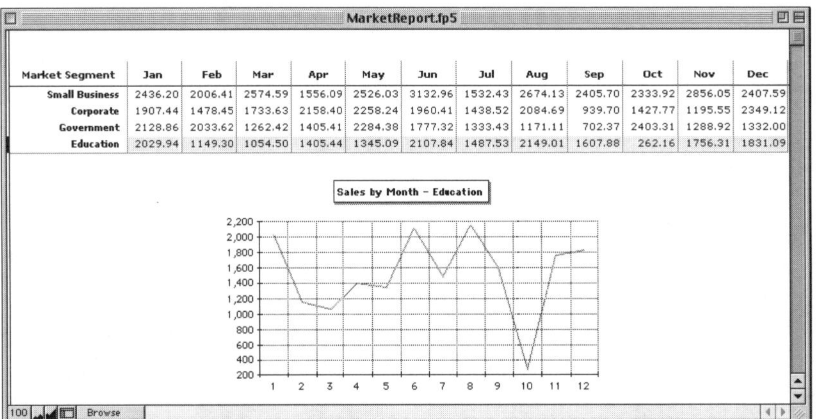

MarketReport.fp5

Market Segment	Jan	Feb	Mar	Apr	May	Jun	Jul	Aug	Sep	Oct	Nov	Dec
Small Business	2436.20	2006.41	2574.59	1556.09	2526.03	3132.96	1532.43	2674.13	2405.70	2333.92	2856.05	2407.59
Corporate	1907.44	1478.45	1733.63	2158.40	2258.24	1960.41	1438.52	2084.69	939.70	1427.77	1195.55	2349.12
Government	2128.86	2033.62	1262.42	1405.41	2284.38	1777.32	1333.43	1171.11	702.37	2403.31	1288.92	1332.00
Education	2029.94	1149.30	1054.50	1405.44	1345.09	2107.84	1487.53	2149.01	1607.88	262.16	1756.31	1831.09

Figure 9.17

Task 1 — Pie Chart

Recall that we said earlier that one of the benefits of creating the bucket report for sales by month as a simple list in a utility table was that it could be viewed while in Browse mode. Now you'll see why this is such a benefit. You can place buttons on the report that allow the user to interact with it in ways that would be impossible in Preview mode.

In order to make a pie chart, the charting plug-in needs to be fed a set of instructions. Each line of the instructions contains information about a particular attribute, such as the title or legend, and has a number of parameters (delimited by semicolons), which can be set to control the behavior of that attribute. The attributes are separated by carriage returns, and the order of the attributes is not significant.

The following is an example of instructions that will generate a pie chart:

```
OpenDrawing(300;250)
    ChartData (24 13 45 23)
    PieChart (oval+shadow+label)
    TitleText ("Test of Pie Chart")
    TitleBackground (;;;;;2;)
    LabelTexts (1;"Pie 1l1\nlf1l%";"Pie 2l1\nlf1l%"; "Pie 3l1\nlf1l%";
         "Pie 4l1\nlf1l%"
Close Drawing()
```

The chart that these instructions generate is shown in Figure 9.18.

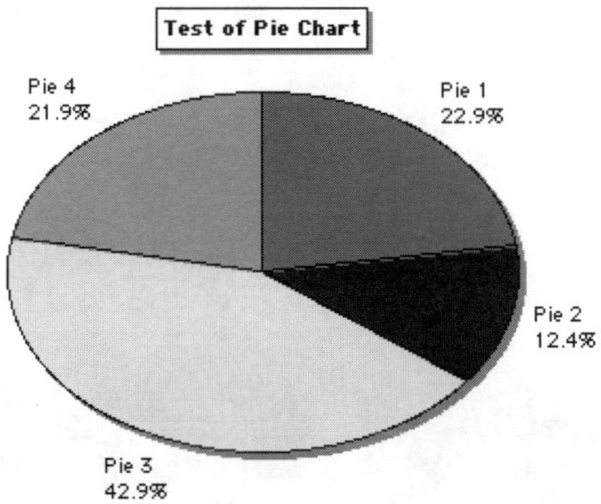

Figure 9.18

The specific meaning of the attributes isn't important here. These instructions will be used as the template for the following pie charts, so it's worth noting a few things. Lines 2 and 4 contain data that will differ from chart to chart depending on what month the user clicks. Line 5, the label texts, is also dynamic in a way, as it needs to list all of the Market Segments. The other lines, however, don't need to change from report to report, as they contain instructions about the overall appearance of the chart.

With that as background, it's time to start scripting. Since there will be 12 buttons the user can click (one for each month), you're going to need at least 12 separate scripts. However, rather than putting all of the charting logic in each script, it makes much more sense to try to have a subscript do the charting, and then to have the 12 scripts simply set variables the charting subscript can use. This way, you're assured of consistency, and if you want to change any of the charting parameters, you only have to change them in one place, not 12.

We think the easiest way to build something like this is to first create one script with all of the logic necessary. Then, try to figure out what you can take out to make it generic, so it can be called as a subscript. For instance, you might start by making a script that would specifically generate a pie chart for the column of January data. It would end up looking something like the following:

```
Go to Layout [Chart Utility]
Set Field [gChart Data, ""]
Set Field [gLegendText, ""]
Go to Record/Request/Page [First]
Loop
     Set Field [gChartData, gChartData & Jan & " "]
     gLegendText &""""& Market Segment & "\nl11f1l%""" % ";"]
     Go to Record/Request/Page [Exit after last, Next]
End Loop
Set Field [gChartInstructions, Open Drawing (300;250)
     ChartData("& gChartData &")
     PieChart(oval+shadow+label)
     TitleText(""Sales by Market - "& gSelection &""")
     LabelTexts(1;" & gLegendText &")
     TitleBackground (;;;;;2;)"]
Set Field [gChartError, External (xmCH-DrawChart, gChartInstructions)]
Paste [Select, Chart]
Go to Layout ["Market Report"]
```

Five new fields were created for this charting routine: four global text fields (gChartData, gLegendText, gChartInstructions, and gChartError) and one container field (Chart). The heart of the script is a simple loop that moves from record to record and collects the January sales for each Market Segment. By the time the loop is complete, gChartData will contain a space-delimited list of the four data points, while gLegendText will contain the corresponding names of the Market Segments. Note that literal text strings like the legend text and the title need to be enclosed in quotes when passed to the plug-in.

The gChartInstructions field then integrates the dynamically generated gChartData and gLegendText data and the hard-coded charting instructions. These instructions get passed to the plug-in in the next script step. The purpose of setting gChartError to the results of the External function, by the way, is that if an error is generated by the plug-in, you've got someplace to view the error. If there are no errors, then gChartError will be left blank. So, you may want to have a step after calling the plug-in that checks to see if gChartError is empty or not and acts accordingly.

Finally, the script pastes the contents of the clipboard (which now has the chart on it) into the Chart container field. Keep in mind when using the Paste function (and the Cut, Copy, and Clear functions for that matter) that the field referenced must be on the current layout, or else the script step will fail. This is why the script goes to a layout called Chart Utility and then back to the report layout at the very end.

You'll notice that the specific references to January are set in bold type. In order to turn this script into a generic script that can be used regardless of month, you have to figure out how to replace these references with variables. Then, you can build 12 scripts that set the variables appropriately and call this script as a subscript.

The first thing to replace is the field referenced within the loop. Right now, it references specifically the "Jan" field. The new GetField function in FileMaker 5.5 will help you turn this into a generic function. GetField returns the contents of a field referenced by a variable. In the current situation, say you have a global text field called gSelection, and that field contains the text string "Jan." Then, GetField (gSelection) will return the value of the field whose name is "Jan."

The other month-specific data that needs to be replaced is the name of the month in the title. This is just literal text (as opposed to field data), so no GetField function is needed.

You could use two separate global variables to eliminate the month-specific data, but since the name of the field containing the sales data is always the first three characters of the name of the month, one field is all that's really needed. Given the name of the month, the name of the field containing that month's sales data can be derived using the Left function.

Your next step, then, is to create a month-specific script called Chart: January which does the following:

```
Set Field [gSelection, "January"]
Perform Script [Sub-scripts, "Sub: Create Pie Chart"]
```

Then, modify the script you wrote earlier so that it references gSelection where appropriate:

```
Go to Layout [Chart Utility]
Set Field [gChart Data, ""]
Set Field [gLegendText, ""]
Go to Record/Request/Page [First]
Loop
   Set Field [gChartData, gChartData & GetField (Left (gSelection,3)) & " "]
   Set Field [gLegendText, gLegendText & """" & Market Segment & """" & ";"]
       Go to Record/Request/Page [Exit after last, Next]
End Loop
Set Field [gChartInstructions, "ChartData (" & gChartData &")¶
PieChart(clipboard;400;225;shadow+label+3D+oval;;;20;max)¶
TitleText(""Sales by Market - " & gSelection & """)¶
LegendTexts(" & gLegendText &")¶
TitleBackground (;;;;;2;)"]
Set Field [gChartError, External (xmCH-DrawChart, gChartInstructions)]
Paste [Select, Chart]
Go to Layout ["Market Report"]
```

All that's left now is to create 11 more scripts, each similar to the Chart: January script, and to attach them to invisible buttons placed over the column headings on the report. It's probably a good idea to stop and test after creating two or three of the scripts. This way, if there's a problem, you've got less rework to do.

Task 2 — Line Chart

A pie chart was the proper representation of the breakdown in sales data by market for a single month. Trend data, however, like sales by month for a particular market, is best represented as a line chart or bar chart. In this example, a user will be clicking on a row heading (that is, a particular Market Segment). For many reasons, this task is easier to accomplish than the last one. First, all of the data lives in a single record, which means you don't need a looping construct to gather the chart data. Also, everything can all be done in a single script, since the button to run the script will be tied to unique record.

Line Chart: Sales by Month

```
Go to Layout [Chart Utility]
Set Field [gSelection, Market Segment]
Set Field [gChartData, Jan & " " & Feb & " " & Mar & " " & Apr & " " & May &
          " " & Jun & " " & Jul & " " & Aug & " " & Sep & " " & Oct & " " &
          Nov & " " & Dec]
Set Field [gChartInstructions, Open Drawing (400;225)
          ChartData("& gChartData &"
          LineChart()
          TitleText(""Sales by Month - "& Market Segment &""")
          LabelTexts(1;" & gLegend & ")
          TitleBackground (;;;;;2;)"]
Set Field [gChartError, External (xmCH-DrawChart, gChartInstructions)]
Paste [Select, Chart]
Go to Layout ["Market Report"]
```

The only reason for setting gSelection in the second line of the script above is for the row and column highlighting that you see in Figures 9.16 and 9.17. There's a global highlight field with a yellow rectangle in it, and 12 calculation fields that evaluate to the highlight field if gSelection is either equal to a specific month or the Market Segment of the current record. See the demo files on the companion CD to learn more about that particular feature.

Summary

Our discussion of reporting techniques is by no means exhaustive. We merely intended to show examples of some of the most interesting reporting techniques that we've come across. We began by presenting two methods for doing year-over-year reporting. Then we discussed using a utility file as a data warehouse and continued by examining two methods of creating what we call bucket reports. We concluded by showing how to use a plug-in to create a graphic representation of your data. Hopefully, the methodology we presented gave you some ideas that you'll be able to incorporate into your own solutions.

Chapter 10

Recursive Data Structures

Have you ever stood between two mirrors and been able to see your reflection in the reflection of the other mirror? And the reflection of the reflection of the reflection? This is a good metaphor to keep in mind when thinking about recursion. Here's another you've likely seen. A TV that shows a picture of a TV that shows a picture of a TV that shows a picture… You get the idea.

In FileMaker, recursive structures are usually modeled with self-relationships, though not all self-relationships are recursive. Just as with "normal" relationships, recursive self-relationships can be either one-to-many relationships or many-to-many relationships. Each of these will be explored in detail in this chapter.

So, how can you recognize recursion when you see it? For one, recursive data structures are usually hierarchical and can be represented using tree diagrams. A truly recursive structure is potentially boundless (meaning the tree can keep extending in either direction), and the rules that govern relationships between levels in the hierarchy are independent of their level in the hierarchy.

Think, for instance, of the file structure of your typical computer system (see Figure 10.1). A folder can contain any number of files or other folders, and any folder or file is contained by at most one parent folder. No matter how deep you go in the structure the rules don't change. A folder is a folder. Further, there's no practical limit on the number of levels to the hierarchy. Because of these rules, we would label this data structure as an example of one-to-many recursion.

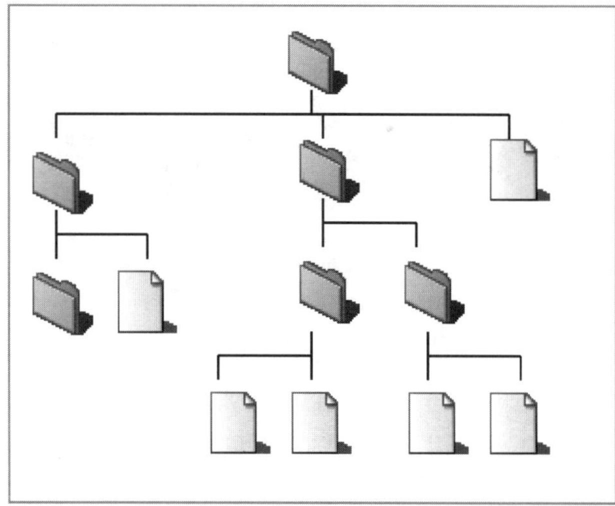

Figure 10.1

In this chapter, we're going to look at two examples of recursive data structures. Now, recursive data structures aren't something that you're going to encounter on a day-to-day basis. When you do, though, you're probably going to end up scratching your head for a fair amount of time trying to figure out the best way to represent the data. Hopefully, this chapter will not only help you to recognize recursive data structures when you see them, but also will give you the tools you need to make the most of them.

One-to-Many Recursion: The Organizational Chart

The classic example of one-to-many recursion is the organizational chart of your average company. Pretend for a while that you've been given the responsibility of maintaining the employee directory for the venerable public speaking firm, Bombast & Invective. The information captured by the database is shown in Figure 10.2.

Employees.FP5

Employee ID	Name First	Name Last	Title
1	Paul	Bombast	CEO
2	Fred	Invective	President
3	Sally	Forth	Vice President
4	Morgan	Sprechen	Account Manager
5	Carl	Louder	Account Manager
6	Holden	Yeller	Account Representative
7	Sandy	Seemore	Account Representative
8	Joe	Schnell	Account Representative

100 Browse

Figure 10.2

The first task you've been given is to produce an organizational chart showing the reporting relationships within the company. It's not uncommon when presented with this scenario for a beginning data modeler to think, "well, there are managers and there are employees, so what I need is another table for managers." Following this logic, you'd probably end up with a data model that looks like Figure 10.3, with a one-to-many relationship between a Manager table and an Employee table.

Figure 10.3

If you were to actually build these tables, there are several problems you'd encounter. The biggest is trying to figure out which records go into which table. After all, managers are also employees, aren't they? If you put the managers into both tables, you end up with data redundancy issues. Another problem is how to deal with the managers of the managers. Do you make yet another table called Senior Managers with a one-to-many relationship to the Manager table?

These problems are clues that should alert you that you're dealing with a recursive data structure. When you have a one-to-many relationship like Customers to Invoices, your tables contain information about two fundamentally different types of objects. Not so with managers and employees. A manager is just an employee. The data fields that you collect about managers are probably the same as those you collect for employees (i.e., data of hire, phone number, birthday, salary). Further, the relationship between employees and managers is analogous to that between managers and senior managers. That is, the rules are independent of the level of hierarchy.

This, then, becomes another example of a one-to-many recursive data structure. It's one-to-many because a manager can have many direct reports, but an employee has only one manager. (Yes, we know that in many organizations you have more complex reporting relationships, but let's keep it simple for now). A one-to-many recursive data structure will actually end up being modeled as a single flat file, with a one-to-many self-relationship as shown in Figure 10.4.

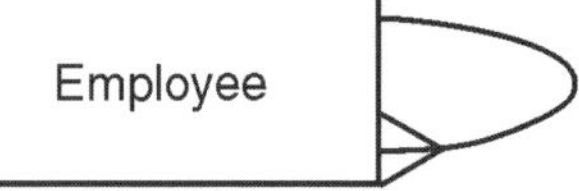

Figure 10.4

OK, so that's how you model it on your ER diagram. Next comes the fun part: making an interface for data entry and displaying this "flat" file as a hierarchical tree structure.

To begin, you need a new field called Manager ID where you can record who reports to whom. This field will hold the Employee ID of the employee's manager. That is, if Sally Forth reports directly to Paul Bombast, the Manager ID field in her record will contain "1," which is Bombast's ID.

It's thus possible to have many people report directly to Bombast. Each of his direct reports, in turn, may be the manager of many other employees. Say that Carl Louder reports to Sally Forth. The Manager ID field in his record, then, will be set to "3." Figure 10.5 shows the results of populating the Manager ID in the Employee table.

Employees.FP5

Employee ID	Name First	Name Last	Title	Manager ID
1	Paul	Bombast	CEO	
2	Fred	Invective	President	1
3	Sally	Forth	Vice President	1
4	Morgan	Sprechen	Account Manager	2
5	Carl	Louder	Account Manager	3
6	Holden	Yeller	Account Representative	4
7	Sandy	Seemore	Account Representative	4
8	Joe	Schnell	Account Representative	5

100 Browse

Figure 10.5

Now for the user interface. To start, you'll want to create a layout to display all of a person's direct reports. Since there are potentially multiple direct reports for a given manager, you'll need a portal to display them. This portal will be based on a self-relationship that matches Employee ID to Manager ID. Relationship naming can get quite confusing when you're dealing with recursion, so we usually try to name these relationships something that will intuitively tell you what the relationship shows. In this case, we'd call this relationship something simple like "Direct Reports." Figure 10.6 shows what your layout might look like with this portal. Keep in mind that there's only one file; the portal displays those records in the Employee file where the Manager ID is equal to the Employee ID of the current record. More concretely, Sally Forth and Fred Invective are those employees whose Manager IDs are 1, so they show up in the portal of direct reports for Paul Bombast, whose Employee ID is 1.

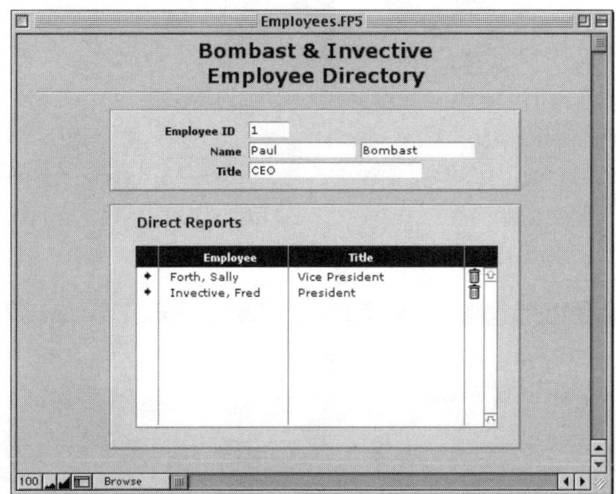

Figure 10.6

Next, you can build another self-relationship to display information about a person's manager. This is the inverse of the "Direct Reports" relationship: it's a self-relationship that matches Manager ID to Employee ID (name the relationship "Manager"). The Manager ID field in any given record points at most to one related record, so you don't need a portal to display this related information; related fields will work just fine.

Figure 10.7 shows Morgan Sprechen's record with her manager's information added. See how the Direct Report portal looks "down" the tree, while the Manager relationship looks "up" the tree.

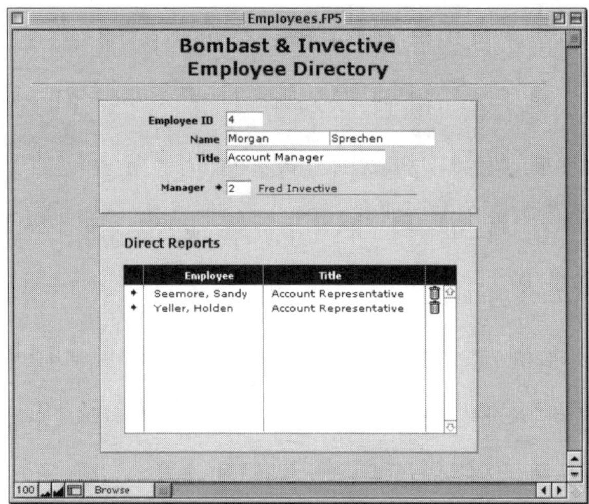

Figure 10.7

At a glance, you're able to tell that Sprechen has two people who report to her, and that her manager is Fred Invective. Since the structure is recursive, you're able to tell these same two pieces of information for anyone in the database, no matter how far down the line they are.

Let's spice up the interface a bit and add some navigational aids. Wouldn't it be nice to jump to the manager's record with a single click, and similarly to jump to a direct report's record?

The script to jump to the manager's record, shown below, is quite basic:

Jump to Manager

```
If [IsValid(Manager::Employee ID)
     Go to Related Record ["Manager"]
End If
```

You can either make a small button, like that shown in Figure 10.7, to run this script, or you can just select the field that displays the manager's name itself and define that as a button. The latter works well in cases like this because you're not doing data entry in that field, and it's one less object to clutter up your layout.

Similarly, the script to jump to a particular direct report is also quite simple:

Jump to Direct Report

```
Go to Related Record ["Direct Report"]
```

Since this script only performs a single step, some might argue that it's easier to define a button that directly performs this step, rather than taking the extra step of creating a script. In general, we prefer to always define buttons that run scripts, even if it is a one-step script, for three reasons. First, consistency is a good thing, and second, there's a good likelihood that eventually you'll want the script to do something else, like error trapping. Third, you might have several layouts that have buttons that perform the same script step. Defining these buttons to perform scripts means that if you ever need to change this action, you change it one place (in the script) rather than needing to edit multiple layouts.

No data entry is being performed in the Direct Reports portal, so you can place an invisible button that performs the script over the entire row. You'll probably also want to go into the Field Format for the fields displayed in the portal and uncheck the Allow entry into field option.

Try navigating through the system now, and you'll see how nice it is. You can "walk" up and down the layers of hierarchy at will. We like this metaphor so much that we often refer to this technique as "portal walking."

Now that the display is working well, let's work on an interface for assigning and removing employees to a manager. Keep in mind that the portal displaying direct reports is a self-relationship — this means that you don't simply want to add or delete portal rows as you normally might. If you did so, you'd be creating and deleting records in the Employee database, which is not desirable here. Rather, you just want to assign and remove people from reporting to that particular manager, and to do this, all you need to do is manipulate the Manager ID field.

You'll also want some error trapping performed when assigning an employee to a particular manager. You don't want to allow people to report to themselves, of course! Nor do you want to allow what's known as a "tangled hierarchy." This would be the equivalent of someone reporting to someone who reports to him or her. Think of a family tree: Your grandmother can't also be your niece. So when you assign an employee to a manager, you must ensure that he or she isn't hierarchically above that manager.

The first step in this process is to create a mechanism for listing all of the available (unassigned) employees. Unassigned employees all share one attribute: Their Manager ID field is empty. You can use this fact to create a selection portal similar to those built in Chapter 8.

1. Add a calculation field, Constant, which is simply equal to 1, with a number result. Constants come in handy in many situations; it's a good idea to add one to every database you make.

2. Next you'll need something for this constant to relate to. Create another calculation field (with number result), Constant Match, with the following definition:

   ```
   IsEmpty(Manager ID)
   ```

   This is a Boolean calculation, mcaning that the statement is evaluated as True (1) or False (0). In this case, if it's true that the Manager ID field is empty, Constant Match will equal 1; if it's not empty, it will equal 0.

3. Create a self-relationship from Constant to Constant Match (called "Unassigned Employees"). If you build a portal based on this relationship (see Figure 10.8), it will always display all employees who haven't been assigned to a manager. Since the front end of the relationship is a constant (… and the constant has the identical value in every record in the database), the contents of such a portal would be the same no matter what record you're viewing.

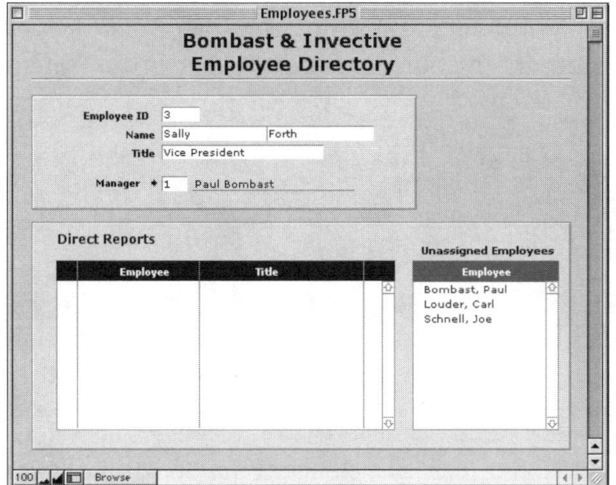

Figure 10.8

4. Finally, create a script that will allow you to click on any unassigned employee and have them assigned to the person whose record you're on. This is much easier than you might think at first. The only thing that differentiates records in the portal on the right from the records in the portal on the left is the value of the Manager ID field. All the script needs to do (for now, at least) is set this field with the Employee ID of the current record.

Assign Employee

```
Set Field [Unassigned Employees::Manager ID, Employee ID]
Set Field [Employee ID, Employee ID]
Exit Record/Request
```

By setting the Manager ID field of the unassigned employee, that employee no longer meets the criteria for being displayed in that portal (which is that the Manager ID field is empty, you'll recall). Instead, he meets the criteria for showing up in the Direct Reports portal of the current record. The other Set Field and the Exit Record/Request will alleviate the screen refresh issues that would otherwise result.

Finish by attaching this script to a button (invisible or otherwise) in the Unassigned Employees portal.

The process for removing an employee from a manager's direct reports is nearly identical to that for assigning them. The only difference is that you'll want to clear out the Manager ID field instead of populating it.

Remove Employee

```
Set Field [Direct Report::Manager ID, ""]
Set Field [Employee ID, Employee ID]
Exit Record/Request
```

You'll want to create a button in the Direct Reports portal (perhaps like the trash can icon in Figure 10.7) that runs this script.

We mentioned earlier the need to avoid "tangled hierarchies" when assigning employees to managers. The Assign Employee script, while adequate for the job of assigning, in no way offers protection against this. To do so complicates the script quite a lot, but it's a good exercise, so read on.

To protect against a tangled hierarchy, you'd need to trap for two situations. First, and easiest to trap, is when someone attempts to assign an employee to herself. The other is when the selected employee is the manager of the current record, or the manager of the manager, or the manager of the manager of the manager, etc. Basically, you need to walk "up" the tree from the current record and make sure you never encounter the selected employee.

You'll need a few new fields and relationships before reworking the script. The first is a global number field (gSelectedEmp ID) where you can store the selected employee's ID while performing the error checks. The other field is another global number called gEmp ID, which will allow you to walk up the tree without ever leaving the current record. The two new relationships you need are self-relationships matching each of these global fields with the Employee ID. They're both purely utilitarian. The revised script, then, is as follows:

Assign Employee

```
Set Field [gSelectedEmp ID, Unassigned Employees::Employee ID]
Exit Record/Request
If [gSelectedEmp ID = Employee ID]
     Show Message ["An employee can't report to themselves!]
     Halt Script
End ID
Set Field [gEmp ID, Employee ID]
```

```
Loop
     Exit Record/Request
     Exit Loop If [IsEmpty (Employee by gEmp ID::Manager ID]
     If [Employee by gEmp ID::Manager ID = gSelectedEmp ID]
         Show Message ["Tangled Hierarchy!! The person you have selected
         cannot report to this employee"]
     Halt Script
     Else
          Set Field [gEmp ID, Employee by gEmp ID::Manager ID]
     End If
End Loop
Set Field [Employee by gSelectedEmp ID::Manager ID, Employee ID]
```

Each pass through the loop represents moving up one level in the hierarchy. If it makes it to the top without finding a tangled hierarchy, then the loop ends (via the Exit Loop If) and the Manager ID of the selected employee is set.

Let's pause here for a moment and take stock of what's been done. We took a very simple flat-file employee database and turned it into a recursive data structure through the addition of the Manager ID field. A few relationships (five!) later, you're able to track and display information about a person's manager and direct reports, as well as all the unassigned employees. You've also added navigation for walking up and down the tree and scripts for assigning and removing employees as direct reports.

It's at this point that someone (usually your boss or the client) asks the fateful question: This is all fine and dandy, but can you display the information as an org chart?

If you're smart, you'll say no. But if you're brave enough to try it, there's a very slick way to display recursive data as a tree structure. We fondly call it the "data accordion." It's a great exercise in scripting and has many other potential uses. As with most things FileMaker, there are probably other ways of displaying data hierarchically, but this method has proven to be fast and extensible.

The Data Accordion

As we've lamented a few times already, even with the advent of global fields which can act as variables, it's impossible to make a true variable array in FileMaker. Recall that an array is just a collection of elements all referenced by a common name. For example, instead of just a variable x, an array might consist of x(0), x(1), x(2), and so on, where the pointer (0,1,2) specifies the location of a value within x. We've seen people try to make repeating fields work like arrays — you can, after all, set and get specified repetition values (like the tenth value of some field named Counter).

The problem is that you can't set a specific repetition based on a variable. The repetition number has to be hard-coded. In other words, you can't be in a loop and set the *n*th repetition of a field each time through the loop. Talk to a real programmer, and they'll be stunned that you can't create arrays in FileMaker (and equally as stunned how easy other stuff is). As before when we've needed arrays for tasks, we'll build our own as delimited lists within global text fields.

A good place to start building the "data accordion" is the end result, the tree, and think backwards about how to get there. Figure 10.9 shows the end product of the process.

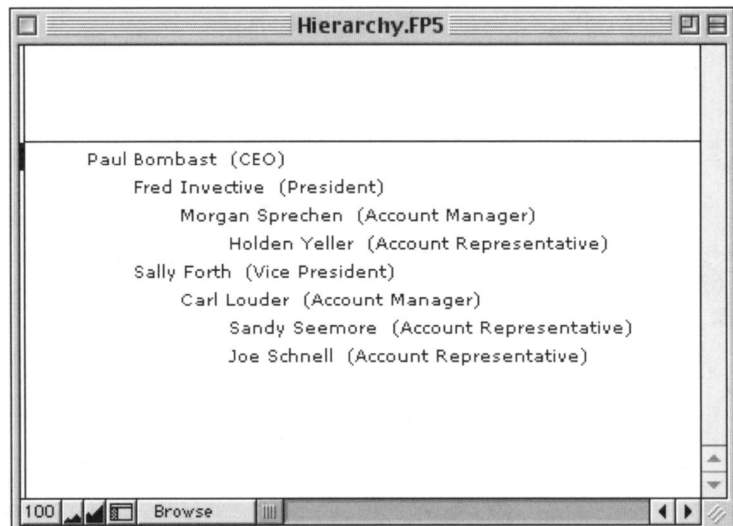

Figure 10.9

Now, this isn't an org chart in the traditional sense, perhaps, but it does accurately and visually convey the hierarchy. At first glance, you might think this is a subsummary report. The problem we've run into every time we've tried to represent hierarchies as subsummaries is that you necessarily have to limit the number of levels in the hierarchy. And coming up with a sort order that would produce the above hierarchy is no small task either.

A far easier way of displaying a hierarchy like this is by writing out records to a utility file. Each record in the utility file simply needs to contain an Employee ID and an Index Level to know how far to indent the name. The Employee ID can even be related back to the Employee table to pull over any and all information (like the name and title) to display in the tree. The Index Level is a simple ordinal number (i.e., 1, 2, 3) that can be used to pad spaces or tabs before their name. In this way, the hierarchy can contain as many levels as can be displayed well on a page. Assigning the level numbers is tricky, though.

Here's why it's tricky. You can start out easily enough at Bombast's record and assign it to level 1. Then you can jump to the set of records containing his direct reports (Fred and Sally) and assign them to level 2. Not too bad so far. You'd go next to Fred's reports (Morgan) and assign her to level 3, and then to Morgan's reports (Holden), and assign him to level 4. But now, you need to climb back up the tree to see if Sally has any people who report to her. When you jumped to the found set of Fred's reports, you lost Sally from the existing found set. Unless you can temporarily store her information somewhere (like an array), you're in trouble.

Now that you understand the problem a bit better, let's turn to the "data accordion" itself. The first step is to create the utility file for displaying the tree, called Hierarchy.fp5. The fields needed at this point are the following:

Field Name	Type
Employee ID	Number
Index Level	Number
Constant	Calculation (=1)

Records will eventually be created in the Hierarchy table in the proper display order, so you won't need to worry about sort order here at all. One of the other nice things about writing out records to the utility table is that it's possible to have someone appear multiple times in the list, possibly even at different levels of hierarchy. It's probably not something you'd want in an org chart, but it can come in handy in other situations.

The script to generate the tree starts, as you might guess, in the Employee table. Whatever record the user is currently viewing will be considered the top node in the tree. That is, the tree will dynamically be built down from the current record. At each node in the tree, the script will be guided by a simple ordering algorithm:

> If a record has child records (… if an employee has direct reports), process those next. If not, or when they've been processed, process the next sibling record in the current generation. If this record is the last (or only) sibling in a generation, then return the parent record after processing.

It's more intuitive than it looks: Simply walk out to the end of each branch, marking the path as you go. At the end of a branch, walk back up until there's a new branch to go down. It's sort of like how you can find your way out of any maze simply by keeping your right hand in contact with the wall at all times.

The script that generates the tree will need a few new global fields and relationships in the Employee table. The global fields all act as temporary storage locations for pieces of the hierarchy.

gAccordion	Global text
gChildren	Global text
gTop Line	Global text
gWaiting List	Global text
gChild	Global number
gIndex Level	Global number
gTree	Global text

The field gAccordion grows and contracts several times during the course of the script. It's used to hold the list of records (employees) to process. It grows when those records have children records and contracts when they don't.

The new relationship that you need (called "Reports of gChild") is a self-relationship from gChild back to the Manager ID. Create also a new layout called Utility and place on it a portal based on this relationship, as well as all of the global fields listed above. The portal is needed by the script; having the rest of the fields makes troubleshooting much simpler. Figure 10.10

shows what this layout might look like. A user will never see it, so aesthetics don't matter.

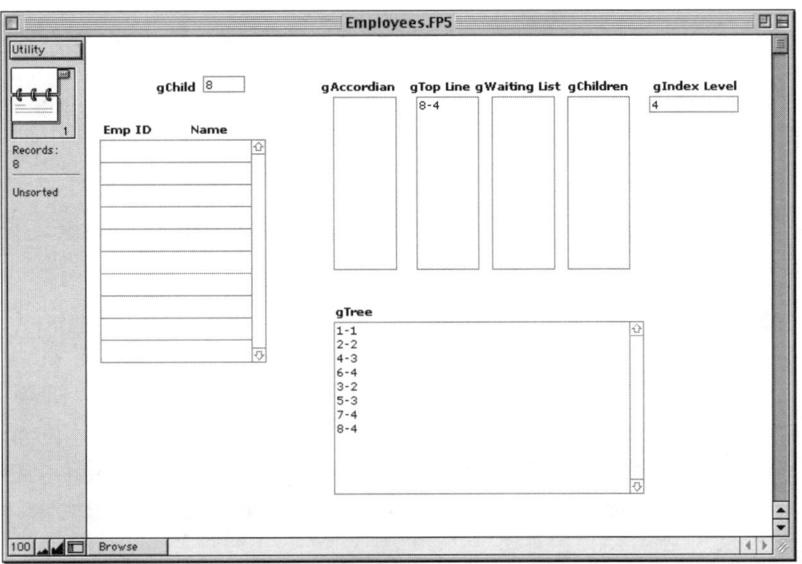

Figure 10.10

Let's finally take a look at the scripts for creating and displaying the hierarchy.

Prepare Tree

```
Go to Layout [Utility]
Set Field [gTree, ""]
Set Field [gAccordion, Employee ID & "-1¶"]
Loop
     Exit Loop If [IsEmpty (gAccordion)]
     Set Field [gTop Line, Left (gAccordion, Position(gAccordion, "¶",
               1,1) - 1)]
     Set Field [gWaiting List, Right (gAccordion, Length(gAccordion) -
               Position(gAccordion, "¶" , 1, 1)]
     Set Field [gChild, Left (gTop Line, Position (gTop Line, "-",1,1)-1)]
     Set Field [gIndex Level, Right (gTop Line, Length (gTop Line) -
               Position (gTop Line, "-", 1, 1)]
     Set Field [gTree, gTree & gTop Line & "¶"]
     Set Field [gChildren, ""]
     Exit Record/Request
     If [IsValid(Reports of gChild::Employee ID)
          Go to Portal Row [Select, First]
```

```
            Loop
                  Set Field [:gChildrend, gChildren & Reports of
                            gChild::Employee ID & "-" & (gIndex Level + 1) & "¶"]
                  Go to Portal Row [Select, Exit after last, Next]
            End Loop
      End If
      Set Field [gAccordion, gChildren & gWaiting List]
End Loop
Go to Layout [original layout]
Perform Script [Sub-scripts, External, "Hierarchy.fp5"]
      - Display tree
```

The script begins innocently enough, going to the Utility layout and clearing out the gTree global, which is where the whole hierarchy will be stored prior to display. The gAccordion field is initialized with the Employee ID and a "-1" which indicates that the current record is at level 1 of the hierarchy. Throughout the script, the format $x - y$ indicates an Employee (x) and an Index Level (y). In the quasi-array that's being created, returns will separate pairs.

The Loop that follows walks through the entire tree below the current record. The only condition for exiting the loop, in fact, is when gAccordion is exhausted. The next two Set Field steps (gTop Line and gWaiting List) split the Accordion into two pieces. The first piece is the top "row" of gAccordion, and the other is everything else. You can see that this is accomplished by finding the position in gAccordion of the return ("¶") and taking respectively everything to the left and right of this character. The two following Set Fields (gChild and gIndex Level) split gTop Line in much the same way, except that the delimiter there is a dash ("-").

Assuming you had started this script from Bombast's record (his Employee ID, you'll recall, is 1), the globals up to this point would read as follows:

gAccordion	1-1
gTop Line	1-1
gWaiting List	<empty>
gChild	1
gIndex Level	1

Each time through the loop, the top line of the accordion (gTop Line) is appended to the end of gTree. Keep in mind that gTop Line contains both an employee ID and an index value.

The next section of the script (starting when gChildren is cleared out) creates a list of the direct reports of gChild. This is done by looping through the rows of the portal and collecting Employee IDs along the way. Notice that as gChildren is set each time through the loop, the index level of each child is set to be one higher than the index level of the top line.

Finally then, the accordion is reset to be this list of child records and the former waiting list, and the whole process starts over. You might think at first to add gChildren to the bottom of gAccordion, and let those records wait their turn to be the top line. In fact, you want to do just the opposite. They need to be inserted at the top of the list. All of the "offspring" of the top line need to be processed before moving on to the next item in the waiting list.

As each branch of the tree is followed out to its end, gTree records the path. And when there are finally no more entries to process in gAccordion, gTree contains all of the information necessary for displaying the hierarchy. For the set of records in the test database, gTree contains the following at the conclusion of the script:

```
1-1
2-2
4-3
6-4
3-2
5-3
7-4
8-4
```

This array next needs to be passed to the Hierarchy table and parsed back out into separate records. An alternative would have been to write records out to this file incrementally within the script above. There's certainly nothing wrong with this approach; either works just fine and the difference in speed would be marginal at best. We find, though, that loading up a global array like gTree helps us modularize our scripts and keeps the logic cleaner: one script to generate the array, one to parse it. The only time the global array gets you into trouble is when it can potentially grow beyond the 64,000-character limit of a text field.

The subscript in the Hierarchy table that parses the array is as follows:

```
Show All Records
Delete All Records [No dialog]
Set Field [gTemp, Employee by Constant::gTree]
Loop
     Exit Loop If [IsEmpty(gTemp)]
     Set Field [gTemp2, Left (gTemp, Position (gTemp,"¶",1,1)-1]
     New Record/Request
     Set Field [Employee ID, Left (gTemp2, Position (gTemp2, "-",1,1)-1]
     Set Field [Index Level, Right (gTemp2, Length (gTemp2) - Position
                               (gTemp2, "-",1,1))]
     Set Field [gTemp, Right (gTemp, Length(gTemp) - Position(gTemp,
                         "¶",1,1)]
End Loop
Go to Layout [Display]
```

At the start, everything that was previously in the table is deleted. In a network environment, you would want to be more careful than that and only delete records, for example, that belonged to the current user. From there, a couple of global fields are used to parse the contents of gTree into new records.

There's one last piece to the puzzle, and that's a calculation field for actually displaying the items in the hierarchy. This calculation should pad spaces (or tabs) before the employee's name based on the value in the Index Level field. If you know you'll never have more than a few levels, you can hard-code the field with conditional statements (e.g., if index level is 1, add one tab; if it's 2, add two, etc.). Making it extensible to an undeterminable level is tougher, since there's no simple calculation formula for creating a string of x number of y's.

The best workaround we know of for creating variable length strings of a certain character involves powers of 10. Imagine, for instance, that you raised 10 to the fifth power. The result is a 1 followed by five zeros (100,000). Take the right five characters of this string and you end up with just the five zeros. And finally, substitute another character, such as "x," for zeros and you end up with a string of five x's.

Employing this workaround, the calculation for the Display field in Hierarchy becomes:

```
Substitute(Right(10^((Index Level-1)*7),((Index Level-1)*7)),"0","
    ")&Employee by ID::Name\Title
```

We've chosen to display a concatenation of Name and Title from the Employee file, but you can, of course, display any fields that would be appropriate to the situation. The layout for viewing the hierarchy, by the way, is nothing other than a simple list view with a single field, as shown below.

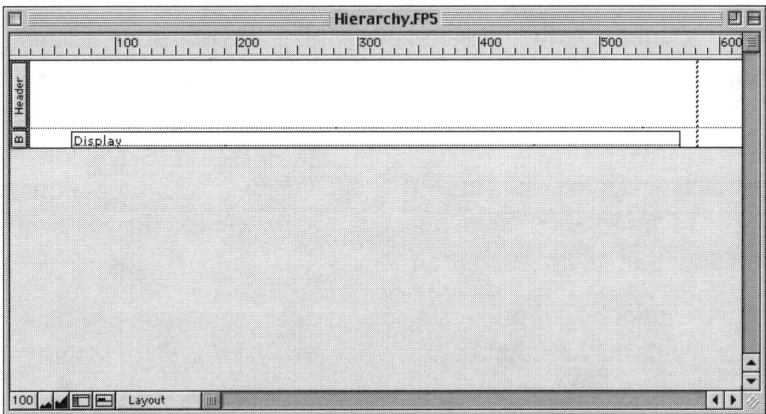

Figure 10.11

You may want to finish off this solution by placing a button on this layout to return to the Employee table. Or, you could even make each Employee's name a button that jumped back to his or her record.

Over the years, we've used recursive relationships and the data accordion in all sorts of situations, ranging from org charts like the one we've presented here to image-tracking systems (hierarchy shows reproductions of images), document creation systems (hierarchy is the outline of the sections of the document), and client management systems (hierarchy shows relationships between companies and their subsidiaries).

Hopefully you'd recognize each of these as a recursive data structure if you came across it now: Images are reproduced to create other images, sections of a document contain other sections of a document, companies own other companies. The key, recall, is that in each case there's only one type of thing (images, documents, companies), but there's a hierarchical ordering among the things themselves.

Many-to-Many Recursion

Just as there can be a one-to-many hierarchical ordering within a set of objects, so too are there many-to-many orderings. Think of these as trees that can extend in either direction. The example in the previous section was one-to-many recursion since each employee reported to a single manager. If the rules were changed slightly so that each employee could report to any number of managers, then that would have become many-to-many recursion (a manager has many employees, an employee has many managers).

Many-to-many recursion seems to pop up most often in manufacturing companies, and often goes by names such as kits, bundles, recipes, blends, or assemblies. One food importer we know, for example, sells such products as peppercorns. Besides selling the individual varieties, though, he also creates blends like the five-peppercorn blend and sells that. So, products can be comprised of multiple other products, and products can also be used in the production of multiple other products.

In this section, we'll present a classic example of many-to-many recursion (assemblies/subassemblies) and show you how it can become the centerpiece of a robust inventory solution.

Imagine that you work for a company that makes and distributes external disk drives and related products. Your two main products are the Alpha drive and the Omega drive. You also sell disks for these, power supplies, carrying cases, and battery packs. Besides selling all of these products individually, you also bundle them. The Basic bundle, for example, consists of a drive, a three-pack of disks, and a power supply. The Developer bundle contains a drive, a 10-pack of disks, a power supply, a carrying case, and a battery pack. Finally, you also sell a Deluxe bundle, which contains both an Alpha and Omega Developer Bundle.

Your goal is to accurately track the inventory level of all of the products you sell, including the bundles, which you assemble from on-hand components. As you produce bundles, the inventory level of the components should decrease accordingly. Also, you'd like the system to be able to tell you how many bundles you're capable of producing from existing inventory.

Believe it or not, you can set up a database to do all of this in a matter of hours. Let's get started.

The Product Database

The first step is to create the Product table, which is really nothing more than a list of the products you sell. The only two fields necessary at this point are Item Number and Item Name, as shown (with data) in Figure 10.12.

Product.fp5

Item Number	Item Name
100	Alpha Drive
101	Omega Drive
102	Universal Power Supply
103	Carrying Case
104	Alpha Disk
105	Alpha Disk 3-pack
106	Alpha Disk 10-pack
107	Omega Disk
108	Omega Disk 3-pack
109	Omega Disk 10-pack
110	Battery Pack
111	Alpha Basic Bundle
112	Alpha Developer Bundle
113	Omega Basic Bundle
114	Omega Developer Bundle
115	Deluxe Bundle

100 Browse

Figure 10.12

This file contains many-to-many recursion, you'll recall, because products can contain many other products, and products can be contained in many other products.

So, how would you model this on an ER diagram, and how would you render the hierarchical organization of products? Figure 10.13 depicts an ER diagram of the Product table with a many-to-many self-relationship.

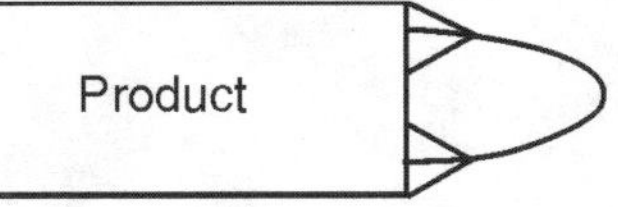

Figure 10.13

Though it ends up looking a bit strange, the rules for resolving this are the same as with any many-to-many relationship. You create a join file. In Figure 10.14, we've called this join file Component, and no, there's no error with the illustration: Both one-to-many relationships point the same direction.

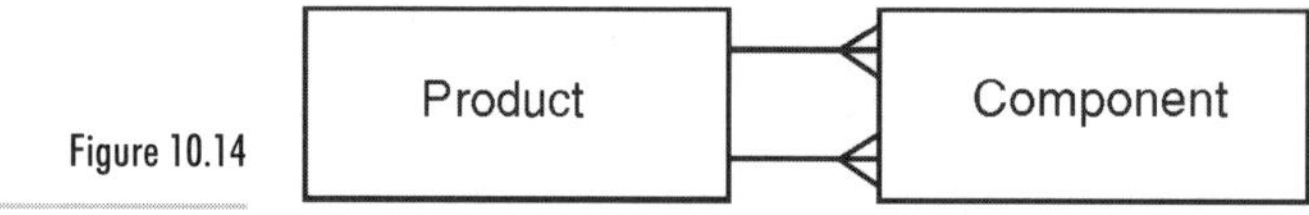

Figure 10.14

It may help to think about a more traditional join file, like that between an Invoice table and a Product table (see Figure 10.15). A record in the Line Item table represents an instance of a Product appearing on an Invoice. The primary key of each of the outside tables becomes a foreign key in the Line Items table.

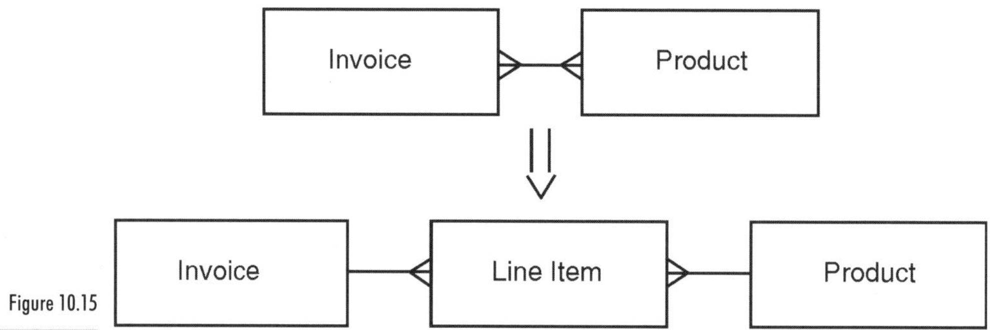

Figure 10.15

The same is true in the product/component scenario. A record in the Component database will represent an instance of an item containing another item. As such, each record will contain two item numbers, one of which acts as the main part and the other which acts as the component part.

From here, things get a bit complicated and may make your brain feel like it's a pretzel. So, let's go step by step through the creation of the Component table and the relationships between products and components.

1. Create a new database, Component.fp5, with two fields: Main Part ID (number) and Component Part ID (number). Add new records with the following data:

Main Part ID	Component Part ID
111	100
111	102
111	105
113	101
113	102
113	108

This data represents the two basic bundles: An Alpha Basic Bundle (Item 111) contains an Alpha drive (Item 100), a Universal Power Supply (Item 102), and a three-pack of Alpha disks (Item 105). Similarly, the Omega Basic Bundle (Item 113) contains an Omega drive (Item 101), a Universal Power Supply (Item 102), and a three-pack of Omega disks (Item 108). Notice that Item 102, the power supply, is a component in both bundles.

2. Return to the Product database, and create two new relationships as shown in Figure 10.16. These are the two one-to-many relationships on the ER diagram in Figure 10.14. In both you should check the options for cascading deletion of related records.

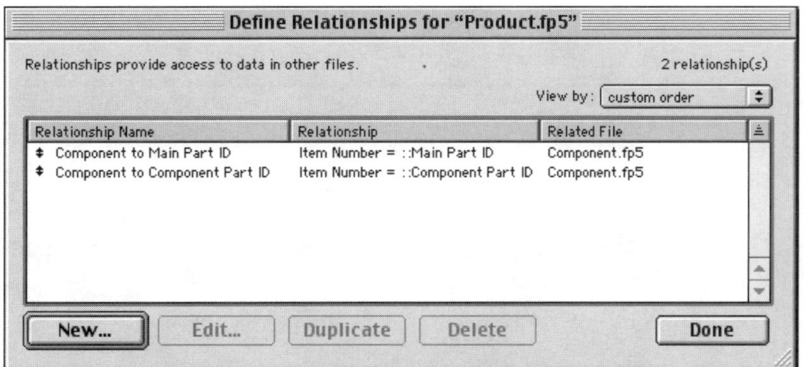

Figure 10.16

The Component to Main Part ID relationship will be used to display all of the components that make up a given item, while the Component to Component Part ID relationship will be used to display all of the items a given component is part of. It may take a few moments for this to sink in. It's a crucial concept, so return to this paragraph after seeing the relationships in action if this isn't crystal clear.

3. Next, create a layout in the Product table with two portals, as shown in Figure 10.17. The portal on the left is based on the Component to Main Part ID relationship. The one on the right is based on the Component to Component Part ID relationship. Put the related field Component to Main Part ID::Component Part ID in the portal on the left, and the Component to Component Part ID::Main Part ID field in the portal on the right.

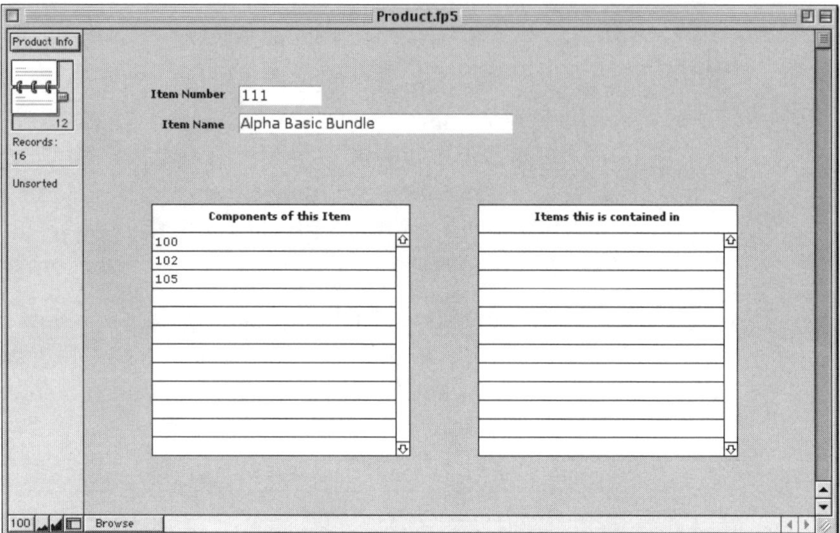

Figure 10.17

Looking at the Alpha Basic Bundle record in the Product table, as in Figure 10.17, you can see that the portal on the left displays the three components of the bundle. The record for the Universal Power Supply, shown in Figure 10.18, shows the two items it's part of in the portal on the right.

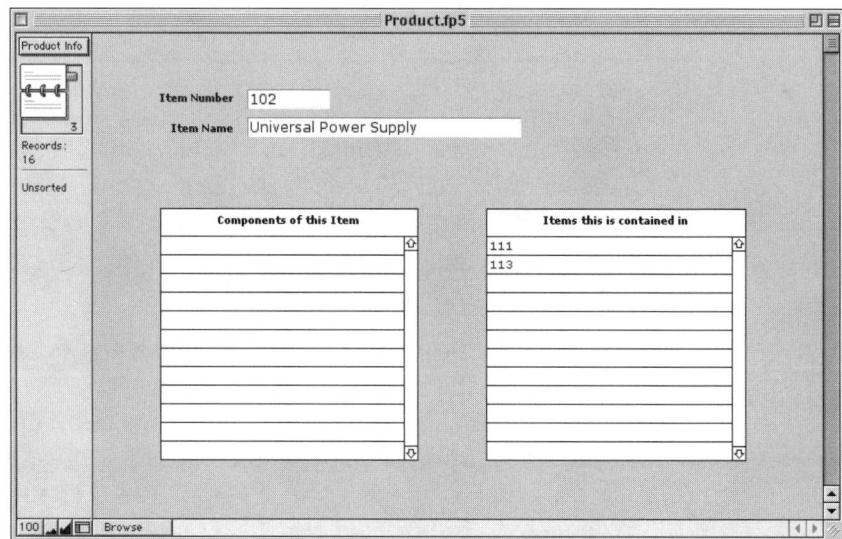

Figure 10.18

4. You've no doubt noticed that these portals only show the ID of the related item. In order to display the actual name of the item, you need to create two unstored calculations in the Component table to pull the name over to there. Whatever you do, don't just put the Item Name field in the portals. Remember that any field you place in a portal has to be through the same relationship as the portal itself. So, the Item Name needs to get over to the Component table.

   To do this, create two new relationships from Component back to Product, as shown in Figure 10.19.

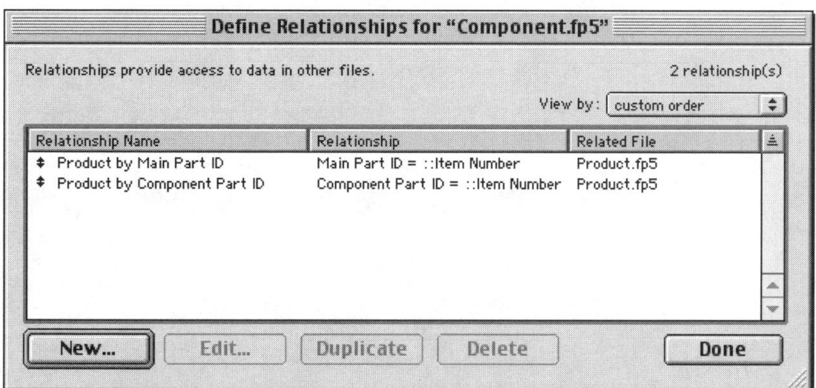

Figure 10.19

Don't turn on cascading delete or allow creation of related records for either relationship. Each of these serves purely to pull information about either a Main Part ID or Component Part ID into the Component file. You're on the "many" side of the one-to-many relationships, so each of these is a foreign key that points back uniquely to the primary key of the Product file.

Next, create two new calculation fields in the Component table, as follows:

```
Main Part Name (text result) = Product by Main Part ID::Item Name
Component Part Name (text result) = Product by Component Part ID::Item Name
```

If you were to place all four fields of the Component table on a layout at this point, you should see something similar to Figure 10.20.

Component.fp5

Main Part ID	Main Part Name	Component ...	Component Part Name
111	Alpha Basic Bundle	100	Alpha Drive
111	Alpha Basic Bundle	102	Universal Power Supply
111	Alpha Basic Bundle	105	Alpha Disk 3-pack
113	Omega Basic Bundle	101	Omega Drive
113	Omega Basic Bundle	108	Omega Disk 3-pack
113	Omega Basic Bundle	102	Universal Power Supply

Figure 10.20

Return to the Product table and add the Component to Main Part ID::Component Part Name field to the portal on the left, and the Component to Component Part ID::Main Part Name field to the portal on the right. Figure 10.21 shows the results of this for the Alpha Basic Bundle record.

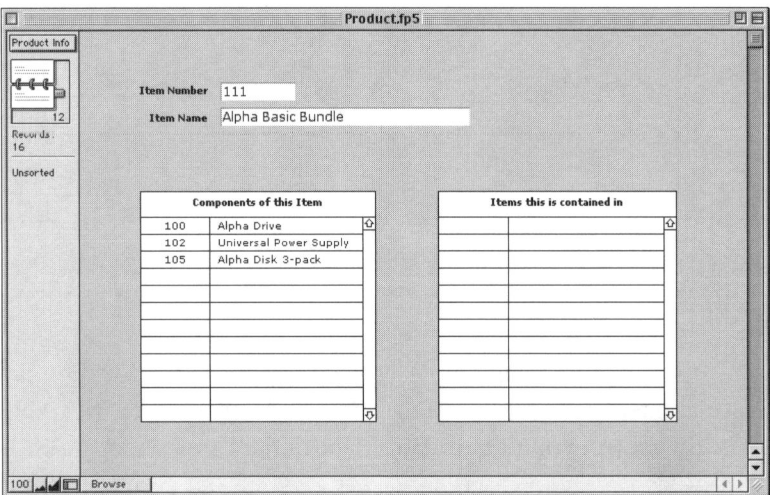

Figure 10.21

5. There's one final piece of data that you need, namely the quantity of each component required to make a part. For instance, it's not enough to know that Alpha Disks are a component in an Alpha Disk three-pack. You also need to know that it takes three of them.

   This quantity is not an attribute of the product itself, but rather of the relationship between two products, and therefore it needs to be a field in the Component database. For the records that were previously created there, you'll want to set the quantity to 1. It might help to think of the assembled part as a recipe. For instance, it takes three widgets and two doorknobs and 1/2 cup of sugar to make one gizmo.

Add the Quantity field (through the proper relationships, of course) to each of the portals in the Product table, so that it looks like Figure 10.22.

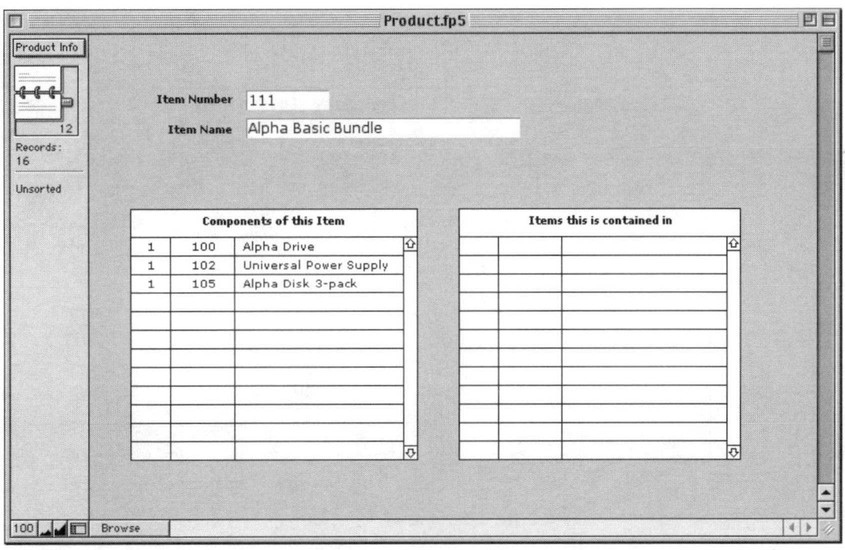

Figure 10.22

Navigating the Hierarchy

Now that the tables and layouts have been created, let's turn to navigating up and down the hierarchy. You'll recall that in the first half of this chapter, buttons were added to jump up or down the org chart. The scripts to do that performed basic Go to Related Records steps. In this case, the desired functionality is similar: Click on a row in either portal and jump to that record. But jumping to related records puts you in the Component file, and you want to stay in the Product file.

There are two ways you can deal with this. The first is what we call the "double hop." That is, jump to related records in the Component table, and then call a subscript there that jumps back to the Product table. The double hop is usually how you'll navigate from one side of a many-to-many relationship over to the other.

The other way, which involves a global field and a self-relationship, is what we'll create here. There's no discernable speed difference between the two methods, but we think this way is a trifle more elegant and requires half as many scripts as the double hop.

Start by creating a global number field called gSelectedItem ID in the Product table. This field doesn't need to appear on any layouts. Then create a self-relationship from this field back to the Item Number, as shown in Figure 10.23.

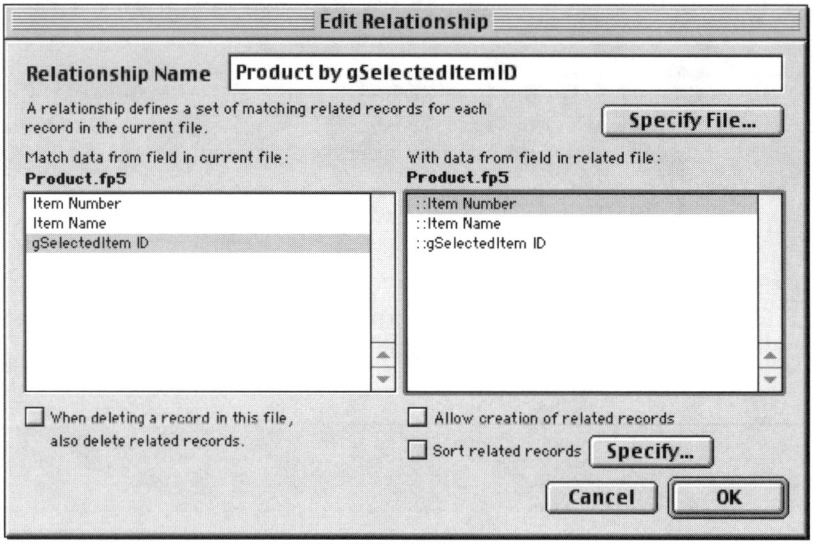

Edit Relationship

Relationship Name: Product by gSelectedItemID

A relationship defines a set of matching related records for each record in the current file.

Specify File...

Match data from field in current file:
Product.fp5

Item Number
Item Name
gSelectedItem ID

With data from field in related file:
Product.fp5

::Item Number
::Item Name
::gSelectedItem ID

When deleting a record in this file, also delete related records.

Allow creation of related records

Sort related records Specify...

Cancel OK

Figure 10.23

Next, you're ready for the actual navigation scripts. In each, the global field is set to the ID of the related record that you've clicked on in the portal, and then you jump to related records through the self-relationship so as to end up on the record in Product that you just selected. You need two scripts because you have two portals. The same global field and self-relationship can be used by each, though.

Jump to Component

```
Set Field [gSelectedItem ID, Component to Main Part ID::Component Part ID]
Exit Record/Request
Go to Related Record [Product by gSelectedItemID]
```

Jump to Main Part

```
Set Field [gSelectedItem ID, Component to Component Part ID::Main Part ID]
Exit Record/Request
Go to Related Record [Product by gSelectedItemID]
```

Create an invisible button over the portal on the left that runs the Jump to Component script, and one over the other portal that runs the Jump to Main Part script.

Now, when you're looking at the Alpha Basic Bundle, you can click on the Universal Power Supply to jump to that record. You should then be able to get back to the Alpha Basic Bundle by clicking it in the right-hand portal.

Calculating Inventory Levels

In the final section of this chapter, we'll show you how you can turn the recursive Product table into a simple, yet robust inventory solution. The easiest way to derive the inventory of a product is as the difference between the quantity received and the quantity sold. The situation becomes slightly more complex, though, when your inventory contains assemblies that are produced from other parts. As you produce something, you need to decrement all of the components' inventory levels accordingly.

The quantity on hand of a product can thus be expressed by the following generic formula:

Qty on Hand = Qty Received + Qty Produced – Qty Shipped
  – Qty Used in Production

Let's look now at what you need to add to the work done in the previous section to derive each of these values.

Quantity Received

To start, there needs to be some mechanism in place to track when new items come into the system. The easiest way to do this is to create a new database table where each record represents the amount of a product received on a certain date. This table is also a good place to make inventory adjustments as either positive or negative amounts received.

You can then relate from the Product file to this new file and total up the amount received. If you wanted, you could even put a portal in the Product database listing all of the receipt transactions for any given item.

1. Create a new database, Receiving.fp5, with the following fields:

Receiving ID	Number (Auto-entered serial number)
Date	Date
Item Number	Number
Quantity	Number

2. Create a list or table view layout with all of these fields.
3. Define a relationship called Product by Item Number from Receiving to Product, where Item Number matches Item Number. You don't need to select any of the options in the relationship setup.
4. This relationship gives you access to information about a given Item Number. Go to Layout Mode and add the Product by Item Number::Item Name field to your list view. Now, as an Item Number is entered into a record in the Receiving table, the name of the item will automatically display.
5. Format the Item Number field as a pop-up list, using a new value list called Items that is based on the contents of the Item Number and Item Name fields from Product (see Figure 10.24).

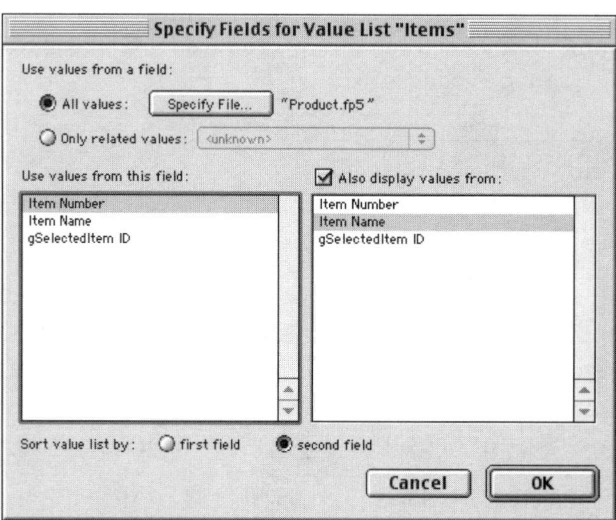

Figure 10.24

6. Return to Browse mode and enter some test data. Your Receiving database should now look similar to Figure 10.25.

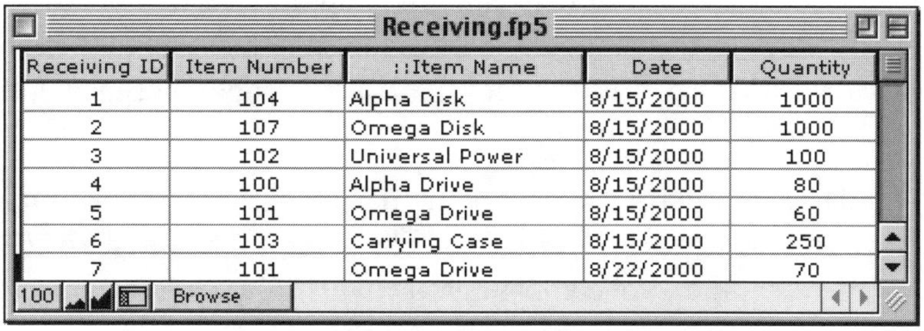

Receiving.fp5

Receiving ID	Item Number	::Item Name	Date	Quantity
1	104	Alpha Disk	8/15/2000	1000
2	107	Omega Disk	8/15/2000	1000
3	102	Universal Power	8/15/2000	100
4	100	Alpha Drive	8/15/2000	80
5	101	Omega Drive	8/15/2000	60
6	103	Carrying Case	8/15/2000	250
7	101	Omega Drive	8/22/2000	70

100 Browse

Figure 10.25

7. Go now to the Product database, and create a new relationship called Receiving by Item Number over to Receiving, matching Item Number to Item Number. You don't need to select any of the relationship options.
8. Create a new calculation field in the Product table called Total Received, which is defined as follows:

```
Total Received (number result) = Sum(Receiving by Item Number::Quantity)
```

9. Add this field to the bottom of the main Product layout. Go to Browse mode, and check that everything is working properly. Using the test data in Figure 10.25, for instance, the Total Received for the Omega Drives should be 130 (60 + 70).

Quantity Produced

The next inventory component we'll derive is the quantity produced. Just as you needed a new database table for logging receipt of products, you'll want to create another new table that tracks product assembly. Keep in mind that as bundles are produced from existing inventory, the number of component parts used in that bundle need to be decreased. For example, if you assemble 20 10-packs of Alpha Disks from inventory, you want to decrease the inventory of Alpha Disks by 200 and add 20 to the inventory of 10-packs.

You might think first of using a script to accomplish this, but there are at least two big reasons to try to avoid scripting in a situation like this. First, scripts require some agent to set them in motion, like the user. If the user neglects or forgets to run a script, then the integrity of the data is compromised. Second, scripts capture the situation at a particular moment in time; if the situation later changes, the data won't automatically reflect the new, current situation. Consider what would happen if a user were to record that they assembled 20 10-packs, run the script to post to inventory, and then they were later to change the quantity assembled to 25. Or were to delete the record entirely! It becomes quite a challenge to predict and allow for any possible scenario of user action.

The other option, of course, is to use unstored calculations to track the use of components in assemblies. Then, even if records are added, changed, or deleted, the total component use will still calculate correctly. The process to implement this is remarkably similar to that used above for the Receiving database.

1. Create a new database, Production.FP3 with the following fields:

Production ID	Number, (auto-entered serial number)
Date	Date
Item Number	Number
Quantity	Number

2. Create a list or table view layout that contains all of these fields.

3. Define a new relationship called Product by Item Number from Production to Product, where Item Number matches Item Number. This relationship gives you access to information about a given item. In Layout mode, add the Product by Item Number::Item Name field to your list or table view.

4. Define the Item Number field as a pop-up list, using a value list named Items that is based on the contents of the Item Number and Item fields from Product.

5. Create some test data, so that your table looks something like Figure 10.26.

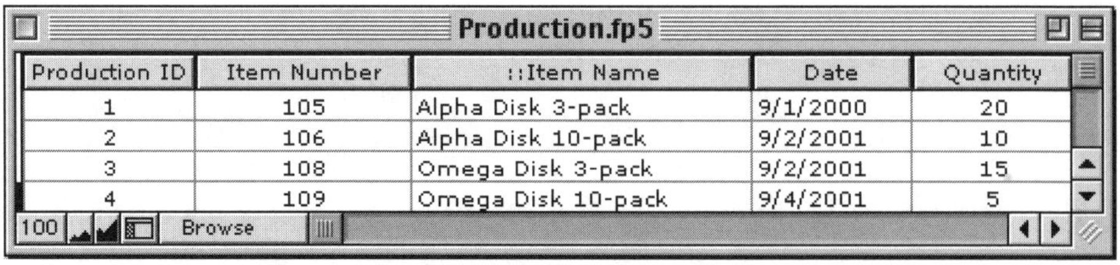

Production.fp5

Production ID	Item Number	::Item Name	Date	Quantity
1	105	Alpha Disk 3-pack	9/1/2000	20
2	106	Alpha Disk 10-pack	9/2/2001	10
3	108	Omega Disk 3-pack	9/2/2001	15
4	109	Omega Disk 10-pack	9/4/2001	5

100 Browse

Figure 10.26

6. Back in the Product table, create a new relationship called Production by Item Number over to Production, matching Item Number to Item Number.
7. Create a new calculation field called Total Produced, defined as follows:

```
Total Produced (number result) = Sum(Production by Item Number::Quantity)
```

8. Add this field to the bottom of the main Product layout. Go to Browse mode, and confirm that the relationship and calculation are both working properly.

Quantity Used in Production

Determining the quantity of an item used in production is the hardest task in this exercise. Let's think about what's known so far: You produced, say, 20 Alpha three-packs, and the Alpha three-pack contains three Alpha Disks. The component use of Alpha Disks is therefore 60. The calculation is simple, yet where does it live? Keep in mind that if you produce 10 more of the three-packs tomorrow, you'll add another record to the Production database, in which case the total component use would be 90 (20*3 + 10*3). Also keep in mind that Alpha Disks are used in other assemblies, like the 10-pack.

The biggest hint for figuring out where to put the component use calculation is that the Quantity field lives in the Component database.

Every time Alpha Disks shows up as a Component Part ID in the Component database, that indicates they're part of an assembly. By relating the Component database to the new Production table by Main Part ID, you can determine the total number of assemblies produced. This, multiplied by the Quantity field, yields the number of components used in production of that particular type of assembly. Then, simply sum up the component usage from Product, thereby taking into account that a part might be used in multiple assemblies. It's complicated, but after going through it step by step, it will start to click.

1. In the Component table, create a new relationship called Production by Main Part ID to Production, matching Main Part ID to Item Number. Don't select any of the relationship options.

2. Also in the Component table, create a new calculation field, Component Use, with the following formula:

```
Component Use (number result) = Quantity* Sum(Production by Main Part
     ID::Quantity)
```

3. Back in the Product database, create a new calculation field, Total Used in Assemblies, with the following formula:

```
Total Used in Assemblies (number result) = Sum(Component to Component
     Part ID::Component Use)
```

4. Place this field on the layout next to the other quantity fields. See what happens to the value in this field as you add production records.

Quantity Shipped

Finally, inventory levels need to reflect shipments and/or orders. Rather than link what's been built up to this point to a full-fledged shipment tracking system, we'll just create another simple little Shipment database, virtually identical to those we made above for Receiving and Production. All you really need to track for inventory purposes, after all, is the Item Number and Quantity Shipped.

1. Create a Shipment database with the following fields:

Shipment ID	Number (auto-entered serial number)
Item Number	Number
Date	Date
Quantity	Number

2. Follow the same process for setting up this file as you did for the Receiving and Production tables, and enter some test data.

3. In the Product table, create a relationship (Shipment by Item Number) to Shipment, matching Item Number to Item Number.

4. Create a new calculation field, Quantity Shipped, with the following formula:

```
Quantity Shipped (number result) = Sum(Shipment by Item Number::Quantity)
```

5. Add this field to your layout next to the other three components that make up the on-hand inventory level.

Finishing the Job

You've now got the four components necessary to compute the quantity on hand. Remember, it's just:

On Hand = Qty Received + Qty Produced – Qty Shipped
– Qty Used in Production

The inventory of every product, no matter if it's the smallest component or largest assembly, can be determined from this formula. If you were building this in real life, there are a few factors that would probably cause complications. You might have to figure out how to deal with returns, waste generated during production, or bundles that need to be disassembled when you run out of a certain component. Write down all the scenarios you'll need to accommodate, then come up with rules to handle them. And don't be afraid to build new layouts or new tables; trying to have an existing routine serve double duty will eventually come back to haunt you. We've got one client who added printers and broom closets to their phone directory database so they could use it for asset tracking. Years later they still have bad memories of "printer people." There's rarely one way to build something. Try at least to think through the limitations of whatever method you choose so you're not taken by surprise.

Extra Credit

There's one other neat feature of the inventory solution presented above. With very little extra work, the system can tell you the maximum number of any given bundle you can produce from the inventory on hand.

The logic is fairly simple. Say you need five widgets to make a doodad, and that you've got 12 widgets in stock. Obviously, you can maximally produce two doodads before running out of widgets. When you've got multiple components in an assembly, you're limited by the part that allows you to create the least number of assemblies. For instance, if, besides five widgets, you also need four pieces of string to produce a doodad, and you've got 12 widgets and six pieces of string, you're limited to production of a single doodad.

Here's how to program this into the inventory system:

1. Start in the Component table, where you'll need a new calculation field called Part Quantity that pulls the on-hand inventory of a component:

   ```
   Part Quantity (number result) = Product by Component Part ID::Inventory
         Level
   ```

2. Create another calculation field in the Component table, Max Possible, and define it as follows:

   ```
   Max Possible (number result) = Int(Part Quantity / Quantity)
   ```

   Don't be scared; this is the same math you did to figure out you could make two doodads if you've got 12 widgets and it takes five widgets per doodad. The Part Quantity of the component, widgets, is 12, and the Quantity is the number of components required in the assembly, 5. And of course, the Int (12/5) = Int (2.4) = 2.

3. Go next to the Product table, and add the related Max Possible field to the left-hand portal. This shows you how each component limits the potential production of the assembly. The lowest number in the list is the maximum number you can produce.

4. So, create a new calculation in the Product table, Quantity Possible, that finds the minimum Max Possible of related components:

   ```
   Quantity Possible (number result) = Min(Component to Main Part ID::Max
         Possible)
   ```

5. Place this field on the layout somewhere. It will tell you how many assemblies you can make given your component inventory.

Figure 10.27 shows the finished layout in the Product table. Remember that all of this started as a simple product list. Now it's chock-full of useful information.

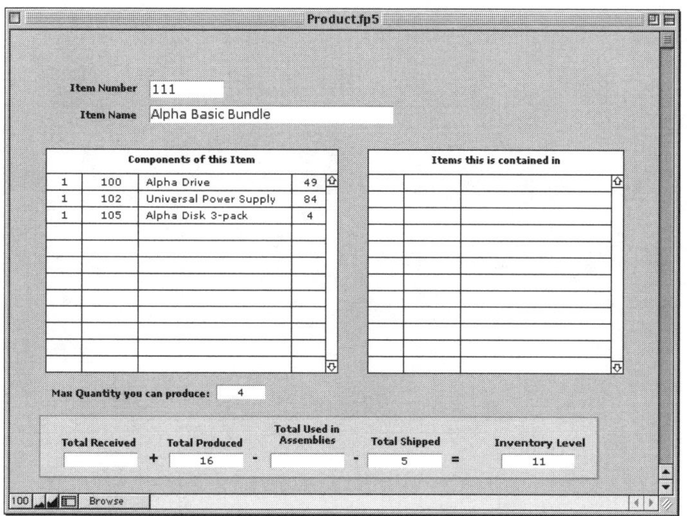

Figure 10.27

Summary

In this chapter, you've probably learned more than you ever thought you'd need to about recursive relationships. The first example, the org chart, taught you how to recognize and deal with one-to-many recursion, and how to use the "data accordion" to display hierarchical data. The other example concerned that classic scenario of many-to-many recursion, assemblies and subassemblies. You learned how to create a join file to resolve the many-to-many relationship, and how to build an entire inventory solution around the Product table.

The files used in this chapter can be found on the CD that accompanies this book. We'd urge you also to try building these files from scratch, as simply reading about how to build something isn't quite the same as creating it yourself.

Chapter 11

Complex Calculations

An essential part of any FileMaker developer's toolbox is a hearty supply of calculation formulas. Calculations, as you undoubtedly have discovered, are the lifeblood of scripting, reporting, and data hygiene. We don't intend what follows to be a comprehensive calculation reference guide. Rather, we present real-world situations that you may find yourself in, and show you some essential building blocks for creating complex calculations. Some functions we'll discuss in depth, while others (like If and Case) we'll assume that you're familiar with. If you need to brush up on any syntax, we recommend a visit to the help system.

For many of the examples in this chapter, there are other formulas that could be used to achieve the same results. When choosing which method to present here, we opted for solutions that were succinct and extensible. By succinct, we mean using a minimal number of functions, favoring elegant constructions over "brute force" methods. And by extensible, we mean solutions that can easily be adapted to variations or extensions of the original problem.

The formulas we present are grouped into three sections:

- Text manipulation tools
- Numbers
- Date and time formulas

As you read through this chapter, you may want to spend a few minutes thinking about how you would approach each scenario before reading our proposed solution. Even if you don't know all the exact syntax for a solution, having the right approach is 87% of the battle. Our goal is not only to teach you some neat formulas, but also to get you thinking more deeply about how to use calculations to solve particular types of problems.

First, a few words about terminology. We use the word *function* to indicate a particular FileMaker calculation. For instance, Position, Int, DateToText, and Case are all functions. Functions usually take one or more *arguments* (also called *parameters*), separated by commas. The Position function, for example, takes four arguments: text, search string, start, and occurrence. Every function returns some sort of *result*. Think of the arguments as the inputs and the result as the output. The result of the Position function is a number that represents the character position at which the requested search string was found. When you learn a new function, be sure you memorize the arguments that you need to define for it as well as the result that you can expect from it. Finally, we'll call all the stuff you write in the calculation window a *formula*.

Text Manipulation Tools

You must learn how to manipulate text strings adroitly. When it comes down to it, all data (except the contents of container fields) can simply be thought of as ordered strings of characters. As such, these strings can be counted, they can be cut into pieces, parts of them can be extracted, and you can locate items within them. Once you are comfortable with the basic moves, you can combine them to fit almost any need you have.

There are 11 functions that we consider basic moves for text manipulation. Let's review these briefly and then move on to some scenarios. Even if you think you know these functions, read over our comments; you'll probably learn a few new subtleties.

In the examples below, consider that the following values apply:

```
myString = "My name is Fred."
n = 5
x = 2
```

The first four functions manipulate strings at the character level.

- **Length(text)** — Returns the number of characters in the specified text string. Keep in mind that spaces, punctuation, and carriage returns all count as characters.

    Example: Length(myString) = 16

- **Left(text, number)** — Returns a text string that contains the first *n* characters of the specified string. If the number argument is larger than the length of the string, the entire string is returned.

  Example: Left(myString, n) = "My na"

- **Right(text, number)** — Similar to the Left function, except that it starts at the end of the specified string instead of the beginning.

  Example: Right(myString, n) = " Fred."

- **Middle(text, start, size)** — Returns a text string that contains some number of characters in the middle of the specified string. Start defines where to start extracting, and size defines how many characters to grab. Size does not specify where to stop extracting, which is a common misconception.

  Example: Middle(myString, n, x) = "am"

NOTE You can always use a Middle function in place of a Left or Right function.

Middle(text, 1, n) = Left (text, n)
Middle(text, Length (text) – n + 1, n) = Right (text, n)

The next four functions are very similar to the previous four, except that they manipulate text at the word level. In general, the word functions are a very clunky way of manipulating strings. We tend to favor character-wise text manipulation over word-wise text manipulation.

- **WordCount(text)** — Returns the number of words in the specified text string. It's important that you know how FileMaker defines a word. There are particular characters that are considered word delimiters. Besides spaces and carriage returns, other word delimiters include the following:

  !@#$%^&*()_+{}[]\|/,<>?;:"~`

  Hyphens, commas, and periods are sometimes word delimiters, and sometimes not. Hyphens next to numbers are delimiters but not between text strings. Commas are the exact opposite; next to text, they're delimiters but not between numbers. Periods are different still. Between two numbers or two pieces of text, they're not delimiters, but between a number and a text character they are. Do you see now why we called these clunky? A word is defined as a group of characters between two word delimiters or between a word delimiter and the beginning or end of the string. This means that if you have multiple delimiters next to one another (like multiple spaces), they are essentially reduced down to a single delimiter.

Example: WordCount(myString) = 4

- **LeftWords(text, number)** — Returns the first *n* words of the specified string.

  Example: LeftWords(myString, x) = "My name"

- **RightWords(text, number)** — Returns the last *n* words of the specified string. Note in the example below that the period following "Fred" is not returned as part of this function. Delimiters themselves are never part of the returned string.

  Example: RightWords(myString, x) = "is Fred"

- **MiddleWords(text, start, size)** — Returns some number of words from the middle of a string.

  Example: MiddleWords(myString, 2, 1) = "name"

The final three functions are essential for analyzing and manipulating strings.

- **Position(text, search string, start, occurrence)** — Returns the character number that the *n*th occurrence of the search string was found in the specified string, starting from the start character. If the search string isn't found, the function returns 0. This function is not case sensitive. The most common use of the function is with start and occurrence arguments both set to 1.

  Example: Position(myString, "is" , 1, 1) = 9

  This finds the position of the first instance of the string "is" in myString. If you wanted to find the position, say, of the second space, you'd use Position(myString, " ", 1, 2) (which is 8). Or, if you wanted to find the position of the first space after the fifth character, you would use Position(myString, " " , 5, 1) (which is also 8).

- **PatternCount(text, search string)** — Returns the number of times that the search string was found in the specified string. This function is not case sensitive.

  Example: PatternCount(myString, " ") = 3.

  That is, there are three spaces in the original text string.

- **Substitute(text, search string, replacement string)** — Returns the original text string, but with all instances of the search string replaced with the replacement string. This function is case sensitive.

  Example: Substitute(myString, "e", "HUH?") = "My namHUH? is FrHUH?d."

Let's look now at three common text manipulation scenarios.

Scenario: You have a field in your database called CSZ that has been used to enter the city, state, and zip code of your clients. For example, a field might contain "Elm Creek, WI 12345." There's always a comma between the city and state. You now want to pull out just the city element from this field.

Solution: Any time you need to parse a text string, you must know the rules about how the string is structured. In this case, you know that a comma always follows the city. Therefore, if you find the position of the first comma in the string, you can simply extract all of the text to the left of it.

```
City = Left(CSZ, Position (CSZ, ",", 1 , 1) – 1)
```

The "–1" is needed so that you don't also get the comma itself as part of your result. Keep in mind when nesting functions inside one another that the inner functions evaluate first. In this case, the Position function returns a number (10 for "Elm Creek, WI 12345"). Subtract one, and this number becomes the second argument of the Left function. Indeed, the left nine characters of "Elm Creek, WI 12345" are "Elm Creek".

You'll use this formula anytime you want to split a string at a certain point. It's one of the workhorses of text manipulation. To generalize, if A is the position of a delimiter, the formula to extract all of the text in front of the delimiter is:

```
Left (text, A – 1)
```

<u>**Scenario**</u>: Using the same CSZ field as the previous example, you now wish to extract the zip code from the field.

<u>**Solution**</u>: Again, the first thing you must do is understand the rules. If you knew that only five-digit zip codes were entered, you could probably get away with something like Right(CSZ, 5) or RightWords(CSZ, 1). However, let's say that some zips were entered as "+4" zips. The RightWords function wouldn't work because it would be considered a word delimiter in this context. As we mentioned before, we find the "words" functions to be clunky for most text manipulation. For fun, let's see how we'd define a formula based on a definition of zip as "everything to the right of the last space in the CSZ field." In the last scenario, you learned how to extract everything to the left of a certain character. The generalized formula for extracting everything to the right of a delimiter is:

```
Right(text, Length(text) – A)
```

where A represents the position of the delimiter.

In this case, you don't want everything to the right of the first space, but rather the last space. To find this, you first find the number of spaces in the string and use this as the fourth argument (occurrence) of the Position function. The finished formula would be as follows:

```
Zip = Right(CSZ, Length(CSZ) – Position(CSZ, " " , 1 , PatternCount(CSZ, "
        ")))
```

<u>**Scenario**</u>: For completeness, let's try to extract the state from the CSZ field.

<u>**Solution**</u>: Let's first look at the generalized formula for extracting text out of the middle of a string. Say that A is the position of the first delimiter, and B is the position of the second delimiter. The formula you'll need is:

```
Middle(text, A + 1 , B – (A + 1))
```

For example, say that you had the string X = "12*45#89" and wished to extract everything between the * and #. The formula you would use would be:

```
Middle(X, Position(X, "*", 1, 1) + 1, Position(X, "#", 1, 1) – (Position
      (X, "*", 1, 1) + 1))
```

Substituting in the actual values, you can see how this works:

```
Middle(X, Position(X, "*", 1, 1) + 1, Position(X, "#", 1, 1) - (Position (X, "*", 1,
      1) + 1))
      = Middle (X, 3 + 1 , 6 - (3 + 1))
      = Middle (X, 4 , 2)
      = "45"
```

Applying this logic to the CSZ field, you can extract the state using the following formula:

```
State = Trim(Middle(CSZ, Position(CSZ, ",", 1, 1) + 1, Position(CSZ, " " , 1 ,
        PatternCount(CSZ, " ")) - (Position(CSZ, ",", 1, 1) + 1)))
```

The Trim function is used to strip any leading or trailing spaces from the extracted characters.

In the preceding three scenarios, we presented three generalized formulas for extracting characters from a text string based on the position of delimiters. One place these formulas prove especially helpful is in setting and retrieving arrays. Unlike other programming tools, FileMaker unfortunately has no built-in support of arrays. The closest it comes is repeating fields, but the tools for setting repetition values are not nearly robust enough to make them useful as arrays.

As a working definition, let's consider an array simply as a delimited string. We would consider all of the following to be examples of arrays.

Example 1:

"26|235|125|8|11|19|" — This is a pipe-delimited array with six values.

Example 2:

"Green
Red
White
Blue" — This is a return-delimited array with four values.

Example 3:

"125:W*|*532:E*|*893:E*|*153:E" — This is a two-dimensional array. One dimension is delimited by *|*, and the other dimension by colons.

When using an array, there are a few things to be aware of. First, the choice of delimiter isn't very important, except that you must be absolutely sure that the delimiter will never appear as part of the data. Second, it's easier in FileMaker to work with well-balanced arrays. By this, we mean arrays that have an equal number of data elements and delimiters. For instance, the array "1*2*3" has three data elements and two delimiters. Better would be to have a delimiter following the last data element, such as "1*2*3*". Finally, even if your data elements are numbers or dates, all arrays should be of type text (or global text). Keep in mind, though, that the maximum amount of text you can put in a text field is 64,000 characters. This may seem like a lot, but we've run into several situations in which we've hit our head on this limit.

There are several FileMaker design functions that actually return an array as their result. For instance, the LayoutNames function, which takes the name of a database as its single argument, returns a return-delimited array of the layout names in the specified database. If you wanted to then, say, create a report that listed the fields that each of these layouts contained, you'd need to walk through the array of layout names one by one and feed each to the FieldNames function. As the final example for this section on text manipulation, let's look at how you can build a simple utility file that will do just this.

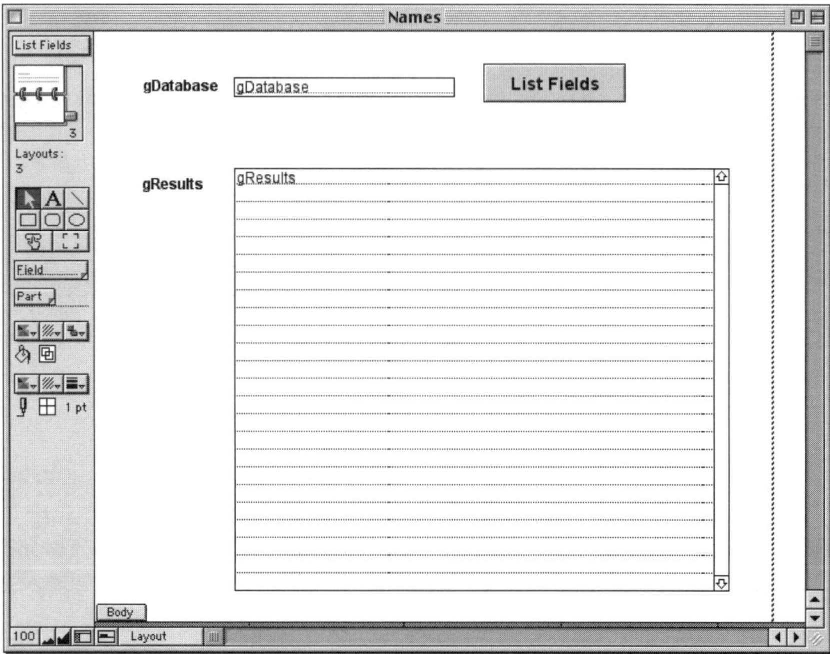

Figure 11.1

Begin with a brand new database that has the following four global text fields: gDatabase, gLayouts, gResults, and gTemp. You'll need to create a layout that has gDatabase and gResults on it, similar to Figure 11.1.

You'll enter the name of some other database into the gDatabase field, and then click the List Fields button. The script is shown below.

```
Set Field ["gLayouts", "LayoutNames(gDatabase) & "¶"]
Set Field ["gResults", " "" "]
Loop
     Exit Loop If ["IsEmpty(gLayouts)"]
     Set Field ["gTemp", "Left(gLayouts, Position(gLayouts, "¶", 1, 1)
               - 1)"]
     Set Field ["gResults", "gResults & "Layout: "& gTemp & Substitute("¶" &
               FieldNames(gDatabase, gTemp), "¶", "¶* ") & "¶¶""]
     Set Field ["gLayouts", "Right(gLayouts, Length(gLayouts) -
               Position(gLayouts, "¶", 1, 1))"]
End Loop
```

At the beginning of the script, gLayouts is set to an array of the layout names of the specified database. Notice that we've added a return ("¶") to the end of the array to ensure proper balance. The loop that follows walks through the items in the array one by one. If there are five layouts in the database you've specified, then there will be five elements in the gLayouts array, and you'll go through the loop five times. Each time through the loop, the variable gTemp is set to the first item in the array (using the first generalized formula we defined above). Then, the results field is set to the name of the current layout (aka gTemp) and a list of the fields that appear on that layout.

Notice that there is a Substitute function wrapped around the FieldNames list. This is purely optional, but we included it so that the field names appear as a bulleted list below the layout name. The FieldNames function returns a return-delimited list of field names. Here, the Substitute function is replacing all instances of returns with returns and a bullet. In order to have a bullet in front of the first item in the list, it's necessary to stick a return at the beginning of the array (it's that balance thing again).

Finally, the last step in the loop simply removes the first item from the gLayouts array by setting it equal to everything to the right of the first return (using the second generalized formula). The loop continues until the gLayout field is empty, which means that all the layouts have been processed.

Figure 11.2 shows an example of what gResults ends up looking like for a simple file.

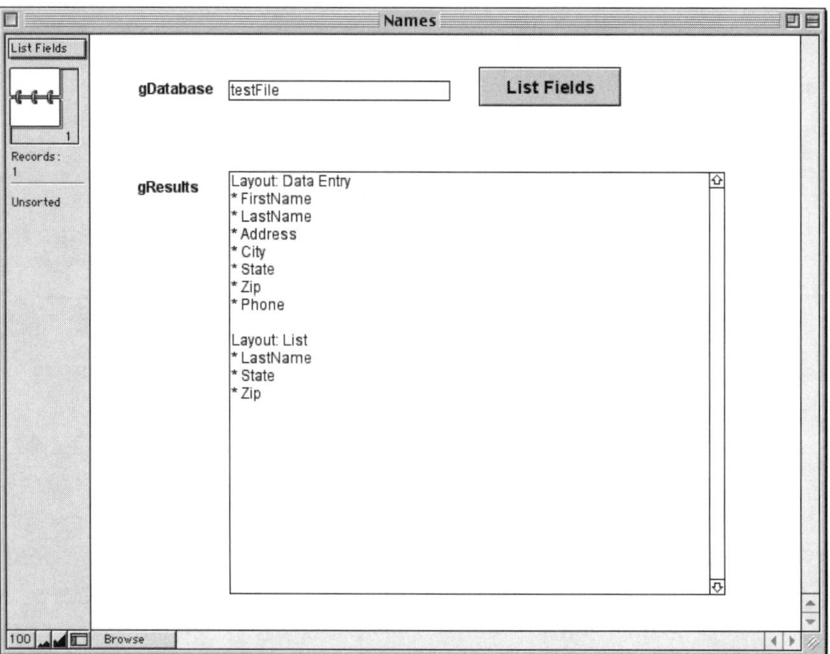

Figure 11.2

A few final notes about this example. The database that you are documenting has to be open in order for the script to work. For clarity, we haven't added any error trapping for this, but it's fairly simple to add an If statement that checks whether gDatabase is found in the list of open databases that's returned by the DatabaseNames function. Also, the FieldNames function will list fields from both the specified database as well as any related fields that happen to be on the layout, which is a good thing. Finally, the utility as built here will only document a single database at a time. It would require only small modifications to have the tool start with a list of databases and create a record for each as it processes them. We'll leave that to you as an exercise.

Number Functions

For the most part, the number functions are easy to understand and use. If you need to know the square root of a number, for instance, all you need to do is use the Sqr(x) function. There are a few functions, however, that aren't quite as intuitive, yet have broad uses. The functions we'll focus on in this section are Int, Mod, and Random.

Let's start again with a syntax review:

- **Int (number)** — Returns the integer portion of a number.

  Example: Int(4.56) = 4

- **Mod(number, divisor)** — Returns the remainder when the number is divided by the divisor.

  Example: Mod(15, 6) = 3 (because 15/6 = 2, remainder 3)

- **Random** — This function, which takes no arguments, returns a decimal number between 0 and 1.

  Example: Random = .0694132922540481

Now let's look at a few scenarios where these come in handy.

<u>**Scenario**</u>: Given some dollar amount, create a calculation that rounds down to the nearest quarter. For instance, $1.25, $1.28, and $1.49 should round to $1.25.

<u>**Solution**</u>: Since the goal is to round, your first approach to this might be to use the Round function. Unfortunately, the Round function only rounds to a certain number of digits (e.g., the nearest whole number, the nearest tenth, the nearest hundredth). Actually, all you need is the Int function:

```
roundDown = Int( Amount * 4) / 4
```

This solution is surprisingly succinct and highly extensible, as we'll see in a moment. But why does it work? Put crudely, the Int function hacks off decimals. If you've used other programming languages, you might have run across something called Floor that does that does the same thing. By multiplying the amount by 4 (the reciprocal of .25), amounts that previously spanned a quarter now span a dollar. That is, the range from $1.25 to $1.50, when multiplied by 4, now spans $5.00 to $6.00. Taking the Int of this forces all the amounts from $5.00 to $5.96 (the original $1.25 to $1.49) to $5.00. Finally, dividing this amount by four maps all of these back to $1.25.

Now let's see how this formula is extensible. Say that instead of rounding down to the nearest quarter, you wanted to round down to the nearest dime or nickel. Simply replace the 4 in the formula with 10 or 20, respectively. The general formula is thus Int (Amount * x) / x, where x is the reciprocal of the rounding factor.

Scenario: Given some dollar amount, create a calculation that rounds to the nearest quarter. For example, $1.37 should round to $1.25, but $1.38 should round to $1.50.

Solution: One solution to this looks quite similar to the last scenario.

```
nearestQuarter = Int((Amount + .12) * 4 ) / 4
```

All that's happening here is that the range is shifted by twelve cents. A move like this is often called a *translation*. We're translating thc initial amount so that each number will behave like another in a formula we already know. For instance, consider $1.38. This amount will behave just like $1.50 did in the last scenario, and hence rounds to $1.50. $1.37, on the other hand, behaves like $1.49 did, and so rounds down to $1.25 as desired.

You might wonder why we add .12 instead of .125 (which, after all, is half of .25, our rounding factor). The answer is that it doesn't matter; both will work. Somehow, though, it's easier (for us) to think of translating by twelve cents rather than twelve and half cents.

Scenario: Indulge us with one more scenario with rounding. Create a calculation that rounds up to the nearest quarter. For example, $1.26 should round up to $1.50.

Solution: After the last example, you might have a good guess as to one solution for this. Yep, that's right, another translation. But by how much? The easiest way to determine this is to think back to how various numbers behaved in the first example and how far you would need to move before you come to the range that behaves like you want. In this case, we want the range from $1.26 to $1.50 to behave like the range from $1.50 to $1.74 did. So that means translating by .24. The formula would thus be:

```
roundUp = Int((Amount + .24) * 4 ) / 4
```

There's another, completely different approach to this scenario that we want to cover as well. It's not quite as succinct as the Int solution, but is similarly extensible. This approach uses the Mod function (which, of course, is why we want to cover it).

First, consider the following specific instance: Mod(1.28, .25) = .03. When you divide 1.28 by .25, you get a remainder of .03. Now, in order to round 1.28 to 1.50, you need to add .22, which is .25 – .03. Let's see how a number like 1.46 fares. Mod (1.46, .25) = .21. 1.46 + (.25 – .21) = 1.50. This suggests the following formula:

```
Amount + (.25 - Mod(Amount, .25)
```

And in fact, this almost works. The problem is with a number like 1.25 itself. Mod(1.25 , .25) = 0, so 1.25 ends up rounding up to 1.50 which isn't what we want. There are a few ways to account for this situation. One is through a translation:

```
roundUp = Amount + (.25 - Mod(Amount - .01, .25)) - .01
```

The way we prefer, however, is to simply use another Mod function.

```
roundUp = Amount + Mod(.25 - Mod(Amount, .25) , .25)
```

The outer Mod function traps for the case where .25 – Mod(Amount, .25) = .25 (like Amount = $1.25) but doesn't touch any other numbers (since they're simply .01 through .24).

Hopefully you can see the extensibility of this function. To round to the nearest nickel or dime would simply require changing all of the instances of .25 to .05 or .1.

We need to mention one big potential problem with the Mod solution. There are times when a particular computer processor returns an incorrect value for the Mod of a fractional value. For instance, if we ask a Mac G3 laptop to evaluate Mod(1.31, .25), it returns .0600000000000001 instead of .06. Because of this, if you find yourself using a decimal number as the divisor for a Mod function, it's good practice to round the result. It rankles us to have to do this since it should work fine without, but that's life. The finished formula would thus end up looking like this:

```
roundUp = Amount + Mod(.25 - Round(Mod(Amount, .25) , 2) , .25)
```

Among the solutions we've presented for this scenario, it's wrong to say that one is better or worse than the others. If one of them makes more intuitive sense to you, that's probably the one you should use. There are probably even other solutions you might know of. The important thing is that you take away a better understanding of the Int and Mod functions.

Scenario: Create a formula that determines whether a whole number is odd or even.

Solution: It might seem like there should be a function that does this, but there isn't. Here again, we're going to present two possible solutions, one using the Int function and the other using the Mod function.

First the Int function. A number is even if it can evenly be divided by 2. We can test this using the following formula:

```
Int(x / 2) = x / 2
```

When this is true, x is even. When it isn't, x is odd. Think of a few examples:

Int(4 / 2) = 4 / 2
Int(2) = 2
2 = 2 (and therefore 4 is even)

Int(7 / 2) = 7 / 2
Int(3.5) = 3.5
3 = 3.5 (and therefore 7 is odd)

Of course, if you wanted a formula that returned "Even" or "Odd," then you'd end up using a conditional statement:

```
If (Int(x / 2) = x / 2, "Even", "Odd")
```

Now let's think about a solution using Mod. First, the universe we're interested in has only two values, "Even" and "Odd." It's a binary universe. As long as we're only considering whole numbers, then a binary universe is also a mod-2 universe. In a mod-2 universe, the only objects that exist are 0 and 1. Notice what happens if we map the domain of whole numbers into a mod-2 universe:

x	Mod(x , 2)
1	1
2	0
3	1
4	0
5	1
6	0
7	1
8	0
9	1
10	0
11	1

We're introducing this concept of a mod-*n* universe for a reason. Before this chapter is out, we'll have presented uses for several other modular universes. In this case, it might be easier to just mention that when you divide any whole number by 2, you either have a remainder of 0 (if the number is even) or a remainder of 1 (if the number is odd). Thus, the formula for determining if a number is even or odd would be:

```
If (Mod(x, 2) , "Odd", "Even")
```

Note that we simply treat the result of the Mod function as a Boolean result (which it is!). You could, of course, write "If(Mod(x , 2) = 1…", but that's redundant, and besides, it's also redundant.

Scenario: Write a calculation that creates a random eight-digit password

Solution: Finally we'll get a chance to see the Random function in action. The Random function by itself is fairly worthless. Usually, what you want is something like "a random whole number between 1 and 6." To produce a random whole number between 1 and x, you'd use the following formula:

```
Int(Random * x ) + 1
```

Since Random produces a number between 0 and 1, Random * x produces a number between 0 and x. Taking the Int of this yields a number between 0 and x–1, which is why the + 1 is necessary.

Armed with this knowledge, let's think about how we can create our random password. First, let's say that we want the password to contain only numbers, lowercase letters, or uppercase letters. There are therefore 62 different symbols to choose from for each character (10 + 26 + 26). To pluck one of these at random, we just need a string that contains all of them, a random number between 1 and 62, and the Middle function:

```
Middle("ABCDEFGHIJKLMNOPQRSTUVWXYZabcdefghijklmnopqrstuvwxyz1234567890",
        Int(Random*62) + 1 , 1)
```

To create a string with eight random characters, simply do this same move eight times:

```
Middle("ABCDEFGHIJKLMNOPQRSTUVWXYZabcdefghijklmnopqrstuvwxyz1234567890",
        Int(Random*62) + 1 , 1) &
Middle("ABCDEFGHIJKLMNOPQRSTUVWXYZabcdefghijklmnopqrstuvwxyz1234567890",
        Int(Random*62) + 1 , 1) &
Middle("ABCDEFGHIJKLMNOPQRSTUVWXYZabcdefghijklmnopqrstuvwxyz1234567890",
        Int(Random*62) + 1 , 1) &
Middle("ABCDEFGHIJKLMNOPQRSTUVWXYZabcdefghijklmnopqrstuvwxyz1234567890",
        Int(Random*62) + 1 , 1) &
Middle("ABCDEFGHIJKLMNOPQRSTUVWXYZabcdefghijklmnopqrstuvwxyz1234567890",
        Int(Random*62) + 1 , 1) &
Middle("ABCDEFGHIJKLMNOPQRSTUVWXYZabcdefghijklmnopqrstuvwxyz1234567890",
        Int(Random*62) + 1 , 1) &
Middle("ABCDEFGHIJKLMNOPQRSTUVWXYZabcdefghijklmnopqrstuvwxyz1234567890",
        Int(Random*62) + 1 , 1) &
Middle("ABCDEFGHIJKLMNOPQRSTUVWXYZabcdefghijklmnopqrstuvwxyz1234567890",
        Int(Random*62) + 1 , 1)
```

Scenario: Create a calculation that will randomly select a color from a list of colors.

Solution: This scenario demonstrates one of our favorite uses of the Random function. In fact, we use it all the time to generate random test data. For now, imagine that you've got a database of employee data, and you want to randomly assign each employee to one of four teams (represented by a color) for the big tug-of-war competition at your upcoming office picnic.

The first thing to do, of course, is generate a random number between 1 and 4. To turn this number into meaningful text, the Choose function comes in quite handy. Let's briefly review how this function works, since it's not one you likely use every day. Choose has a single test and multiple results:

```
Choose(test, result zero, result one, result two…)
```

The test should result in a number. If that number is 0, the function returns whatever is in the zero result slot; if the number is 1, then it returns the contents of the result one, and so on. The test, by the way, doesn't have to result in a whole number. Any decimal portion of a number will simply be ignored in determining which result to return.

Since the Choose function is zero-based and ignores decimals, all we really need to accomplish the goal is the following:

```
Choose(Random * 4 , "Blue", "Red", "Green", "Mauve")
```

If you don't want your teams to constantly be shifting, we'd suggest using this formula in a script or calculated replace rather than as a calculation field.

Scenario: Given some dollar amount, create a string of "check words" appropriate for printing checks.

Solution: If you've ever tried to create accounting systems in FileMaker, you've likely come across this problem: How can you turn numbers into words to print checks? We've seen a number of solutions for this problem, all of which involve large, messy calculations. There is a plug-in that's been written to eliminate the messiness, but we think there are a few things you can learn from the messy solution and possibly apply to other situations. The solution we present below is good for numbers up to 10 million dollars.

To begin, let's define three "helper" calculations that will store the various text elements that can appear on a check. Notice that the spacing in these is very important: The entries get padded to a set width, creating an array of sorts.

```
Ones = "One  Two  ThreeFour Five Six  SevenEightNine "
Tens = "Twenty    Thirty    Forty     Fifty     Sixty     Seventy   Eighty
       Ninety    "
Teens = "Ten       Eleven    Twelve    Thirteen  Fourteen  Fifteen   Sixteen
        Seventeen Eighteen  Nineteen  "
```

The Ones string is padded to five characters, the Tens to 10, and the Teens to 10.

Now, we need to establish a methodology for parsing a number into its ones, tens, hundreds, etc., digits. One school of thought is to treat the number like a string. The character to the left of the decimal is the ones place, two away is the tens place, and so on. Another method, which we prefer and will demonstrate here, uses the Mod function. It's going to be a mod-10 universe, which is the one that we most often live in, so it should feel comfortable to work with. The only elements in a mod-10 universe are the numbers 0 through 9.

For any x, Mod(Int(x) , 10) will return the ones digit of the number. For instance, consider x = 43. Mod(43, 10) = 3. And, for any x, Mod(Int(x/10), 10) will return the tens digit of the number. Consider again x = 43. Mod (Int(43/10)), 10 = Mod(Int(4.3), 10) = Mod(4 , 10) = 4. Using this logic, we can easily parse out any particular digit that we need from the original number. The millions place, for example, can be extracted from a number as Mod(Int (x / 1000000), 10).

Since the elements in the Ones array are spaced at five-character intervals, if we are given some x which represents the ones digit of a number, we can extract the part of the Ones array that contains the corresponding text by the following formula:

```
Trim(Middle(Ones, (x-1) * 5 + 1 , 5))
```

An example will help clarify this. Consider the case where x = 6:

Trim(Middle(Ones, (6–1) * 5 + 1, 5))
= Trim(Middle(Ones, 26, 5))
= Trim("Six ")
= "Six"

So much for the ones place then. When decoding the tens digit, however, there are two different scenarios to take into account. If the tens digit is a 1, we need text from the Teens array based on what the ones digit was. However, if the tens digit is greater than 1, then we need appropriate text from the Tens array, a hyphen (if the ones digit is not zero), and appropriate text from the Ones array. Thus, the following formula will work for values of x up to $99:

```
Case(
 Mod(Int(x/10), 10) > 1,
   Trim(Middle(Tens, (Mod(Int(x/10), 10) -2)*10 + 1, 10)) & If(Mod(Int(x),
         10) > 0, "-", " "),

 Mod(Int(x/10), 10) = 1 ,
   Trim(Middle(Teens, Mod(Int(x), 10) * 10 + 1, 10)) & " ") &

Case(
 Mod(Int(x), 10)> 0 and not Mod(Int(x/10), 10) = 1,
```

```
        Trim(Middle(Ones, (Mod(Int(x),10)-1 )* 5 + 1, 5)) & " ") &

    "and " & Right(x * 100, 2) & "/100"
```

Figure 11.3 shows some test data that's been run through this formula.

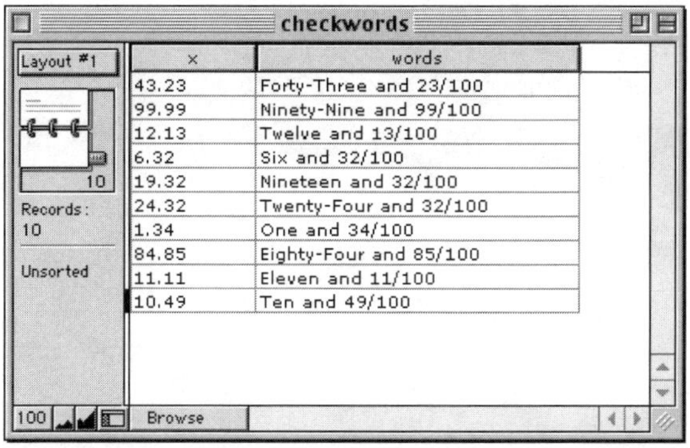

checkwords

Layout #1

Records: 10

Unsorted

x	words
43.23	Forty-Three and 23/100
99.99	Ninety-Nine and 99/100
12.13	Twelve and 13/100
6.32	Six and 32/100
19.32	Nineteen and 32/100
24.32	Twenty-Four and 32/100
1.34	One and 34/100
84.85	Eighty-Four and 85/100
11.11	Eleven and 11/100
10.49	Ten and 49/100

100 Browse

Figure 11.3

Similar logic can be applied to extend this formula out to any number of digits. As for the decimal part of the number, notice in the above formula that we're multiplying the number by 100 and taking the right two characters of the resulting string. Another option would have been to take the Mod(x, 1) * 100. Either should work just fine.

The entire calculation for decoding numbers up to 9,999,999.99 is given below:

```
Case(
 Mod(Int(x/1000000),10)>0,
   Trim(Middle(Ones,(Mod(Int(x/1000000),10)-1)*5+1,5)) &" Million ") &

Case(
 Mod(Int(x/100000),10)>0,
   Trim(Middle(Ones,(Mod(Int(x/100000),10)-1)*5+1,5)) &" Hundred ") &

Case(
  Mod(Int(x/10000),10)=0 and Mod(Int(x/1000),10)=0 and not
       Mod(Int(x/100000),10)=0,
      "Thousand " ,

  Mod(Int(x/10000),10)=1,
    Trim(Middle(Teens,(Mod(Int(x/1000),10))*10+1,10)) &" Thousand ",
```

```
  Mod(Int(x/10000),10)>1,
   Trim(Middle(Tens,(Mod(Int(x/10000),10)-2)*10+1,10)) &
     Case(
       Mod(Int(x/1000),10)>0,
          "-" & Trim(Middle(Ones,(Mod(Int(x/1000),10)-1)*5+1,5))) &
                 " Thousand " ,

  Mod(Int(x/10000),10)=0 and Mod(Int(x/1000),10)>0,
    Trim(Middle(Ones,(Mod(Int(x/1000),10)-1)*5+1,5))&" Thousand " ) &

Case(
  Mod(Int(x/100),10)>0,
   Trim(Middle(Ones,(Mod(Int(x/100),10)-1)*5+1,5))&" Hundred ") &

Case(
 Mod(Int(x/10), 10) > 1,
   Trim(Middle(Tens, (Mod(Int(x/10), 10) -2)*10 + 1, 10)) & If(Mod(Int(x),
         10) > 0, "-", " "),

 Mod(Int(x/10), 10) = 1 ,
   Trim(Middle(Teens, Mod(Int(x), 10) * 10 + 1, 10)) & " ") &

Case(
 Mod(Int(x), 10)> 0 and not Mod(Int(x/10), 10) = 1,
     Trim(Middle(Ones, (Mod(Int(x),10)-1 )* 5 + 1, 5)) & " ") &

"and " & Right(x * 100, 2) & "/100"
```

If you ever need to sit down and write a calculation of this magnitude and complexity from scratch, the best way is to start with a simple example and then gradually work your way up. Refine the solution by trial and error until you're satisfied with the results.

Date and Time Formulas

As the last topic for this chapter, let's take a close look at several useful date and time formulas. Date calculations can drive you crazy. Unfortunately, they're an essential part of most any database system, whether it's for payroll or scheduling classes. Before looking at the functions we'll be highlighting, let's review how dates and times are stored in a FileMaker database.

Dates are actually stored in the database as an integer number that represents the number of days since 1/1/0001. For instance, November 19, 2001 is stored as 730808. You may have seen a number like this if you've forgotten to format a calculation that returns a date as a date result. Times are stored internally as the number of seconds since midnight. This means that every time is a number from 0 to 86399.

Below are the main functions we'll be using in the scenarios to follow. In these examples, assume that you have a date field called myDate with the value "6/29/1969."

- **Date(month, day, year)** — This function returns a date based on the arguments you pass it. It's one of the most crucial functions for manipulating dates.

  Example: Date(myDate) = "6/29/1969"

NOTE If any of the arguments are out of range, FileMaker will adjust the result accordingly. So, Date(13, 4, 2001) = "1/4/2002."

- **Day(date)** — Returns a number that represents the day portion of the specified date.

  Example: Day(myDate) = 29

- **DayOfWeek(date)** — Returns an integer from 1 to 7 that represents what day the specified date falls on. 1 represents Sunday, 2 represents Monday, and so on.

  Example: DayOfWeek(myDate) = 1

- **Month(date)** — Returns an integer from 1 to 12 that represents the month of the specified date

  Example: Month(myDate) = 6

- **Year(date)** — Returns a four-digit number that represents the year portion of the specified date.

  Example: Year(myDate) = 1969

- **Status(CurrentDate)** — Returns the current date according to the system clock of the user's machine. We make this distinction so that you understand that in a client/server setup, the Status(CurrentDate) function does not return the server's date. Also, be sure that if you use this function in a calculation that you explicitly define the formula to be unstored, or else the function will evaluate once and remain static thereafter. Status(CurrentDate) has the advantage over the Today function in that it does not need to be recalculated each day. In general, you should prefer to use Status(CurrentDate) instead of the Today function.

  Example: Status(CurrentDate) = "11/23/01"

- **Time(hour, minute, second)** — Returns a time based on the three specified parameters

  Example: Time(14, 30, 0) = "14:30:00"

- **Hour(time)** — Returns the number of hours in the specified time. For times that represent a time of day, the Hour function will return a value from 0 to 23. If the time argument represents a duration, however, the value of the Hour function may return a larger number.

  Example: Hour("10:30:00") = 10
  Example: Hour("30:15:34") = 30

- **Minute(time)** — Returns the minute portion of the specified time. As such, the Minute function always returns a value from 0 to 59.

  Example: Minute("10:30:00") = 30

- **Seconds(time)** — Returns the second portion of the specified time. Similar to the Minute function, this range of this function is 0 to 59.

  Example: Seconds("16:45:23") = 23

- **Status(CurrentTime)** — Returns the current time. See the discussion on Status(CurrentDate) above. The same comments about server time versus client time apply, as does the reminder to define calculations using Status(CurrentTime) to be unstored.

Scenario: Imagine that you're importing data from a spreadsheet where the dates are formatted as an eight-digit number (MMDDYYYY). Convert this data into a format that FileMaker can understand.

Solution: It's quite common to get dates in all sorts of weird formats from other systems. If you try to import directly something formatted MMDDYYYY into a FileMaker date field, you'll be disappointed with the result. Rather, in a situation like this, the best thing to do is import the data into a text field and then run some sort of data conversion routine to format it as a proper FileMaker date. Essentially, you just need to treat the imported data as a string and use the parsing tools we covered earlier in this chapter to feed the Date function:

```
cleanDate = Date(Left(ImportedDate, 2), Middle(ImportedDate, 3, 2), Right
                (ImportedDate, 4))
```

Scenario: Given a date, create a calculation that returns the date of the last day of that month. For instance, if date = "9/23/01," then the calculation should return "9/30/01."

Solution: Most people usually approach this problem by creating a huge conditional statement: If the month of myDate is January, then the last day is... if the month of myDate is February (and it's not a leap year), then... That's a pretty good example of "brute force" thinking. It will indeed work, but it's definitely not succinct, nor extensible.

Instead, take a different approach. While it's tough to know the last day of a month, it's utterly simple to find the first day of the following month. Just use:

```
Date(Month(myDate) + 1 , 1, Year(myDate))
```

... and, of course, the last day of this month is simply the day before the first day of next month, right? Let FileMaker do the heavy lifting. The solution below works in all situations, including leap years:

```
lastDay = Date(Month(myDate) + 1 , 1, Year(myDate)) - 1
```

Scenario: Given a date, create a calculation that returns the date of the next Friday.

Solution: We see this situation come up a lot, especially in time and expense tracking systems that need to subsummarize by week.

Now, the DayOfWeek function will tell you what day of the week a given date falls on. Let's say that myDate is a Wednesday. DayOfWeek(myDate) would return a 4. Using this information, one approach you might have would be to hard-code conditional statements to say that if myDate is a Wednesday, then add 2 to myDate to get the date of the following Friday; if myDate is a Tuesday, then add 3, and so on.

Since the DayOfWeek of any Friday is 6, you can also just subtract the DayOfWeek of myDate from 6 to determine the number of days you are from Friday. For instance, if myDate is a Monday, then 6 – DayOfWeek(myDate) would be 6 – 2 = 4, which is the number of days you'd need to add to myDate to get to the following Friday.

This works great until you get to Saturday. Saturday is a 7, and if you subtract that from 6, you get –1, which, when added to myDate, results in the previous Friday. You could simply have a conditional test for Saturday and treat it differently than the other days, but that's kludgy and not very extensible.

We talked earlier about modular universes. Well, the days of the week fairly obviously constitute a mod-7 universe. As you try to envision modular universes, it's best to picture the elements in a circular arrangement.

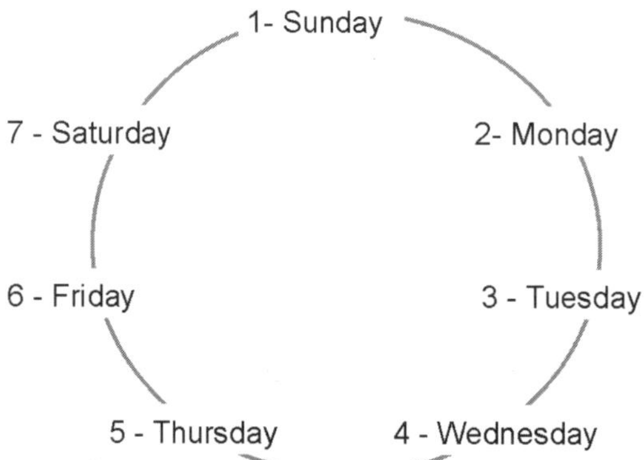

Figure 11.4

On this circle, addition can be thought of as moving so many places clockwise, while subtraction would be represented by counterclockwise movement. Now, let's see how this might help with the dilemma of Saturday. Notice first that from any day Sunday through Friday, the formula 6 – DayOfWeek(myDate) represents the number of clockwise moves you have to make to land on Friday. To move clockwise from Saturday to Friday, however, would require moving six places clockwise, which would mean changing the formula to something like 13 – DayOfWeek(myDate). But, in a mod-7 universe, 6 and 13 are equivalent. The two formulas aren't so different after all. So as long as we're in a mod-7 universe, it doesn't matter what we subtract from as long as it's 6 plus some multiple of 7 and doesn't return any negative numbers (which keeps us moving in a clockwise direction, which is forward in time). The final formula you need, therefore, is:

```
weekEndingFriday = myDate + Mod(13 - DayOfWeek(myDate) , 7)
```

The following table shows how this plays out over the course of an entire week:

```
Sunday 11/18/2001:      11/18/01 + Mod(13 – 1, 7) = 11/18/01 + 5 = 11/23/01
Monday 11/19/2001:      11/19/01 + Mod(13 – 2, 7) = 11/19/01 + 4 = 11/23/01
Tuesday 11/20/2001:     11/20/01 + Mod(13 – 3, 7) = 11/20/01 + 3 = 11/23/01
Wednesday 11/21/2001:   11/21/01 + Mod(13 – 4, 7) = 11/21/01 + 2 = 11/23/01
Thursday 11/22/2001:    11/22/01 + Mod(13 – 5, 7) = 11/22/01 + 1 = 11/23/01
Friday 11/23/2001:      11/23/01 + Mod(13 – 6, 7) = 11/23/01 + 0 = 11/23/01
Saturday 11/24/2001:    11/24/01 + Mod(13 – 7, 7) = 11/24/01 + 6 = 11/30/01
```

This solution is extensible in that you can easily adapt it to figure out week ending Thursday, week ending Saturday, or whatever. Simply change the constant (13) to 7 plus the day of the week you are interested in. So, week ending Thursday would be myDate + Mod(12 – DayOfWeek(myDate), 7).

To go backwards in time to find the date of, say, the week beginning Monday, requires a slightly different approach. You'd need to take myDate minus the difference of DayOfWeek(myDate) and 2 (the DayOfWeek of Monday). You'll run into problems with Sundays in this case, and will once again need to add 7 before doing the subtraction (and take the mod-7 of the result):

```
weekBeginningMonday = myDate – Mod(DayOfWeek(myDate) + 7 – 2, 7)
```

which can be reduced to:

```
weekBeginningMonday = myDate – Mod(DayOfWeek(myDate) + 5, 7)
```

The constant here will always be the mod-7 complement of the day you are interested in. For example, the weekBeginningWednesday would be myDate – Mod(DayOfWeek(myDate) + 3, 7), since 3 is the mod-7 complement of 4.

As a final extension of this formula, consider how easy it would be to find the date of the first Monday of any given month. Instead of starting at myDate, figure out the DayOfWeek of the first day of the month, and then add the appropriate number of days following the weekEnding formula above:

```
firstMondayOfMonth = Date(Month(myDate), 1, Year(myDate)) + Mod(9–
    DayofWeek(Date(Month(myDate), 1, Year(myDate))), 7)
```

How about the last Monday in any given month (… perhaps to schedule your bingo group)? Well, that's just the first Monday of the following month less 7, right? Piece of cake.

Scenario: Given a date, create a calculation that returns the calendar quarter of that date. That is, dates in January, February, or March should return a 1, dates in April, May, or June should return a 2, and so on.

Solution: This is another calculation that's needed quite often for summary reports. Typical situations would include things like wanting to get total product sales by quarter or total hours billed by quarter. Once you map all your dates to their respective quarters, that becomes the break field in your summary report.

Again, your first inclination might be to use a brute force method, which would look something like this:

```
calendarQuarter = Case(Month(myDate) <= 3, 1, Month(myDate) <=6, 2,
    Month(myDate) <=9, 3, 4)
```

As brute force methods go, this isn't a bad one. Since a Case statement stops evaluating once it finds a true test, you don't need to explicitly test for a range of months. Still, there's a more elegant and interesting formula:

```
calendarQuarter = Int((Month(myDate) + 2) / 3)
```

Test it out. Think of some date ("August 16th"). Take its month number ("8") and add 2 ("10"). Divide this by 3 ("3.33"), and then take the integer of the result ("3"). Neat, huh? Moreover, this is the kind of thing that will amaze your friends in your bowling league, trust us.

It's really not that hard to derive from scratch a formula like this. Start by thinking of what it is you're trying to accomplish. Here, you're trying to map a range of numbers from 1 to 12 into a range of 1 to 4. Division by 3 is a natural candidate. So you write out on scratch paper what division by 3 gets you:

	1	2	3	4	5	6	7	8	9	10	11	12
Div 3	.3	.6	1	1.3	1.6	2	2.3	2.6	3	3.3	3.6	4

Hopefully at this point you notice that the integer portions of the results are very close to the desired goal, but that things just line up wrong. Time for another translation. If you simply extend the scale and consider 3 through 14 instead of 1 to 12, things start to line up better:

	1	2	3	4	5	6	7	8	9	10	11	12		
plus 2			3	4	5	6	7	8	9	10	11	12	13	14
div 3	.3	.6	1	1.3	1.6	2	2.3	2.6	3	3.3	3.6	4	4.3	4.6
int			1	1	1	2	2	2	3	3	3	4	4	4

Then it's just a matter of translating the logic into symbols.

Scenario: Given a date, create a calculation that returns the fiscal quarter of that date.

Solution: Many organizations operate on a fiscal calendar that begins July 1 or September 1. For them, the first quarter is months 7-9 or 10-12. The calculation derived in the previous scenario to yield the calendar quarter can easily be extended to take this into consideration.

Let's look first at the situation of a fiscal year that begins in July. The following table illustrates how the calendar quarters map to the fiscal quarters:

Calendar Quarter	**Fiscal Quarter (beginning July 1)**
1	3
2	4
3	1
4	2

Do you recognize that we're operating in a mod-4 universe here? The transformation that maps the calendar quarter into the fiscal quarter is simply a modular translation. If you picture a dial with four positions on it, rotating the dial by two clicks (either direction) achieves the desired mapping. To generalize, rotating the calendar quarter by some number in mod-4 space yields the fiscal quarter. Or, as the outline of a formula: fiscalQuarter = Mod(calendarQuarter + x , 4). The value we choose for x determines whether we end up mapped to fiscal July, fiscal September, or even fiscal April.

Let's look at what happens if x is 1:

Calendar quarter:	1	2	3	4
+ 1	2	3	4	5
mod–4	2	3	0	1

In a mod-4 universe, the only elements are 0, 1, 2, and 3. This means that in order to return a value from 1 to 4, we'll need to add 1 to the result of the Mod function. In the specific case above where x = 1, this would have produced a final result of:

+ 1	3	4	1	2

... which is exactly the result we want for fiscal July.

The table below shows how varying x from 0 to 3 yields the four possibilities of fiscal quarter:

x	Fiscal Calendar	Formula
0	September	Mod (Int((Month(myDate) + 2) / 3)) , 4) + 1
1	July	Mod (Int((Month(myDate) + 2) / 3) + 1) , 4) + 1
2	Jan**	Mod (Int((Month(myDate) + 2) / 3) + 2) , 4) + 1
3	April	Mod (Int((Month(myDate) + 2) / 3) + 3) , 4) + 1

** Of course, it would be easier for this to just use the formula for calendar quarter. We've included it here merely for completeness.

Scenario: Given someone's birthdate, calculate his or her age.

Solution: We'll assume for our solution that we want to find the person's age as of today. To keep the formulas we're going to generate more manageable, assume that you've got an unstored calculation called curDate:

```
curDate = Status(CurrentDate)
```

Now, let's think about a few possible formats for the result of an age calculation. If someone is 32 years old, you may want any of the following age formats:

1. 32
2. 32 years and 64 days
3. 32 years, 2 months, and 3 days

Let's derive calculations that yield each of these.

1. This, not surprisingly, is the easiest of the three formats to generate. Think about a person born, say, in 1969. To calculate her age you first need to subtract the year of her birth from the year of the current date. If this year is 2001, then that evaluates to 32. However, during the year 2001, someone who was born in 1969 is 31 for part of the year prior to

her birthday, and is 32 for the remainder of the year. The calculation we need, then, starts by finding the difference in years, and then subtracts 0 or 1 depending on whether it's past the person's birthday:

```
ageInYears = Year(curDate) – Year(birthDate) – (DayofYear(curDate)
            < DayofYear(birthDate))
```

Notice that we're using a Boolean comparison to do the final subtraction. If the DayofYear of curDate is less than the DayofYear of the person's birthdate, then the statement is true, and 1 will be subtracted from the difference in years. You could also use an If or Case statement to do this test, but anytime you're going to return a 0 or 1, a Boolean test works just the same.

2. To achieve this result, you'll use the same logic developed above to generate the year portion, and then you'll calculate either the number of days the current date is past the birthdate, or, if the current date is past the person's birthdate, the number of days so far elapsed in the year plus the number of days between the birthdate and the end of the year. Two examples will help clarify this. Say that the person's birthdate is June 29, 1969. If today is June 30, 2001, then this person is 32 years and 1 day old. The day portion is easy to calculate by subtracting the DayofYear of each of the dates. But, if today were June 28, 2002, then you'd want to figure out how many days there were between June 29, 2001, and December 31, 2001, and add this to the number of days from January 1, 2002, to June 28, 2002. The formula ends up looking like this:

```
ageInYears\Days =
Year(curDate)-Year(birthDate) - (DayofYear(curDate) < DayofYear
    (birthDate)) & " years and " &
Case(DayofYear(curDate) >= DayofYear(birthDate),
     DayofYear(curDate) - DayofYear(birthDate),
     DayofYear(curDate) + (DayofYear(Date(12, 31, Year(curDate)) -
              DayofYear(birthDate))) & " days"
```

Notice that we don't just assume that there are 365 days in a year. Rather, we explicitly calculate how many days there are by using DayofYear(Date(12, 31, Year(curDate)).

3. Returning the age in years, months, and days is the most complicated scenario, but the logic is an extension of that above. To figure out the number of whole months that have passed since the last birth date, you can use mod-12 subtraction. The months of the year, after all, form a nice mod-12 universe. So, the number of months past the person's birthdate is:

   ```
   Mod(Month(curDate) – Month(birthDate) + 12, 12)
   ```

   The + 12 is necessary to ensure that the result of the subtraction is a positive number. Remember that in a mod-12 universe, 12 is the same thing as 0 (as is 24, 36, 48, etc.). Adding 12 here is a necessary evil because of how FileMaker (incorrectly, in our opinion) handles the mod of a negative number.

Just as we potentially needed to subtract 1 from the difference in years, we also need to subtract 1 from the difference in months if the day of the current month is less than the day of the birth month (i.e., it hasn't been a complete month yet). Taking these things into account, the final formula ends up as:

```
age =
     Year(curDate)-Year(birthDate) - (DayofYear(curDate) < DayofYear
        (birthDate)) & " years, " &
     Mod (Month(curDate) - Month(birthDate) + 12 - (Day(curDate) <
         Day(birthDate)), 12) & " months, and " &
     (curDate - Date(Month(curDate) - (Day(curDate) < Day(birthDate)),
         Day(birthDate), Year (curDate))) & " days"
```

Scenario: Imagine that you have a workshop database that contains, among other things, a time field for the start time of the workshop. Create a calculation field that can be used as the body of a confirmation email to display information about the workshop, including the start time. For instance, the calculation should return something like "Workshop 23 is scheduled to begin at 8:30 am".

Solution: Just for the heck of it, let's look at an obvious, but wrong solution.

```
emailBody = "Workshop " & WorkshopID & " is scheduled to begin at " &
     startTime
```

This would actually return "Workshop 23 is scheduled to begin at 30600". The problem, of course, is that if you use a time field in a calculation that has a text result, it is displayed in its "natural" form, as seconds since midnight. Wrapping the start time in a TimeToText function doesn't quite get you there either. That would return "Workshop 23 is scheduled to begin at 8:30:00". Moreover, the time here is actually military time, so a 2 P.M. workshop would come out as 14:00:00.

To come up with a solution, let's look separately at the various segments we need to compose. First, let's consider the hour. Above you learned that the Hour function returns a value from 0 to 23. For our email confirmation, however, we want all times to begin with a number from 1 to 12. Now, time is a fairly obvious (and common) mod-12 universe. If it's 10 in the morning and someone asks you what time it will be in five hours, you unhesitatingly reply 3 P.M., since 10 + 5 = 3 in a mod-12 universe. But, if you try to simply map military time into regular time with the mod-12 function, you end up with one small problem, namely the zeros, which need to evaluate as 12. The result needs to be a range of 1-12 and not 0-11. You can account for this by adding 1 to the result of the Mod function, but need to have an offsetting translation within the function itself. So, this part of our formula ends up as:

```
Mod(Hour(startTime) +11, 12) + 1
```

Since we doubt you'll take the time to test this yourself right now, let's look at how this plays out.

Hour	0	1	2	3	4	5	6	7	8	9	10	11	12	13	14	15	16	17	18	19	20	21	22	23
+ 11	11	12	13	14	15	16	17	18	19	20	21	22	23	24	25	26	27	28	29	30	31	32	33	34
mod-12	11	0	1	2	3	4	5	6	7	8	9	10	11	0	1	2	3	4	5	6	7	8	9	10
+ 1	12	1	2	3	4	5	6	7	8	9	10	11	12	1	2	3	4	5	6	7	8	9	10	11

Your first inclination for the translation might be to subtract 1, so as to offset the + 1 outside the function. As we've discussed a few times already, however, this would have resulted in negative numbers, which the Mod function doesn't handle well. But in a mod-12 universe, subtracting 1 and adding 11 are the same thing.

That takes care of the hour portion of the formula; let's move on to the minutes. The Minute function, of course, returns a value from 0 to 59. The only difficulty we encounter when using this function to build a text rendition of a time is with leading zeros. That is, if the minute function returns a 6, we don't want a 6 displayed, we want "06" displayed.

There's a fairly standard and well-known routine for padding leading zeros on a string. Simply concatenate a string of zeros with your string, and take the right x characters of the resulting string. In our case, we want to pad up to two leading zeros, so this part of our formula would look like this:

```
Right("00" & Minute(startTime) , 2)
```

All that remains is to appropriately display "am" or "pm." Nothing complex here. Just test whether the hour (which returns 0 to 23) is less than 12.

Putting all these pieces together, the final formula ends up as:

```
"Workshop " & WorkshopID & " is scheduled to begin at " &
(Mod(Hour(startTime) +11, 12) + 1)& ":" & Right("00" & Minute(startTime),2)
      & Case(Hour(startTime) < 12, " am", " pm")
```

Scenario: Calculate the elapsed time between two events that might occur over a day apart.

Solution: We'll explore several variations of this scenario. First, let's take a simple case. Let's say that you have a Time & Expense system where your users can log time on various projects. The time they start is logged as startTime; the time they finish is entered as endTime (both time fields, of course).

Now, as long as both times occur in the same day, and they've been properly entered (i.e., the end time is greater than the start time), then the following is sufficient to determine the elapsed time:

```
elapsedTime = endTime – startTime
```

You have to be careful, though, when selecting the type for the calculation result. Say that startTime is 8:00 am and endTime is 11:45 am. If you set elapsedTime to have a text result, the formula will return the string "3:45:00." This might look okay, but you'll have plenty of problems when you try to add up a list of times later on, and hence this method should be avoided. As a number result, the formula would yield "13500," which represents the number of seconds between the two times. In some cases, this might be an appropriate format. More frequently, you'd use a number format if you wanted to return the elapsed time in a decimal format (i.e., 3.75). To achieve this, you would just need to divide (endTime–startTime) by 3600 (the number of seconds in an hour). Finally, if you set the result type to time, the formula returns “3:45:00.” This is probably the best of the three options. Keep in mind as you're formatting this field on the layout that this represents a duration and not an actual time.

Let's complicate things. What happens if someone begins work at, say, 10 P.M., and ends at 2 A.M.? The simple formula above would yield –20:00. That might make a client happy, but probably not your accountant. To get the correct result (4:00), you would need to add 24 hours. There are two equally good ways to do this. Either add 86400 (the number of seconds in a day) or add Time (24, 0, 0). The formula to take this into account would be:

```
elapsedTime = endTime – startTime + Case(endTime < startTime, 86400)
```

For many purposes, this would be quite sufficient. As a final bit of complication, let's say that the startTime and endTime refer to events that happen potentially several days apart, like a long sailboat race. How, given also a startDate and endDate, can you calculate the elapsed time (in hours and minutes) a boat took to finish the race? If you try to solve this using conditional statements, you'll end up with a mess. The easier way is to get everything to use a common unit, namely seconds. If you multiply the date by 86400 and then add the time, you'll have a unique number that represents the number of seconds since January 1, 0001. The formula ends up looking like this:

```
elapsedTime = (endDate * 86400 + endTime) – (startDate * 86400 + startTime)
```

Format the result as time, and you're done.

Summary

In this chapter, we've covered a number of important and useful complex calculations for manipulating text, numbers, dates, and times. Our approach has been to discuss at length the thought process that goes into a given formula. Undoubtedly, there are other formulas that could have been used to solve particular problems we've presented. We've tried to present solutions that are elegant and extensible, so that you would learn to strive for these goals in your own calculations. Obviously, the ultimate test of any calculation is whether it does what it's supposed to do, no matter how inelegant or kludgy.

Nonetheless, we think you'll agree after reading this chapter that there are certain ideas and moves that come up repeatedly in quite diverse situations. Having these at your fingertips will allow you to solve new challenges more quickly and with less effort.

Appendix A

References

Books

If you'd like to read up on the roots of the relational model, a pretty readable math book is *Discrete Mathematics* by Richard Johnsonbaugh (ISBN: 0-13-089008-1). It gets terrible reviews on Amazon, but we found it to be very succinct on the topics we cared about.

If you're looking for a great overview of the entire subject of relational databases, our longtime favorite is *An Introduction to Database Systems* by C.J. Date (ISBN: 0-20-138590-2).

Here are some good and varied data modeling books:

Data Modeling for Information Professionals by Bob Schmidt (ISBN: 0-13-080450-9). This gets into way more than just data modeling, but the content is great.

The Data Modeling Handbook by Michael Reingruber and William Gregory (ISBN: 0-471-05290-6). This one gets a lot more into process.

Handbook of Relational Database Design by Candace Fleming and Barbara von Halle (ISBN: 0-201-11434-8). Great coverage of design methodologies.

For those of you who are more interested in process, try:

The Rational Unified Process, An Introduction by Philippe Kruchten (ISBN: 0-201-70710-1) or *The Unified Modeling Language User Guide* by Grady Booch, James Rumbaugh, and Ivar Jacobson (ISBN: 0-201-57168-4).

If the quick taste of extreme programming (aka XP) piqued your interest, you should look at:

Extreme Programming Explained by Kent Beck (ISBN: 0-201-61641-6) and *Extreme Programming in Practice* by James Newkirk and Robert C. Martin (ISBN: 0-201-70937-6).

Here are a couple of books that are slightly off-topic, but are still good to read:

Managing the Professional Service Firm by David H. Maister (ISBN: 0-684-83431-6). If you run or work in a consulting company, this is a fantastic book that will open your eyes. It explores every aspect of the running of a service firm.

Just in case you have terrible positioning at your desk (if your back is to the door), read *The Personal Feng Shui Manual* by Master Lam Kam Chuen (ISBN: 0-8050-5558-4). After reading several books on the topic, Chris likes this one best.

Discussion Lists

FileMaker Café
http://www.maclane.com/cgi-bin/ultimatebb.cgi

FM Forums
http://www.fmforums.com/

Forums@FileMakerWorld.com
http://forum.filemakerworld.com

Listservers

Filemaker Pro Talk
http://www.blueworld.com/blueworld/lists/filemaker.html

FileMaker Pro-CGI Talk
http://www.listsearch.com

FMAnnounce
http://www.databasepros.com/fmannounce.html

FMPexperts
http://www.ironclad.net.au/lists/lasso.html

Searchable Listserver Archives from Blueworld
http://www.blueworld.com/blueworld/lists/FMPro-CGI.html

Magazines

FileMaker Pro Advisor
http://www.advisor.com/whome.nsf/w/ZFMP

ISO FileMaker Magazine
http://www.filemakermagazine.com/

General Reference

Aberdeen Group
FileMaker TCO Study
http://www.filemaker.com/it/index.html

Software

Filemaker Solutions Directory
Search the Filemaker database for pre-made solutions
http://www.filemaker.com/solutions/find_solution.html

FileMaker, Inc.
FileMaker collection
Free templates for starting out your filemaker solutions
http://www.filemaker.com/collection/

FileMaker, Inc.
FileMaker templates
http://www.filemaker.com/solutions/templates.html

User Groups

FileMaker User Group List
http://www.filemaker.com/support/usergroups.html

FileVille
http://www.fileville.com/

Web Sites

A FileMaker Affliction
http://www.afilemakeraffliction.com/

Chris Moyer Consulting
http://www.fmpro.com

ClickWorld
http://www.clickworld.com

Data Concepts Tips and Tricks
http://dwdataconcepts.com/dwdcgames.htm

FileMaker ISPs
http://www.filemaker.com/products/isp.html

FileMaker Now
http://www.filemaker.com/news/newsletter.html

FileMaker World Web Ring
http://www.webring.org/cgi-bin/webring?ring=fmpring;list

FileMaker XML Central
http://www.filemaker.com/xml/index.html
http://www.flemaker.com/xml/index.html

FM NewsWire
http://www.fmnewswire.com

FMP Archives Search Engine
http://mcnilith.unix-ag.uni-hannover.de/filemaker/fmp_faq/search.html

FMPasap
http://www.fmpasap.com/

FMPro.org
http://www.fmpro.org/

John Mark Osborne
ISO FileMaker World
http://www.filemakerworld.com

Plug-ins

Waves in Motion
http://www.wmotion.com

Troi Automatisering
www.troi.com

New Millenium
http://www.newmillennium.com/

FileMaker's plug-in directory
http://www.filemaker.com/plugins/index.html

Appendix B

Keyboard Shortcuts and Other Time-Saving Techniques

Studies have shown that FileMaker developers who use keyboard shortcuts tend to develop much more quickly than developers who don't. OK, so not actual published studies, but we're still convinced this is the case, and you should be, too. Most people who have been developing database applications with FileMaker for a while tend to know and use a smattering of keyboard shortcuts. Most of the shortcuts are intuitive, and don't take long to memorize. But beyond straight keyboard shortcuts, there are numerous other time-saving "tricks of the trade" that we've picked up over the years. In this appendix, we'll share these with you.

We don't intend this to be a comprehensive list of keyboard shortcuts. It would be almost embarrassing to just print a list of commands and what they do. After all, you can find such a list on the back cover of the manual. (People are always amazed to learn this!) Instead, we have organized this appendix into sections based on functionality. We discuss in depth what we feel are the most important shortcuts to learn. Also, we're counting on you to already know (and therefore we don't discuss) keyboard shortcuts that are common to most every application, like open, close, quit, print, cut, copy, and paste. Nor do we discuss all of the shortcuts available by right-clicking (Ctrl-clicking on Mac) on an object. You can discover all of those on your own.

The functional areas we cover are:

- The essentials
- Navigation
- Layouts
- Scripting
- Field definitions
- Text formatting
- Other miscellaneous stuff

Even if you think you know a lot of shortcuts, we'd encourage you to read this appendix fairly carefully. There are probably a few surprises even for veteran developers.

Most of the shortcuts we'll show you work the same on Windows and Mac. We'll always give the Windows shortcut first, followed by the Mac shortcut in parentheses.

The Essentials

The shortcuts in this section are the lifeblood of a FileMaker developer. There's really no excuse for not knowing these.

Ctrl-Shift-D (Cmd-Shift-D) takes you to the Define Fields dialog. This works no matter what mode you're in. More on field definitions in the "Field Definitions" section.

Every developer should know (and use!) the shortcuts to enter the four modes:

Ctrl-B (Cmd-B) — Browse mode

Ctrl-F (Cmd-F) — Find mode

Ctrl-L (Cmd-L) — Layout mode

Ctrl-U (Cmd-U) — Preview mode (This is the one people forget. Just think "PrevU".)

Similarly, the essential shortcuts for working with records are:

Ctrl-N (Cmd-N) — New record

Ctrl-D (Cmd-D) — Duplicate record/request

Ctrl-E (Cmd-E) — Delete record. Hold down the Shift (Option) key to suppress the confirmation dialog. This holds true of all delete confirmation dialogs. You can also delete find requests with a Ctrl-E.

Ctrl-S (Cmd-S) — Sort

Navigation

The shortcuts in this section all mostly intended to help you navigate more quickly through sets of records. Many of them are things you'll want to teach users of your system.

Ctrl-up/down arrows (Cmd-up/down) — This is one of our favorites, and we're surprised that more developers (and users) don't know this one. In Browse mode, Ctrl-up arrow and Ctrl-down arrow will navigate to the next and previous record of the found set. These work similarly in the other modes. In Layout mode, you can move from layout to layout; in Find mode, from request to request; and in Preview mode, from page to page. On Windows, if you have a mouse with a wheel on it, you can use the wheel to do this too.

Ctrl-J (Cmd-J) — Show All Records

Ctrl-Shift-S (Cmd-Option-S) — Hide/unhide the status area

Ctrl-Shift-Z (Cmd-Option-Z) — Zoom/unzoom the window

Ctrl-M (Cmd-M) — Omit the current record from the found set

Ctrl-Shift-M (Cmd-Shift-M) — Omit multiple records from the found set. If you ever want to omit all the records from the current record to the end of the found set, just do a Ctrl-Shift-M, and when prompted for the number of records to omit, type in a large number (like 99999). FileMaker will tell you that it can only omit x number of records, and will then fill this in as the number to omit, saving you the trouble of that complicated subtraction.

Layouts

The shortcuts in this section all pertain to designing layouts.

The arrow keys — When you have an object selected in Layout mode, you can use all of the arrow keys on your keyboard to "nudge" the object a pixel at a time. This is much, much easier than trying to, say, drag an object exactly on top of another object.

Shift drag — If you hold down the Shift key while dragging an object, you'll restrict its motion to either the vertical or horizontal plane. This really helps keep things aligned as you replicate objects.

Control drag (Option drag) — Holding down the Option key whil dragging an object will create a copy of the object. We almost always use this method of duplication rather than selecting an object and doing a Ctrl-D (Cmd-D). Ctrl-D creates a copy 6 pixels down and to the right of the original object. Option dragging is also a much better way of adding fields to a layout than dragging them from the status area, because you'll get an object with the same properties as the one you're copying. The one time that using Ctrl-D is nice is when you want to create lists of fields all at the same offset from one another. If you dupe once, then move the item where you want it, duping again will create the next copy with the same offset of the first moved item.

The Autogrid — Many people are passionate about the use or non-use of the autogrid feature. You can toggle between using and not using it by doing a Ctrl-Y(Cmd-Y). We almost always develop with the autogrid on. Objects move in 6-pixel increments, making it much easier to get consistent spacing between objects, and helps also when you need to temporarily move layered objects. Moving it back into place is much simpler with the autogrid on. Also, if you have the autogrid on, you can suspend it by holding down the Alt (Command) key as you're dragging an object. Given this, there's really no reason not to leave it on.

Selecting objects — There are several shortcuts that come in handy for selecting objects. First, in FileMaker 5.5, if you hit the Tab key while in Layout mode, the focus will cycle through all of the objects on the layout (in the order they were created). Shift-clicking will allow you to select multiple objects, as will clicking somewhere on the background and dragging entirely around the objects you want to select. As a variation on this, holding down the Control (Cmd) key will select any object that you touch (instead of just those you completely surround). Ctrl-A (Cmd-A) will select every object on the layout. If you've selected a single object, then Ctrl-Shift-A (Cmd-Option-A) will select all similar objects on the layout (i.e., all the fields or all of the text labels). It's often helpful to select all the objects on the layout and deselect items you don't want to include by Cmd dragging or Shift-clicking.

Alignment — If you've selected multiple objects and want to align them, do a Ctrl-Shift-K (Cmd-Shift-K). Once you've aligned objects, FileMaker remembers the last alignment settings, so if you want to align some other objects similarly, you just need to do a Ctrl-K (Cmd-K). Only use the Shift when you want to change the default settings.

Finally, you should know the commands for grouping, locking and layering:

Ctrl-G (Cmd-G) and Ctrl Shift G (Cmd-Shift-G) — Group and ungroup items

Ctrl-H (Cmd-H) and Ctrl Shift H (Cmd-Shift-H) — Lock and unlock items

Ctrl-Shift-J (Cmd-Shift-J) — Send backward one layer. If you also hold down the Alt (Option) key, it will send the object all the way to the back.

Ctrl-Shift-F (Cmd-Shift-F) — Bring forward one layer. If you also hold down the Alt (Option) key, it will bring the object all the way to the front.

Scripting

There are a whole bunch of tricks you can use to speed up your scripting. There's unfortunately no shortcut to get to the ScriptMaker itself (OK… on Windows, you can do an Alt-S-S). Once you have the ScriptMaker open, the fun begins.

- The Tab key will toggle the focus between the existing list of scripts to the new script name area.
- When the existing script names are active, you can use type-ahead to quickly find a script you're interested in.
- Ctrl-up arrow (Cmd-up arrow) and Ctrl-down arrow (Cmd-down arrow) will change the order of the scripts.
- The space bar will toggle the check box to include the script in the script menu.
- You can select multiple scripts by Shift-clicking. This comes in handy if you want to duplicate or delete a bunch of scripts. Just as when deleting records, holding down Shift (Option) when deleting a script will bypass the usual delete warning.

- When creating new scripts, just hit the Return key after you've typed the name of the script. Create will always be the default button when you're typing in the script name area.
- Finally, whenever you're ready to exit the ScriptMaker, don't bother with the Done button; just hit the Escape key.

After you're into an actual script definition, there are even more shortcuts you can use.

- If you're on Windows, anytime you create a new script, immediately hit Alt-A to delete all of the default script steps. No such luck for Mac users; you'll have to click the button.
- If you can't remember where a particular script step is, you can always click over on the left to activate the list of steps (or hit the Tab key) and then use type-ahead to find the step you want. On a Mac, once a step is highlighted, just tap the space bar and it will be inserted into your script.
- The same trick for reordering scripts works with script steps, too. Ctrl-up and down arrow are very handy, especially when you add an If or a Loop that has its close tag with it.

If you have a script step selected, the backspace key will delete that step. That's much more convenient (and much faster) than using the Clear button.

- To exit the script definition, use either the Enter key (if you wish to save your changes) or the Escape key (if you don't).

There are a few more platform-specific shortcuts worth mentioning. On a Mac, most times when a script step has an option to select a field or file (like Set Field, Import, Copy, etc.), you can access the field or file dialog by hitting the space bar. This works also with script steps that have a single "Specify" dialog, like If, Show Message, and Comment. On a Windows machine, take advantage of the Alt-key sequences available for things like duplicating script steps and getting into the specification dialogs.

Field Definitions

The keyboard shortcuts for working with field definitions are similar in many ways to those for scripting. For instance, you can use the Tab key to change the focus to various areas of the dialog. Also, you can use type-ahead to find a field easily.

Once you've done a Ctrl-Shift-D to open field definitions, the focus will be on the field name area. If you want to add a new field, just start typing, and hit the Return key when you're done. If the field you're adding is of type text, number, date, or time, then hitting the Return key again will take you immediately into the field options.

We'll assume that since the shortcuts for the various field types are right on the screen and that you've seen them hundreds of times, that you always use Cmd-T, N, D, I, O, L, S, or G to select your field type. If not, then you're probably not even reading this section because saving time doesn't matter to you.

On Windows, after you've defined a new field as a global field and are asked to select the data type, use the up and down arrows to change the selection and just hit the Return key when you're done.

When you're working on a calculation definition, there are two ways to exit the calculation dialog. Either hit the Enter key (not the Return) to keep any changes you've made, or the Escape key to exit without saving them. The Escape key also closes the field definition dialog itself, but there's nothing to worry about saving first, so you should always use that.

Also while working on calculations, on Windows if you want to change the data type of the calculation result, hit the Tab key and then use the up and down arrow to make your selection.

Text Formatting

The shortcuts in this section mostly apply both to working with text elements on layouts and actual text that you enter into a field in Browse mode.

First, hopefully everyone knows Command-Shift-B/U/I to make selected text bold, underlined, or italics. Other shortcuts of the Command-Shift variety include Command-Shift-< and Command-Shift->, which make the selected text smaller or bigger. With the Alt (Option) key held down also, it increments one pixel at a time. Without, it goes to the next size defined for that font (i.e., 10-12-14-18).

Command-[— Left justify selected text

Command-| — Center selected text

Command-] — Right justify selected text

You can insert the current date anywhere you want by doing a Command-hyphen. The current time is Command-;.

Other Miscellaneous Stuff

The shortcuts in this section didn't fit nicely into any of the sections above, so we just punted and decided to put them in a section of their own.

- In the Sort dialog, you can use the Tab key to change the focus from side to side. You can type ahead to find a field on either side. On a Mac, once a field is highlighted, the space bar will move it to the other side. The Return key will perform the sort; Escape will exit without performing it. The same holds true of the export records dialog.
- There's no keyboard shortcut to get to the define relationships dialog. (OK, on Windows, you can do Alt-F-R.)
- In the import field mapping, you can use Ctrl-up arrow (Cmd-up arrow) or Ctrl-down arrow (Cmd-down arrow) to move fields up or down in the order. Hitting the space bar toggles between importing and not importing the selected field.
- When you're clicked into a field, Ctrl-I (Cmd-I) will pull up the index of a field (if it's indexable, of course). This works in Find mode also.
- There are a number of interesting things you can do to copy sets of records. Say that you're looking at a list of records. A Ctrl-Shift-C (Cmd-Option-C) performs a Copy All, and you'll get a tab- and return-delimited array of all of the fields on the current layout for the current found set. A Ctrl-C (Cmd-C) while you're not clicked into a field gives you the same thing, but only for the current record. A Ctrl-C (Cmd-C) while in Preview mode creates a bitmap graphic of the current page and places it on your clipboard. This last one comes in handy for creating your own print preview routines.

Appendix C

Glossary

atomic values

Also known as scalar values, these values cannot be meaningfully divided into smaller pieces. "10" is an atomic value, while "10 Veggie Dogs" is not, since you have both quantity and description information in the same value.

attribute

An attribute corresponds to a field. An attribute is part of a table in the relational model, as a field is part of a database table in physical reality. The terms attribute and field (or column) are often used interchangeably.

authentication

The process by which a database system verifies the identity of a user.

base tables

The "permanent" tables that contain persistent data, as opposed to tables that are created to temporarily display a report or total values, and then are discarded. The persistent data contained in base tables may differ from temporary data that is generated for display to the user in a web browser or other client application.

Boyce-Codd Normal Form (BCNF)

A table is in Boyce-Codd Normal Form when it meets the criteria for First through Third Normal Form and allows candidate keys to be determinants.

candidate key

A value or set of values that, taken as a group, uniquely identify a row in a table. Every primary key must be a candidate key, but a candidate key may or may not be chosen as the primary key.

cardinality

The number of rows in a table.

Cartesian product

One of the relational operators that generates all possible combinations of the rows of two argument (input) tables. See Chapter 2 for specific examples.

client/server

In a client/server database implementation, a powerful server runs the database system while a client piece of software (often a web browser) interacts with the user and retrieves data from the server.

closure property

If the result of a mathematical expression is of the same data type as the arguments of that expression, then the expression exhibits the closure property.

column

The same thing as a field.

compound key

A key (candidate, primary, or foreign) that consists of more than one attribute.

data modeling

A process used to gather and represent the business logic and rules that a database system must codify.

DBA

Database administrator

DBMS

Database management system

degree

The number of attributes in a particular table. A table with six fields is of degree 6.

denormalization

The opposite of normalization. After a data model has been completely normalized, it is sometimes necessary to add redundancy back into the model for performance reasons. As an example, think of searching on an unstored calculation field in a large table. The performance can be greatly improved if you create a field that looks up the related value and then search on that stored value instead.

derived tables

Generated by the user interface, or client software, for display to the user. They are derived in that they use data from base tables and then reinterpret it to add meaning for the user. Examples would be to reinterpret a 1, 2, or 3 as East, Central, and Western regions, or to total values from multiple base records.

difference

A set operator and a relational operator. It's used when you want to find the difference between two tables. The result will be records that the two tables don't have in common. The difference operator is useful when you need to synchronize two tables with similar sets of records. A field sales database system would be a good candidate.

direct materialization

This happens when a single underlying base value is directly reinterpreted, such as a 1 or 0 being presented to the user as Yes or No.

divide

A relational operator that's used to identify rows in one table that match all rows in another. A good example would be if you wanted to find all invoices that contained red widgets, blue widgets, and green widgets. The invoice table would be your dividend, and the widgets table would be your divisor.

domain

The set of all possible values that a particular field can contain. Somewhat analagous to validating a field as a member of a value list, domains can be described more abstractly by stating some criteria for domain membership, such as "All species of animals that live in the Hudson River Valley." Try putting that in a value list.

entity

An entity is something about which you need to record information, such as a customer or a product.

equijoin

A join between two tables that is based on the key fields in each table being equal to each other, as opposed to being greater than or not equal. This is the only type of join that FileMaker is currently capable of.

existential quantifier

A concept from predicate logic, it means that if you have a result from a predicate, at least one of those values is true.

Fifth Normal Form (5NF)

Most tables that are in Third or Fourth Normal Form are already in Fifth Normal Form. Fifth Normal Form exists to address a special case where a table cannot be decomposed (in a non-loss fashion, or so that the resulting tables can be joined to recreate the original table) into two tables, but can be decomposed into three or more tables. A table is in Fifth Normal Form if it has met the criteria for First through Fourth Normal Forms, and every join dependency is implied by the table's candidate key(s). See Chapter 3 for more information.

First Normal Form (1NF)

A table is in First Normal Form if all of its values are atomic (scalar).

foreign key

A key that references a primary key in another table. For example, an invoice might contain a Customer ID field. This might be the match field for a relationship to a Customer table, and would thus be acting as a foreign key.

Fourth Normal Form (4NF)

A table is in Fourth Normal Form when it meets the criteria for First through Boyce-Codd Normal Form and is free from multivalued dependencies, which are repeating groups that repeat across records. See the example in Chapter 3.

functional dependence

A relationship between two or more attributes where one or more of the attributes uniquely determines the other. For example, a phone number might uniquely identify Molly Thorsen in an employee phone number table. In that case, we'd say that phone number functionally determines employee name, or that employee name is functionally dependent on phone number.

index

A de-duplicated list of all values contained in a field. Indexed fields respond to sorting and searching operations more quickly than unindexed fields. In order to create a valid relationship in FileMaker, you must match to an indexed field in the related file.

indirect materialization

This happens when underlying base values are indirectly reinterpreted, such as when a collection of extended price values are totaled to produce an invoice subtotal.

integrity

See referential integrity

intersection

A set and relational operator. Intersection yields the records that two tables have in common.

join

A relational operator. A relationship in FileMaker is a specific type of join called an equijoin where the foreign key and the related primary key are equal. In other database systems, it's possible to join based on other operators such as <, >, and ≠. A join is used to display values from multiple related tables.

join dependency

If you take a table and subdivide it into smaller tables using subsets of the fields (perform a project operation), and only certain subsets can be joined to recreate the original table, that fact is a constraint on the table, and that constraint is called a join dependency.

key

There are four different kinds of keys: primary, candidate, alternate, and foreign. A primary key is a field or set of fields that can be used to uniquely indentify a record in a table. In some tables, there may be multiple sets of fields that can accomplish this. In that case, those sets of fields (a set might contain only one member) are all known as candidate keys. One of them is chosen to be the primary key, and the rest are alternate keys. A foreign key is a set of fields in one table that references a primary key in another table. If an invoice table had an invoice ID and a customer ID, the invoice ID would be the primary key and the customer ID would be a foreign key that referenced the primary key in the customer table.

normalization

The process of restructuring tables so that they conform to the normal forms (First Normal Form, Second Normal Form, Third Normal Form, Boyce-Codd Normal Form, Fourth Normal Form, Fifth Normal Form).

This conformance will ensure that operations performed on the tables will not lead to update anomalies.

null values
: Empty values, not to be confused with zeros. Null values are an important problem for database developers, since there needs to be agreement among a group of users on what a particular null value means. Primary key fields can never contain null values.

ODBC
: Open database connectivity. ODBC is the almost universal language that database systems made by different vendors can use to exchange data.

persistent data
: Data that is actually "stored." In the case of FileMaker, this means any text, number, date, or time field, as well as any calculations whose storage option is set to Stored. Calculations that reference global fields or related fields (or other calculations that reference either of these) are always unstored.

predicate logic
: One of the roots of the relational model, it actually provides a construct that allows a database designer to enforce the insertion of only acceptable values into the database system.

primary key
: A field or set of fields that can be used to uniquely identify a record in a table.

product
: A relational operator. See Cartesian product.

project
: A relational operator that's used to display a subset of fields from a table. The FileMaker equivalent is to put certain fields onto a layout.

RDBMS
: Relational database management system, which is the software product that runs a database system.

redundancy
: A description of a database that has multiple instances of the same piece of data. Redundancy can never be entirely eliminated from a relational da-

tabase since redundant copies of foreign keys are necessary to maintain relationships between tables. Redundancy should be minimized when performance and structural considerations allow it to be.

referential integrity
: A foreign key in one table must reference a value that exists in the related table. To prevent the creation of "orphaned" records, database designers must use integrity constraints to restrict updates and deletions or cascade updates and deletions when the record in question is related to a record in another table.

relation
: A theoretical construct that roughly corresponds to a table.

relational closure property
: This means that given relations as arguments in an expression, you need to get a relation as the result. Relations in, relations out.

relational model
: Invented by Dr. E.F. Codd, and first introduced in his paper "A Relational Model of Data for Large Shared Data Banks." It is the basis for most database products on the market today. Its mathematical roots are in set theory and first order predicate logic.

relational operators
: The original relational operators are project, restrict, join, product, difference, divide, intersection, and union. See the definitions for each of these for more detail.

relational system
: A system built on the principles of the relational model.

relationship
: An association between two tables based on primary and foreign keys. A table may have one or more relationships with one or more other tables.

restrict
: A relational operator that's used to generate a row subset of a table. In other words, it's a find operation. You restrict the number of rows that a user sees.

row
: A record in a table.

scalar values

The same as atomic values. Values that contain only one fact; they cannot be meaningfully subdivided.

Second Normal Form (2NF)

A table is in Second Normal Form if all of the non-key fields are functionally dependent on the entire primary key. This means that if you have a compound primary key, all other fields have to be functionally determined by all fields that comprise the key, not just some of them.

SELECT

A SQL command that performs the same function as the restrict operator: it finds a subset of records in a table.

SQL

Originally an acronym for Structured Query Language, it's now just a name for a standard query language. Used for creating queries in client/server environments. ODBC is a superset of SQL.

stored field

A stored field is any FileMaker Pro text, number, date, or time field, and any calculation field that references only stored information (not global fields or related fields) and that hasn't been forced into an unstored state by means of its storage options.

stored procedure

In the client/server world, this is a script that runs on the server. It can be invoked by a SQL or ODBC command. In the FileMaker world, this is a script.

table

The same as a file or database in FileMaker Pro.

table fields

Since FileMaker stores non-table information in its file format, we distinguish between base values (text, number, date, time, and container fields) and derived values (calculation, summary, and global fields) by referring to the base fields as table fields and the derived fields as view fields.

theta join (Θ-join)

A join which uses some type of operator: =, ≠, <, >

tuple

The same as a record or row of a table. This is a term from the relational model.

union

A set and relational operator. As a relational operator, it combines the records from two indentically structured tables. Importing records from one table to another is a union operation.

universal quantifier

A concept from predicate logic, it means that if you have a result from a predicate, all of those result values are true.

update anomaly

A problem that has to do with either the insertion, deletion, or update of a record in a table. Since each of these actions updates the table, they all get lumped together under the same name. The anomaly occurs when you perform one of these operations on an incompletely normalized table. See Chapter 3 for specific examples.

view

A new table that is derived from one or more base tables by a client application. In FileMaker Pro, views are analagous to layouts, and this unified file structure causes the derived and base table to "live" in the same place.

view fields

See table fields

virtual field

A field that's just created for presentation to the user but isn't actually stored in any underlying database tables. In FileMaker, the page number symbol or date symbol might be considered as virtual fields.

Index

About the CD

The companion CD contains files and examples used in the book. These are organized by chapter, as follows:

Chapter 4
- AuditTrail

Chapter 7
- AdvancedSystem
- BasicSystem

Chapter 8
- Events
- Portals
- Sorting
- Students
- TypeAhead

Chapter 9
- Invoices

Chapter 10
- Hierarchy
- Inventory

Chapter 11
- Checkwords
- Age
- DateTimes

Warning:

By opening the CD package, you accept the terms and conditions of the CD/Source Code Usage License Agreement on the following page.

Opening the CD package makes this book nonreturnable.

CD/Source Code Usage License Agreement

Please read the following CD/Source Code usage license agreement before opening the CD and using the contents therein:

1. By opening the accompanying software package, you are indicating that you have read and agree to be bound by all terms and conditions of this CD/Source Code usage license agreement.
2. The compilation of code and utilities contained on the CD and in the book are copyrighted and protected by both U.S. copyright law and international copyright treaties, and is owned by Wordware Publishing, Inc. Individual source code, example programs, help files, freeware, shareware, utilities, and evaluation packages, including their copyrights, are owned by the respective authors.
3. No part of the enclosed CD or this book, including all source code, help files, shareware, freeware, utilities, example programs, or evaluation programs, may be made available on a public forum (such as a World Wide Web page, FTP site, bulletin board, or Internet news group) without the express written permission of Wordware Publishing, Inc. or the author of the respective source code, help files, shareware, freeware, utilities, example programs, or evaluation programs.
4. You may not decompile, reverse engineer, disassemble, create a derivative work, or otherwise use the enclosed programs, help files, freeware, shareware, utilities, or evaluation programs except as stated in this agreement.
5. The software, contained on the CD and/or as source code in this book, is sold without warranty of any kind. Wordware Publishing, Inc. and the authors specifically disclaim all other warranties, express or implied, including but not limited to implied warranties of merchantability and fitness for a particular purpose with respect to defects in the disk, the program, source code, sample files, help files, freeware, shareware, utilities, and evaluation programs contained therein, and/or the techniques described in the book and implemented in the example programs. In no event shall Wordware Publishing, Inc., its dealers, its distributors, or the authors be liable or held responsible for any loss of profit or any other alleged or actual private or commercial damage, including but not limited to special, incidental, consequential, or other damages.
6. One (1) copy of the CD or any source code therein may be created for backup purposes. The CD and all accompanying source code, sample files, help files, freeware, shareware, utilities, and evaluation programs may be copied to your hard drive. With the exception of freeware and shareware programs, at no time can any part of the contents of this CD reside on more than one computer at one time. The contents of the CD can be copied to another computer, as long as the contents of the CD contained on the original computer are deleted.
7. You may not include any part of the CD contents, including all source code, example programs, shareware, freeware, help files, utilities, or evaluation programs in any compilation of source code, utilities, help files, example programs, freeware, shareware, or evaluation programs on any media, including but not limited to CD, disk, or Internet distribution, without the express written permission of Wordware Publishing, Inc. or the owner of the individual source code, utilities, help files, example programs, freeware, shareware, or evaluation programs.
8. You may use the source code, techniques, and example programs in your own commercial or private applications unless otherwise noted by additional usage agreements as found on the CD.

Warning:

By opening the CD package, you accept the terms and conditions of the CD/Source Code Usage License Agreement.

Additionally, opening the CD package makes this book non-returnable.